THE ENGLISH TRADITION:
DRAMA

THE ENGLISH TRADITION: FICTION

THE ENGLISH TRADITION: NONFICTION

THE ENGLISH TRADITION: POETRY

THE ENGLISH TRADITION: DRAMA

THE ENGLISH TRADITION: DRAMA

Marjorie Wescott Barrows
Formerly, General Editor
Macmillan Literary Heritage

Robert P. Bletter
Director, Teachers College Press
New York City

Donald G. Kobler
Chairman, English Department
Housatonic Valley Regional High School
Falls River, Connecticut

Bertrand Evans
Professor Emeritus of English
University of California
Berkeley, California

James E. Frey
Associate Professor of English
California State University
Fresno, California

Matthew Dolkey
Professor of English
Kean College of New Jersey
Union, New Jersey

Nelda B. Kubat
English Coordinator
Lansing High School
Ludlowville, New York

James G. Magill
Formerly, Chairman, English Department
Lincoln High School
Manitowoc, Wisconsin

A revision of *Spenser to Goldsmith* and *Modern English Drama*,
previously published by Macmillan Publishing Co., Inc.

MACMILLAN PUBLISHING COMPANY
NEW YORK

COLLIER MACMILLAN PUBLISHERS
LONDON

ACKNOWLEDGMENTS

For permission to reprint copyright material in this volume, grateful acknowledgment is made to the following:

Brandt & Brandt: For *The Browning Version* by Terence Rattigan, Copyright, 1949, by Terence Rattigan. CAUTION: *The Browning Version* is the sole property of the author and is fully protected by copyright. It may not be acted by professionals or amateurs without formal permission and the payment of a royalty. All rights, including professional, amateur, stock, radio and television, broadcasting, motion picture, recitation, lecturing, public reading, and the rights of translation into foreign languages are reserved. All inquiries should be addressed to the author's agent: Harold Freedman, Brandt & Brandt Dramatic Department, Inc., 101 Park Avenue, New York, New York 10017.

Robert Lantz Literary Agency: For *White Lies* by Peter Shaffer. Copyright © 1967 by Reath Enterprises.

St. Martin's Press: For *The Plough and the Stars* by Sean O'Casey. Reprinted by special arrangement with St. Martin's Press, Inc. Renewal copyright © Sean O'Casey 1953. Play production rights controlled by The Richard J. Madden Play Company, Inc., 52 Vanderbilt Avenue, New York, New York 10017.

The Society of Authors and the Public Trustee (London): For *Arms and the Man*, by George Bernard Shaw, copyright 1898 by George Bernard Shaw. Renewal copyright 1926 by George Bernard Shaw. All rights fully protected and reserved.

Cover design by William S. Shields

Macmillan Publishing Company
866 Third Avenue, New York, New York 10022
Collier Macmillan Canada, Inc.
Printed in the United States of America
ISBN 0-02-194150-5
9 8 7 6 5 4 3 2 1

Contents

Introduction

English drama had its earliest beginnings in the medieval miracle plays. These religious productions gradually evolved into secular dramas that were based on ancient Greek and Roman models. However, it was not until the Renaissance reached England in the early years of the sixteenth century that English drama began to flourish. During the century that followed, some of the finest English plays ever written were penned by a number of talented and creative dramatists. Unique among these playwrights was William Shakespeare, who produced a series of masterpieces unequaled in English literature or in any other of the world's literatures. In Shakespeare's plays, we find a maturity and power unhampered by classical or religious restraints. They represent a culmination of the long evolutionary process of English drama.

Perhaps it is indicative of the extent of Shakespeare's influence that English drama languished for nearly three hundred years after his death in 1616. Most of the palys that were written during this period are examples of superlative drama. Restoration drama of the late seventeenth and early eighteenth centuries wallowed in a sea of petty concerns, and nineteenth century drama was so ponderous and poorly staged that it fell victim to the rising popularity of the Victorian novel. There was one brief period during the final three decades of the eighteenth century when the witty, original comedies of Oliver Goldsmith and Richard Brinsley Sheridan relieved the general mediocrity affecting British drama.

English drama was finally taken out of these doldrums during the final two decades of the nineteenth century when the dramatic art of Western civilization experienced the beginnings of a revolution. A Norwegian dramatist, Henrik Ibsen, was largely responsible for this revitalization of the drama. His new drama of ideas was dynamic in its concern with the social and moral problems of contemporary life. Its influence was soon felt in England where early twentieth-century playwrights found, in the works of Ibsen, a way to restore excellence to English drama.

Set against the backdrop of Victorian drama, which had consisted largely of heavy, uninspired melodrama, sentimental comedy, and farce, the early productions of Ibsen's realistic plays aroused a storm of controversy in England. For some time, there was open hostility from critics, moralists, and segments of the general public. Nevertheless, his plays gradually won acceptance as a new critical, corrective spirit began to emerge. Following the example of Ibsen's realism, English dramatists began to turn to science, philosophy, economics, and social criticism for ideas that would give vitality and significance to their plays.

The first of the English playwrights to translate the new realism of Ibsen into successful British dramatic productions was George Bernard Shaw. His genius transformed the drama of ideas into a witty, sophisticated vehicle for social criticism and reform. Shaw's large output of notable plays soon made him the dominant figure of English drama of the first half of the twentieth century.

Meanwhile, across the Irish sea, a new variety of English drama was developing. English ideas, concerns, and attitudes had dominated Irish theater to such an extent that before the final years of the nineteenth century, there had been no real Irish drama. However, by the end of the century, an "Irish Renaissance" began to take place. Following the nationalistic leadership of the Abbey Theater in Dublin, Irish dramatists began to turn to their own heritage of Gaelic folktales and myths and to the everyday life of the Irish countryside for the subject matter of their plays. The result was a series of plays about the "common folk," which had dialogue that incorporated the strong cadences and rich imagery of native Irish language and lore.

This, however, was not the only direction the new Irish drama took. Sean O'Casey chose instead to dramatize the harsh political and economic realities of city life and the contemporary Irishman's struggle against them. His plays are saved from being overly harsh in their social criticism by the inherent exuberance of the Irish spirit. In addition, his prose dialogue employs many poetic devices to capture the rich rhythm and ripe imagery of Irish speech. This poetic quality, also found in the work of John Millington Synge and William Butler Yeats, accounts for much of the power of Irish drama in the twentieth century.

During the early part of the twentieth century, Shaw was still the most influential playwright representing English drama. However, some English and Irish playwrights followed the direction of the French and other Continental naturalistic dramatists who portrayed the more gritty aspects of real life. Other playwrights of this period reacted against the new realism and utilized their talents to create lighthearted, imaginative plays such as J. M. Barrie's *Peter Pan*. These whimsical and often tender dramas added variety to English theater.

English and Irish poets also contributed to the new English theater. William Butler Yeats, T. S. Eliot, Christopher Fry, and others developed verse techniques that brought a rich, elevated tone to dialogue yet did not make it seem too far removed from the language of daily life.

From the turn of the century to the beginning of the reign of Elizabeth II, English playwrights excelled in comedy. The witty comedies of Shaw, the polished drawing-room satires of Somerset Maugham, the brittle situation comedies of Noel Coward, and the farces of the young Terence Rattigan are characteristic of the English plays of this period. Unfortunately, by continued use of the same dramatic formulas over several decades by the end of World War II, left English theater moving toward stagnation.

Among the younger playwrights were those who saw a need for a revitalization of drama. Terence Rattigan, for example, turned to serious drama and became one of England's most skillful exponents of the realistic form. John Osborne and other "angry young men" of the English theater reintroduced the type of provocative drama that focuses on the problems of contemporary life. Their wrathful social dramas often show the younger generation in rebellion against the conditions in the world around them. Though these plays reflect a general disenchantment with the materialistic life, they are remarkably diverse in both style and content.

Another kind of experimental drama developed after World War II. Plays of this kind have been labelled as belonging to the "theater of the absurd." These plays grew out of a widespread sense of the utter meaninglessness of human existence that was produced by the terrible horrors of the war. The authors of these plays often abandoned the traditional dramatic devices of logical plot development, coherent dialogue, and easily understood characters. In their plays, man is portrayed as a dupe who is at the mercy of unfathomable forces over which he has little or no control. Plays of the "theater of the absurd," such as Samuel Beckett's *Waiting for Godot* and Harold Pinter's *The Caretaker*, portray modern man's feelings of alienation and bewilderment. They often conveyed a sense of the unreality of life itself.

English theater today shows a great vitality and a capacity for innovation. The large number of new productions, the many accomplished younger playwrights as well as actors and directors, and the development of new theater techniques hold much promise for the future. The popularity of the plays being produced in England extends beyond its shores, and we frequently find the hit drama of the London season is also the hit drama of New York when it reaches Broadway.

THE ENGLISH TRADITION: DRAMA

William Shakespeare

In 1592, in London, a dramatist and prose writer named Robert Greene died leaving an unpublished pamphlet in which one angry passage clearly refers to William Shakespeare:

> ... there is an upstart crow, beautified with our feathers that with his *Tygers heart wrapt in a Players hide,* suppose he is as well able to bumbast out a blanke verse as the best of you; and being an absolute *Johannes Factotum,* is in his own conceit the only Shak-scene in a countrie.[1]

This bitter comment is of enormous importance to Shakespeare scholars because it provides the first evidence that the boy born twenty-eight years earlier in Stratford had made his way to London, had "broken into" the theater, and had begun to do well enough to attract the jealousy of an established playwright.

Why Shakespeare left Stratford for London, and at what date, is unknown. When he was about thirteen, his father, a man of civic importance, suffered financial difficulties; the future poet may have left school at that time to help out. Later, as a twenty-one-year-old father of three, he may have gone to

---

[1] Robert Greene, *A Groatsworth of Wit, Bought with a Million of Repentance* (New Shakespeare Society, Series IV, Vol. I; London: N. Trübner & Co., 1874), p. 30.

London for the quite ordinary reason of finding the means to support his family. It is conceivable that he arrived there as a member of a company of touring players.

Shakespeare's London was a bustling metropolis of about 200,000 people. At the time, England was enjoying both peace and prosperity. In 1588, perhaps three years after Shakespeare's arrival, Sir Francis Drake and his light, gallant ships defeated the dreaded Spanish Armada. England was no longer threatened with invasion and English ships were free to sail all the seas. At home and abroad Englishmen were infected with the spirit of their country's greatness, proud of her past, confident of her present, and hopeful of what seemed her boundless future. They had time and money for culture and entertainment, and men great enough to give them all they wanted of both. In all the world's history there was never a more propitious moment for a young poet of extraordinary genius to appear on the scene.

THE ELIZABETHAN THEATER

For Shakespeare the immediate center of activity was The Theatre, a towering, circular structure built in 1576. It had no roof, but it did have several stages. The main stage was a great, square platform that projected far out, so that the audience stood or sat around three sides of it. At the rear of this platform was an inner stage with a curtain that could be used as need required. Above the main stage, set back to the wall at the second-story level, was an upper stage. Above this, at the third-story level, was yet another acting area where, for example, a guard might stand as on a tower or where heralds might trumpet the arrival of a king. Doorways to the right and left of the main stage, as well as usable windows to the right and left of the upper stage, provided actors with ample facilities for speedy entrances and exits.

Shakespeare's three-level theater differed greatly from the present-day conventional theater. It was not walled in on three sides, nor did it have a curtain and footlights to separate audience and actors. Scene followed scene in swift succession and without interruptions. As one group of actors swept out through the doorways at either side, their flying banners and coattails frequently still visible, a second group could enter on another level, or on the inner stage at the rear, already speaking the opening lines of the next scene. Thus, in two action-packed hours, plays were presented which, in most modern theaters, require three or four hours. No wonder drama meant excitement not only for the lords and ladies from Queen Elizabeth's court but also for those who came in from the streets of London.

Indeed, for such an audience, drama *had* to be exciting. Here, in part, is a famous French historian's portrayal of the crowds for whom Shakespeare wrote:

On a dirty site, on the banks of the Thames, rose the principal theatre, the Globe, a sort of hexagonal tower, surrounded by a muddy ditch, surmounted by a red flag. The common people could enter as well as the rich: there were sixpenny, twopenny, even penny seats; but they could not see it without money. If it rained, and it often rains in London, the people in the pit, butchers, mercers, bakers, sailors, apprentices, received the streaming rain upon their heads. . . . While waiting for the piece, they amuse themselves after their fashion, drink beer, crack nuts, eat fruits, howl, and now and then resort to their fists; they have been known to fall upon the actors and turn the theatre upside down. At other times they have gone in disgust to the tavern to give the poet a hiding, or toss him in a blanket. . . . Above them, on the stage, were the spectators able to pay a shilling, the elegant people, the gentlefolk. These were sheltered from the rain, and if they chose to pay an extra shilling could have a stool. . . . It often happened that stools were lacking; then they stretched themselves on the ground: they were not dainty at such times. They play cards, smoke, insult the pit, who give it them back without stinting, and throw apples at them into the bargain. As for the gentlefolk, they gesticulate, swear in Italian, French, English; crack aloud jokes in dainty, composite, high-colored words: in short, they have the energetic, original, gay manners of artists, the same humor, the same absence of constraint, and, to complete the resemblance, the same desire to make themselves singular, the same imaginative cravings, the same absurd and picturesque devices, beards cut to a point, into the shape of a fan, a spade, the letter T, gaudy and expensive dresses, copied from five or six neighboring nations, embroidered, laced with gold, motley, continually heightened in effect, or changed for others: there was, as it were, a carnival in their brains as on their backs.[2]

Before this kind of audience Shakespeare's plays were acted with virtually no scenery and without visual indication of changes in location other than the rapid shifts from one playing area to another. The same platform might stand, in swift succession and without change in furnishings, for a room in a duke's palace, a seacoast, or a mansion in the suburbs. The lines spoken by the actors often identified the location of the scene, but all else was left to the abundant imagination of the audience.

The freedom allowed by multiple stages and absence of scenery is reflected in the action of Shakespeare's plays. The dramatist could follow his story wherever his imagination led, leaping from Rome to Egypt, from a king's court to the battlements outside, from a palace in Sicily to the seacoast of Bohemia. At the end of each scene, however, he had to get all the living actors and the dead bodies off the stage so that they would not interfere with the next action. Surprisingly, he managed to capitalize on this very necessity, making a virtue out of what might have been a fault; the action flows freely from scene to scene, yet each scene is in a fundamental way *complete:* it begins with actors entering upon some specific business; it ends with their departure, when this business is finished.

Probably, when the young Shakespeare first arrived from Stratford, he accepted an apprenticeship with the professional company of players who operated The Theatre. He played minor roles and, perhaps, women's roles, since custom required that their parts be played by boys and young men. By 1592 Shakespeare was a writer as well as an actor, and by 1598 was receiving, as a part-owner of the company, a share of the profits. When The Theatre was torn down in 1599, Shakespeare's company used its timbers to build the Globe, the

[2]H. A. Taine, *History of English Literature,* tr. Henri Van Laun (Edinburgh: Edmonston and Douglas, 1873), pp. 360–362.

theater that is most closely associated with his name. Except for winter performances at the indoor Blackfriars theater after 1608, his company continued to perform at the Globe until it burned down in 1613.

THE PLAYS AND POEMS

During Shakespeare's twenty years of residence in London he wrote thirty-seven plays (ten tragedies, ten histories, seventeen comedies); more than one hundred and fifty sonnets; and two long narrative poems totaling more than 3000 lines (roughly the length of one of his longer plays). The order of the plays is still in doubt, for no one knows the exact year in which any single play was written. To create that many, he must have completed them at an average rate of nearly two each year. Occasionally, if our figures are right, he managed to complete three. During that same period—particularly in the decade before 1600—he also wrote the sonnets and long poems. He was intimately engaged in other aspects of dramatic production as well, including acting.

Such a prodigious accomplishment was extraordinary even in an age known for its energy and aspiration. Together, the thirty-seven plays exhibit the full range of human experience, human character, and human emotion.

SHAKESPEARE'S LANGUAGE

In displaying the potential of his subject matter, Shakespeare's indispensable ally was language. Like other poets, dramatists, and prose writers of the Renaissance, he was an experimenter and innovator, fascinated by the possibilities of expression that were being discovered in the English language. He revelled in its sounds, delighting in the effects achieved by combinations of vowels and consonants. He played elaborate tricks with the flexible structure of the language, contriving new and striking patterns. If he needed a verb and had none, he made one from a noun; if he needed a

noun and had none, he made one from a verb. Like an archi-
tect constructing intricate forms, either delicate or ponderous,
he balanced word against word, phrase against phrase, sentence against sentence.

Shakespeare took up the toy of language and never tired of
playing with it. He exploited it for all that it could be made to
yield—fun, music, beauty, terror, grief, harshness, tenderness,
excitement, profundity. In his works, everyone plays with
language—kings, princes, heroes, heroines, villains, old men
and boys, professional jesters and country bumpkins, men in a
happy mood and men at the point of death. One of Shakespeare's favorite ways of playing with words is the pun. His
characters, it appears, can never resist the opportunities af-
forded by such pairs of words as *heart–hart, soul–sole, deer–
dear, knight–night.* Though word-play obviously flourishes
most in comic scenes, it is used with effect even at tragic
moments.

Since the spelling of Shakespeare's language has been
modernized in most present-day editions, it does not look
formidably different from ours. Some words have become ob-
solete; some are now archaic. Others have undergone a slight,
or even a drastic, change in meaning. On the whole the differences in vocabulary are relatively slight and can be noted
without much difficulty. The reader must be alert for unexpected shifts of meaning, but he need not labor over each line
as if he were deciphering a foreign language.

Shakespeare's dramatic verse is predominantly blank verse
—unrhymed iambic pentameter:

> So sháken ás we áre, so wán with cáre
> Find wé a tíme for fríghted péace to pánt.

Of course, not every line of every play has this unvaried
rhythm pattern. As Shakespeare matured, he learned to match
the accents with the thought expressed and with the manner
and mood of the speaker. Note the change in rhythm when
Macbeth cries out:

> Whénce is that knócking?

or when Horatio, in *Hamlet* (Act I, scene 1), addresses the ghost of Hamlet's father:

Stáy! spéak, spéak! I chárge thee, spéak!

In some of the supremely great passages, the verse resembles potent prose, even though certain of the lines can be scanned as flawless blank verse.

Shakespeare frequently used both prose and poetry in his plays. Low characters, comic characters, and ordinary persons often speak in prose when discussing situations about which the audience must be informed. Kings and princes generally speak in blank verse. Whatever form of expression is more appropriate to the level of the speakers, to the occasion, and to the matter being presented, this is the form Shakespeare used. In *Macbeth*, there are few occasions suited to prose; thus, its use is severely limited. This fact alone suggests the unbroken, terrifying intensity of its dramatic impact.

Macbeth

Of the tragedies that are often called Shakespeare's "Big Four" *(Hamlet, Othello, King Lear, Macbeth), Macbeth* is the last, the shortest, and the most concentrated in power. As in a short story by Poe, the language, characters, and settings combine to produce a single predominant effect of moving horror. The first breath of this horror is conveyed in less than a dozen lines (Scene 1). In thunder and lightning, the Witches meet, mutter the name "Macbeth," and depart on an ominous note that will be echoed and re-echoed until the very end of the tragedy:

> Fair is foul, and foul is fair.
> Hover through the fog and filthy air.

This same breath of horror is felt again when, after the Witches have told their prophecies, the specific idea of murder first intrudes into the mind of Macbeth:

> . . . why do I yield to that suggestion
> Whose horrid image doth unfix my hair.
> And make my seated heart knock at my ribs,
> Against the use of nature?

Before the spell of horror is broken (at the very end of the play) with the ecstatic cry, "the time is free," it has afflicted the whole land under King Macbeth's tyranny and has caused the murderers excruciating torment. At no time in *Macbeth*, however, is horror created for the sake of horror, as in the traditional melodrama. This play is a tragedy and, unlike melodrama, is concerned primarily with the magnitude and fullness of the human experience it presents. In tragedy, action and outcome are intimately bound to human character and determined by it. A basic principle of Shakespearean tragedy is that the hero (protagonist), being as he is, must therefore do as he does. Moreover, in the particular situation in which the dramatist places him, the decisions that he makes and the actions that he takes prove inevitably fatal. Thus, in the final analysis, his own character is the cause of his destruction.

In the course of presenting the story of Macbeth and his eventual downfall, Shakespeare explores the human mind and will, raising old and new questions about man's relation to the universe outside himself. Is man free, or not free, to exercise his will? How free is Macbeth? True, he is deeply influenced by Lady Macbeth and by the prophecies of the Witches who confront him on the "blasted heath," yet the decisions he makes are his own. Are they, however, "free" decisions when they are dictated as surely by what he himself is — by the tyrant, one may say, within his own breast — as are those of a slave by his master?

The unfathomable question of "fate" looms larger in this tragedy than in any other of Shakespeare's except, possibly, *Romeo and Juliet*. Frequently, spiritual and psychological forces within Macbeth seem to be in league with mysterious forces outside himself — forces of which the Witches are only the visible figureheads. Macbeth unconsciously reveals this league in the first words he speaks in the play:

So foul and fair a day I have not seen.

Note how directly they echo the Witches' paradoxical chant of the opening scene: "Fair is foul, and foul is fair." Tempted by the Witches' prophecies, Macbeth himself quickly responds to the riddle with which, it seems, "fate" has confronted him:

> If chance will have me King, why, chance may crown me
> Without my stir.

Shall he, therefore, bide his time? Or does "chance" expect him to take things into his own hands—to "help fate out," so to speak, in bringing about what is destined? By choosing the second course, he becomes king. Would he also have become king if he had not acted? Being exactly as he is, was he free to make any other choice? Did fate, then, "know" that he would act, and thus bring about the destined end?

Great tragedy always raises questions which, in the words of John Keats, "tease us out of thought as doth eternity." As you are drawn into the world of Macbeth, you may hate him for his wickedness—and that he is a wicked man there is little room for doubt. Still, because of the depth of Shakespeare's portrayal of him, you can understand him. You may even feel compassion for him as a suffering fellow-being. What could be more paradoxical than that because of our good impulses we feel pity and terror for a tyrant like Macbeth!

The play is rich in paradoxes that go deeper than the mere words that point them out: "Fair is foul, and foul is fair," "Nothing is but what is not." It poses, too, some of the central riddles of life. Shakespeare did not attempt to solve them for us. It is enough that by the force of his poetic and dramatic art he urged them upon our consciousness and made us want to wrestle with them.

CHARACTERS

DUNCAN, king of Scotland

MALCOLM,
DONALBAIN, } his sons

MACBETH, } generals of the
BANQUO, } King's army

MACDUFF,
LENNOX,
ROSS,
MENTEITH, } noblemen of
ANGUS, } Scotland
CAITHNESS,

FLEANCE, son to BANQUO

SIWARD, earl of Northumberland, general of the English forces

YOUNG SIWARD, his son

SEYTON, an officer attending on MACBETH

BOY, son to MACDUFF
An English Doctor
A Scotch Doctor
A Sergeant
A Porter
An Old Man
LADY MACBETH
LADY MACDUFF
Gentlewoman attending on LADY MACBETH

HECATE
Three Witches
Apparitions
Lords, Gentlemen, Officers, Soldiers, Murderers, Attendants, and Messengers

SCENE: *Scotland and England around the middle of the eleventh century.*

Act I SCENE 1

A deserted place. Thunder and lightning. Enter three Witches.

FIRST WITCH.   When shall we three meet again?
    In thunder, lightning, or in rain?
SECOND WITCH.   When the hurlyburly's° done,   uproar
    When the battle's lost and won.

11

THIRD WITCH.   That will be ere the set of sun.   5
FIRST WITCH.   Where the place?
SECOND WITCH.   Upon the heath.
THIRD WITCH.   There to meet with Macbeth.
FIRST WITCH.   I come, Graymalkin.°   gray cat
ALL.   Paddock° calls:—anon!°   toad; right away
    Fair is foul, and foul is fair.   10
    Hover through the fog and filthy air.   *(Exeunt.)*

Act I SCENE 2

A camp near Forres¹. Alarum within². Enter DUNCAN,
MALCOLM, DONALBAIN, LENNOX, *with* Attendants, *meeting a bleeding* Sergeant.

DUNCAN.   What bloody man is that? He can report,
    As seemeth by his plight, of the revolt
    The newest state.
MALCOLM.   This is the sergeant
    Who like a good and hardy soldier fought
    'Gainst my captivity. Hail, brave friend!   5
    Say to the king the knowledge of the broil°   battle
    As thou didst leave it.
SERGEANT.   Doubtful it stood,
    As two spent swimmers that do cling together
    And choke their art. The merciless Macdonwald—
    Worthy to be a rebel, for to that   10
    The multiplying villainies of nature
    Do swarm upon him—from the western isles³
    Of kerns° and gallowglasses° is supplied;   light infantry; armored men
    And fortune, on his damned quarrel smiling,

·*Forres:* town in northern Scotland
²*Alarum:* trumpet call
³*western isles:* Ireland and the Hebrides

Show'd like a rebel's whore. But all's too weak,   15
For brave Macbeth—well he deserves that name—
Disdaining fortune, with his brandish'd steel,
Which smok'd with bloody execution,
Like valor's minion° carved out his passage   favorite
Till he fac'd the slave,   20
Which° ne'er shook hands, nor bade farewell to him,   who
Till he unseam'd him from the nave° to the chaps,°   navel;
And fix'd his head upon our battlements.   jaw

DUNCAN.   O valiant cousin! Worthy gentleman!

SERGEANT.   As whence the sun 'gins his reflection   25
Shipwrecking storms and direful thunders break,
So from that spring whence comfort seem'd to come
Discomfort swells. Mark, king of Scotland, mark:
No sooner justice had, with valor arm'd,
Compell'd these skipping kerns to trust their heels,   30
But the Norweyan lord,⁴ surveying vantage,
With furbish'd arms and new supplies of men
Began a fresh assault.

DUNCAN.   Dismay'd not this
Our captains, Macbeth and Banquo?

SERGEANT.   Yes—
As sparrows eagles, or the hare the lion.   35
If I say sooth,° I must report they were   truth
As cannons overcharg'd with double cracks;° so they   loads
Doubly redoubled strokes upon the foe.
Except° they meant to bathe in reeking wounds,   unless
Or memorize° another Golgotha,⁵   make memorable
I cannot tell—   41
But I am faint; my gashes cry for help.

DUNCAN.   So well thy words become thee as thy wounds;
They smack of honor both. Go get him surgeons.
                         (*Exit* Sergeant, *attended.*)
Who comes here?

(*Enter* ROSS.)

⁴*Norweyan lord:* Sweno, King of Norway
⁵*Golgotha:* where Christ was crucified; a place of skulls

MALCOLM. The worthy thane° of Ross.   earl   45
LENNOX. What a haste looks through his eyes! So should
    he look
    That seems° to speak things strange.   seems ready
ROSS.   God save the king!
DUNCAN. Whence cam'st thou, worthy thane?
ROSS.   From Fife, great king,
    Where the Norweyan banners flout° the sky   insult
    And fan our people cold. Norway himself,   50
    With terrible numbers,
    Assisted by that most disloyal traitor
    The thane of Cawdor, began a dismal° conflict,   fearful
    Till that Bellona's bridegroom,[6] lapp'd in proof,°   armor
    Confronted him with self-comparisons,   clad in 55
    Point against point, rebellious arm 'gainst arm,
    Curbing his lavish° spirit. And, to conclude,   insolent
    The victory fell on us.
DUNCAN.   Great happiness!
ROSS. That° now   so that
    Sweno, the Norways' king, craves composition;°   peace t .....
    Nor would we deign him burial of his men   61
    Till he disbursed, at Saint Colme's inch,[7]
    Ten thousand dollars to our general use.
DUNCAN. No more that thane of Cawdor shall deceive
    Our bosom interest. Go pronounce his present°   immediate
    death,   65
    And with his former title greet Macbeth.
ROSS. I'll see it done.
DUNCAN. What he hath lost, noble Macbeth hath won.
                                 (Exeunt.)

---

[6]*Bellona's bridegroom:* Macbeth. Bellona was the Roman goddess of war.
[7]*Saint Colme's inch:* Isle of St. Columba near Edinburgh, Scotland

Act I SCENE 3

A heath. Thunder. Enter the three Witches.

FIRST WITCH.   Where has thou been, sister?
SECOND WITCH.   Killing swine.
THIRD WITCH.   Sister, where thou?
FIRST WITCH.   A sailor's wife had chestnuts in her lap,
   And munch'd, and munch'd, and munch'd.   5
   "Give me," quoth I.
   "Aroint thee ° witch!" the rump-fed ronyon° cries.   begone; hussy
   Her husband's to Aleppo[1] gone, master o' the *Tiger;*
   But in a sieve I'll thither sail,
   And, like a rat without a tail,   10
   I'll do, I'll do, and I'll do.
SECOND WITCH.   I'll give thee a wind.
FIRST WITCH.   Thou'rt kind.
THIRD WITCH.   And I another.
FIRST WITCH.   I myself have all the other,°   other winds 15
   And the very ports they blow,
   All the quarters that they know
   I' the shipman's card.°   compass
   I will drain him dry as hay;
   Sleep shall neither night nor day   20
   Hang upon his pent-house lid;°   eyelid
   He shall live a man forbid.°   accursed
   Weary se'nnights° nine times nine   weeks
   Shall he dwindle, peak,° and pine.   waste away
   Though his bark° cannot be lost,   ship 25
   Yet it shall be tempest-tost.
   Look what I have.
SECOND WITCH.   Show me, show me.
FIRST WITCH.   Here I have a pilot's thumb,
   Wreck'd as homeward he did come.   *(Drum within.)* 30
THIRD WITCH.   A drum, a drum!
   Macbeth doth come.

[1]*Aleppo:* city in Syria

ALL.　The weird sisters, hand in hand,
　　Posters° of the sea and land,　　　　　　　swift travelers
　　Thus do go about, about:　　　　　　　　　35
　　Thrice to thine, and thrice to mine,
　　And thrice again, to make up nine.
　　Peace! The charm's wound up.

(*Enter* MACBETH *and* BANQUO.)

MACBETH.　So foul and fair a day I have not seen.
BANQUO.　How far is't call'd to Forres? What are these,　40
　　So wither'd and so wild in their attire,
　　That look not like the inhabitants o' the earth,
　　And yet are on't? Live you? Or are you aught
　　That man may question? You seem to understand me.
　　By each at once her choppy° finger laying　　chapped 45
　　Upon her skinny lips. You should be women,
　　And yet your beards forbid me to interpret
　　That you are so.
MACBETH.　　　　Speak, if you can. What are you?
FIRST WITCH.　All hail, Macbeth! Hail to thee, thane of
　　Glamis!
SECOND WITCH.　All hail, Macbeth! Hail to thee, thane of
　　Cawdor!　　　　　　　　　　　　　　　　50
THIRD WITCH.　All hail, Macbeth, that shalt be king
　　hereafter!
BANQUO.　Good sir, why do you start, and seem to fear
　　Things that do sound so fair? I' the name of truth,
　　Are ye fantastical,° or that indeed　　　imaginary
　　Which outwardly ye show? My noble partner　55
　　You greet with present grace and great prediction
　　Of noble having and of royal hope,
　　That he seems rapt withal.° To me you speak not.　spellbound thereby
　　If you can look into the seeds of time,
　　And say which grain will grow and which will not,　60
　　Speak then to me, who neither beg nor fear
　　Your favors nor your hate.
FIRST WITCH.　Hail!
SECOND WITCH.　Hail!

THIRD WITCH.   Hail!   65
FIRST WITCH.   Lesser than Macbeth, and greater.
SECOND WITCH.   Not so happy, yet much happier.
THIRD WITCH.   Thou shalt get° kings, though thou   beget
    be none.
    So all hail, Macbeth and Banquo!
FIRST WITCH.   Banquo and Macbeth, all hail!   70
MACBETH.   Stay, you imperfect speakers, tell me more.
    By Sinel's[2] death I know I am thane of Glamis;
    But how of Cawdor? The thane of Cawdor lives,
    A prosperous gentleman. And to be king
    Stands not within the prospect of belief,   75
    No more than to be Cawdor. Say from whence
    You owe this strange intelligence, or why
    Upon this blasted heath you stop our way
    With such prophetic greeting. Speak, I charge you.
                        (Witches vanish.)
BANQUO.   The earth hath bubbles as the water has,   80
    And these are of them. Wither are they vanish'd?
MACBETH.   Into the air, and what seem'd corporal°   corporeal
    melted
    As breath into the wind. Would they had stay'd!
BANQUO.   Were such things here as we do speak about?
    Or have we eaten on the insane° root   causing insanity 85
    That takes the reason prisoner?
MACBETH.   Your children shall be kings.
BANQUO.   You shall be king.
MACBETH.   And thane of Cawdor too. Went it not so?
BANQUO.   To the selfsame tune and words. Who's here?

(Enter ROSS *and* ANGUS.)

ROSS.   The king hath happily receiv'd, Macbeth,   90
    The news of thy success; and when he reads
    Thy personal venture in the rebels' fight,
    His wonders and his praises do contend
    Which should be thine or his. Silenc'd° with that,   struck dumb
    In viewing o'er the rest o' the selfsame day,   95

---

[2]*Sinel:* Macbeth's father

He finds thee in the stout Norweyan ranks,
Nothing afeard of what thyself didst make—
Strange images of death. As thick as hail
Came post with post, and every one did bear
Thy praises in his kingdom's great defense,   100
And pour'd them down before him.

ANGUS.   We are sent
To give thee, from our royal master, thanks;
Only to herald thee into his sight,
Not pay thee.

ROSS. And for an earnest° of a greater honor, token payment 105
He bade me, from him, call thee thane of Cawdor:
In which addition,° hail, most worthy thane! title
For it is thine.

BANQUO.   What, can the devil speak true?

MACBETH. The thane of Cawdor lives. Why do you dress
  me
In borrow'd robes?

ANGUS.   Who was the thane lives yet, 110
But under heavy judgment bears that life
Which he deserves to lose. Whether he was combin'd
With those of Norway, or did line° the rebel support
With hidden help and vantage, or that with both
He labor'd in his country's wreck, I know not. 115
But treasons capital, confess'd and proved,
Have overthrown him.

MACBETH (*aside*).   Glamis, and thane of Cawdor:
The greatest is behind.°—Thanks for your pains.— yet to
come
Do you not hope your children shall be kings,
When those that give the thane of Cawdor to me 120
Promis'd no less to them?

BANQUO.   That, trusted home,° fully
Might yet enkindle you unto the crown,
Besides the thane of Cawdor. But 'tis strange,
And oftentimes, to win us to our harm,
The instruments of darkness tell us truths, 125
Win us with honest trifles, to betray 's
In deepest consequence.
Cousins, a word, I pray you.

MACBETH *(aside).*   Two truths are told,
  As happy prologues to the swelling act
  Of the imperial theme. — I thank you, gentlemen. —   130
  (Aside.) This supernatural soliciting°   bidding
  Cannot be ill, cannot be good. If ill,
  Why hath it given me earnest of success,
  Commencing in a truth? I am thane of Cawdor.
  If good, why do I yield to that suggestion   135
  Whose horrid image doth unfix° my hair   stand on end
  And make my seated heart knock at my ribs,
  Against the use of nature? Present fears
  Are less than horrible imaginings:
  My thought, whose murder yet is but fantastical,   140
  Shakes so my single state of man that function
  Is smother'd in surmise, and nothing is
  But what is not.
BANQUO.   Look, how our partner's rapt.
MACBETH *(aside).* If chance will have me king, why,
      chance may crown me
  Without my stir.
BANQUO.   New honors come upon him,   145
  Like our strange° garments, cleave not to their mold   new
  But with the aid of use.
MACBETH *(aside).*   Come what come may,
  Time and the hour runs through the roughest day.
BANQUO. Worthy Macbeth, we stay upon your leisure.
MACBETH. Give me your favor:° my dull brain was   pardon
      wrought   150
  With things forgotten. Kind gentlemen, your pains
  Are register'd where every day I turn
  The leaf to read them. Let us toward the king.
  Think upon what hath chanc'd, and at more time,
  The interim having weigh'd it, let us speak   155
  Our free hearts each to other.
BANQUO.   Very gladly.
MACBETH. Till then, enough. Come, friends.   *(Exeunt.)*

Act I SCENE 4

Forres. The palace. Flourish. Enter DUNCAN, MALCOLM,
DONALBAIN, LENNOX, *and* Attendants.

DUNCAN.   Is execution done on Cawdor? Are not
    Those in commission yet return'd?
MALCOLM.   My liege,
    They are not yet come back. But I have spoke
    With one that saw him die, who did report
    That very frankly he confess'd his treasons,   5
    Implor'd your highness' pardon, and set forth
    A deep repentance. Nothing in his life
    Became him like the leaving it; he died
    As one that had been studied in his death,
    To throw away the dearest thing he ow'd°   owned 10
    As 'twere a careless trifle.
DUNCAN.   There's no art
    To find the mind's construction° in the face: intention
    He was a gentleman on whom I built
    An absolute trust.

    (Enter MACBETH, BANQUO, ROSS, *and* ANGUS.*)*

                O worthiest cousin!
    The sin of my ingratitude even now   15
    Was heavy on me. Thou art so far before,
    That swiftest wing of recompense is slow
    To overtake thee. Would thou hadst less deserv'd,
    That the proportion both of thanks and payment
    Might have been mine! Only I have left to say,   20
    More is thy due than more than all can pay.
MACBETH.   The service and the loyalty I owe,
    In doing it, pays itself. Your highness' part
    Is to receive our duties, and our duties
    Are to your throne and state children and servants,   25
    Which do but what they should by doing everything
    Safe toward° your love and honor.   to safeguard

DUNCAN.   Welcome hither.
   I have begun to plant thee, and will labor
   To make thee full of growing. Noble Banquo,
   That hast no less deserv'd, nor must be known   30
   No less to have done so, let me infold thee
   And hold thee to my heart.
BANQUO.   There if I grow,
   The harvest is your own.
DUNCAN.   My plenteous joys,
   Wanton° in fullness, seek to hide themselves   unrestrained
   In drops of sorrow. Sons, kinsmen, thanes,   35
   And you whose places are the nearest, know
   We will establish our estate upon
   Our eldest, Malcolm, whom we name hereafter
   The Prince of Cumberland,[1] which honor must
   Not unaccompanied invest him only,   40
   But signs of nobleness, like stars, shall shine
   On all deservers. From hence to Inverness,[2]
   And bind us further to you.
MACBETH.   The rest is labor, which is not used for you.
   I'll be myself the harbinger,° and make joyful   messenger 45
   The hearing of my wife with your approach;
   So humbly take my leave.
DUNCAN.   My worthy Cawdor!
MACBETH *(aside).*   The Prince of Cumberland! That is a
     step
   On which I must fall down, or else o'erleap,
   For in my way it lies. Stars, hide your fires;   50
   Let not light see my black and deep desires.
   The eye wink at the hand; yet let that be
   Which the eye fears, when it is done, to see.   *(Exit.)*
DUNCAN.   True, worthy Banquo, he is full so valiant,
   And in his commendations I am fed;   55
   It is a banquet to me. Let's after him,
   Whose care is gone before to bid us welcome.
   It is a peerless kinsman.   *(Flourish. Exeunt.)*

   [1]*Prince of Cumberland:* This title establishes Malcolm as successor to
Duncan's throne, thus making it impossible for Macbeth to receive the crown
of Scotland legitimately.
   [2]*Inverness:* Macbeth's castle

Act I SCENE 5

Inverness. MACBETH's *Castle. Enter* LADY MACBETH *reading a letter.*

LADY MACBETH. "They met me in the day of success; and I
have learned by the perfectest report, they have more in
them than mortal knowledge. When I burned in desire to
question them further, they made themselves air, into
which they vanished. Whiles I stood rapt in the wonder   5
of it, came missives from the king, who all-hailed me
'Thane of Cawdor'; by which title, before, these weird
sisters saluted me, and referred me to the coming on of
time, with 'Hail, king that shalt be!' This have I thought
good to deliver thee, my dearest partner of greatness, that 10
thou mightst not lose the dues of rejoicing, by being ignorant of what greatness is promised thee. Lay it to thy
heart, and farewell."
Glamis thou art, and Cawdor, and shalt be
What thou art promis'd. Yet do I fear thy nature;   15
It is too full o' the milk of human kindness
To catch° the nearest way. Thou wouldst be great,   take
Art not without ambition, but without
The illness should attend it. What thou wouldst highly,
That wouldst thou holily; wouldst not play false,   20
And yet wouldst wrongly win; thou'dst have, great
    Glamis,
That which cries "Thus thou must do,' if thou have it;
And that which rather thou dost fear to do
Than wishest should be undone. Hie thee hither,
That I may pour my spirits in thine ear,   25
And chastise with the valor of my tongue
All that impedes thee from the golden round,°   crown
Which fate and metaphysical° aid doth seem   supernatural
To have thee crown'd withal.

(Enter a Messenger.*)*

LADY MACBETH.   What is your tidings?
MESSENGER.   The king comes here tonight.
LADY MACBETH.   Thou'rt mad to say it. 30
    Is not thy master with him? Who, were 't so,
    Would have inform'd for preparation.
MESSENGER.   So please you, it is true; our thane is
      coming.
    One of my fellows had the speed of° him,   outran
    Who, almost dead for breath, had scarcely more   35
    Than would make up his message.
LADY MACBETH.   Give him tending;
    He brings great news.   *(Exit* Messenger.*)*
                The raven himself is hoarse
    That croaks the fatal entrance of Duncan
    Under my battlements. Come, you spirits
    That tend on mortal thoughts, unsex me here,   40
    And fill me, from the crown to the toe, top-full
    Of direst cruelty! Make thick my blood,
    Stop up th' access and passage to remorse,
    That no compunctious visitings of nature
    Shake my fell° purpose, nor keep peace between   cruel 45
    Th' effect and it! Come to my woman's breasts,
    And take° my milk for gall, you murd'ring ministers,   exchange
    Wherever in your sightless° substances   invisible
    You wait on nature's mischief! Come, thick night,
    And pall° thee in the dunnest° smoke of hell,   cover; 50
                                     darkest
    That my keen knife see not the wound it makes,
    Nor heaven peep through the blanket of the dark
    To cry "Hold, hold!"

    (Enter MACBETH.*)*

                Great Glamis! Worthy Cawdor!
    Greater than both, by the all-hail hereafter!
    Thy letters have transported me beyond   55
    This ignorant present, and I feel now
    The future in the instant.
MACBETH.   My dearest love,
    Duncan comes here tonight.

LADY MACBETH.   And when goes hence?

MACBETH.   Tomorrow, as he purposes.

LADY MACBETH.   O, never
   Shall sun that morrow see!   60
   Your face, my thane, is as a book where men
   May read strange matters. To beguile° the time,   deceive
   Look like the time; bear welcome in your eye,
   Your hand, your tongue; look like the innocent flower,
   But be the serpent under 't. He that's coming   65
   Must be provided for; and you shall put
   This night's great business into my dispatch,°   care
   Which shall to all our nights and days to come
   Give solely sovereign sway° and masterdom.   rule 69

MACBETH.   We will speak further.

LADY MACBETH.   Only look up clear;   look
                                             innocent
   To alter favor° ever° is to fear.   facial expression; always
   Leave all the rest to me.   *(Exeunt.)*

Act I SCENE 6

Before MACBETH's *Castle. Hautboys and torches. Enter*
DUNCAN, MALCOLM, DONALBAIN, BANQUO, LENNOX, MAC-
DUFF, ROSS, ANGUS, *and* Attendants.

DUNCAN.   This castle hath a pleasant seat;° the air   site
   Nimbly and sweetly recommends itself
   Unto our gentle senses.

BANQUO.   This guest of summer,
   The temple-haunting martlet,° does approve°   swallow;
                                         prove
   By his lov'd mansionry that the heaven's breath   5
   Smells wooingly here. No jutty, frieze,
   Buttress, nor coign of vantage,° but this bird   handy niche
   Hath made his pendant bed and procreant cradle.°   breeding
                                         place
   Where they most breed and haunt, I have observ'd
   The air is delicate.

(Enter LADY MACBETH.*)*

DUNCAN.   See, see, our honor'd hostess!   10
  The love that follows us sometime is our trouble,
  Which still we thank as love. Herein I teach you
  How you shall bid God 'ield° us for your pains,   reward
  And thank us for your trouble.
LADY MACBETH.   All our service
  In every point twice done, and then done double,   15
  Were poor and single business to contend
  Against those honors deep and broad wherewith
  Your majesty loads our house. For those of old,
  And the late dignities heap'd up to them,
  We rest your hermits.[2]
DUNCAN.   Where's the thane of Cawdor?   20
  We cours'd° him at the heels, and had a purpose   followed
  To be his purveyor;° but he rides well,   announcer
  And his great love, sharp as his spur, hath holp° him   helped
  To his home before us. Fair and noble hostess,
  We are your guest tonight.
LADY MACBETH.   Your servants ever   25
  Have theirs, themselves, and what is theirs, in compt,°   trust
  To make their audit° at your highness' pleasure,   account
  Still° to return your own.   always
DUNCAN.   Give me your hand;
  Conduct me to mine host. We love him highly,
  And shall continue our graces toward him.   30
  By your leave, hostess.   *(Exeunt.)*

Act I SCENE 7

Hautboys and torches. Enter a Sewer,[1] *and divers* Servants *with dishes and service, and pass over the stage.*
Then enter MACBETH.

MACBETH.   If it were done when 'tis done, then 'twere well
  It were done quickly. If th' assassination

[1]*Sewer:* butler
[2]*rest your hermits:* remain in your debt

Could trammel up° the consequence, and catch,   enmesh
With his surcease,° success; that but this blow   its ending
Might be the be-all and the end-all here,   5
But here, upon this bank and shoal of time,
We'd jump° the life to come. But in these cases   risk
We still have judgment here, that we but teach
Bloody instructions, which being taught return
To plague th' inventor. This even-handed justice   10
Commends th' ingredients of our poison'd chalice
To our own lips. He's here in double trust:
First, as I am his kinsman and his subject,
Strong both against the deed; then, as his host,
Who should against his murderer shut the door,   15
Not bear the knife myself. Besides, this Duncan
Hath borne his faculties° so meek, hath been   powers
So clear in his great office, that his virtues
Will plead like angels, trumpet-tongu'd against
The deep damnation of his taking-off;   20
And pity, like a naked newborn babe
Striding the blast,° or heaven's cherubin hors'd   riding the wind
Upon the sightless couriers° of the air,   invisible carriers
Shall blow the horrid deed in every eye,
That° tears shall drown the wind. I have no spur so that 25
To prick the sides of my intent, but only
Vaulting ambition, which o'erleaps itself
And falls on th' other.°   other side

(*Enter* LADY MACBETH.)

               How now! What news?
LADY MACBETH.   He has almost supp'd. Why have you
    left the chamber?
MACBETH.   Hath he ask'd for me?
LADY MACBETH.   Know you not he has?   30
MACBETH.   We will proceed no further in this business.
    He hath honor'd me of late, and I have bought
    Golden opinions from all sorts of people,
    Which would be worn now in their newest gloss,
    Not cast aside so soon.

LADY MACBETH.   Was the hope drunk   35
   Wherein you dress'd yourself? Hath it slept since?
   And wakes it now, to look so green and pale
   At what it did so freely? From this time
   Such I account thy love. Art thou afeard
   To be the same in thine own act and valor   40
   As thou art in desire? Would'st thou have that
   Which thou esteem'st the ornament of life,
   And live a coward in thine own esteem,
   Letting "I dare not" wait upon "I would,"
   Like the poor cat i' th' adage?[2]

MACBETH.   Prithee, peace.   45
   I dare do all that may become a man;
   Who dares do more is none.

LADY MACBETH.   What beast was't then
   That made you break this enterprise to me?
   When you durst do it, then you were a man;
   And, to be more than what you were, you would   50
   Be so much more the man. Nor time nor place
   Did then adhere,° and yet you would make both.   suit
   They have made themselves, and that their fitness now
   Does unmake you. I have given suck, and know
   How tender 'tis to love the babe that milks me;   55
   I would, while it was smiling in my face,
   Have pluck'd my nipple from his boneless gums
   And dash'd the brains out, had I so sworn as you
   Have done to this.

MACBETH.   If we should fail?

LADY MACBETH.   We fail!
   But screw° your courage to the sticking place,°   fix; notch 60
   And we'll not fail. When Duncan is asleep—
   Whereto the rather shall his day's hard journey
   Soundly invite him—his two chamberlains
   Will I with wine and wassail° so convince,°   ale; impair
   That memory, the warder of the brain,   65
   Shall be a fume, and the receipt° of reason   receptacle
   A limbec° only. When in swinish sleep   distiller

[3]*th' adage:* proverb which says: "The cat would eat fish, but would not
wet her feet."

Their drenched natures lie as in a death,
What cannot you and I perform upon
Th' unguarded Duncan? What not put upon   7c
His spongy officers, who shall bear the guilt
Of our great quell?°   killing

MACBETH.   Bring forth men-children only,
For thy undaunted mettle should compose
Nothing but males. Will it not be receiv'd,
When we have mark'd with blood those sleepy two   75
Of his own chamber, and us'd their very daggers,
That they have done't?

LADY MACBETH.   Who dares receive it other,
As we shall make our griefs and clamor roar
Upon his death?

MACBETH.   I am settled, and bend up°   stiffen
Each corporal° agent to this terrible feat.   bodily 80
Away, and mock° the time with fairest show: deceive
False face must hide what the false heart doth
    know.

(Exeunt.)

Act II Scene 1

Inverness. Court of MACBETH'*s Castle. Enter* BANQUO,
and FLEANCE *bearing a torch before him.*

BANQUO.   How goes the night, boy?
FLEANCE.   The moon is down; I have not heard the clock.
BANQUO.   And she goes down at twelve.
FLEANCE.   I take 't, 'tis later, sir.
BANQUO.   Hold, take my sword. There's husbandry°   thrift
    in heaven,   5
Their candles are all out. Take thee that too.
A heavy summons lies like lead upon me,
And yet I would not sleep. Merciful powers,
Restrain in me the cursed thoughts that nature
Gives way to in repose!

(Enter MACBETH, *and a* Servant *with a torch.)*

                         Give me my sword.
Who's there?   10
MACBETH.   A friend.
BANQUO.   What, sir, not yet at rest? The king's abed.
   He hath been in unusual pleasure, and
   Sent forth great largess° to your offices.°   gifts;
                                 servants' quarters
   This diamond he greets your wife withal,   15
   By the name of most kind hostess; and shut up° retired
   In measureless content.
MACBETH.   Being unprepar'd,
   Our will became the servant to defect,°   lack of means
   Which else° should free have wrought.   otherwise
BANQUO.   All's well.
   I dreamt last night of the three weird sisters.   20
   To you they have show'd some truth.
MACBETH.   I think not of them.
   Yet, when we can entreat an hour to serve,
   We would spend it in some words upon that business,
   If you would grant the time.
BANQUO.   At your kind'st leisure.   24
MACBETH If you shall cleave to my consent,°   follow
      when 'tis,   my advice
   It shall make honor for you.
BANQUO.   So I lose none
   In seeking to augment it, but still keep
   My bosom franchis'd° and allegiance clear,   free
   I shall be counsel'd.
MACBETH.   Good repose the while!
BANQUO.   Thanks, sir. The like to you!   30

(Exeunt BANQUO *and* FLEANCE.)

MACBETH.   Go bid thy mistress, when my drink is ready,
   She strike upon the bell. Get thee to bed.
                           (Exit Servant.)
   Is this a dagger which I see before me,
   The handle toward my hand? Come, let me clutch
     thee.

I have thee not, and yet I see thee still.   35
Art thou not, fatal vision, sensible°   perceptible
To feeling as to sight? Or art thou but
A dagger of the mind, a false creation,
Proceeding from the heat-oppressèd brain?
I see thee yet, in form as palpable   40
As this which now I draw.
Thou marshal'st° me the way that I was going,   leadest
And such an instrument I was to use.
Mine eyes are made the fools o' th' other senses,
Or else worth all the rest. I see thee still,   45
And on thy blade and dudgeon° gouts° of blood, handle; drops
Which was not so before. There's no such thing:
It is the bloody business which informs°   creates images
Thus to mine eyes. Now o'er the one half-world
Nature seems dead, and wicked dreams abuse   50
The curtain'd sleep; witchcraft celebrates
Pale Hecate's¹ offerings; and wither'd murder,
Alarum'd by his sentinel, the wolf,
Whose howl's his watch, thus with his stealthy pace,
With Tarquin's² ravishing strides, towards his design 55
Moves like a ghost. Thou sure and firm-set earth,
Hear not my steps, which way they walk, for fear
Thy very stones prate of my whereabout,
And take the present horror from the time,
Which now suits with° it. Whiles I threat, he lives: befits
Words to the heat of deeds too cold breath gives.   61
                                   (A bell rings.)
I go, and it is done. The bell invites me.
Hear it not, Duncan, for it is a knell
That summons thee to heaven, or to hell.   *(Exit.)*

¹*Hecate:* goddess of magic and witchcraft
²*Tarquin:* Roman ruler overthrown by the people for his wicked deeds

Act II SCENE 2

Scene: the same. Enter LADY MACBETH.

LADY MACBETH.   That which hath made them drunk
    hath made me bold;
  What hath quench'd them hath given me fire. Hark!
    Peace!
  It was the owl that shriek'd, the fatal bellman
  Which gives the stern'st good night. He is about it.
  The doors are open, and the surfeited grooms°   drunken servants 5
  Do mock their charge with snores. I have drugg'd
    their possets,°   drinks
  That death and nature do contend about them,
  Whether they live or die.
MACBETH *(within).*   Who's there? What, ho!
LADY MACBETH.   Alack, I am afraid they have awak'd
  And 'tis not done. Th' attempt and not the deed   10
  Confounds° us. Hark! I laid their daggers ready; ruins
  He could not miss 'em. Had he not resembled
  My father as he slept, I had done 't.

    (Enter MACBETH.*)*

                        My husband!
MACBETH.   I have done the deed. Didst thou not hear a
    noise?
LADY MACBETH.   I heard the owl scream and the crickets
    cry.   15
  Did not you speak?
MACBETH.   When?
LADY MACBETH.   Now.
MACBETH.   As I descended?
LADY MACBETH.   Aye.
MACBETH.   Hark!
  Who lies i' the second chamber?
LADY MACBETH.   Donalbain.

MACBETH.   This is a sorry sight. *(Looking on his hands.)* 20
LADY MACBETH.   A foolish thought, to say a sorry sight.
MACBETH.   There's one did laugh in 's sleep, and one
     cried "Murder!"
   That they did wake each other. I stood and heard
      them;
   But they did say their prayers, and address'd them
   Again to sleep.
LADY MACBETH.   There are two lodg'd together.   25
MACBETH.   One cried "God bless us!" and "Amen" the other,
   As they had seen me with these hangman's hands.
   List'ning their fear, I could not say "Amen"
   When they did say "God bless us!"
LADY MACBETH.   Consider it not so deeply.   30
MACBETH.   But wherefore could not I pronounce "Amen"?
   I had most need of blessing, and "Amen"
   Stuck in my throat.
LADY MACBETH.   These deeds must not be thought
   After these ways; so, it will make us mad.   34
MACBETH.   Methought I heard a voice cry "Sleep no more!
   Macbeth does murder sleep"—the innocent sleep,
   Sleep that knits up the ravel'd sleeve° of care,   thread
   The death of each day's life, sore labor's bath,
   Balm of hurt minds, great nature's second course,°   main course
   Chief nourisher in life's feast—
LADY MACBETH.   What do you mean?   40
MACBETH.   Still it cried "Sleep no more!" to all the house:
   "Glamis hath murder'd sleep, and therefore Cawdor
   Shall sleep no more: Macbeth shall sleep no more."
LADY MACBETH.   Who was it that thus cried? Why, worthy
     thane,
   You do unbend your noble strength, to think   45
   So brainsickly of things. Go get some water,
   And wash this filthy witness from your hand.
   Why did you bring these daggers from the place?
   They must lie there. Go carry them, and smear
   The sleepy grooms with blood.
MACBETH.   I'll go no more.   50
   I am afraid to think what I have done;
   Look on 't again I dare not.

LADY MACBETH.   Infirm of purpose!
　Give me the daggers. The sleeping and the dead
　Are but as pictures; 'tis the eye of childhood
　That fears a painted devil. If he do bleed,   55
　I'll gild° the faces of the grooms withal,   smear
　For it must seem their guilt. *(Exit. Knocking within.)*
MACBETH.   Whence is that knocking?
　How is 't with me, when every noise appals me?
　What hands are here? Ha! They pluck out mine eyes!
　Will all great Neptune's ocean wash this blood   60
　Clean from my hand? No; this my hand will rather
　The multitudinous seas incarnadine,°
　Making the green one red.   redden

(Re-enter LADY MACBETH.)

LADY MACBETH.   My hands are of your color, but I shame
　To wear a heart so white. *(Knocking within.)* I hear a
　　knocking   65
　At the south entry. Retire we to our chamber.
　A little water clears us of this deed.
　How easy it is then! Your constancy°   resolute purpose
　Hath left you unattended. *(Knocking within.)* Hark!
　　More knocking.   70
　Get on your nightgown, lest occasion call us
　And show us to be watchers. Be not lost
　So poorly in your thoughts.
MACBETH.   To know my deed, 'twere best not know myself.
                    (Knocking within.)
　Wake Duncan with thy knocking! I would thou could'st!
                    (Exeunt.)

Act II SCENE 3

Scene: The same. Enter a Porter. *Knocking within.*

PORTER.   Here's a knocking indeed! If a man were porter of
hell gate, he should have old[1] turning the key. *(Knocking
within.)* Knock, knock, knock! Who's there, i' the name of
Beelzebub?[2] Here's a farmer, that hanged himself on th'
expectation of plenty. Come in time; have napkins enow[3]   5
about you; here you'll sweat for 't. *(Knocking within.)*
Knock, knock! Who's there, in th' other devil's name?
Faith, here's an equivocator, that could swear in both the
scales against either scale; who committed treason enough
for God's sake, yet could not equivocate to heaven. O,   10
come in, equivocator. *(Knocking within.)* Knock, knock,
knock! Who's there? Faith, here's an English tailor come
hither, for stealing out of a French hose.[4] Come in, tailor;
here you may roast your goose.[5] *(Knocking within.)* Knock,
knock; never at quiet! What are you? But this place is too   15
cold for hell. I'll devil-porter it no further. I had thought to
have let in some of all professions, that go the primrose
way to the everlasting bonfire. *(Knocking within.)* Anon,
anon! I pray you, remember the porter.*(Opens the gate.)*

(Enter MACDUFF *and* LENNOX.*)*

MACDUFF.   Was it so late, friend, ere you went to bed,   20
That you do lie so late?
PORTER.   Faith, sir, we were carousing till the second cock.
And drink, sir, is a great provoker.
MACDUFF.   I believe drink gave thee the lie last night.
PORTER.   That it did, sir, i' the very throat on me. But I re-   25
quited him for his lie, and, I think, being too strong for

---

[1]*old:* plenty of
[2]*Beelzebub:* Prince of Devils and Satan's assistant
[3]*enow:* enough
[4]*French hose:* tight-fitting knee breeches fashionable in France
[5]*goose:* smoothing iron with a gooseneck handle

him, though he took up my leg sometime, yet I made a
shift to cast him.
MACDUFF. Is thy master stirring?

(Enter MACBETH.*)*

Our knocking has awak'd him; here he comes.   30
LENNOX. Good morrow, noble sir.
MACBETH.   Good morrow, both.
MACDUFF. Is the king stirring, worthy thane?
MACBETH.   Not yet.
MACDUFF. He did command me to call timely on him. I had
almost slipp'd the hour.
MACBETH.   I'll bring you to him.
MACDUFF. I know this is a joyful trouble to you;   35
But yet 'tis one.
MACBETH. The labor we delight in physics° pain.   cures
This is the door.
MACDUFF.   I'll make so bold to call,
For 'tis my limited° service.   appointed
                                          (Exit.)

LENNOX. Goes the king hence today?
MACBETH.   He does; he did appoint so. 40
LENNOX. The night has been unruly. Where we lay,
Our chimneys were blown down, and, as they say,
Lamentings heard i' th' air, strange screams of death,
And prophesying with accents terrible
Of dire combustion° and confus'd events   uproar 45
New hatch'd to the woeful time. The obscure bird° owl
Clamor'd the livelong night. Some say the earth
Was feverous and did shake.
MACBETH.   'Twas a rough night.
LENNOX. My young remembrance cannot parallel
A fellow to it.   50

(Re-enter MACDUFF.*)*

MACDUFF. O horror, horror, horror! Tongue nor heart
Cannot conceive nor name thee.

 ⁶*Gorgon:* female monster who turned all who gazed on her to stone

MACBETH.⎫   What's the matter?
LENNOX. ⎭

MACDUFF.   Confusion now hath made his masterpiece.
  Most sacrilegious murder hath broke ope
  The Lord's anointed temple, and stole thence   55
  The life o' the building.

MACBETH.   What is 't you say? The life?

LENNOX.   Mean you his majesty?

MACDUFF.   Approach the chamber, and destroy your sight
  With a new Gorgon.[6] Do not bid me speak;
  See, and then speak yourselves.

  (*Exeunt* MACBETH *and* LENNOX.)

                                 Awake, awake!   60
  Ring the alarum bell. Murder and treason!
  Banquo and Donalbain! Malcolm! Awake!
  Shake off this downy sleep, death's counterfeit,
  And look on death itself! Up, up, and see
  The great doom's° image! Malcolm! Banquo!   doomsday's 65
  As from your graves rise up, and walk like
      sprites,°   spirits
  To countenance° this horror. Ring the bell.   look on
                                   (*Bell rings.*)

  (*Enter* LADY MACBETH.)

LADY MACBETH.   What's the business,
  That such a hideous trumpet calls to parley
  The sleepers of the house? Speak, speak!

MACDUFF.   O gentle lady,
  'Tis not for you to hear what I can speak.   71
  The repetition, in a woman's ear,
  Would murder as it fell.

  (*Enter* BANQUO.)

                     O Banquo, Banquo!
  Our royal master's murder'd.

LADY MACBETH.   Woe, alas!
  What, in our house?
BANQUO.   Too cruel anywhere.   75
  Dear Duff, I prithee, contradict thyself,
  And say it is not so.

  (Re-enter MACBETH *and* LENNOX, *with* ROSS.*)*

MACBETH.   Had I but died an hour before this chance,° happen-
  I had liv'd a blessed time; for from this instant   ing
  There's nothing serious in mortality.   80
  All is but toys; renown and grace is dead;
  The wine of life is drawn, and the mere lees°   dregs
  Is left this vault° to brag of.   world

  (Enter MALCOLM *and* DONALBAIN.*)*

DONALBAIN.   What is amiss?
MACBETH.   You are, and do not know 't.
  The spring, the head, the fountain of your blood   85
  Is stopp'd; the very source of it is stopp'd.
MACDUFF.   Your royal father's murder'd.
MALCOLM.   O, by whom?
LENNOX.   Those of his chamber, as it seem'd, had done 't.
  Their hands and faces were all badg'd with blood;
  So were their daggers, which unwip'd we found   90
  Upon their pillows.
  They star'd, and were distracted; no man's life
  Was to be trusted with them.
MACBETH.   O, yet I do repent me of my fury,
  That I did kill them.
MACDUFF.   Wherefore did you so?   95
MACBETH.   Who can be wise, amaz'd, temp'rate and furious,
  Loyal and neutral, in a moment? No man.
  The expedition° of my violent love   speed
  Outrun the pauser, reason. Here lay Duncan,
  His silver skin lac'd with his golden blood,   100
  And his gash'd stabs look'd like a breach in nature
  For ruin's wasteful entrance; there, the murderers,

Steep'd in the colors of their trade, their daggers
Unmannerly breech'd° with gore. Who could   clothed
   refrain,
That had a heart to love, and in that heart   105
Courage to make 's love known?
LADY MACBETH.   Help me hence, ho!
MACDUFF.   Look to the lady.
MALCOLM *(aside to* DONALBAIN*).*   Why do we hold our
   tongues,
That most may claim this argument° for ours?   subject
DONALBAIN *(aside to* MALCOLM*).*   What should be spoken
   here, where our fate,
Hid in an auger hole,° may rush and seize us?   small hole 110
Let's away;
Our tears are not yet brew'd.
MALCOLM *(aside to* DONALBAIN*).*   Nor our strong sorrow
Upon the foot of motion.°   set in motion
BANQUO.   Look to the lady.

   *(*LADY MACBETH *is carried out.)*

And when we have our naked frailties hid,
That suffer in exposure, let us meet   115
And question this most bloody piece of work
To know it further. Fears and scruples shake us.
In the great hand of God I stand, and thence
Against the undivulg'd pretense° I fight   plot
Of treasonous malice.
MACDUFF.   And so do I.
ALL.   So all.   120
MACBETH.   Let's briefly put on manly readiness,
And meet i' the hall together.
ALL.   Well contented.

   (Exeunt all but MALCOLM *and* DONALBAIN*.)*

MALCOLM.   What will you do? Let's not consort with them.
To show an unfelt sorrow is an office
Which the false man does easy. I'll to England.   125
DONALBAIN.   To Ireland, I; our separated fortune

Shall keep us both the safer. Where we are,
There's daggers in men's smiles. The near in blood,
The nearer bloody.
MALCOLM.   This murderous shaft that's shot
Hath not yet lighted, and our safest way   130
Is to avoid the aim. Therefore to horse;
And let us not be dainty of leave-taking,
But shift° away; there's warrant in° that   steal; justification for
    theft
Which steals itself when there's no mercy left.
                                        (Exeunt.)

Act II SCENE 4

Outside MACBETH'S *Castle. Enter* ROSS *with an* Old Man.

OLD MAN.   Three score and ten I can remember well,
Within the volume of which time I have seen
Hours dreadful and things strange, but this sore night
Hath trifled° former knowings.   made trifles of
ROSS.   Ah, good father,
Thou seest the heavens, as troubled with man's act,   5
Threaten his bloody stage. By the clock 'tis day,
And yet dark night strangles the traveling lamp.°   the sun
Is 't night's predominance, or the day's shame,
That darkness does the face of earth entomb
When living light should kiss it?
OLD MAN.   'Tis unnatural,   10
Even like the deed that's done. On Tuesday last
A falcon tow'ring in her pride of place
Was by a mousing owl hawk'd at and kill'd.
ROSS.   And Duncan's horses—a thing most strange and
    certain—
Beauteous and swift, the minions° of their race,   darlings 15
Turn'd wild in nature, broke their stalls, flung out,
Contending 'gainst obedience, as they would make
War with mankind.

OLD MAN.   'Tis said they eat each other.
ROSS.   They did so, to the amazement of mine eyes
    That look'd upon 't.

(Enter MACDUFF.*)*

                    Here comes the good Macduff.   20
    How goes the world, sir, now?
MACDUFF.   Why, see you not?
ROSS.   Is 't known who did this more than bloody deed?
MACDUFF.   Those that Macbeth hath slain.
ROSS.   Alas, the day!
    What good could they pretend?
MACDUFF.   They were suborn'd.°   bribed
    Malcolm and Donalbain, the king's two sons,   25
    Are stol'n away and fled, which puts upon them
    Suspicion of the deed.
ROSS.   'Gainst nature still!
    Thriftless ambition, that wilt ravin up°   devour
    Thine own life's means! Then 'tis most like
    The sovereignty will fall upon Macbeth.   30
MACDUFF.   He is already nam'd, and gone to Scone[1]
    To be invested.°   crowned
ROSS.   Where is Duncan's body?
MACDUFF.   Carried to Colme-kill,[2]
    The sacred storehouse° of his predecessors   tomb
    And guardian of their bones.
ROSS.   Will you to Scone?   35
MACDUFF.   No, cousin, I'll to Fife.[3]
ROSS.   Well, I will thither.
MACDUFF.   Well, may you see things well done there. Adieu!
    Lest our old robes sit easier than our new!
ROSS.   Farewell, father.
OLD MAN.   God's benison° go with you, and with those   blessing
    That would make good of bad and friends of foes!   41
                                  (Exeunt.)

---

[1]*Scone:* city in Scotland where Scottish kings were crowned
[2]*Colme-kill:* burial ground for Scottish kings
[3]*Fife:* Macduff's castle

Act III SCENE 1

Forres. The palace. Enter BANQUO.

BANQUO.   Thou hast it now: King, Cawdor, Glamis, all,
  As the weird women promised; and I fear
  Thou play'dst most foully for 't. Yet it was said
  It should not stand in thy posterity,
  But that myself should be the root and father   5
  Of many kings. If there come truth from them—
  As upon thee, Macbeth, their speeches shine—
  Why, by the verities on thee made good,
  May they not be my oracles as well
  And set me up in hope? But hush, no more.   10

  (Sennet sounded. Enter MACBETH, *as king;* LADY MAC-
BETH *as queen;* LENNOX, ROSS, Lords, Ladies, *and* Attendants.*)*

MACBETH.   Here's our chief guest.
LADY MACBETH.   If he had been forgotten,
  It had been as a gap in our great feast,
  And all-thing° unbecoming.   in all ways
MACBETH.   Tonight we hold a solemn° supper, sir,   formal
  And I'll request your presence.
BANQUO.   Let your highness   15
  Command upon me, to the which my duties
  Are with a most indissoluble tie
  For ever knit.
MACBETH.   Ride you this afternoon?
BANQUO.   Aye, my good lord.   20
MACBETH.   We should have else desir'd your good advice,
  Which still° hath been both grave and prosperous,   always
  In this day's council; but we'll take tomorrow.
  Is 't far you ride?
BANQUO.   As far, my lord, as will fill up the time   25
  'Twixt this and supper. Go not my horse the better,
  I must become a borrower of the night
  For a dark hour or twain.

MACBETH.   Fail not our feast.
BANQUO.   My lord, I will not.
MACBETH.   We hear ou bloody cousins are bestow'd   30
   In England and in Ireland, not confessing
   Their cruel parricide, filling their hearers
   With strange invention.° But of that tomorrow,   falsehood
   When therewithal we shall have cause of state
   Craving us jointly. Hie you to horse. Adieu,   35
   Till you return at night. Goes Fleance with you?
BANQUO.   Aye, my good lord. Our time does call upon 's.
MACBETH.   I wish your horses swift and sure of foot,
   And so I do commend you to their backs.
   Farewell.   40

(Exit BANQUO.*)*

   Let every man be master of his time
   Till seven at night; to make society
   The sweeter welcome, we will keep ourself
   Till suppertime alone. While° then, God be with you!   until

(Exeunt all but MACBETH *and an* Attendant.*)*

   Sirrah, a word with you. Attend those men   45
   Our pleasure?
ATTENDANT.   They are, my lord, without the palace gate.
MACBETH.   Bring them before us.

(Exit Attendant.*)*

               To be thus is nothing;
   But to be safely thus! Our fears in Banquo
   Stick deep, and in his royalty of nature   50
   Reigns that which would be fear'd. 'Tis much he dares,
   And, to that dauntless temper° of his mind,   disposition
   He hath a wisdom that doth guide his valor
   To act in safety. There is none but he
   Whose being I do fear; and under him   55
   My Genius is rebuk'd, as it is said

Mark Antony's was by Cæsar.[1] He chid the sisters,
When first they put the name of king upon me,
And bade them speak to him; then prophet-like
They hail'd him father to a line of kings.   60
Upon my head they plac'd a fruitless crown
And put a barren scepter in my gripe,
Thence to be wrench'd with an unlineal hand,
No son of mine succeeding. If 't be so,   64
For Banquo's issue° have I fil'd° my mind;   offspring; defiled
For them the gracious Duncan have I murder'd;
Put rancors in the vessel of my peace
Only for them, and mine eternal jewel°   soul
Given to the common enemy of man,°   the devil
To make them kings, the seed° of Banquo kings!   sons 70
Rather than so, come, Fate, into the list,°   arena
And champion° me to the utterance!° Who's there?   fight; uttermost

(Re-enter Attendant, with two Murderers.)

Now go to the door, and stay there till we call.

(Exit Attendant.)

Was it not yesterday we spoke together?
FIRST MURDERER.   It was, so please your highness.
MACBETH.   Well then, now 75
Have you consider'd of my speeches? Know
That it was he in the times past which held you
So under fortune, which you thought had been
Our innocent self. This I made good to you
In our last conference; pass'd in probation° with you   gave proofs
How you were borne in hand,° how cross'd,   deceived
    the instruments,   81
Who wrought with them, and all things else that might
To half a soul and to a notion craz'd
Say "Thus did Banquo."
FIRST MURDERER.   You made it known to us.

[1]*and under him . . . Cæsar:* Octavius Cæsar continually outmaneuvered
Mark Antony in their struggle for control of the Roman world.

MACBETH.   I did so, and went further, which is now   85
    Our point of second meeting. Do you find
    Your patience so predominant in your nature
    That you can let this go? Are you so gospel'd,°   Christianized
    To pray for this good man and for his issue,
    Whose heavy hand hath bow'd you to the grave   90
    And beggar'd yours for ever?
FIRST MURDERER.   We are men, my liege.
MACBETH.   Aye, in the catalogue ye go for men
    As hounds and greyhounds, mongrels, spaniels, curs,
    Shoughs, waterrugs, and demiwolves are clept°   called
    All by the name of dogs. The valu'd file   95
    Distinguishes the swift, the slow, the subtle,
    The housekeeper, the hunter, every one
    According to the gift which bounteous nature
    Hath in him clos'd, whereby he does receive
    Particular addition° from the bill   distinction 100
    That writes them all alike. And so of men.
    Now if you have a station in the file
    Not i' the worst rank of manhood, say it,
    And I will put that business in your bosoms
    Whose execution takes your enemy off,   105
    Grapples you to the heart and love of us,
    Who wear our health but sickly in his life,
    Which in his death were perfect.
SECOND MURDERER.   I am one, my liege,
    Whom the vile blows and buffets of the world
    Have so incens'd that I am reckless what   110
    I do to spite the world.
FIRST MURDERER.   And I another
    So weary with disasters, tugg'd with° fortune,   pulled about by
    That I would set my life on any chance
    To mend it or be rid on 't.
MACBETH.   Both of you
    Know Banquo was your enemy.
BOTH MURDERERS.   True, my lord.   115
MACBETH.   So is he mine, and in such bloody distance°   close proximity
    That every minute of his being thrusts
    Against my near'st of life. And though I could

With barefac'd power sweep him from my sight
And bid my will avouch° it, yet I must not,   condone 120
For certain friends that are both his and mine,
Whose loves I may not drop, but wail his fall
Who I myself struck down. And thence it is
That I to your assistance do make love,
Masking the business from the common eye   125
For sundry weighty reasons.

SECOND MURDERER.   We shall, my lord,
Perform what you command us.

FIRST MURDERER.   Though our lives—

MACBETH. Your spirits shine through you. Within this hour
     at most
I will advise you where to plant yourselves,   precise
Acquaint you with the perfect spy o' the time,°   moment 130
The moment on 't; for 't must be done tonight,
And something° from the palace; always thought   somewhat
That I require a clearness.° And with him—   freedom
                                             from suspicion
To leave no rubs nor botches in the work—
Fleance his son, that keeps him company,   135
Whose absence is no less material to me
Than is his father's, must embrace the fate
Of that dark hour. Resolve yourselves apart;
I'll come to you anon.

BOTH MURDERERS.   We are resolv'd, my lord.

MACBETH. I'll call upon you straight; abide within.   140

(Exeunt Murderers.*)*

It is concluded, Banquo, thy soul's flight,
If it find heaven, must find it out tonight.   *(Exit.)*

Act III scene 2

Enter LADY MACBETH *and a* Servant.

LADY MACBETH.   Is Banquo gone from court?
SERVANT.   Aye, madam, but returns again tonight.
LADY MACBETH.   Say to the king I would attend his leisure
   For a few words.
SERVANT.   Madam, I will.   *(Exit.)*
LADY MACBETH.   Naught's had, all's spent,
   Where our desire is got without content.   5
   'Tis safer to be that which we destroy
   Than by destruction dwell in doubtful joy.

   (Enter MACBETH.*)*

   How now, my lord! Why do you keep alone,
   Of sorriest fancies your companions making,
   Using those thoughts which should indeed have died   10
   With them they think on? Things without all remedy
   Should be without regard: what's done is done.
MACBETH.   We have scotch'd° the snake, not kill'd it.   slashed
   She'll close° and be herself, whilst our poor malice   heal
   Remains in danger of her former tooth.   15
   But let the frame of things disjoint, both the worlds
     suffer,
   Ere we will eat our meal in fear, and sleep
   In the affliction of these terrible dreams
   That shake us nightly. Better be with the dead,
   Whom we, to gain our peace, have sent to peace,   20
   Than on the torture of the mind to lie
   In restless ecstasy.° Duncan is in his grave;   frenzy
   After life's fitful fever he sleeps well.
   Treason has done his worst; nor steel, nor poison,
   Malice domestic, foreign levy, nothing,   25
   Can touch him further.
LADY MACBETH.   Come on;

Gentle my lord, sleek o'er your rugged looks.
Be bright and jovial among your guests tonight.
MACBETH.   So shall I, love; and so, I pray, be you.   29
Let your remembrance apply to Banquo;
Present him eminence,° both with eye and tongue.   do him honor
Unsafe the while, that we
Must lave our honors in these flattering streams,
And make our faces vizards° to our hearts,   masks
Disguising what they are.
LADY MACBETH.   You must leave this.   35
MACBETH.   O, full of scorpions is my mind, dear wife!
Thou know'st that Banquo, and his Fleance, lives.
LADY MACBETH.   But in them nature's copy's not eterne.
MACBETH.   There's comfort yet; they are assailable.   39
Then be thou jocund.° Ere the bat hath flown   gay
His cloister'd flight, ere to black Hecate's summons
The shard-borne beetle with his drowsy hums
Hath rung night's yawning peal, there shall be done
A deed of dreadful note.
LADY MACBETH.   What's to be done?
MACBETH.   Be innocent of the knowledge, dearest chuck, 45
Till thou applaud the deed. Come, seeling° night,   blinding
Scarf up the tender eye of pitiful day,
And with thy bloody and invisible hand
Cancel and tear to pieces that great bond
Which keeps me pale! Light thickens, and the crow   50
Makes wing to the rooky wood.
Good things of day begin to droop and drowse,
Whiles night's black agents to their preys do rouse.
Thou marvel'st at my words, but hold thee still;
Things bad begun make strong themselves by ill.   55
So, prithee, go with me.   *(Exeunt.)*

Act III scene 3

A park near the palace. Enter three Murderers.

FIRST MURDERER.   But who did bid thee join with us?
THIRD MURDERER.   Macbeth.
SECOND MURDERER.   He needs not our mistrust, since
     he delivers
     Our offices,° and what we have to do,   duties
     To the direction just.°   in detail
FIRST MURDERER.   Then stand with us.
     The west yet glimmers with some streaks of day.   5
     Now spurs the lated° traveler apace   belated
     To gain the timely inn, and near approaches
     The subject of our watch.
THIRD MURDERER.   Hark! I hear horses.
BANQUO *(within).*   Give us a light there, ho!
SECOND MURDERER.   Then 'tis he. The rest
     That are within the note of expectation   10
     Already are i' the court.
FIRST MURDERER.   His horses go about.
THIRD MURDERER.   Almost a mile; but he does usually—
     So all men do—from hence to the palace gate
     Make it their walk.
SECOND MURDERER.   A light, a light!

(Enter BANQUO, *and* FLEANCE *with a torch.)*

THIRD MURDERER.   'Tis he.
FIRST MURDERER.   Stand to 't.   15
BANQUO.   It will be rain tonight.
FIRST MURDERER.   Let it come down.

(They set upon BANQUO.*)*

BANQUO.   O, treachery! Fly, good Fleance, fly, fly, fly!
     Thou mayst revenge. O slave!
                         (Dies. FLEANCE *escapes.)*

THIRD MURDERER.　Who did strike out the light?
FIRST MURDERER.　　　　　　　　　　Was 't not the way?
THIRD MURDERER.　There's but one down; the son is fled.
SECOND MURDERER.　　　　　　　　We have lost 20
　　Best half of our affair.
FIRST MURDERER.　Well, let's away and say how much
　　is done.

　　　　　　　　　　　　　　　　　　(Exeunt.)

Act III Scene 4

A hall in the palace. A banquet prepared. Enter MACBETH,
LADY MACBETH, ROSS, LENNOX, Lords, *and* Attendants.

MACBETH.　You know your own degrees;° sit down. At first ranks
　　And last a hearty welcome.
LORDS.　　　　　　　　　　Thanks to your majesty.
MACBETH.　Ourself will mingle with society
　　And play the humble host.
　　Our hostess keeps her state,° but in best time throne 5
　　We will require her welcome.
LADY MACBETH.　Pronounce it for me, sir, to all our friends,
　　For my heart speaks they are welcome.

(Enter First Murderer *to the door.)*

MACBETH.　See, they encounter° thee with their heart's greet
　　thanks.
　　Both sides are even; here I'll sit i' the midst.　　　　10
　　Be large in mirth; anon we'll drink a measure° draught
　　The table round. *(Approaching the door.)* There's blood
　　upon thy face.
MURDERER.　'Tis Banquo's then.
MACBETH.　'Tis better thee without than he within.
　　Is he dispatch'd?° killed 15
MURDERER.　My lord, his throat is cut; that I did for him.
MACBETH.　Thou art the best o' the cutthroats; yet he's good

That did the like for Fleance. If thou didst it,
Thou art the nonpareil.
MURDERER.   Most royal sir,
    Fleance is 'scaped.   20
MACBETH *(aside).*   Then comes my fit again. I had else
        been perfect,
    Whole as the marble, founded as the rock,
    As broad and general as the casing° air.   surrounding
    But now I am cabin'd, cribb'd, confin'd, bound in
    To saucy doubts and fears.—But Banquo's safe?   25
MURDERER.   Aye, my good lord: safe in a ditch he bides,
    With twenty trenched gashes on his head,
    The least a death to nature.
MACBETH.   Thanks for that.
    (Aside.) There the grown serpent lies; the worm°   snake
        that's fled
    Hath nature that in time will venom breed,   30
    No teeth for the present. Get thee gone. Tomorrow
    We'll hear ourselves° again.   confer

(Exit Murderer.*)*

LADY MACBETH.   My royal lord,
    You do not give the cheer. The feast is sold
    That is not often vouch'd, while 'tis a-making,° proceeding
    'Tis given with welcome. To feed were best
        at home;   35
    From thence° the sauce to meat is ceremony;   away from home
    Meeting were bare° without it.   barren
MACBETH.   Sweet remembrancer!
    Now good digestion wait on° appetite,   accompany
    And health on both!
LENNOX.   May 't please your highness sit.

(The Ghost of BANQUO *enters and sits in* MACBETH'S
place.)*

MACBETH.   Here had we now our country's honor
        roof'd,°   under
    Were the grac'd person of our Banquo present—   one roof   41

Who may I rather challenge° for unkindness   reprove
Than pity for mischance!
ROSS.   His absence, sir,
Lays blame upon his promise. Please 't your highness
To grace us with your royal company.   45
MACBETH.   The table's full.
LENNOX.   Here is a place reserv'd, sir.
MACBETH.   Where?
LENNOX.   Here, my good lord. What is 't that moves
      your highness?
MACBETH.   Which of you have done this?
LORDS.   What, my good lord?
MACBETH.   Thou canst not say I did it. Never shake   50
Thy gory locks at me.
ROSS.   Gentlemen, rise; his highness is not well.
LADY MACBETH.   Sit, worthy friends. My lord is often thus,
And hath been from his youth. Pray you, keep seat;
The fit is momentary; upon a thought°   suddenly 55
He will again be well. If much you note him,
You shall offend him and extend his passion.
Feed, and regard him not. Are you a man?
MACBETH.   Aye, and a bold one, that dare look on that
Which might appal the devil.
LADY MACBETH.   O proper stuff!°   a fine thing! 60
This is the very painting of your fear.
This is the air-drawn dagger which you said
Led you to Duncan. O, these flaws and starts,
Impostors to true fear, would well become
A woman's story at a winter's fire,   65
Authoriz'd° by her grandam. Shame itself!   told
Why do you make such faces? When all 's done,
You look but on a stool.
MACBETH.   Prithee, see there! Behold! Look! Lo!
      How say you?
Why, what care I? If thou canst nod, speak too.   70
If charnel houses° and our graves must send   tombs
Those that we bury back, our monuments
Shall be the maws of kites.°   vultures' stomachs

(Exit Ghost.)

LADY MACBETH.   What, quite unmann'd in folly?

MACBETH.   If I stand here, I saw him.

LADY MACBETH.   Fie, for shame!

MACBETH.   Blood hath been shed ere now, i' th' olden time, 75
Ere humane statute purg'd° the gentle weal;°   civilized; state
Aye, and since too, murders have been perform'd
Too terrible for the ear. The time has been
That when the brains were out, the man would die,
And there an end; but now they rise again,   80
With twenty mortal murders on their crowns,
And push us from our stools. This is more strange
Than such a murder is.

LADY MACBETH.   My worthy lord,
Your noble friends do lack you.

MACBETH.   I do forget.
Do not muse° at me, my most worthy friends;   wonder 85
I have a strange infirmity, which is nothing
To those that know me. Come, love and health to all;
Then I'll sit down. Give me some wine, fill full.
I drink to the general joy o' the whole table,
And to our dear friend Banquo, whom we miss.   90
Would he were here! To all and him we thirst,
And all to all.

LORDS.   Our duties, and the pledge.

(Re-enter Ghost.)

MACBETH.   Avaunt, and quit my sight! Let the earth hide
thee!
Thy bones are marrowless, thy blood is cold;
Thou hast no speculation° in those eyes   vision 95
Which thou dost glare with.

LADY MACBETH.   Think of this, good peers,
But as a thing of custom:° 'tis no other,   usual thing
Only it spoils the pleasure of the time.

MACBETH.   What man dare, I dare.
Approach thou like the rugged Russian bear,   100
The arm'd rhinoceros, or the Hyrcan tiger;[1]

¹*Hyrcan tiger:* the kind of tiger that roamed near the Caspian Sea

Taken any shape but that, and my firm nerves
Shall never tremble. Or be alive again,
And dare me to the desert with thy sword;   104
If trembling I inhabit° then, protest° me   live on; proclaim
The baby of a girl. Hence, horrible shadow!
Unreal mockery, hence!

(Exit Ghost.)

                        Why, so: being gone,
I am a man again. Pray you, sit still.
LADY MACBETH.   You have displac'd the mirth, broke
    the good meeting,
With most admir'd° disorder.   wondered at
MACBETH.   Can such things be,   110
And overcome us like a summer's cloud,
Without our special wonder? You make me strange
Even to the disposition that I owe,°   own
When now I think you can behold such sights,
And keep the natural ruby of your cheeks,   115
When mine is blanch'd with fear.
ROSS.   What sights, my lord?
LADY MACBETH.   I pray you, speak not; he grows worse
    and worse.
Question enrages him. At once, good night.
Stand not upon the order of your going,
But go at once.
LENNOX.   Good night; and better health   120
Attend his majesty!
LADY MACBETH.   A kind good night to all!

(Exeunt all but MACBETH *and* LADY MACBETH.*)*

MACBETH.   It will have blood. They say blood will have
    blood.
Stones have been known to move and trees to speak;
Augurs° and understood relations° have   auguries; revelations
By maggot-pies° and choughs and rooks brought   magpies
    forth
                                       125

The secret'st man of blood. What is the night?

LADY MACBETH.   Almost at odds with morning, which is
which.

MACBETH.   How say'st thou that Macduff denies his person
At our great bidding?

LADY MACBETH.   Did you send to him, sir?

MACBETH.   I hear it by the way,° but I will send.   indirectly 130
There's not a one of them but in his house
I keep a servant fee'd.° I will tomorrow,   as a paid spy
And betimes I will, to the weird sisters.
More shall they speak, for now I am bent to know,
By the worst means, the worst. For mine own good   135
All causes shall give way. I am in blood
Stepp'd in so far that, should I wade no more,
Returning were as tedious as go o'er:
Strange things I have in head that will to hand,
Which must be acted ere they may be scann'd.   140

LADY MACBETH.   You lack the season° of all natures,   preservative
sleep.

MACBETH.   Come, we'll to sleep. My strange and
self-abuse°   hallucination
Is the initiate fear that wants hard use.°   lacks experience
We are yet but young in deed.   *(Exeunt.)*

Act III   SCENE 5

A *heath. Thunder. Enter the three* Witches, *meeting*
HECATE.

FIRST WITCH.   Why, how now, Hecate! You look angerly.

HECATE.   Have I not reason, beldams° as you are,   hags
Saucy and overbold? How did you dare
To trade and traffic with Macbeth
In riddles and affairs of death,   5
And I, the mistress of your charms,

The close° contriver of all harms,   secret
Was never call'd to bear my part,
Or show the glory of our art?
And, which is worse, all you have done   10
Hath been but for a wayward son,
Spiteful and wrathful, who, as others do,
Loves for his own ends, not for you.
But make amends now. Get you gone,
And at the pit of Acheron¹   15
Meet me i' the morning. Thither he
Will come to know his destiny.
Your vessels and your spells provide,
Your charms and every thing beside.
I am for the air; this night I'll spend   20
Unto a dismal and fatal end.
Great business must be wrought ere noon.
Upon the corner of the moon
There hangs a vaporous drop profound;
I'll catch it ere it comes to ground,   25
And that distill'd by magic sleights
Shall raise such artificial sprites
As by the strength of their illusion
Shall draw him on to his confusion.
He shall spurn fate, scorn death, and bear   30
His hopes 'bove wisdom, grace, and fear.
And you all know security°   false confidence
Is mortals' chiefest enemy.

*(Music and a song within: "Come away, come away,"
etc.)*

Hark! I am call'd; my little spirit, see,
Sits in a foggy cloud, and stays for me.   *(Exit.)* 35
FIRST WITCH.   Come, let's make haste; she'll soon be back
     again.
                              (Exeunt.)

¹*Acheron:* a river of the underworld which leads to Hades

Act III SCENE 6

Forres. The palace. Enter LENNOX *and another* Lord.

LENNOX.   My former speeches have but hit your thoughts,
Which can interpret farther. Only I say
Things have been strangely borne.° The gracious   managed
   Duncan
Was pitied of° Macbeth. Marry, he was dead.   by
And the right-valiant Banquo walk'd too late—   5
Whom you may say, if 't please you, Fleance kill'd,
For Fleance fled. Men must not walk too late.
Who cannot want the thought° how monstrous   help thinking
It was for Malcolm and for Donalbain
To kill their gracious father? Damned fact!   10
How it did grieve Macbeth! Did he not straight,
In pious rage, the two delinquents tear,
That were the slaves of drink and thralls° of sleep?   slaves
Was not that nobly done? Aye, and wisely too;
For 'twould have anger'd any heart alive   15
To hear the men deny 't. So that, I say,
He has borne all things well, and I do think
That, had he Duncan's sons under his key—
As, an 't° please heaven, he shall not—they should find   if it
What 'twere to kill a father; so should Fleance.   20
But, peace! For from° broad words and 'cause   because of
   he fail'd
His presence at the tyrant's feast, I hear,
Macduff lives in disgrace. Sir, can you tell
Where he bestows himself?
LORD.   The son of Duncan,
From whom this tyrant holds the due° of birth,   usurps 25
                                                   the right
Lives in the English court, and is receiv'd
Of° the most pious Edward[1] with such grace   by
That the malevolence of fortune nothing
Takes from his high respect. Thither Macduff

[1]*Edward:* Edward the Confessor, King of England (1004-1066)

Is gone to pray the holy King upon his aid°   behalf 30
To wake Northumberland and warlike Siward,
That by the help of these, with Him above
To ratify the work, we may again
Give to our tables meat, sleep to our nights,
Free from our feasts and banquets bloody knives,   35
Do faithful homage, and receive free honors —
All which we pine for now. And this report
Hath so exasperate the King that he
Prepares for some attempt of war.
LENNOX.   Sent he to Macduff?
LORD.   He did, and with an absolute "Sir, not I,"   40
The cloudy° messenger turns me his back   surly
And hums, as who would say "You'll rue the time
That clogs° me with this answer."   burdens
LENNOX.   And that well might
Advise him to a caution, to hold what distance
His wisdom can provide. Some holy angel   45
Fly to the court of England and unfold
His message ere he come, that a swift blessing
May soon return to this our suffering country
Under a hand accurs'd!
LORD.   I'll send my prayers with him.
                                   (*Exeunt.*)

Act IV   SCENE 1

*A cavern. In the middle, a boiling Cauldron. Thunder.
Enter the three* Witches.

FIRST WITCH.   Thrice the brinded° cat hath mew'd.   striped
SECOND WITCH.   Thrice and once the hedgepig whin'd.
THIRD WITCH.   Harpier[1] cries "'Tis time, 'tis time."
FIRST WITCH.   Round about the cauldron go;
  In the poison'd entrails throw.   5

[1]*Harpier:* mythical monster — half woman, half bird

Toad, that under cold stone
Days and nights has thirty-one
Swelter'd° venom sleeping got,   oozed out
Boil thou first i' the charmed pot.
ALL. Double, double, toil and trouble; 10
Fire burn and cauldron bubble.
SECOND WITCH. Fillet of a fenny° snake, swamp (fen)
In the cauldron boil and bake;
Eye of newt and toe of frog,
Wool of bat and tongue of dog, 15
Adder's fork° and blindworm's° sting, forked tongue; snake's
Lizard's leg and howlet's° wing, owlet's
For a charm of powerful trouble,
Like a hell-broth boil and bubble.
ALL. Double, double, toil and trouble; 20
Fire burn and cauldron bubble.
THIRD WITCH. Scale of dragon, tooth of wolf,
Witches' mummy, maw and gulf° stomach and throat
Of the ravin'd° salt-sea shark, ravenous
Root of hemlock digg'd i' the dark, 25
Liver of blaspheming Jew,
Gall of goat and slips of yew° yew tree
Sliver'd in the moon's eclipse,
Nose of Turk and Tartar's lips,
Finger of birth-strangled babe 30
Ditch-deliver'd° by a drab, ditch-born
Make the gruel thick and slab.° slab-like
Add thereto a tiger's chaudron° entrails
For the ingredients of our cauldron.
ALL. Double, double, toil and trouble; 35
Fire burn and cauldron bubble.
SECOND WITCH. Cool it with a baboon's blood,
Then the charm is firm and good.

(Enter HECATE *to the other three* Witches.*)*

HECATE. O, well done! I commend your pains,
And every one shall share i' the gains. 40
And now about the cauldron sing,

Like elves and fairies in a ring,
Enchanting all that you put in.

(Music and a song: "Black spirits," etc. HECATE *retires.)*

SECOND WITCH. By the pricking of my thumbs,
Something wicked this way comes.   45
Open, locks,
Whoever knocks!

(Enter MACBETH.*)*

MACBETH. How now, you secret, black, and midnight hags!
What is 't you do?
ALL.   A deed without a name.
MACBETH. I conjure you by that which you profess,   50
Howe'er you come to know it, answer me.
Though you unite the winds and let them fight
Against the churches, though the yesty° waves   foamy
Confound and swallow navigation up,
Though bladed corn be lodg'd° and trees blown   beaten flat
    down,   55
Though castles topple on their warders' heads,
Though palaces and pyramids do slope
Their heads to their foundations, though the treasure
Of nature's germens° tumble all together   seeds
Even till destruction sicken,° answer me   is satiated 60
To what I ask you.
FIRST WITCH.   Speak.
SECOND WITCH.   Demand.
THIRD WITCH.   We'll answer.
FIRST WITCH. Say if thou 'dst rather hear it from our
    mouths,
Or from our masters.
MACBETH.   Call 'em, let me see 'em.
FIRST WITCH. Pour in sow's blood, that hath eaten
Her nine farrow; grease that's sweaten   65
From the murderer's gibbet throw
Into the flame.

ALL.   Come, high or low;
  Thyself and office° deftly show!   function

(Thunder. First Apparition: *an armed Head.)*

MACBETH.   Tell me, thou unknown power—
FIRST WITCH.   He knows thy thought.
  Hear his speech, but say thou nought.   70
FIRST APPARITION.   Macbeth! Macbeth! Macbeth! Beware
   Macduff!
  Beware the thane of Fife! Dismiss me. Enough.
                       (Descends.)
MACBETH.   Whate'er thou art, for thy good caution thanks;
  Thou hast harp'd° my fear aright. But one word more— hit
FIRST WITCH.   He will not be commanded. Here's another,
  More potent than the first.   76

(Thunder. Second Apparition: *a bloody Child.)*

SECOND APPARITION.   Macbeth! Macbeth! Macbeth!
MACBETH.   Had I three ears, I'd hear thee.
SECOND APPARITION.   Be bloody, bold, and resolute; laugh
   to scorn
  The power of man, for none of woman born   80
  Shall harm Macbeth.   *(Descends.)*
MACBETH.   Then live, Macduff. What need I fear of thee?
  But yet I'll make assurance doubly sure,
  And take a bond° of fate. Thou shalt not live,   guarantee
  That I may tell palehearted fear it lies,   85
  And sleep in spite of thunder.

(Thunder. Third Apparition: *a Child crowned, with a tree in his hand.)*

                    What is this,
  That rises like the issue of a king,
  And wears upon his baby-brow the round°   the crown
  And top of sovereignty?
ALL.   Listen, but speak not to t.

THIRD APPARITION.   Be lion-mettled, proud, and take
    no care   90
  Who chafes, who frets, or where conspirers are.
  Macbeth shall never vanquish'd be until
  Great Birnam wood to high Dunsinane hill
  Shall come against him.   *(Descends.)*
MACBETH.   That will never be.
  Who can impress° the forest, bid the tree   compel 95
  Unfix his earth-bound root? Sweet bodements!°   omens
    Good!
  Rebellion's head, rise never, till the wood
  Of Birnam rise, and our high-plac'd Macbeth
  Shall live the lease of nature,° pay his breath   a lifetime
  To time and mortal custom. Yet my heart   100
  Throbs to know one thing. Tell me, if your art
  Can tell so much, shall Banquo's issue ever
  Reign in this kingdom?   *(Hautboys.)*
ALL.   Seek to know no more.
MACBETH.   I will be satisfied. Deny me this,
  And an eternal curse fall on you! Let me know!   105
  Why sinks that cauldron, and what noise is this?
FIRST WITCH.   Show!
SECOND WITCH.   Show!
THIRD WITCH.   Show!
ALL.   Show his eyes, and grieve his heart;   110
  Come like shadows, so depart!

(A show of eight Kings,[2] the last with a glass in his hand;
BANQUO'S *Ghost following.)*

MACBETH.   Thou art too like the spirit of Banquo. Down!
  Thy crown does sear mine eyeballs. And thy hair,
  Thou other gold-bound brow, is like the first.
  A third is like the former. Filthy hags!   115
  Why do you show me this? A fourth! Start, eyes!
  What, will the line stretch out to the crack of doom?
  Another yet! A seventh! I'll see no more.

  [2]*eight Kings:* the Stuart kings of Scotland, thought to be descended from
Banquo

And yet the eighth appears, who bears a glass
Which shows me many more; and some I see   120
That twofold balls and treble scepters[3] carry.
Horrible sight! Now I see 'tis true,
For the blood-bolter'd° Banquo smiles upon me,   smeared
And points at them for his. What, is this so?
FIRST WITCH.   Aye, sir, all this is so. But why   125
Stands Macbeth thus amazedly?
Come, sisters, cheer we up his sprites,
And show the best of our delights.
I'll charm the air to give a sound,
While you perform your antic round,°   grotesque dance   130
That this great king may kindly say
Our duties did his welcome pay.

(*Music. The* Witches *dance, and then vanish, with*
HECATE.)

MACBETH.   Where are they? Gone? Let this pernicious hour
Stand aye accursed in the calendar!
Come in, without there!

(*Enter* LENNOX.)

LENNOX.   What's your grace's will?   135
MACBETH.   Saw you the weird sisters?
LENNOX.   No, my lord.
MACBETH.   Came they not by you?
LENNOX.   No indeed, my lord.
MACBETH.   Infected be the air whereon they ride,
And damn'd all those that trust them! I did hear
The galloping of horse. Who was 't came by?   140
LENNOX.   'Tis two or three, my lord, that bring you word
Macduff is fled to England.
MACBETH.   Fled to England!
LENNOX.   Aye, my good lord.
MACBETH (*aside*).   Time, thou anticipat'st my dread exploits.
The flighty purpose never is o'ertook   145
Unless the deed go with it. From this moment
The very firstlings° of my heart shall be   first impulses

[3]*Twofold . . . scepters:* symbols of James I of England (1603-1625)

The firstlings° of my hand. And even now,   first deeds
To crown my thoughts with acts, be it thought and done.
The castle of Macduff I will surprise,   150
Seize upon Fife, give to the edge o' the sword
His wife, his babies, and all unfortunate souls
That trace him in his line. No boasting like a fool;
This deed I'll do before this purpose cool.
But no more sights!—Where are these gentlemen?   155
Come, bring me where they are.   *(Exeunt.)*

Act IV SCENE 2

Fife. MACDUFF'S *Castle. Enter* LADY MACDUFF, *her* SON, *and* ROSS.

LADY MACDUFF.   What had he done, to make him fly the
     land?
ROSS.   You must have patience, madam.
LADY MACDUFF.   He had none.
     His flight was madness. When our actions do not,
     Our fears do make us traitors.
ROSS.   You know not
     Whether it was his wisdom or his fear.   5
LADY MACDUFF. Wisdom! To leave his wife, to leave
     his babes,
     His mansion and his titles in a place
     From whence himself does fly? He loves us not;
     He wants° the natural touch.° For the poor wren,   lacks;
                                                         instinct
     The most diminutive of birds, will fight,   10
     Her young ones in° her nest, against the owl.   being in
     All is the fear and nothing is the love,
     As little is the wisdom, where the flight
     So runs against all reason.
ROSS.   My dearest coz,°   cousin 14
     I pray you, school° yourself. But, for your husband, control

He is noble, wise, judicious, and best knows
The fits° o' the season.° I dare not speak much   ^{quirks;}
   further,   ^{times}
But cruel are the times, when we are traitors
And do not know ourselves; when we hold° rumor   interpret
From what we fear, yet know not what we fear,   20
But float upon a wild and violent sea
Each way and move. I take my leave of you;
Shall not be long but I'll be here again.
Things at the worst will cease, or else climb upward
To what they were before. My pretty cousin,   25
Blessing upon you!

LADY MACDUFF.   Father'd he is, and yet he's fatherless.

ROSS.   I am so much a fool, should I stay longer,
It would be my disgrace and your discomfort.
I take my leave at once.   *(Exit.)*

LADY MACDUFF.   Sirrah, your father's dead.   30
And what will you do now? How will you live?

SON.   As birds do, mother.

LADY MACDUFF.   What, with worms and flies?

SON.   With what I get, I mean; and so do they.

LADY MACDUFF.   Poor bird! Thou'dst never fear the net
   nor lime,°   ^{birdlime}
The pitfall nor the gin.°   ^{trap} 35

SON.   Why should I, mother? Poor birds they are not set for.
My father is not dead, for all your saying.

LADY MACDUFF.   Yes, he is dead. How wilt thou do for a
   father?

SON.   Nay, how will you do for a husband?

LADY MACDUFF.   Why, I can buy me twenty at any market.

SON.   Then you'll buy 'em to sell again.   41

LADY MACDUFF.   Thou speak'st with all thy wit, and yet,
   i' faith,
With wit enough for thee.

SON.   Was my father a traitor, mother?

LADY MACDUFF.   Aye, that he was.   45

SON.   What is a traitor?

LADY MACDUFF.   Why, one that swears and lies.

SON.   And be all traitors that do so?

LADY MACDUFF.   Every one that does so is a traitor, and
   must be hanged.
SON.   And must they all be hanged that swear and lie?   50
LADY MACDUFF.   Every one.
SON.   Who must hang them?
LADY MACDUFF.   Why, the honest men.
SON.   Then the liars and swearers are fools, for there are liars
   and swearers enow° to beat the honest men   enough
   and hang up them.   56
LADY MACDUFF.   Now, God help thee, poor monkey!
   But how wilt thou do for a father?
SON.   If he were dead, you'd weep for him. If you would not,
   it were a good sign that I should quickly have a new
   father.   60
LADY MACDUFF.   Poor prattler, how thou talk'st!

(Enter a Messenger.*)*

MESSENGER.   Bless you, fair dame! I am not to you
   known,
   Though in your state of honor° I am perfect.°   of your nobility; informed
   I doubt° some danger does approach you nearly.   fear
   If you will take a homely° man's advice,   humble   65
   Be not found here; hence, with your little ones.
   To fright you thus, methinks I am too savage;
   To do worse to you were fell° cruelty,   fierce
   Which is too nigh your person. Heaven preserve you!
   I dare abide no longer.   *(Exit.)*
LADY MACDUFF.   Whither should I fly?   70
   I have done no harm. But I remember now
   I am in this earthly world, where to do harm
   Is often laudable, to do good sometime
   Accounted dangerous folly. Why then, alas,
   Do I put up that womanly defense,   75
   To say I have done no harm?—What are these faces?

(Enter Murderers.*)*

FIRST MURDERER.   Where is your husband?

LADY MACDUFF.   I hope, in no place so unsanctified
    Where such as thou mayst find him.
FIRST MURDERER.   He's a traitor.
SON.   Thou liest, thou shag-ear'd° villain!   shaggy-haired
FIRST MURDERER.   What, you egg!
                                        (Stabbing him.)
    Young fry° of treachery!   spawn
SON.   He has kill'd me, mother.
    Run away, I pray you!   *(Dies.)*

(Exit LADY MACDUFF, *crying 'Murder!' Exeunt* Murderers,
following her.)

Act IV   SCENE 3

England. Before the King's palace. Enter MALCOLM *and*
MACDUFF.

MALCOLM.   Let us seek out some desolate shade, and there
    Weep our sad bosoms empty.
MACDUFF.   Let us rather
    Hold fast the mortal° sword, and like good men   deadly
    Bestride our downfall'n birthdom.° Each new morn   home-
                                                          land
    New widows howl, new orphans cry, new sorrows   5
    Strike heaven on the face, that it resounds
    As if it felt with Scotland and yell'd out
    Like syllable of dolor.°   grief
MALCOLM.   What I believe, I'll wail;
    What know, believe; and what I can redress,
    As I shall find the time to friend,° I will.   to be favorable 10
    What you have spoke, it may be so perchance.
    This tyrant, whose sole° name blisters our tongues,   very
    Was once thought honest. You have lov'd him well;
    He hath not touch'd you yet. I am young; but something
    You may deserve of him through me, and wisdom   15
    To offer up a weak, poor, innocent lamb
    T' appease an angry god.

MACDUFF. I am not treacherous.
MALCOLM.   But Macbeth is.
   A good and virtuous nature may recoil°   yield
   In an imperial charge. But I shall crave your pardon; 20
   That which you are, my thoughts cannot transpose.
   Angels are bright still, though the brightest fell.
   Though all things foul would wear the brows of grace,
   Yet grace must still look so.°   like herself
MACDUFF.   I have lost my hopes.
MALCOLM. Perchance even there where I did find my
     doubts.   25
   Why in the rawness left you wife and child,
   Those precious motives, those strong knots of love,
   Without leave-taking? I pray you,
   Let not my jealousies° be your dishonors,   suspicions
   But mine own safeties.° You may be rightly just, safeguards
   Whatever I shall think.   31
MACDUFF.   Bleed, bleed, poor country.
   Great tyranny, lay thou thy basis sure,
   For goodness dare not check thee. Wear thou thy
     wrongs;
   The title is affeer'd.° Fare thee well, lord.   confirmed
   I would not be the villain that thou think'st   35
   For the whole space that's in the tyrant's grasp
   And the rich East to boot.
MALCOLM.   Be not offended.
   I speak not as in absolute fear of you.
   I think our country sinks beneath the yoke;
   It weeps, it bleeds, and each new day a gash   40
   Is added to her wounds. I think withal°   moreover
   There would be hands uplifted in my right,
   And here from gracious England have I offer
   Of goodly thousands. But for all this,
   When I shall tread upon the tyrant's head,   45
   Or wear it on my sword, yet my poor country
   Shall have more vices than it had before,
   More suffer and more sundry ways than ever,
   By him that shall succeed.
MACDUFF.   What should he be?
MALCOLM. It is myself I mean, in whom I know   50

All the particulars of vice so grafted
That, when they shall be open'd, black Macbeth
Will seem as pure as snow, and the poor state
Esteem him as a lamb, being compar'd
With my confineless° harms.   boundless

MACDUFF.   Not in the legions   55
Of horrid hell can come a devil more damn'd
In evils to top Macbeth.

MALCOLM.   I grant him bloody,
Luxurious,° avaricious, false, deceitful,   lustful
Sudden, malicious, smacking of every sin
That has a name. But there's no bottom, none,   60
In my voluptuousness. Your wives, your daughters,
Your matrons, and your maids could not fill up
The cistern of my lust, and my desire
All continent impediments° would o'erbear   decent restraints
That did oppose my will. Better Macbeth   65
Than such an one to reign.

MACDUFF.   Boundless intemperance
In nature is a tyranny; it hath been
Th' untimely emptying of the happy throne,
And fall of many kings. But fear not yet
To take upon you what is yours. You may   70
Convey° your pleasures in a spacious plenty,   carry on
And yet seem cold, the time you may so hoodwink.
We have willing dames enough; there cannot be
That vulture in you, to devour so many
As will to greatness dedicate themselves,   75
Finding it so inclin'd.

MALCOLM.   With this there grows
In my most ill-compos'd affection such
A stanchless avarice that, were I king,
I should cut off the nobles for their lands,
Desire his jewels and this other's house.   80
And my more-having would be as a sauce
To make me hunger more, that I should forge
Quarrels unjust against the good and loyal,
Destroying them for wealth.

MACDUFF.   This avarice
  Sticks deeper, grows with more pernicious root   85
  Than summer-seeming lust, and it hath been
  The sword° of our slain kings. Yet do not fear;   death
  Scotland hath foisons° to fill up your will   abundant resources
  Of your mere own. All these are portable,°   bearable
  With other graces weigh'd.   90
MALCOLM.   But I have none. The king-becoming graces,
  As justice, verity, temperance, stableness,
  Bounty, perseverance, mercy, lowliness,
  Devotion, patience, courage, fortitude,
  I have no relish for them, but abound   95
  In the division of each several crime,
  Acting in many ways. Nay, had I power, I should
  Pour the sweet milk of concord into hell,
  Uproar the universal peace, confound
  All unity on earth.
MACDUFF.   O Scotland, Scotland!   100
MALCOLM.   If such a one be fit to govern, speak.
  I am as I have spoken.
MACDUFF.   Fit to govern!
  No, not to live. O nation miserable!
  With an untitled tyrant bloody-scepter'd,
  When shalt thou see thy wholesome days again,   105
  Since that the truest issue of thy throne
  By his own interdiction° stands accurs'd   accusation
  And does blaspheme his breed?° Thy royal father   parents
  Was a most sainted king; the queen that bore thee,
  Oftener upon her knees than on her feet,   110
  Died every day she lived. Fare thee well!
  These evils thou repeat'st upon thyself
  Have banish'd me from Scotland. O my breast,
  Thy hope ends here!
MALCOLM.   Macduff, this noble passion,
  Child of integrity, hath from my soul   115
  Wip'd the black scruples, reconcil'd my thoughts
  To thy good truth and honor. Devilish Macbeth
  By many of these trains° hath sought to win me   stratagems

Into his power, and modest wisdom plucks me
From overcredulous haste. But God above   120
Deal between thee and me! For even now
I put myself to thy direction, and
Unspeak mine own detraction; here abjure°   renounce
The taints and blames I laid upon myself,
For strangers to my nature. I am yet   125
Unknown to woman, never was forsworn,°   broke a vow
Scarcely have coveted what was mine own,
At no time broke my faith, would not betray
The devil to his fellow, and delight
No less in truth than life. My first false speaking   130
Was this upon myself. What I am truly
Is thine and my poor country's to command—
Whither indeed, before thy here-approach,°   arrival
Old Siward, with ten thousand warlike men,
Already at a point,° was setting forth.   ready for battle 135
Now we'll together, and the chance of goodness
Be like° our warranted quarrel. Why are you silent? equal to
MACDUFF.   Such welcome and unwelcome things at once
   'Tis hard to reconcile.

   (Enter a Doctor.*)*

MALCOLM.   Well, more anon. Comes the king forth, I pray
     you?   140
DOCTOR.   Aye, sir; there are a crew of wretched souls
   That stay° his cure. Their malady convinces°   await; conquers
   The great assay° of art;° but at his touch,   efforts; medicine
   Such sanctity hath heaven given his hand,
   They presently amend.
MALCOLM.   I thank you, doctor.   145

   (Exit Doctor.*)*

MACDUFF.   What's the disease he means?
MALCOLM.   'Tis call'd the evil—
   A most miraculous work in this good king,
   Which often, since my here-remain° in England,   stay
   I have seen him do. How he solicits heaven,

Himself best knows. But strangely visited° people,   afflicted
All swoln and ulcerous, pitiful to the eye,   151
The mere despair of surgery, he cures,
Hanging a golden stamp° about their necks,   medal
Put on with holy prayers. And 'tis spoken,
To the succeeding royalty he leaves   155
The healing benediction. With this strange virtue
He hath a heavenly gift of prophecy,
And sundry blessings hand about his throne
That speak him full of grace.

(Enter ROSS.*)*

MACDUFF.   See, who comes here?
MALCOLM.   My countryman; but yet I know him not.   160
MACDUFF.   My ever gentle cousin, welcome hither.
MALCOLM.   I know him now. Good God, betimes° remove   soon
The means that makes us strangers!
ROSS.   Sir, amen.
MACDUFF.   Stands Scotland where it did?
ROSS.   Alas, poor country!
Almost afraid to know itself! It cannot   165
Be call'd our mother, but our grave, where nothing,
But who knows nothing, is once seen to smile;
Where sighs and groans and shrieks that rend the air
Are made, not mark'd; where violent sorrow seems
A modern ecstasy.° The dead man's knell   madness 170
Is there scarce ask'd for who, and good men's lives
Expire before the flowers in their caps,
Dying or ere° they sicken.   before
MACDUFF.   O, relation
Too nice,° and yet too true!   precise
MALCOLM.   What's the newest grief? 174
ROSS.   That of an hour's age doth hiss the speaker;° seem outmoded
Each minute teems° a new one.   brings forth
MACDUFF.   How does my wife?
ROSS.   Why, well.
MACDUFF.   And all my children?
ROSS.   Well too.
MACDUFF.   The tyrant has not batter'd at their peace?

ROSS.   No; they were well at peace when I did leave
     'em.

MACDUFF.   Be not a niggard° of your speech. How
     goes 't?   miser

ROSS.   When I came hither to transport the tidings,   181
     Which I have heavily borne, there ran a rumor
     Of many worthy fellows that were out;°   up in arms
     Which was to my belief witness'd the rather,
     For that I saw the tyrant's power afoot.   185
     Now is the time of help; your eye° in Scotland   appearance
     Would create soldiers, make our women fight,
     To doff° their dire distresses.   throw off

MALCOLM.   Be 't their comfort
     We are coming thither. Gracious England hath
     Lent us good Siward and ten thousand men;   190
     An older and a better soldier none
     That Christendom gives out.

ROSS.   Would I could answer
     This comfort with the like! But I have words
     That would be howl'd out in the desert air,   194
     Where hearing should not latch them.

MACDUFF.   What concern they?
     The general cause? Or is it a fee-grief°   private woe
     Due to some single breast?

ROSS.   No mind that's honest
     But in it shares some woe, though the main part
     Pertains to you alone.

MACDUFF.   If it be mine,
     Keep it not from me; quickly let me have it.   200

ROSS.   Let not your ears despise my tongue for ever,
     Which shall possess them with the heaviest sound
     That ever yet they heard.

MACDUFF.   Hum! I guess at it.

ROSS.   Your castle is surpris'd; your wife and babes
     Savagely slaughter'd. To relate the manner   205
     Were, on the quarry° of these murder'd deer,   carcasses
     To add the death of you.

MALCOLM.   Merciful heaven!
     What, man! Ne'er pull your hat upon your brows;

Give sorrow words. The grief that does not speak   209
Whispers the o'erfraught° heart, and bids it break.   over-laden

MACDUFF.   My children too?

ROSS.   Wife, children, servants, all
That could be found.

MACDUFF.   And I must be from thence!
My wife kill'd too?

ROSS.   I have said.

MALCOLM.   Be comforted.
Let's make us med'cines of our great revenge,
To cure this deadly grief.   215

MACDUFF.   He has no children. All my pretty ones?
Did you say all? O hell-kite! All?
What, all my pretty chickens and their dam
At one fell swoop?

MALCOLM.   Dispute° it like a man.   avenge

MACDUFF.   I shall do so;   220
But I must also feel it as a man.
I cannot but remember such things were,
That were most precious to me. Did heaven look on,
And would not take their part? Sinful Macduff,   224
They were all struck for thee! Naught° that I am,   wicked
Not for their own demerits, but for mine,
Fell slaughter on their souls. Heaven rest them now!

MALCOLM.   Be this the whetstone of your sword. Let grief
Convert to anger; blunt not the heart, enrage it.

MACDUFF.   O, I could play the woman with mine eyes,   230
And braggart with my tongue! But, gentle heavens,
Cut short all intermission.° Front to front   interval
Bring thou this fiend of Scotland and myself.
Within my sword's length set him. If he 'scape,
Heaven forgive him too!

MALCOLM.   This tune goes manly.   235
Come, go we to the king; our power is ready;
Our lack is nothing but our leave. Macbeth
Is ripe for shaking, and the powers above
Put° on their instruments.° Receive what cheer   urge; agents
    you may;   239
The night is long that never finds the day.   *(Exeunt.)*

Act V   SCENE 1

Dunsinane.   Anteroom in the Castle.   Enter a Doctor
of Physic *and a* Waiting Gentlewoman.

DOCTOR.   I have two nights watched with you, but can perceive no truth in your report. When was it she last walked?
GENTLEWOMAN.   Since his majesty went into the field, I have
seen her rise from her bed, throw her nightgown upon
her, unlock her closet, take forth paper, fold it, write   5
upon 't, read it, afterwards seal it, and again return to bed;
yet all this while in a most fast sleep.
DOCTOR.   A great perturbation in nature, to receive at once
the benefit of sleep and do the effects of watching! In this
slumbery agitation, besides her walking and other actual 10
performances, what, at any time, have you heard her say?
GENTLEWOMAN.   That, sir, which I will not report after her.
DOCTOR.   You may to me, and 'tis most meet you should.
GENTLEWOMAN.   Neither to you nor any one, having no
witness to confirm my speech.   15

(Enter LADY MACBETH, *with a taper.)*

Lo you, here she comes! This is her very guise, and, upon
my life, fast asleep. Observe her; stand close.
DOCTOR.   How came she by that light?
GENTLEWOMAN.   Why, it stood by her. She has light by her
continually; 'tis her command.   20
DOCTOR.   You see, her eyes are open.
GENTLEWOMAN.   Aye, but their sense is shut.
DOCTOR.   What is it she does now? Look, how she rubs her
hands.
GENTLEWOMAN.   It is an accustomed action with her, to seem 25
thus washing her hands. I have known her continue in this
a quarter of an hour.
LADY MACBETH.   Yet here's a spot.
DOCTOR.   Hark! She speaks. I will set down what comes from
her, to satisfy my remembrance the more strongly.   30

LADY MACBETH.   Out, damned spot! Out, I say! One, two.
Why, then 'tis time to do 't. Hell is murky. Fie, my lord,
fie! A soldier, and afeard? What need we fear who knows
it, when none can call our power to account? Yet who
would have thought the old man to have had so much 35
blood in him?

DOCTOR.   Do you mark that?

LADY MACBETH.   The thane of Fife had a wife; where is she
now? What, will these hands ne'er be clean? No more o'
that, my lord, no more o' that. You mar all with this
starting.   40

DOCTOR.   Go to, go to; you have known what you should not.

GENTLEWOMAN.   She has spoke what she should not, I am
sure of that. Heaven knows what she has known.

LADY MACBETH.   Here's the smell of the blood still. All the
perfumes of Arabia will not sweeten this little hand. Oh, 45
oh, oh!

DOCTOR.   What a sigh is there! The heart is sorely charged.

GENTLEWOMAN.   I would not have such a heart in my bosom
for the dignity of the whole body.

DOCTOR.   Well, well, well—   50

GENTLEWOMAN.   Pray God it be, sir.

DOCTOR.   This disease is beyond my practice. Yet I have
known those which have walked in their sleep who have
died holily in their beds.

LADY MACBETH.   Wash your hands; put on your nightgown; 55
look not so pale. I tell you yet again, Banquo's buried;
he cannot come out on 's grave.

DOCTOR.   Even so?

LADY MACBETH.   To bed, to bed; there's knocking at the gate.
Come, come, come, come, give me your hand. What's 60
done cannot be undone. To bed, to bed, to bed.   *(Exit.)*

DOCTOR.   Will she go now to bed?

GENTLEWOMAN.   Directly.

DOCTOR.   Foul whisp'rings are abroad. Unnatural deeds
Do breed unnatural troubles. Infected minds   65
To their deaf pillows will discharge their secrets.
More needs she the divine than the physician.
God, God forgive us all! Look after her;
Remove from her the means of all annoyance,°   injury

And still keep eyes upon her. So good night.   70
My mind she has mated° and amaz'd my sight.   stupefied
I think, but dare not speak.
GENTLEWOMAN.   Good night, good doctor.

                                            (Exeunt.)

Act V SCENE 2

The country near Dunsinane.   Drum and colors.   Enter
MENTEITH, CAITHNESS, ANGUS, LENNOX, *and* Soldiers.

MENTEITH.   The English power is near, led on by Malcolm,
    His uncle Siward and the good Macduff.
    Revenges burn in them, for their dear° causes   heartfelt
    Would to the bleeding and the grim alarm°   call to battle
    Excite the mortified° man.   dead
ANGUS.   Near Birnam wood   5
    Shall we well meet them; that way are they coming.
CAITHNESS.   Who knows if Donalbain be with his brother?
LENNOX.   For certain, sir, he is not. I have a file
    Of all the gentry. There is Siward's son,
    And many unrough° youths, that even now   unbearded   10
    Protest their first° of manhood.   make first trial
MENTEITH.   What does the tyrant?
CAITHNESS.   Great Dunsinane he strongly fortifies.
    Some say he's mad; others, that lesser hate him,
    Do call it valiant fury. But, for certain,
    He cannot buckle his distemper'd cause°   sick rage   15
    Within the belt of rule.°   self-control
ANGUS.   Now does he feel
    His secret murders sticking on his hands;
    Now minutely revolts upbraid his faith-breach.
    Those he commands move only in command,
    Nothing in love. Now does he feel his title   20

Hang loose about him, like a giant's robe
Upon a dwarfish thief.
MENTEITH.   Who then shall blame
His pester'd senses to recoil and start,
When all that is within him does condemn
Itself for being there?
CAITHNESS.   Well, march we on,   25
To give obedience where 'tis truly ow'd.
Meet we the med'cine of the sickly weal,
And with him pour we, in our country's purge,
Each drop of us.
LENNOX.   Or so much as it needs   29
To dew° the sovereign flower and drown the weeds.   water
Make we our march toward Birnam. (*Exeunt, marching.*)

Act V SCENE 3

Dunsinane. A room in the Castle. Enter MACBETH,
Doctor, *and* Attendants.

MACBETH.   Bring me no more reports; let them fly all.
Till Birnam wood remove to Dunsinane
I cannot taint° with fear. What's the boy Malcolm?   be tainted
Was he not born of woman? The spirits that know
All mortal consequences have pronounc'd me thus: 5
"Fear not, Macbeth; no man that's born of woman
Shall e'er have power upon thee." Then fly, false thanes,
And mingle with the English epicures.°   gluttons
The mind I sway by and the heart I bear
Shall never sag with doubt nor shake with fear.   10

(*Enter a* Servant.)

The devil damn thee black, thou cream-fac'd loon!
Where got'st thou that goose look?

SERVANT.   There is ten thousand—
MACBETH.   Geese, villain?
SERVANT.   Soldiers, sir.
MACBETH.   Go prick thy face and over-red thy fear,
    Thou lily-liver'd boy. What soldiers, patch!°   fool   15
    Death of my soul! Those linen cheeks of thine
    Are counselors to fear. What soldiers, wheyface?
SERVANT.   The English force, so please you.
MACBETH.   Take thy face hence.

(*Exit* Servant.)

    Seyton!—I am sick at heart,   20
    When I behold—Seyton, I say!—This push
    Will cheer me ever, or disseat me now.
    I have liv'd long enough. My way of life
    Is fall'n into the sear,° the yellow leaf,   withered
    And that which should accompany old age,   25
    As honor, love, obedience, troops of friends,
    I must not look to have; but, in their stead,
    Curses, not loud but deep, mouth-honor, breath,
    Which the poor heart would fain deny, and dare not.
    Seyton!   30

(*Enter* SEYTON.)

SEYTON.   What's your gracious pleasure?
MACBETH.   What news more?
SEYTON.   All is confirm'd, my lord, which was reported.
MACBETH.   I'll fight, till from my bones my flesh be hack'd.
    Give me my armor.
SEYTON.   'Tis not needed yet.
MACBETH.   I'll put it on.   35
    Send out moe° horses, skirr° the country round;   more; scour
    Hang those that talk of fear. Give me mine armor.
    How does your patient, doctor?
DOCTOR.   Not so sick, my lord,
    As she is troubled with thick-coming fancies
    That keep her from her rest.

MACBETH.   Cure her of that.   40
   Canst thou not minister to a mind diseas'd,
   Pluck from the memory a rooted sorrow,
   Raze out the written troubles of the brain,
   And with some sweet oblivious antidote
   Cleanse the stuff'd bosom of that perilous stuff   45
   Which weighs upon the heart?
DOCTOR.   Therein the patient
   Must minister to himself.
MACBETH.   Throw physic° to the dogs, I'll none of it.   medicine
   Come, put mine armor on; give me my staff.
   Seyton, send out. Doctor, the thanes fly from me.   50
   Come, sir, dispatch. If thou couldst, doctor, cast°   examine
   The water of my land, find her disease
   And purge it to a sound and pristine health,
   I would applaud thee to the very echo,
   That should applaud again, Pull 't off, I say.   55
   What rhubarb, senna, or what purgative drug
   Would scour these English hence? Hear'st thou of them?
DOCTOR.   Aye, my good lord; your royal preparation
   Makes us hear something.
MACBETH.   Bring it after me.   destruction
   I will not be afraid of death and bane°   60
   Till Birnam forest come to Dunsinane.
DOCTOR.   *(Aside.)* Were I from Dunsinane away and clear,
   Profit again should hardly draw me here.   *(Exeunt.)*

Act V scene 4

Country near Birnam Wood. Drum and colors. Enter
MALCOLM, *old* SIWARD *and his Son,* MACDUFF, MENTEITH,
CAITHNESS, ANGUS, LENNOX, ROSS, *and* Soldiers, *march-*
ing.

MALCOLM.   Cousins, I hope the days are near at hand
   That chambers will be safe.

MENTEITH.   We doubt it nothing.
SIWARD.   What wood is this before us?
MENTEITH.   The wood of Birnam.
MALCOLM.   Let every soldier hew him down a bough,
    And bear 't before him. Thereby shall we shadow   5
    The numbers of our host, and make discovery
    Err in report of us.
SOLDIERS.   It shall be done.
SIWARD.   We learn no other but the confident tyrant
    Keeps still in Dunsinane, and will endure
    Our setting down° before 't.   laying siege
MALCOLM.   'Tis his main hope;   10
    For where there is advantage° to be given,   opportunity
    Both more and less° have given him the revolt,   high and low
    And none serve with him but constrained things
    Whose hearts are absent too.
MACDUFF.   Let our just censures°   judgments
    Attend° the true event,° and put we on   await; outcome 15
    Industrious soldiership.
SIWARD.   The time approaches
    That will with due decision make us know
    What we shall say we have and what we owe.°   actually
                                                       possess
    Thoughts speculative their unsure hopes relate,
    But certain issue° strokes must arbitrate.   outcome 20
    Towards which advance the war.°   army
                                    (Exeunt, marching.)

Act V SCENE 5

Dunsinane. Within the Castle. Enter MACBETH, SEYTON,
and Soldiers, *with drum and colors.*

MACBETH.   Hang out our banners on the outward walls.
    The cry is still, 'They come!' Our castle's strength
    Will laugh a siege to scorn. Here let them lie
    Till famine and the ague eat them up.

Were they not forc'd° with those that should be   reinforced
   ours,   5
We might have met them dareful, beard to beard,
And beat them backward home. *(A cry of women within.)*
                          What is that noise?
SEYTON.   It is the cry of women, my good lord.   *(Exit.)*
MACBETH.   I have almost forgot the taste of fears.
   The time has been, my senses would have cool'd   10
   To hear a night-shriek, and my fell of hair°   scalp
   Would at a dismal treatise° rouse and stir   tale
   As life were in 't. I have supp'd full with horrors.
   Direness,° familiar to my slaughterous thoughts,   horror
   Cannot once start me.

   (Re-enter SEYTON.)

                         Wherefore was that cry?   15
SEYTON.   The queen, my lord, is dead.
MACBETH.   She should have died hereafter;
   There would have been a time for such a word.
   Tomorrow, and tomorrow, and tomorrow
   Creeps in this petty pace from day to day   20
   To the last syllable of recorded time,
   And all our yesterdays have lighted fools
   The way to dusty death. Out, out, brief candle!
   Life's but a walking shadow, a poor player
   That struts and frets his hour upon the stage   25
   And then is heard no more. It is a tale
   Told by an idiot, full of sound and fury,
   Signifying nothing.

   (Enter a Messenger.)*

   Thou com'st to use thy tongue; thy story quickly.
MESSENGER.   Gracious my lord,   30
   I should report that which I say I saw,
   But know not how to do it.
MACBETH.   Well, say, sir.
MESSENGER.   As I did stand my watch upon the hill,

I look'd toward Birnam, and anon, methought,
The wood began to move.
MACBETH.   Liar and slave!   35
MESSENGER.   Let me endure your wrath, if 't be not so.
Within this three mile may you see it coming;
I say, a moving grove.
MACBETH.   If thou speak'st false,
Upon the next tree shalt thou hang alive
Till famine cling° thee. If thy speech be sooth,   shrivel 40
I care not if thou dost for me as much.
I pull in resolution,° and begin   confidence
To doubt° the equivocation of the fiend   suspect
That lies like truth: "Fear not, till Birnam wood
Do come to Dunsinane." And now a wood   45
Comes toward Dunsinane. Arm, arm, and out!
If this which he avouches does appear,
There is nor flying hence nor tarrying here.
I 'gin to be aweary of the sun,
And wish the estate o' the world were now undone.   50
Ring the alarum bell! Blow, wind! Come, wrack!° destruction
At least we'll die with harness° on our back.   armor
                                                    (*Exeunt.*)

Act V SCENE 6

Dunsinane. Before the Castle. Drum and colors. Enter
MALCOLM, *old* SIWARD, MACDUFF, *and their Army, with*
boughs.

MALCOLM.   Now near enough; your leavy screens throw
        down,
And show like those you are. You, worthy uncle,
Shall, with my cousin, your right noble son,
Lead our first battle.° Worthy Macduff and we   battalion
Shall take upon 's what else remains to do,   plan 5
According to our order.°

SIWARD.   Fare you well.
  Do we but find the tyrant's power tonight,
  Let us be beaten, if we cannot fight.
MACDUFF.   Make all our trumpets speak; give them all breath,
  Those clamorous harbingers of blood and death. *(Exeunt.)*   10

Act V SCENE 7

Another part of the field. Alarums. Enter MACBETH.

MACBETH.   They have tied me to a stake; I cannot fly,
  But bear-like I must fight the course. What's he
  That was not born of woman? Such a one
  Am I to fear, or none.

(Enter YOUNG SIWARD.*)*

YOUNG SIWARD.   What is thy name?
MACBETH.   Thou 'lt be afraid to hear it.   5
YOUNG SIWARD.   No; though thou call'st thyself a hotter name
  Than any is in hell.
MACBETH.   My name's Macbeth.
YOUNG SIWARD.   The devil himself could not pronounce a title
  More hateful to mine ear.
MACBETH.   No, nor more fearful.
YOUNG SIWARD.   Thou liest, abhorred tyrant; with my sword   10
  I'll prove the lie thou speak'st.
  (They fight, and YOUNG SIWARD *is slain.)*
MACBETH.   Thou wast born of woman.
  But swords I smile at, weapons laugh to scorn,
  Brandish'd by man that's of a woman born.   *(Exit.)*

(Alarums. Enter MACDUFF.*)*

MACDUFF.   That way the noise is. Tyrant, show thy face!

If thou be'st slain and with no stroke of mine,   15
My wife and children's ghosts will haunt me still.
I cannot strike at wretched kerns, whose arms
Are hir'd to bear their staves.° Either thou, Macbeth,   spears
Or else my sword, with an unbatter'd edge,
I sheathe again undeeded. There thou shouldst be;   20
By this great clatter, one of greatest note
Seems bruited.° Let me find him, fortune,   reported
And more I beg not.   *(Exit Alarums.)*

(Enter MALCOLM *and old* SIWARD.)

SIWARD.   This way, my lord; the castle's gently render'd.
The tyrant's people on both sides do fight;   25
The noble thanes do bravely in the war;
The day almost itself professes yours,
And little is to do.
MALCOLM.   We have met with foes
That strike° beside us.   fight
SIWARD.   Enter, sir, the castle.
                             (Exeunt. Alarum.)

Act V SCENE 8

Another part of the field. Enter MACBETH.

MACBETH.   Why should I play the Roman fool, and die
On mind own sword? Whiles I see lives, the gashes
Do better upon them.

(Enter MACDUFF.)

MACDUFF.   Turn, hell-hound, turn!
MACBETH.   Of all men else I have avoided thee.
But get thee back; my soul is too much charg'd   5
With blood of thine already.

MACDUFF.   I have no words:
   My voice is in my sword, thou bloodier villain
   Than terms can give thee out!   *(They fight.)*
MACBETH.   Thou losest labor.
   As easy mayst thou the intrenchant° air   invulnerable
   With thy keen sword impress as make me bleed.   10
   Let fall thy blade on vulnerable crests;°   heads
   I bear a charmed life, which must not yield
   To one of woman born.
MACDUFF.   Despair thy charm,
   And let the angel whom thou still° hast serv'd   always
   Tell thee, Macduff was from his mother's womb   15
   Untimely ripp'd.
MACBETH.   Accursed be that tongue that tells me so,
   For it hath cow'd my better part of man!
   And be these juggling fiends no more believ'd,
   That palter with us in a double sense,   20
   That keep the word of promise to our ear,
   And break it to our hope. I'll not fight with thee.
MACDUFF.   Then yield thee, coward,
   And live to be the show and gaze o' the time.
   We'll have thee, as our rarer monsters are,   25
   Painted upon a pole, and underwrit,
   "Here may you see the tyrant."
MACBETH.   I will not yield
   To kiss the ground before young Malcolm's feet,
   And to be baited° with the rabble's curse.   bear-baited
   Though Birnam wood be come to Dunsinane,   30
   And thou oppos'd, being of no woman born,
   Yet I will try the last. Before my body
   I throw my warlike shield. Lay on, Macduff,
   And damn'd be him that first cries "Hold, enough!"

*(Exeunt, fighting. Alarums. Retreat. Flourish. Enter with
drum and colors.* MALCOLM, *old* SIWARD, ROSS, *the other*
Thanes *and* Soldiers.)

MALCOLM.   I would the friends we miss were safe arriv'd.
SIWARD.   Some must go off. And yet, by these I see,   36

So great a day as this is cheaply bought.
MALCOLM.   Macduff is missing, and your noble son.
ROSS.   Your son, my lord, has paid a soldier's debt.
    He only liv'd but till he was a man,   40
    The which no sooner had his prowess confirm'd
    In the unshrinking station where he fought,
    But like a man he died.
SIWARD.   Then he is dead?
ROSS.   Aye, and brought off the field. Your cause of sorrow
    Must not be measur'd by his worth, for then   45
    It hath no end.
SIWARD.   Had he his hurts before?
ROSS.   Aye, on the front.
SIWARD.   Why then, God's soldier be he!
    Had I as many sons as I have hairs,
    I would not wish them to a fairer death:
    And so his knell is knoll'd.
MALCOLM.   He's worth more sorrow,   50
    And that I'll spend for him.
SIWARD.   He's worth no more.
    They say he parted well and paid his score,°   account
    And so God be with him! Here comes newer comfort.

(Re-enter MACDUFF, *with* MACBETH'S *head.)*

MACDUFF.   Hail, King, for so thou art. Behold, where stands
    Th' usurper's cursed head. The time is free.   55
    I see thee compass'd with thy kingdom's pearl,°   nobility
    That speak my salutation in their minds,
    Whose voices I desire aloud with mine:
    Hail, King of Scotland!
ALL.   Hail, King of Scotland! *(Flourish.)*
MALCOLM.   We shall not spend a large expense of time   60
    Before we reckon with your several loves
    And make us even with you. My thanes and kinsmen,
    Henceforth be earls, the first that ever Scotland
    In such an honor named. What's more to do
    Which would be planted newly with the time—   65
    As calling home our exil'd friends abroad

That fled the snares of watchful tyranny,
Producing forth the cruel ministers°   agents
Of this dead butcher and his fiend-like queen,
Who, as 'tis thought, by self and violent hands   70
Took off her life; this, and what needful else
That calls upon us, by the grace of Grace
We will perform in measure, time, and place.
So thanks to all at once and to each one,
Whom we invite to see us crown'd at Scone.   75
                                (Flourish. Exeunt.)

FOR DISCUSSION

Act I SCENE 1

1. The opening scene of *Macbeth* differs from typical first scenes
    in its brevity and its lack of explicitness. Yet it is one of Shake-
    speare's finest openings. What does it *foreshadow* (see Glossary)?
    What other purpose does it serve? Which statements are para-
    doxical?
2. The predominant rhythm of these lines is not iambic. What is it?
    Tell why it is appropriate to what the Witches say and what it
    suggests for the way they would say these lines.

Act I SCENE 2

1. This scene is more typical of Shakespeare's opening scenes in
    that it provides the *exposition* (see Glossary). First you learn the
    enveloping situation; namely, that a state of war exists between
    the Scottish crown (King Duncan) and a rebel lord (Macdonwald),
    aided by other forces including those of Sweno, King of Norway.
    From the accounts of the Sergeant and Ross, what do you learn
    about the battles being fought against the two main enemies?
    Describe in your own words what happened on each battlefront
    and the outcome.
2. Note the beginning of the *characterization* (see Glossary) of
    Macbeth through what others say about him. What qualities are
    mentioned or clearly implied?

3. Examine the Sergeant's three speeches. Point out the lines or passages which you think best illustrate his manner of speaking. Would you call it plain, economical, and direct? Choose whatever word or phrase you can defend. Many readers consider it improbable that a man who is faint from his wounds and recent exertions would present his account in such high style. What purpose, in addition to presenting information, did Shakespeare want the Sergeant's speeches to serve? Does this purpose justify the sacrifice of probability? Give reasons for your opinion.

4. In lines 21-23, the antecedents for the pronouns (including *which*) are indefinite. To whom do you think each pronoun refers? What is the grim ironical humor in line 21?

5. Point out the relation between lines 25 and 26 and lines 27 and 28. Then show the relation between these and the five lines which follow.

6. Compare the style of Ross's lines (49-58) with the Sergeant's style. Are they similar? Why may they appropriately be so, even though two different speakers are involved? Do Ross's lines also serve Shakespeare's purpose (see question 3)?

7. The closing speeches in this scene give you significant facts about the Thane of Cawdor which relate to Macbeth. What are these facts? What similarity do you see between line 68 and the Witches' paradoxical statement in Scene 1?

Act I SCENE 3

1. What new sense of the Witches' character do you gain in the moments before Macbeth enters? What aspect of their nature is illustrated by the First Witch's tale of the sailor and his wife?

2. In line 33, the Witches are called "weird sisters." No doubt they are "weird" enough, in our colloquial sense, but that is not the point. This "weird" derives from the Old English *wyrd*, which means Fate. Yet the Witches are themselves not Fate, but its interpreters. Two specific lines in the First Witch's account make it clear that though the Witches know what Fate holds, they cannot themselves change ultimate outcomes. These lines are of first importance to the whole play. What are they?

3. What insights into the characters of Macbeth and Banquo do you gain from the way each reacts to the Witches and their prophecies? Which lines in this scene would lead you to believe that the idea of being king was already in Macbeth's mind? If so, what purpose would the Witches be serving (see question 2)? Why is the irony of lines 74-76 evident to you but not to Macbeth?

4. Banquo does not share Macbeth's elation over the first proof of the Witches prophecy. Why? Note especially lines 123-127. Are they also, in a sense, a prophecy of things to come? How do you interpret them? What thoughts (expressed in *asides*—see Glossary) so occupy Macbeth's attention that he keeps the King's messengers waiting? How do you interpret lines 128-130? Note the word *murder* in line 140. What brings it to his mind? Have the Witches spoken of murder or even implied it? What bearing do you see here on the question of Macbeth's final responsibility for what follows? What lines, spoken by Macbeth, express the terrible dilemma with which he is confronted and the torment in store for whoever chooses to play a guessing game with Fate?

Act I SCENE 4

1. The words exchanged among King Duncan, Macbeth, and Banquo are rich in *dramatic irony* (see Glossary). How do you explain Macbeth's speech (lines 22-27)? What is ironical in Duncan's reply? What emotion is expressed in lines 33-35?
2. Duncan sees his visit to Macbeth's castle as a strengthening of the bond between him and Macbeth. What evidence in lines 44-53 indicates that Macbeth has other purposes in mind? Does the word *rest* (line 44) mean "remainder" or "repose"? If "repose," why does he speak of it as "labor"?
3. A messenger could have informed Lady Macbeth of Duncan's visit. Discuss the relation between Macbeth's serving as "the harbinger" and the thoughts he expresses in the *aside*. What weakness does Macbeth reveal that Lady Macbeth has reason to deplore later in the play?

Act I SCENE 5

1. Why is it important for Lady Macbeth to receive and read aloud this portion of Macbeth's letter? Compare her reactions to the Witches' prophecies with Macbeth's. How are they similar and different? What does she fear will impede him "from the golden round"? Does she consider it a weakness? Why? How do you interpret lines 28 and 29?
2. Do you think that Lady Macbeth's plea to the spirits is evidence of her essential cruelty and hardness of nature? Could this plea be given a very different interpretation? If so, what qualities of her nature would it reveal?

3. Note the implications of Macbeth's greeting and Lady Macbeth's reply in lines 57-69. What is revealed about the rapport between them? How does she know what he is thinking? What is the double meaning of her remark, "He that's coming must be provided for"? What echo, or echoes, of "Fair is foul" do you find in her advice?

Act I   SCENE 6

1.. What potent irony is implied in the first two speeches?
2. Lady Macbeth and Duncan appear to vie with each other in courtly manner. Knowing what you do about the situation, what *dramatic purpose* (see Glossary) do you think Shakespeare intended this display of courtesy to serve?
3. In lines 11-14, Duncan uses the royal plural *we* instead of *I*, and *us* instead of *me*. Do you interpret lines 11 and 12 to mean "The love my subjects have for me sometimes puts them to great trouble, which I always thank as love, not trouble"? Or does it mean, "The love I have causes me to visit you and, thus, causes trouble for you"? Is there a touch of humor in his closing remark (lines 12-14)? If you interpret the entire passage differently, what do you think it means?
4. From Lady Macbeth's speech (lines 25-28) what do you learn of the relation of subject to sovereign? What does she mean by "still to return your own"?

Act I   SCENE 7

1. The *soliloquy* (see Glossary) which opens this scene is of basic importance in understanding the character of Macbeth. Study it closely to find what it actually *says*. It represents the best reasoning, presumably, of which Macbeth is capable on the question, "to murder, or not to murder." Plainly, his craving for the throne urges him to kill Duncan; but at the end of the speech he has talked himself out of doing so. What are his objections to murder? Is it that to kill a man is morally wrong? Is it that he fears punishment in the life after death? Is it that, by committing murder, a person is in danger of getting "caught"? Do you consider all these reasons equally commendable?
2. "Upon this bank and shoal of time" means right here, on this earth. What is the meaning of "We'd jump the life to come" (line 7)?

3. Does it, in your opinion, speak well for Macbeth as a moral man that he argues against killing Duncan because Duncan is his guest, kinsman, and sovereign?

4. In lines 16-18, Macbeth seems on the verge of arguing that one should especially not kill a good man, like Duncan, because it is worse to kill a good man. Look closely at the lines that follow. Precisely why does Macbeth think it worse to kill a saintly king? What will be the effect on people? What will be the effect on one's likelihood of getting caught?

5. What connection do you see between lines 25 and 26 and the entrance of Lady Macbeth?

6. Macbeth tells his wife flatly, "We will proceed no further in this business." But some forty lines later she has completely changed his mind. How does she do so? Does she convince him that it is not, after all, morally wrong to commit murder? Do you think she knows what is *really* holding back Macbeth? What is it that finally, and quite suddenly, convinces him?

7. Do you consider "conscience" and the "fear of being caught" one and the same? Does Macbeth have a true conscience?

8. What paradoxical (see Glossary for *paradox*) statements occur in this scene?

Act II SCENE 1

1. Though Banquo is deathly tired, he resists the summons (like a court summons) to sleep. Why? What "cursed thoughts" do you suppose might afflict him in sleep?

2. What point do you think Shakespeare intends to make—somewhat awkwardly—by Banquo's speech revealing the king's generosity and his own possession of the diamond to be presented to Lady Macbeth?

3. What evidence do you find in lines 20-30 that Banquo guesses what Macbeth is "up to"? What does Macbeth hope to discover by his statement (lines 25 and 26)? How do you interpret Banquo's reply? Is he just making his position clear or do you detect a note of warning?

4. Macbeth's "dagger speech" (lines 33-64) is one of the high points of the play. From what he says, do you think the dagger is real or imaginary? If the latter, what does this "fatal vision" foretell of his state of mind *after* the murder? What evidence do you find in this speech that Macbeth is "the wrong man for the job"—the kind of murderer who "can't get away with it"?

5. Beginning with line 49, note the way in which Shakespeare builds up the emotional intensity of the situation and of the conflict within Macbeth as he prepares to carry out "the bloody business." Discuss the effect of the figurative language — metaphor, simile, and other imagery — and of the sound — rhythm and language — on the meaning and the intensity of feeling and mood.

Act II SCENE 2

1. Lady Macbeth's speech continues — even raises — the intensity to a degree hardly matched elsewhere, even in Shakespeare. Note that what is happening inside the chamber is reported rather than staged, but not to spare the audience the gruesome sight. What advantage does Shakespeare gain by presenting the grim event in this manner?
2. The "fatal bellman" of line 3 refers to the watchman who, at night, announced the executions scheduled for the morning. Besides the owl's "shriek," what other sounds, directly heard or referred to, occur in the scene? What effects are thus gained? Remember that the main event itself is an affair of silence and secrecy.
3. What view of the deep interior of Lady Macbeth's nature is revealed by lines 12 and 13?
4. Macbeth refers to his "hangman's hands" (line 27) because they are covered with blood. The Elizabethan hangman not only hanged his victim, but also removed his vital organs. At what points in the scene do images of blood occur? The full significance of this emphasis will become evident later.
5. In his earlier soliloquy (Act I, Scene 7), Macbeth brushed aside the idea of punishment in the hereafter, concerned only with whether or not he could escape punishment in the mortal life. In short, he snapped his fingers at Heaven. Which lines in this scene suggest that he learns better while in the very act of murder?
6. So shaken is Macbeth that he stands as in a trance, the bloody daggers in his hand. It is Lady Macbeth who, when her husband refuses to go back in the chamber, returns them. Look closely at lines 53-57. Is it fear or bravery that impels her to act? What evidence do you find in these lines and in lines 67 and 68 that she speaks in this manner to reassure herself?
7. In line 56, why do you think Shakespeare used "gild" rather than "smear" or "paint"?

8. The knocking that begins at line 57 and continues at intervals serves to link this scene with the next. More important, it helps to sustain the intensity achieved at the end of Macbeth's dagger soliloquy. Describe the effect you think this sudden, loud, and repeated sound would have on the characters and the audience.

9. What evidence do you find in Macbeth's final speech in this scene that he is a wiser man than he was at the time he debated the question of murder?

Act II SCENE 3

1. The Porter's speech is the first in the play to be written in prose. Also it is the only comic passage of any length. Moreover, it follows immediately after a scene of horror. What dramatic purpose do you think Shakespeare intended this speech to serve? Why is it both appropriate and ironic that the porter amuses himself by pretending to be the gatekeeper of hell?

2. In lines 24-26, Shakespeare indulged in a play on words with the word *lie*. In Elizabethan times, to give someone "the lie in the throat" was to call him a downright liar. Explain the various meanings implied by *lie* in this play on words.

3. How do lines 41-50 heighten the atrociousness of Duncan's assassination? Why is the place in which these lines are spoken especially appropriate and dramatic?

4. In speaking of the "Lord's anointed temple" (line 55), Macduff is expressing in figurative language the sacredness of the King who was anointed as ruler by divine right. Macduff customarily expresses himself in plain, blunt language. Tell why the poetic language used in lines 53-67 is appropriate to the occasion and not out of character. Comment on the effectiveness of the imagery.

5. What is ironic about Macduff's speech to Lady Macbeth (lines 70-73)?

6. Look closely at the lines spoken by Macbeth and Lady Macbeth in which they attempt to convey the impression that they know nothing of the crime and had no part in it. In your opinion, how successful are they in their attempt? Is her reaction in lines 74 and 75 psychologically sound? Would a "perfect hostess" be likely to think first of the social embarrassment of this tragic event?

7. Look, also, at the manner in which Macbeth describes the dead Duncan, his own feelings, and his "execution" of the grooms

whom he accuses of the murder (lines 78-106). Give reasons to support your opinion (1) that Macbeth does, or does not, do a good job of "covering" and (2) that the poetic language in which he speaks rings true or sounds "phony."

8. Macduff's speech "Look to the lady" (line 107) refers to Lady Macbeth's fainting, a favorite question for debate. Is it real or feigned? Before expressing your opinion, consider the following: (1) the signs of inner weakness she revealed before the murder, despite her outward show of strength; (2) the result which her fainting would achieve — namely, to draw attention from her husband, on whom all eyes were riveted; and (3) the effect which Macbeth's florid speech, filled with images of blood, might have had on her already strained nerves.

9. In line 114, Banquo speaks of hiding "our naked frailties"; in line 121, Macbeth speaks of putting on "manly readiness." The obvious interpretation is that they are referring to changing from their night clothes into more appropriate attire. What other interpretation is possible?

10. Study closely the lines which reveal the reactions of Malcolm and Donalbain to their father's murder and to Macbeth's speech. What, exactly, are their suspicions or fears? Contrast their show of grief with that of the murderers. How do you interpret Donalbain's remark, "The near in blood, the nearer bloody"?

Act II SCENE 4

1. This brief scene accomplishes much. The action is shifted from the scene of the murder to the world outside, thus providing a new view of the tragic event, particularly the repercussions in state and universe which the murder has produced. What details confirm the suspicion that, as in *Hamlet*, "the time is out of joint"? What other information are you given that applies to events at that time or foreshadows future events?

2. From Macduff's lines, what would you say is his attitude? What is the implication of his veiled remark (line 38)? What is suggested by the very fact that it *is* veiled?

Act III SCENE 1

1. From Banquo's equivocal remarks in lines 1-10, and from what you already know, what action would he be most likely to take:

(1) say nothing and bide his time; (2) blackmail Macbeth by allusions and insinuations (see lines 15-18) until given his share of the spoils of murder; or (3) expose Macbeth publicly?

2. In his conversation with Banquo, Macbeth asks three pointed questions as though they are merely incidental. What are they, and what is their purpose? At what point in this scene do you suspect what Macbeth has in mind? Point out the two basic fears, revealed in his soliloquy (lines 48-72), that make his kingship seem a hollow glory.

3. This scene marks a turning point in the action of the play. Hitherto Macbeth has "gone along" with Fate—indeed, by murdering Duncan, he has "helped" Fate to bring about what the Witches prophesied. Hereafter he must attempt to move things in a direction contrary to what Fate intended—even if, by so doing, he must fight against Fate, like challenger against champion in a knightly joust (lines 71 and 72). From the evidence thus far, tell why you do, or do not, think he will succeed in his attempt.

4. By what line of argument does Macbeth persuade the Murderers? The charges he makes against Banquo could be true or false. What do you suspect? On what do you base your opinion?

5. To interpret certain lines in this scene, you will need to work out the meaning conveyed by the imagery. Note especially lines 67, 83, 88 and 89, 92, 99-101, 116 ("bloody distance"), and 130. State in your own words the meaning you think is conveyed by these lines or by the images in them.

Act III SCENE 2

1. Describe Lady Macbeth's attitude before and after her husband joins her. What reason can you give for the change?

2. This is the first husband-wife scene since Duncan's murder. Which images in the scene most strikingly reveal the effects on them of the terrible predicament in which they placed themselves with such apparent confidence? Which of the two would you say is "bearing up" better?

3. Why do you think Macbeth does not take his wife into his confidence in the planned murder of Banquo and Fleance? What suggestion is there that she would favor it? What, specifically, is implied in line 38?

4. Besides being a murderer, Macbeth is an extraordinary poet, who habitually thinks and speaks in figurative language. More-

over, as he gains a deeper insight through experience, his poetic insight also deepens. His imagery becomes even more vivid, controlling the *mood* and *tone* (see Glossary) of the situation, as well as revealing his innermost thoughts and feelings. Note especially Macbeth's last two speeches in this scene. Describe the dominant impression they create. Point out the figurative language—metaphor, simile, image—which largely controls what these impressions are.

Act III SCENE 3

1. Critics have variously interpreted the presence of the Third Murderer. Is he Macbeth, in disguise, checking on his hired assassins since he trusts no one? Is he a creature sent by Fate to make sure that Macbeth fails? Is he simply another murderer? When Macbeth interviewed the Murderers earlier, were you given any hint that more than two might undertake the deed? Does *he* in line 2 refer to Macbeth or to the Third Murderer? Explain.
2. Lines 9-11 refer to other invited guests ("within the note of expectation") who have come for Macbeth's banquet. What explanation is given for the arrival of Banquo and Fleance on foot rather than on horses, when in a previous scene it was revealed that they were going for a ride? Is this explanation perfectly convincing? What, however, is the real, or practical, reason for their being on foot—about which, of course, the dramatist should be expected to say nothing?
3. Some critics hold that the stage direction FLEANCE *escapes* is the exact *climax* (see Glossary) of *Macbeth*. Explain why it is unquestionably an event of momentous significance.
4. The Second Murderer's statement (lines 20 and 21) is certainly true, but how could he possibly know enough to make this statement? Why do you think Shakespeare has him make it?

Act III SCENE 4

1. A case could be made that the climax of the play occurs in this scene at the moment when Macbeth learns of Fleance's escape. Why might this be a more significant turning point than the moment of the escape itself? Or the climax might be Macbeth's fit of guilty terror at the sight of Banquo's ghost. Discuss each of the three possible climaxes, pointing out why each is significant. Which do you favor? Tell why.

2. Macbeth's comment (line 14) is grimly humorous when you discover the meaning. (Try substituting *him* for *he*.) How do you interpret line 28?
3. Lady Macbeth's speech urging her husband to be a jolly host (lines 32-37) does not, at first, make sense. Note the contrast she is making between a "sold" feast and one that is "given with welcome." The clause, "that is not often vouch'd," could be interpreted, "for which assurance is not frequently made." She is also contrasting the difference between eating for nourishment and dining for pleasure. Now state in your own words the meaning of her speech.
4. If you were directing the play, would you have Banquo's ghost actually appear on stage? If so, why could not others besides Macbeth see it? If you used a "real" ghost, would you also, in Macbeth's dagger soliloquy, use a "real" dagger? Usually, the directors show the ghost but not the dagger. Can you justify such a practice?
5. Lines 100-106 reveal much about the nature of Macbeth's courage. Why, then, is he "overcome" by Banquo's ghost? Lines 112-116, addressed to Lady Macbeth, reveal his dismay that she is not also overcome. Why isn't she?
6. During Macbeth's "fit," how does Lady Macbeth react? What is her attitude toward him? Point out the way in which she again takes over when Macbeth is unequal to the situation.
7. Look carefully at each line Lady Macbeth speaks to her husband after the guests depart. How do you account for the difference between these remarks and those she made when the guests were present?

Act III   SCENES 5 and 6

1. What reason does Hecate have for being angry with the Witches? Of all they have done, what does she consider worst? How does she plan to correct the mischief which the Witches have begun?
2. What things "strangely borne" does Lennox point out? Is the *tone* of his irony mild, jesting, bitter? Which phrases convey his *mood*?
3. How does Scene 6, and the specific information it provides, confirm Hecate's foreshadowing of dark days ahead for Macbeth? What is the main function of this scene?
4. Lines 40-43 of Scene 6 are difficult but can be made clear by imaginative application. Who is the *he* of line 40? Whose is the "cloudy messenger"? Why does he personally resent the

kind of message that Macduff has given him to deliver? How would you expect Macbeth to treat the bearer of bad news?

Act IV SCENE 1

1. The dance of the Witches and their chant was so effective theatrically that Elizabethan audiences sometimes insisted on its repetition before continuing with the scene. In your opinion, what makes it so?
2. Macbeth's speech to the Witches (lines 50-61) shows that he knows he is leagued with evil in a game of tinkering with universal spirits. What is it that he wants to learn? What truths does he learn from the four apparitions? Are all four truths "good" or do they cancel out one another?
3. What evidence do you find in this scene of Macbeth's deep-lying fault; namely, that he is all too willing to accept the good and, at the same time, to assume that he can, by his own actions, prevent the bad that has been promised? Has Hecate succeeded in her intention to bring about his ruin by making him over-confident? Discuss.

Act IV SCENE 2

1. Macbeth's threat at the end of Scene 1 adds to the emotional impact of the first seventy-five lines of this scene. How do you explain Lady Macduff's condemnation of her husband's actions? Does "traitors" (line 4) refer to betrayal of country, of family, or of self? What justification does Ross give for Macduff's behavior? How does he try to reassure Lady Macduff?
2. What purpose, if any, is served by the exchange of words between Lady Macduff and her son? If you were directing this play, would you omit these lines? If not, why not?
3. Macbeth attempted earlier to thwart Fate by hiring the Murderers to kill Banquo and Fleance. Ironically, he defeated his own purpose. What reason do you have for believing that the outcome of his attempt to eliminate Macduff will also prove ironical? In both cases, what would Macbeth gain?

1. Again, the closing of the preceding scene affects your reaction to the opening lines in this scene. Malcolm, Duncan's elder

son, naturally assumes that he is more in danger than Macduff. In lines 11-17, he even suggests that he mistrusts Macduff. What is the implied connection between "you have lov'd him well" and "he hath not touch'd you yet"? In view of what you learned in the preceding scene, why do these words have added force? The meaning of lines 14-17 is clearer if you interpret *young* as "inexperienced," *deserve of* as "gain from," and *wisdom* as "political shrewdness." With these clues, express in your own words what Malcolm is implying.

2. Malcolm's next speech (lines 19-24) also requires study. An "imperial charge" suggests royal pressure, and "the brightest" refers to Lucifer, the angel hurled from heaven for rebelling against God. The phrase "would wear the brows" suggests that the true features are covered by a mask. Using these clues, give your interpretation of the entire speech.

3. Despite Macduff's protests that he is honest and that his only concern is Scotland's welfare, Malcolm requires further proof. Describe the way in which he tests Macduff. In what lines does Macduff pass the test? How does his reaction prove his integrity?

4. Lines 140-159 are a digression, in which, by alluding to Edward the Confessor's supposed gift of healing scrofula ("the evil") by touch, Shakespeare complimented his own king, James I, who had been persuaded to revive the practice. Which precise lines in Malcolm's long speech indirectly convey the compliment?

5. Ross's account of the horror under which Scotland is living is packed with exceptionally potent and telling lines. Perhaps it is best summed up in "where violent sorrow seems a modern ecstasy." But what does this mean? "Ecstasy" in Shakespeare regularly means "madness," and "modern ecstasy" is sometimes taken as "ordinary emotion." Does the whole, then, mean that since grief is now so commonplace, to show violent sorrow is to appear mad?

6. On the stage, the moment of Macduff's reaction to the news of his family's slaughter is emotionally very powerful. For one thing, Shakespeare has kept the audience waiting until the end of the longest scene before disclosing what it knows must be revealed. Discuss the way in which Shakespeare conveys Macduff's grief.

7. In line 216, does *he* refer to Malcolm or to Macbeth? Which interpretation better suggests Macduff's grief? What is implied by his statement, "He has no children"?

Act V   SCENE 1

1. For the actress playing Lady Macbeth, the high point is the "sleep-walking scene." Earlier, Lady Macbeth expressed confidence that if one were clever enough to avoid detection, he could commit murder without suffering the consequences. With this in mind, what would you say is the main function of her sleepwalking scene? Which lines specifically bring out the irony of her present condition?
2. Try to identify the "bits and pieces" which Shakespeare has Lady Macbeth speak. What possible event is foreshadowed in lines 69 and 70? Why does the Doctor say "God forgive us all"? At the end of this scene, what do you think Shakespeare intends us to feel toward Lady Macbeth?
3. Much of this scene, like that of the drunken Porter, is in prose. Tell why you do, or do not, think its purpose is also to provide relaxation from intensity.

Act V   SCENE 2

1. The men entering here are Scottish forces. At what point do you discover on which side they will fight?
2. Two place-names of significance are mentioned conspicuously in this scene. What are they, and what is their significance?
3. What reason does Caithness give for the actions of the tyrant Macbeth? What is the meaning of the "clothes" imagery in lines 20-22?
4. Who is the "med'cine of the sickly weal" (state)? What does the figurative "sovereign flower" represent? These are extravagant metaphors of compliment. Under the circumstances, why might they be dramatically appropriate?

Act V   SCENE 3

1. Macbeth's last appearance was his meeting with the Witches in Act IV, Scene 1. What has happened to his condition of mind and spirit since? Point out specific lines, phrases, or ejaculations which reveal his condition.
2. Do you interpret Macbeth's references to the Witches' prophecies as a sign of his basic confidence in them, despite reports, or just the opposite? You know that he is a drowning man clutching at straws. What reason do you have to believe that, in his heart, he also knows it?

3. Which passages in this scene reveal Macbeth's growing poetic powers as his troubles deepen? Discuss the "poetic" conception of these passages and the figurative language used in developing them. Note especially lines 8, 10, 14, and 28.

4. What is the meaning of line 41, one of the greatest in the play? What image is suggested in line 42? How do you interpret "written troubles" (line 43) and the three lines which follow? The word *pristine* (line 53) has been a favorite of poets. Which of the meanings given in the dictionary is best suited to the use of the word here?

5. Macbeth has proved himself a tyrant and a multiple murderer. What evidence do you find in this scene that Shakespeare intended to arouse some sympathy for him? Is it the situation itself, his handling of it, or both?

Act V   SCENE 4

1. This short scene is another example of Shakespeare's use of *dramatic irony* (see Glossary) by which he reveals an important truth or event to the audience while the character most involved remains ignorant of it. What purpose does this scene serve?

2. Malcolm states in line 2, that his "chambers will be safe." Is this a general, figurative statement, or does Malcolm have particular cases in mind? Explain.

3. The statement has been made that the *protagonist* (see Glossary) of a Shakespearean tragedy is, at the last, always alone. In no other tragedy is this truer than in *Macbeth*. In what ways does Macbeth find himself "alone"? How does this "aloneness" affect your feelings toward him?

4. To understand Siward's last speech, you may need to arrange the words in the normal order of prose. What observation is he making about the events at hand?

Act V   SCENE 5

1. Of all the bad news Macbeth has received, which do you think is most shattering to him? Judging by his words (lines 10-15), what is the condition of his mind and spirit? Is this condition similar to, or different from, that revealed in Scene 3?

2. Compare the tone of Macbeth's famous speech (lines 17-28) with the tone of his plea to the Doctor (Scene 3, lines 40-46). What insight does this give you into the importance of Lady Macbeth to her husband?

3. Two interpretations of lines 17 and 18 are possible. What are they? Which do you consider preferable? Which interpretation better suits the attitude toward life that is expressed in the remainder of the passage?

4. When Shakespeare needed to write at his "absolute best," *i.e.*, when he had to supply lines for a great character at a critical instant in his life, he often drew images from his own occupation as a man of the theater. Which lines use such images here, and what conception of the value of life do they express?

5. At the end of the scene, Macbeth is torn by two conflicting attitudes. What are they? Which wins out? Does your own attitude toward Macbeth grow more sympathetic as a result, or less so?

Act V   SCENES 6, 7, and 8

1. On the stage, the action of these three scenes is continuous, as the battle itself is continuous. Thus it must be imagined in reading. The "alarums" serve as bridges between the spoken segments of continuous battle as little knots of men meet, fight and, pursuing the enemy, make room for those who are involved in the next scene. How would the Elizabethan stage better serve the purpose here than the conventional modern stage?

2. In Scene 7, lines 1 and 2, Macbeth compares his predicament to that of a bear tied to a stake and set upon by a pack of savage dogs, as in the Elizabethan sport of bear-baiting. How appropriate is this comparison? At this point, what are your feelings toward Macbeth and his attackers? When he wins a momentary victory by killing young Siward, are you glad or are you more eager for his destruction?

3. Macbeth has nothing but contempt for a man who, following the Roman code of honor, would take his own life rather than accept defeat. Tell why you think this does him credit or discredit.

4. How do you interpret Macbeth's reply to Macduff (Scene 8, lines 4-6)? At what point does he fully realize that he has been duped by the Witches? What is his immediate reaction? In line 18, is he revealing a lack of physical courage? How do you explain his remark "I'll not fight with thee"? If, for a moment, Macbeth does lose his courage, what restores it? What feelings do you think his last words and final exit are intended to arouse?

5. How do you explain Siward's question about his son (line 46)? Why, as an old soldier, is he gratified by the reply?

6. At the end of each of Shakespeare's tragedies, someone is always around to "pick up the pieces." Also, as in the stirring salutation "Hail, King of Scotland!" there is promise of a better day ahead; thus, what has passed seems not to have been in vain. Note, too, the "lift" provided by Malcolm's final speech, which is a characteristic of the very end of all of Shakespeare's tragedies. In one way, however, *Macbeth* is unique; no one has strong words of praise for the dead *protagonist* (see Glossary). What "honor" is accorded Macbeth and Lady Macbeth?
7. Though Shakespeare obviously could not praise Macbeth, he could, if he liked, find a way of implying praise. Look closely again at the heavy emphasis given to the manner of Young Siward's death. In no other tragedy does Shakespeare give precious time in the closing minutes to such a minor figure. Why do you think he did so in this one instance? What is the marked similarity in the deaths of Young Siward and Macbeth?

FOR COMPOSITION

1. Macbeth is rich in imagery which, in addition to enhancing the poetry of the lines, also serves such dramatic purposes as revealing character, creating atmosphere and mood, or heightening the emotional intensity of a scene or incident. Images dealing with clothes, sleep, and blood recur throughout the play. When you have formulated a general thesis about the nature and use of imagery in this play—based on study—present and develop this thesis in an essay.
2. It has been said that the tragic protagonist should be neither wholly good nor wholly bad. Macbeth comes the closest of all Shakespearean protagonists to being the latter. Yet he has certain qualities which, in different circumstances, would be commendable. In a composition of several paragraphs, analyze both his good and bad qualities. In your conclusion, make clear your opinion of him as a person.
3. Unless the playwright can arouse the sympathy of the audience for the protagonist, he will not achieve the classical effects of tragedy—pity and terror—and the drama will not deserve the title of true tragedy. His problem is doubly hard when the protagonist is, like Macbeth, not only a tyrant but also a murderer. Analyze the ways in which Shakespeare attempted to evoke

sympathy for Macbeth. Orally or in writing, present your evidence and be able to support your opinion that he succeeded or failed in his attempt.

4. Make a study of Macbeth's major speeches throughout the play to discover their poetic qualities and to observe how they developed as he became more deeply experienced in the struggles of life. In an essay, present your ideas and opinions, citing evidence from the speeches.

5. It has been said that in Shakespearean tragedy the character of the protagonist is more responsible for his downfall than external agents or forces. In *Macbeth* one cannot overlook such forces as the Witches, Lady Macbeth, and a variety of external circumstances. When you have weighed the evidence for and against character as being more responsible, present your opinion—with support—orally or in writing.

6. In *Macbeth,* Shakespeare probably made more use of *irony* (see Glossary) than in any other play. There is *verbal irony* when Macbeth says "Fail not our feast," at the same time knowing that Banquo will be murdered before dinnertime. There is *irony of situation* when Macduff inquires about the latest horrors in Scotland, not knowing that all his loved ones have been murdered. And there is *irony of Fate* when Macbeth attempts to gain "security" by having Banquo killed and then, on seeing Banquo's ghost, reacts so violently that he arouses the suspicion of everyone present. Write an essay on the forms and uses of irony in the play, making clear what its frequent presence adds to the force of the tragedy.

7. Write a character sketch of Lady Macbeth in which you reveal her strengths and weaknesses and, in addition, the way in which Shakespeare prepares the audience, even in Act I, for her final disintegration in mind and spirit.

8. Much of the action of *Macbeth,* as well as its dramatic impact, is due in large part to the feelings of Macbeth and Lady Macbeth toward each other, to their mutual understandings and dependencies, and to their individual strengths and weaknesses. Orally or in writing, present your evaluation of the relationship between these two and its significance to your own response to the play.

9. Despite its serious tone, *Macbeth* is not devoid of comedy, sometimes in a scene or passage, more often in a line of "grim humor." Write a critical essay in which you evaluate the use of comedy in this play and the purpose it serves.

10. Macbeth and Lady Macbeth so dominate this tragedy that it is easy to overlook the fact that they live in a world of other people, some of whom are almost as completely characterized. Write an essay in which you both distinguish the individual characteristics of at least three of these other people and show their full relation to the story of Macbeth and his downfall. Your problem will be that of presenting a unified essay rather than a succession of unrelated character sketches.

Oliver Goldsmith

Oliver Goldsmith was unquestionably the most versatile man of letters of his day, being equally at home in each of the four major literary genres — essay, novel, poetry, and drama. His novel, *The Vicar of Wakefield* (1766); his long poem, *The Deserted Village* (1770); and his comedy, *She Stoops to Conquer* (1773), are widely read even today. Surprisingly enough, of all the drama produced during the eighteenth century, only *She Stoops to Conquer* and several comedies of the later Richard Sheridan continue to be read and performed today. Many critics agree that, except for the work of these two men, very little drama of merit was produced in England from 1700 up to the time of George Bernard Shaw.

To understand the general mediocrity of English drama during this period, it is helpful to cast a backward glance over dramatic development after Shakespeare. As the brilliant period of Elizabethan drama was drawing to a close, religious and political disunity — between Anglican supporters of the monarchy, known as Cavaliers, and Puritan advocates of Parliamentary rule — was threatening to plunge England into civil war. By 1642 all theaters had been closed by the Puritans, and they remained closed throughout the nearly two decades of civil war and subsequent Commonwealth austerity. With the Restoration of Charles II to the throne in

1660, a general reaction against the recent Puritan austerity took the form of widespread frivolity and licentiousness. The drama of the Restoration period reflected this general trend in its witty, sophisticated comedies with their shallow outlook on life and their utter lack of morality. Indeed, the drama was so preoccupied with sex and debauchery that the final years of the seventeenth century ushered in a reaction against the "rampant immorality" of the English stage.

In opposition to both the Puritan fanaticism and the Cavalier debauchery of the previous century, the eighteenth century became the Age of Reason. Whereas the dissolute drama of the Restoration period had belonged largely to the Cavalier aristocracy, the drama of the eighteenth century became the property of the rising middle classes. The somewhat smug gentility and morality of the middle class gradually imposed their refinement upon the "barbarism" of Restoration drama, and the theater took on an air of grim respectability. A heavy-handed inclination toward moral reform caused a decline in comic effect while an increasing emphasis on sentimentality drowned the former liveliness of English comedy in a welter of maudlin tears.

By 1770, Oliver Goldsmith had achieved a considerable reputation in London as an essayist, novelist, and poet. Having attracted the interest of Dr. Samuel Johnson while a penniless young essayist, he became a member of Johnson's famous Literary Club. For Goldsmith, the stagnation of the English theater was a source of great concern. He deplored the lack of humor and gaiety in English comedy. Although an earlier play had not been wholly successful, he continued his efforts to restore laughter to the stage. He hoped to revive the wit and gaiety of Restoration comedy, while avoiding its lack of morality.

In 1773, *She Stoops to Conquer* was presented at Covent Garden in London. In spite of his literary reputation, Goldsmith was not entirely confident of success. After years of sentimental comedy, the audience might not approve of this boisterous, rollicking play. To boost his confidence, Goldsmith coaxed his friends, including Dr. Johnson, to scatter themselves in the audience and to laugh and applaud at the appropriate times. He need not have worried, however, for the play was an instant success. The audience was delighted with the amusing situations of this unsentimental, entertaining comedy.

Goldsmith died the following year, and it could not have been expected that this one comedy alone would revamp the English theater. Nevertheless, the play is significant historically because it represents the earliest successful attempt to revitalize eighteenth-century drama.

She Stoops to Conquer
or, The Mistakes of a Night

CHARACTERS

MR. HARDCASTLE, a country squire

MRS. HARDCASTLE, his wife

MISS KATE HARDCASTLE, Hardcastle's daughter by a previous marriage

TONY LUMPKIN, Mrs. Hardcastle's son by a previous marriage

MISS CONSTANCE NEVILLE, Mrs. Hardcastle's niece

SIR CHARLES MARLOW, friend of Hardcastle

YOUNG CHARLES MARLOW, his son and suitor of Miss Hardcastle

GEORGE HASTINGS, friend of Young Marlow and suitor of Miss Neville

DIGGORY, a servant

Landlord, Maid, Servants, etc.

Act I SCENE 1

A chamber in an old-fashioned house. Enter MRS. HARD-
CASTLE *and* MR. HARDCASTLE.

MRS. HARDCASTLE.   I vow, Mr. Hardcastle, you're very particular. Is there a creature in the whole country but ourselves that does not take a trip to town now and then to
rub off the rust a little? There's the two Miss Hoggs and
our neighbour, Mrs. Grigsby, go to take a month's polish-
ing every winter.

HARDCASTLE.   Ay, and bring back vanity and affectation to
last them the whole year. I wonder why London cannot
keep its own fools at home. In my time, the follies of the
town crept slowly among us, but now they travel faster
than a stage-coach. Its fopperies come down, not only
as inside passengers, but in the very basket.[1]

MRS. HARDCASTLE.   Ay, your times were fine times, indeed;
you have been telling us of them for many a long year.
Here we live in an old rumbling mansion that looks for
all the world like an inn, but that we never see company.
Our best visitors are old Mrs. Oddfish, the curate's wife,
and little Cripplegate, the lame dancing-master. And all
our entertainment your old stories of Prince Eugene and
the Duke of Marlborough.[2] I hate such old-fashioned
trumpery.

HARDCASTLE.   And I love it. I love every thing that's old:
old friends, old times, old manners, old books, old wine;
and, I believe, Dorothy, *(taking her hand)* you'll own I
have been pretty fond of an old wife.

MRS. HARDCASTLE.   Lord, Mr. Hardcastle, you're for ever
at your Dorothy's and your old wife's. You may be a
Darby, but I'll be no Joan,[3] I promise you. I'm not so old

[1]*basket:* outside compartment for luggage at back of stagecoach
[2]*Prince . . . Marlborough:* leaders of the Grand Alliance armies against
the French in the War of the Spanish Succession (1701-1713)
[3]*Darby and Joan:* the "happy old couple" of eighteenth-century ballad
and tradition

as you'd make me, by more than one good year. Add twenty, and make money of that.

HARDCASTLE. Let me see; twenty added to twenty, makes just fifty and seven.

MRS. HARDCASTLE. It's false, Mr. Hardcastle: I was but twenty when I was brought to bed of Tony, that I had by Mr. Lumpkin, my first husband; and he's not come to years of discretion yet.

HARDCASTLE. Nor ever will, I dare answer for him. Ay, you have taught him finely!

MRS. HARDCASTLE. No matter, Tony Lumpkin has a good fortune. My son is not live by his learning. I don't think a boy wants too much learning to spend fifteen-hundred a year.

HARDCASTLE. Learning, quotha!⁴ A mere composition of tricks and mischief.

MRS. HARDCASTLE. Humor, my dear: nothing but humor. Come, Mr. Hardcastle, you must allow the boy a little humor.

HARDCASTLE. I'd sooner allow him an horse-pond. If burning the footmen's shoes, frighting the maids, and worrying the kittens, be humor, he has it. It was but yesterday he fastened my wig to the back of my chair, and when I went to make a bow I popped my bald head in Mrs. Frizzle's face.

MRS. HARDCASTLE. And am I to blame? The poor boy was always too sickly to do any good. A school would be his death. When he comes to be a little stronger, who knows what a year or two's Latin may do for him?

HARDCASTLE. Latin for him! A cat and fiddle. No, no, the ale-house and the stable are the only schools he'll ever go to.

MRS. HARDCASTLE. Well, we must not snub the poor boy now, for I believe we shan't have him long among us. Anybody that looks in his face may see he's consumptive.

HARDCASTLE. Ay, if growing too fat be one of the symptoms.

MRS. HARDCASTLE. He coughs sometimes.

---

⁴*quotha:* indeed! Forsooth!

HARDCASTLE.   Yes, when his liquor goes the wrong way.

MRS. HARDCASTLE.   I'm actually afraid of his lungs.

HARDCASTLE.   And truly, so am I; for he sometimes whoops like a speaking trumpet—(TONY *hallooing behind the scenes.*)—Oh, there he goes—A very consumptive figure, truly.

(Enter TONY, *crossing the stage.)*

MRS. HARDCASTLE.   Tony, where are you going, my charmer? Won't you give papa and I a little of your company, lovee?

TONY.   I'm in haste, mother, I cannot stay.

MRS. HARDCASTLE.   You shan't venture out this raw evening, my dear. You look most shockingly.

TONY.   I can't stay, I tell you. The Three Pigeons expects me down every moment. There's some fun going forward.

HARDCASTLE.   Ay; the ale-house, the old place. I thought so.

MRS. HARDCASTLE.   A low, paltry set of fellows.

TONY.   Not so low neither. There's Dick Muggins the exciseman, Jack Slang the horse doctor, Little Aminadab that grinds the music box, and Tom Twist that spins the pewter platter.

MRS. HARDCASTLE.   Pray, my dear, disappoint them for one night at least.

TONY.   As for disappointing *them*, I should not so much mind; but I can't abide to disappoint *myself*.

MRS. HARDCASTLE *(detaining him).*   You shan't go.

TONY.   I will, I tell you.

MRS. HARDCASTLE.   I say you shan't.

TONY.   We'll see which is strongest, you or I. *(Exit hauling her out.)*

HARDCASTLE.   Ay, there goes a pair that only spoil each other. But is not the whole age in a combination to drive sense and discretion out of doors? There's my pretty darling, Kate; the fashions of the times have almost infected her too. By living a year or two in town, she is as fond of gauze, and French frippery, as the best of them.

(*Enter* MISS HARDCASTLE.)

HARDCASTLE. Blessings on my pretty innocence! Dressed out as usual, my Kate. Goodness! What a quantity of superfluous silk hast thou got about thee, girl! I could never teach the fools of this age, that the indigent world could be clothed out of the trimmings of the vain.

MISS HARDCASTLE. You know our agreement, sir. You allow me the morning to receive and pay visits and to dress in my own manner; and in the evening, I put on my housewife's dress to please you.

HARDCASTLE. Well, remember, I insist on the terms of our agreement; and, by the bye, I believe I shall have occasion to try your obedience this very evening.

MISS HARDCASTLE. I protest, sir, I don't comprehend your meaning.

HARDCASTLE. Then, to be plain with you, Kate, I expect the young gentleman I have chosen to be your husband from town this very day. I have his father's letter in which he informs me his son is set out and that he intends to follow himself shortly after.

MISS HARDCASTLE. Indeed! I wish I had known something of this before. Bless me, how shall I behave? It's a thousand to one I shan't like him. Our meeting will be so formal and so like a thing of business that I shall find no room for friendship or esteem.

HARDCASTLE. Depend upon it, child, I'll never control your choice; but Mr. Marlow, whom I have pitched upon, is the son of my old friend, Sir Charles Marlow, of whom you have heard me talk so often. The young gentleman has been bred a scholar, and is designed for an employment in the service of his country. I am told he's a man of excellent understanding.

MISS HARDCASTLE. Is he?

HARDCASTLE. Very generous.

MISS HARDCASTLE. I believe I shall like him.

HARDCASTLE. Young and brave.

MISS HARDCASTLE. I'm sure I shall like him.

HARDCASTLE. And very handsome.

MISS HARDCASTLE. My dear papa, say no more; *(kissing his hand)* he's mine, I'll have him.

HARDCASTLE. And to crown all, Kate, he's one of the most bashful and reserved young fellows in all the world.

MISS HARDCASTLE. Eh! you have frozen me to death again. That word "reserved" has undone all the rest of his accomplishments. A reserved lover, it is said, always makes a suspicious husband.

HARDCASTLE. On the contrary, modesty seldom resides in a breast that is not enriched with nobler virtues. It was the very feature in his character that first struck me.

MISS HARDCASTLE. He must have more striking features to catch me, I promise you. However, if he be so young, so handsome, and so everything, as you mention, I believe he'll do still. I think I'll have him.

HARDCASTLE. Ay, Kate, but there is still an obstacle. It's more than an even wager he may not have *you*.

MISS HARDCASTLE. My dear Papa, why will you mortify one so?—Well, if he refuses, instead of breaking my heart at his indifference, I'll only break my glass for its flattery, set my cap to some newer fashion, and look out for some less difficult admirer.

HARDCASTLE. Bravely resolved! In the mean time I'll go prepare the servants for his reception; as we seldom see company they want as much training as a company of recruits, the first day's muster. *(Exit.)*

MISS HARDCASTLE. Lud,[5] this news of Papa's puts me all in a flutter. Young, handsome; these he put last; but I put them foremost. Sensible, good-natured; I like all that. But then reserved, and sheepish, that's much against him. Yet, can't he be cured of his timidity by being taught to be proud of his wife? Yes, and can't I—But I vow I'm disposing of the husband, before I have secured the lover.

(Enter MISS NEVILLE.)

MISS HARDCASTLE. I'm glad you're come, Neville, my dear.

[5]*Lud:* Lord

Tell me, Constance, how do I look this evening? Is th
any thing whimsical about me? Is it one of my wel
looking days, child? Am I in face today?

MISS NEVILLE.   Perfectly, my dear. Yet now I look again—
bless me!—sure no accident has happened among the
canary birds or the gold-fishes. Has your brother or the
cat been meddling? Or has the last novel been too
moving?

MISS HARDCASTLE.   No; nothing of all this. I have been
threatened—I can scarce get it out—I have been threatened with a lover.

MISS NEVILLE.   And his name—

MISS HARDCASTLE.   Is Marlow.

MISS NEVILLE.   Indeed!

MISS HARDCASTLE.   The son of Sir Charles Marlow.

MISS NEVILLE.   As I live, the most intimate friend of Mr.
Hastings, *my* admirer. They are never asunder. I believe
you must have seen him when we lived in town.

MISS HARDCASTLE.   Never.

MISS NEVILLE.   He's a very singular character, I assure you.
Among women of reputation and virtue, he is the modestest man alive; but his acquaintance give him a very different character among creatures of another stamp:
you understand me.

MISS HARDCASTLE.   An odd character, indeed. I shall never
be able to manage him. What shall I do? Pshaw, think
no more of him, but trust to occurrences for success. But
how goes on your own affair, my dear? has my mother
been courting you for my brother Tony, as usual?

MISS NEVILLE.   I have just come from one of our agreeable
tête-à-têtes.[6] She has been saying a hundred tender things
and setting off her pretty monster as the very pink of
perfection.

MISS HARDCASTLE.   And her partiality is such that she
actually thinks him so. A fortune like yours is no small
temptation. Besides, as she has the sole management of
it, I'm not surprised to see her unwilling to let it go out
of the family.

[6]*tête-à-têtes:* intimate conversation between two people (French)

fortune like mine, which chiefly consists
o such mighty temptation. But at any rate,
tings be but constant, I make no doubt to
her at last. However, I let her suppose that
ove with her son, and she never once dreams
that my affections are fixed upon another.

MISS HARDCASTLE.   My good brother holds out stoutly. I
could almost love him for hating you so.

MISS NEVILLE.   It is a good natured creature at bottom, and
I'm sure would wish to see me married to anybody but
himself. But my aunt's bell rings for our afternoon's
walk round the improvements. *Allons.*[7] Courage is necessary as our affairs are critical.

MISS HARDCASTLE.   Would it were bedtime and all were
well.[8]   (*Exit.*)

Act I SCENE 2

*An ale-house room. Several shabby fellows with punch
and tobacco.* TONY *at the head of the table.*

ALL.   Hurrea, hurrea, hurrea, bravo!

FIRST FELLOW.   Now, gentlemen, silence for a song. The
Squire is going to knock himself down[1] for a song.

ALL.   Ay, a song, a song.

TONY.   Then I'll sing you, gentlemen, a song I made upon
this ale-house, The Three Pigeons.

SONG

Let school-masters puzzle their brain
    With grammar, and nonsense, and learning;

[7]*Allons:* Let's go. (French)
[8]*Would . . . well:* refers to Falstaff's remark upon entering battle, *Henry IV,
Part I*, Act V, Scene I

[1]*Knock himself down:* call upon himself

Good liquor, I stoutly maintain,
  Gives genius a better discerning.
Let them brag of their heathenish gods,
  Their Lethes, their Styxes,[2] and Stygians;
Their quis, and their quœs, and their quods,[3]
  They're all but a parcel of pigeons.[4]
                    Toroddle, toroddle, toroll!

When Methodist preachers come down,
  A-preaching that drinking is sinful,
I'll wager the rascals a crown,
  They always preach best with a skinful.
But when you come down with your pence,
  For a slice of their scurvy religion,
I'll leave it to all men of sense,
  But you, my good friend, are the pigeon.
                    Toroddle, toroddle, toroll!

Then come, put the jorum[5] about,
  And let us be merry and clever,
Our hearts and our liquors are stout,
  Here's the Three Jolly Pigeons for ever.
Let some cry up woodcock or hare,
  Your bustards, your ducks, and your widgeons;
But of all the birds in the air,
  Here's a health to the Three Jolly Pigeons.
                    Toroddle, toroddle, toroll!

ALL.   Bravo, bravo.

FIRST FELLOW.   The squire has got spunk in him.

SECOND FELLOW.   I loves to hear him sing, bekeays he never
  gives us nothing that's low.

THIRD FELLOW.   O damn anything that's low, I cannot bear it.

FOURTH FELLOW.   The genteel thing is the genteel thing at
  any time. If so be that a gentleman bees in a concatenation[6] accordingly.

---

[2]*Lethes . . . Styxes:* the Lethe and the Styx, two rivers of Hades
[3]*quis . . . quœs . . . quods:* who, whats, whiches
[4]*pigeons:* simpletons
[5]*jorum:* large drinking bowl
[6]*concatenation:* in this case, a gathering

THIRD FELLOW. I like the maxum of it, Master Muggins. What, though I am obligated to dance a bear, a man may be a gentleman for all that. May this be my poison if my bear ever dances but to the very genteelest of tunes — *Water Parted*, or the minuet in *Ariadne*.[7]

SECOND FELLOW. What a pity it is the squire is not come to his own. It would be well for all the publicans[8] within ten miles round of him.

TONY. Ecod, and so it would, Master Slang. I'd then show what it was to keep choice of company.

SECOND FELLOW. Oh, he takes after his own father for that. To be sure old squire Lumpkin was the finest gentleman I ever set my eyes on. For winding the straight horn, or beating a thicket for a hare or a wench he never had his fellow. It was a saying in the place, that he kept the best horses, dogs and girls in the whole country.

TONY. Ecod, and when I'm of age I'll be no bastard, I promise you. I have been thinking of Bett Bouncer and the miller's grey mare to begin with. But come, my boys, drink about and be merry, for you pay no reckoning. Well, Stingo, what's the matter?

(Enter LANDLORD*)*

LANDLORD. There be two gentlemen in a post-chaise at the door. They have lost their way upo' the forest; and they are talking something about Mr. Hardcastle.

TONY. As sure as can be, one of them must be the gentleman that's coming down to court my sister. Do they seem to be Londoners?

LANDLORD. I believe they may. They look woundily[9] like Frenchmen.

TONY. Then desire them to step this way, and I'll set them right in a twinkling. *(Exit* LANDLORD.*)* Gentlemen, as they mayn't be good enough company for you, step down for a moment, and I'll be with you in the squeezing of a lemon. *(Exeunt Mob.)*

[7]*Water . . . Ariadne:* songs from operas
[8]*publicans:* tavern keepers
[9]*woundily:* exceedingly, extremely

TONY. Father-in-law[10] has been calling me whelp and hound, this half year. Now if I pleased, I could be so revenged upon the old grumbletonian. But then I'm afraid — afraid of what? I shall soon be worth fifteen hundred a year, and let him frighten me out of that if he can.

(Enter LANDLORD, *conducting* MARLOW *and* HASTINGS.*)*

MARLOW. What a tedious, uncomfortable day have we had of it! We were told it was but forty miles across the country, and we have come above threescore.

HASTINGS. And all, Marlow, from that unaccountable reserve of yours that would not let us enquire more frequently on the way.

MARLOW. I own, Hastings, I am unwilling to lay myself under an obligation to every one I meet; and often, stand the chance of an unmannerly answer.

HASTINGS. At present, however, we are not likely to receive any answer.

TONY. No offense, gentlemen. But I'm told you have been enquiring for one Mr. Hardcastle in these parts. Do you know what part of the country you are in?

HASTINGS. Not in the least, sir, but should thank you for information.

TONY. Nor the way you came?

HASTINGS. No, sir; but if you can inform us —

TONY. Why gentlemen, if you know neither the road you are going, nor where you are, nor the road you came, the first thing I have to inform you is, that — you have lost your way.

MARLOW. We wanted no ghost to tell us that.[11]

TONY. Pray, gentlemen, may I be so bold as to ask the place from whence you came?

MARLOW. That's not necessary towards directing us where we are to go.

TONY. No offense; but question for question is all fair, you know. Pray, gentlemen, is not this the same Hardcastle a

---

[10]*father-in-law:* stepfather
[11]*We . . . that:* Horatio's reply to Hamlet, *Hamlet,* Act I, Scene 5

cross-grained, old-fashioned, whimsical fellow, with an ugly face, a daughter, and a pretty son?

HASTINGS. We have not seen the gentleman, but he has the family you mention.

TONY. The daughter, a tall, traipsing, trolloping, talkative maypole—The son, a pretty, well-bred, agreeable youth that everybody is fond of.

MARLOW. Our information differs in this. The daughter is said to be well-bred and beautiful; the son, an awkward booby, reared up and spoiled at his mother's apron-string.

TONY. He-he-hem—Then, gentlemen, all I have to tell you is, that you won't reach Mr. Hardcastle's house this night, I believe.

HASTINGS. Unfortunate!

TONY. It's a damn'd long, dark, boggy, dirty, dangerous way. Stingo, tell the gentlemen the way to Mr. Hardcastle's; *(Winking upon the* LANDLORD.*)* Mr. Hardcastle's, of Quagmire Marsh, you understand me.

LANDLORD. Master Hardcastle's! Lack-a-daisy, my masters, you're come a deadly deal wrong! When you came to the bottom of the hill, you should have crossed down Squash-lane.

MARLOW. Cross down Squash-lane!

LANDLORD. Then you were to keep straight forward, 'till you came to four roads.

MARLOW. Come to where four roads meet!

TONY. Ay; but you must be sure to take only one of them.

MARLOW. O sir, you're facetious.[12]

TONY. Then keeping to the right, you are to go side-ways till you come upon Crack-skull Common. There you must look sharp for the track of the wheel and go forward 'till you come to farmer Murrain's barn. Coming to the farmer's barn, you are to turn to the right, and then to the left, and then to the right about again, till you find out the old mill—

MARLOW. Zounds, man! we could as soon find out the longitude!

HASTINGS. What's to be done, Marlow?

[12]*facetious:* joking, especially at an inappropriate time

MARLOW.   This house promises but a poor reception; though perhaps the Landlord can accommodate us.

LANDLORD.   Alack, master, we have but one spare bed in the whole house.

TONY.   And to my knowledge, that's taken up by three lodgers already. *(After a pause in which the rest seem disconcerted.)* I have hit it. Don't you think, Stingo, our landlady could accommodate the gentlemen by the fire-side, with—three chairs and a bolster?[13]

HASTINGS.   I hate sleeping by the fire-side.

MARLOW.   And I detest your three chairs and a bolster.

TONY.   You do, do you?—then let me see—what—if you go on a mile further to the Buck's Head; the old Buck's Head on the hill, one of the best inns in the whole county?

HASTINGS.   O ho! so we have escaped an adventure for this night, however.

LANDLORD *(apart to* TONY*)*.   Sure, you ben't sending them to your father's as an inn, be you?

TONY.   Mum, you fool you. Let *them* find that out. *(To them.)* You have only to keep on straight forward till you come to a large old house by the road side. You'll see a pair of large horns over the door. That's the sign. Drive up the yard and call stoutly about you.

HASTINGS.   Sir, we are obliged to you. The servants can't miss the way?

TONY.   No, no. But I tell you though, the landlord is rich and going to leave off business; so he wants to be thought a gentleman, saving your presence, he! he! he! He'll be for giving you his company, and, ecod, if you mind him, he'll persuade you that his mother was an alderman, and his aunt a justice of peace.

LANDLORD.   A troublesome old blade, to be sure; but he keeps as good wines and beds as any in the whole country.

MARLOW.   Well, if he supplies us with these, we shall want no further connection. We are to turn to the right, did you say?

TONY.   No, no; straight forward. I'll just step myself, and show you a piece of the way. *(To the* LANDLORD*.)* Mum.

[13]*bolster:* long, narrow cushion or pillow

LANDLORD. Ah, bless your heart, for a sweet, pleasant—damned mischievous son.   *(Exeunt.)*

Act II

An old-fashioned house. Enter HARDCASTLE *followed by three or four awkward servants.*

HARDCASTLE. Well, I hope you're perfect in the table exercise I have been teaching you these three days. You all know your posts and your places and can show that you have been used to good company, without ever stirring from home.

ALL. Ay, ay.

HARDCASTLE. When company comes, you are not to pop out and stare, and then run in again, like frightened rabbits in a warren.

ALL. No, no.

HARDCASTLE. You, Diggory, whom I have taken from the barn, are to make a show at the side-table; and you, Roger, whom I have advanced from the plough, are to place yourself behind my chair. But you're not to stand so, with your hands in your pockets. Take your hands from your pockets, Roger; and from your head, you blockhead you. See how Diggory carries his hands. They're a little too stiff indeed, but that's no great matter.

DIGGORY. Ay, mind how I hold them. I learned to hold my hands this way when I was upon drill for the militia. And so being upon drill—

HARDCASTLE. You must not be so talkative, Diggory. You must be all attention to the guests. You must hear us talk and not think of talking; you must see us drink and not think of drinking; you must see us eat and not think of eating.

DIGGORY. By the laws, your worship, that's perfectly unpossible. Whenever Diggory sees yeating going forward, ecod, he's always wishing for a mouthful himself.

HARDCASTLE. Blockhead! Is not a bellyful in the kitchen as good as a bellyfull in the parlor? Stay your stomach with that reflection.

DIGGORY. Ecod, I thank your worship, I'll make a shift to stay my stomach with a slice of cold beef in the pantry.

HARDCASTLE. Diggory, you are too talkative. Then, if I happen to say a good thing, or tell a good story at table, you must not all burst out a-laughing, as if you made part of the company.

DIGGORY. Then, ecod, your worship must not tell the story of Ould Grouse in the gunroom: I can't help laughing at that—he! he! he!—for the soul of me. We have laughed at that these twenty years—ha! ha! ha!

HARDCASTLE. Ha! ha! ha! The story is a good one. Well, honest Diggory, you may laugh at that—but still remember to be attentive. Suppose one of the company should call for a glass of wine; how will you behave? A glass of wine, sir, if you please. *(To* DIGGORY.*)*—Eh, why don't you move?

DIGGORY. Ecod, your worship, I never have courage till I see the eatables and drinkables brought upo' the table, and then I'm as bauld as a lion.

HARDCASTLE. What, will nobody move?

FIRST SERVANT. I'm not to leave this pleace.

SECOND SERVANT. I'm sure it's no pleace of mine.

THIRD SERVANT. Nor mine, for sartain.

DIGGORY. Wauns,[1] and I'm sure it canna be mine.

HARDCASTLE. You numbskulls! And so while, like your betters, you are quarrelling for places, the guests must be starved. O you dunces! I find I must begin all over again. —But don't I hear a coach drive into the yard? To your posts, you blockheads. I'll go in the meantime and give my old friend's son a hearty reception at the gate. *(Exit.)*

DIGGORY. By the elevens, my pleace is gone quite out of my head.

---

[1]*Wauns:* wounds (a mild oath)

ROGER.   I know that my pleace is to be everywhere.

FIRST SERVANT.   Where the devil is mine?

SECOND SERVANT.   My pleace is to be nowhere at all; and so I'ze go about my business.

(Exeunt SERVANTS, *running about as if frightened, different ways.)*

(Enter SERVANT *with candles, showing in* MARLOW *and* HASTINGS.*)*

SERVANT.   Welcome, gentlemen, very welcome. This way.

HASTINGS.   After the disappointments of the day, welcome once more, Charles, to the comforts of a clean room and a good fire. Upon my word, a very well-looking house; antique, but creditable.

MARLOW.   The usual fate of a large mansion. Having first ruined the master by good housekeeping, it at last comes to levy contributions as an inn.

HASTINGS.   As you say, we passengers are to be taxed to pay all these fineries. I have often seen a good sideboard, or a marble chimney-piece, though not actually put in the bill, inflame a reckoning[2] confoundedly.

MARLOW.   Travelers, George, must pay in all places. The only difference is that in good inns you pay dearly for luxuries; in bad inns you are fleeced and starved.

HASTINGS.   You have lived pretty much among them. In truth, I have been often surprised that you who have seen so much of the world, with your natural good sense, and your many opportunities, could never yet acquire a requisite share of assurance.

MARLOW.   The Englishman's malady. But tell me, George, where could I have learned that assurance you talk of? My life has been chiefly spent in a college or an inn, in seclusion from that lovely part of the creation that chiefly teach men confidence. I don't know that I was ever

---

[2]*inflame a reckoning:* increase the amount of a bill

familiarly acquainted with a single modest woman—
except my mother—But among females of another class,
you know—

HASTINGS. Ay, among them you are impudent enough of
all conscience.

MARLOW. They are of *us*, you know.

HASTINGS. But in the company of women of reputation I
never saw such an idiot, such a trembler; you look for all
the world as if you wanted an opportunity of stealing out
of the room.

MARLOW. Why, man. that's because I *do* want to steal out
of the room. Faith, I have often formed a resolution to
break the ice, and rattle away at any rate. But, I don't
know how, a single glance from a pair of fine eyes has
totally overset my resolution. An impudent fellow may
counterfeit modesty, but I'll be hanged if a modest man
can ever counterfeit impudence.

HASTINGS. If you could but say half the fine things to them
that I have heard you lavish upon the bar-maid of an inn,
or even a college bed maker—

MARLOW. Why, George, I can't say fine things to them.
They freeze, they petrify me. They may talk of a comet,
or a burning mountain, or some such bagatelle.[3] But to me,
a modest woman, dressed out in all her finery, is the most
tremendous object of the whole creation.

HASTINGS. Ha! ha! ha! At this rate, man, how can you ever
expect to marry!

MARLOW. Never, unless, as among kings and princes, my
bride were to be courted by proxy. If, indeed, like an
Eastern bridegroom, one were to be introduced to a
wife he never saw before, it might be endured. But to go
through all the terrors of a formal courtship, together
with the episode of aunts, grandmothers and cousins,
and at last to blurt out the broad staring question of,
Madam, will you marry me? No, no, that's a strain much
above me, I assure you.

---

[3]*bagatelle:* trifle

HASTINGS. I pity you. But how do you intend behaving to the lady you are come down to visit at the request of your father?

MARLOW. As I behave to all other ladies. Bow very low. Answer yes, or no, to all her demands—But for the rest, I don't think I shall venture to look in her face till I see my father's again.

HASTINGS. I'm surprised that one who is so warm a friend can be so cool a lover.

MARLOW. To be explicit, my dear Hastings, my chief inducement down was to be instrumental in forwarding your happiness, not my own. Miss Neville loves you, the family don't know you; as my friend you are sure of a reception, and let honor do the rest.

HASTINGS. My dear Marlow! But I'll suppress the emotion. Were I a wretch, meanly seeking to carry off a fortune, you should be the last man in the world I would apply to for assistance. But Miss Neville's person is all I ask, and that is mine, both from her deceased father's consent and her own inclination.

MARLOW. Happy man! You have talents and art to captivate any woman. I'm doomed to adore the sex, and yet to converse with the only part of it I despise. This stammer in my address, and this awkward, unprepossessing visage of mine can never permit me to soar above the reach of a milliner's 'prentice, or one of the duchesses of Drury Lane. Pshaw! this fellow here to interrupt us.

(*Enter* HARDCASTLE.)

HARDCASTLE. Gentlemen, once more you are heartily welcome. Which is Mr. Marlow? Sir, you're heartily welcome. It's not my way, you see, to receive my friends with my back to the fire. I like to give them a hearty reception in the old style, at my gate. I like to see their horses and trunks taken care of.

MARLOW (*aside*). He has got our names from the servants already. (*To him.*) We approve your caution and hospitality, sir. (*To* HASTINGS.) I have been thinking, George, of changing our travelling dresses in the morning. I am grown confoundedly ashamed of mine.

HARDCASTLE.   I beg, Mr. Marlow, you'll use no ceremony in this house.

HASTINGS.   I fancy, Charles, you're right: the first blow is half the battle. I intend opening the campaign with the white and gold.

MR. HARDCASTLE.   Mr. Marlow—Mr. Hastings—gentlemen—pray be under no constraint in this house. This is Liberty-Hall, gentlemen. You may do just as you please here.

MARLOW.   Yet, George, if we open the campaign too fiercely at first, we may want ammunition before it is over. I think to reserve the embroidery to secure a retreat.

HARDCASTLE.   Your talking of a retreat, Mr. Marlow, puts me in mind of the Duke of Marlborough, when we went to besiege Denain. He first summoned the garrison—

MARLOW.   Don't you think the *ventre d'or*[4] waistcoat will do with the plain brown?

HARDCASTLE.   He first summoned the garrison, which might consist of about five thousand men—

HASTINGS.   I think not: brown and yellow mix but very poorly.

HARDCASTLE.   I say, gentlemen, as I was telling you, he summoned the garrison, which might consist of about five thousand men—

MARLOW.   The girls like finery.

HARDCASTLE.   Which might consist of about five thousand men, well appointed with stores, ammunition, and other implements of war. "Now," says the Duke of Marlborough, to George Brooks, that stood next to him—You must have heard of George Brooks—"I'll pawn my Dukedom," says he, "but I take that garrison without spilling a drop of blood." So—

MARLOW.   What, my good friend, if you gave us a glass of punch in the mean time; it would help us to carry on the siege with vigor.

---

[4] *ventre d'or:* gold-fronted (French)

HARDCASTLE. Punch, sir! (*Aside.*) This is the most unaccountable kind of modesty I ever met with.

MARLOW. Yes, sir, punch. A glass of warm punch, after our journey, will be comfortable. This is Liberty-Hall, you know.

HARDCASTLE. Here's cup,[5] sir.

MARLOW (*aside*). So this fellow, in his Liberty-Hall, will only let us have just what he pleases.

HARDCASTLE (*taking the cup*). I hope you'll find it to your mind. I have prepared it with my own hands, and I believe you'll own the ingredients are tolerable. Will you be so good as to pledge me, sir? Here, Mr. Marlow, here is to our better acquaintance. (*Drinks.*)

MARLOW (*aside*). A very impudent fellow this! but he's a character and I'll humor him a little. Sir, my service to you. (*Drinks.*)

HASTINGS (*aside*). I see this fellow wants to give us his company, and forgets that he's an innkeeper, before he has learned to be a gentleman.

MARLOW. From the excellence of your cup, my old friend, I suppose you have a good deal of business in this part of the country. Warm work, now and then, at elections, I suppose?

HARDCASTLE. No, sir, I have long given that work over. Since our betters have hit upon the expedient of electing each other, there's no business *for us that sell ale.*[6]

HASTINGS. So, then you have no turn for politics, I find.

HARDCASTLE. Not in the least. There was a time, indeed, I fretted myself about the mistakes of government, like other people; but finding myself every day grow more angry, and the government growing no better, I left it to mend itself. Since that, I no more trouble my head about Heyder Ally, or Ally Cawn, than about Ally Croaker.[7] Sir, my service to you.

HASTINGS. So that with eating above stairs, and drinking

[5]*cup:* sweetened, iced wine
[6]*us that sell ale:* us common people
[7]*Heyder Ally . . . Croaker:* Hyder Ali Khan—a formidable ruler of India and opponent of England; "Ally Croaker"—a popular Irish song

below, with receiving your friends within, and amusing
them without you lead a good, pleasant, bustling life of it.

HARDCASTLE.   I do stir about a great deal, that's certain. Half
the differences of the parish are adjusted in this very
parlor.

MARLOW *(after drinking)*.   And you have an argument in
your cup, old gentleman, better than any in Westminster
Hall.

HARDCASTLE.   Ay, young gentleman, that, and a little philosophy.

MARLOW *(aside)*.   Well, this is the first time I ever heard of
an innkeeper's philosophy.

HASTINGS.   So then, like an experienced general, you attack
them on every quarter. If you find their reason manage-
able, you attack it with your philosophy; if you find they
have no reason, you attack them with this. Here's your
health, my philosopher. *(Drinks.)*

HARDCASTLE.   Good, very good, thank you; ha! ha! Your gen-
eralship puts me in mind of Prince Eugene, when he
fought the Turks at the battle of Belgrade. You shall
hear—

MARLOW.   Instead of the battle of Belgrade, I believe it's
almost time to talk about supper. What has your philosophy got in the house for supper?

HARDCASTLE.   For supper, sir! *(Aside.)* Was ever such a request to a man in his own house!

MARLOW.   Yes, sir, supper, sir; I begin to feel an appetite.
I shall make devilish work tonight in the larder, I promise
you.

HARDCASTLE *(aside)*.   Such a brazen dog sure never my eyes
beheld. *(To him.)* Why really, sir, as for supper I can't
well tell. My Dorothy, and the cook-maid, settle these
things between them. I leave these kind of things entirely
to them.

MARLOW.   You do, do you?

HARDCASTLE.   Entirely. By the by, I believe they are in
actual consultation upon what's for supper this moment
in the kitchen.

MARLOW.   Then I beg they'll admit *me* as one of their privy council. It's a way I have got. When I travel, I always choose to regulate my own supper. Let the cook be called. No offense, I hope, sir.

HARDCASTLE. O no, sir, none in the least; yet I don't know how: our Bridget, the cook maid, is not very communicative upon these occasions. Should we send for her, she might scold us all out of the house.

HASTINGS. Let's see your list of the larder then. I ask it as a favor. I always match my appetite to my bill of fare.

MARLOW (to HARDCASTLE, *who looks at them with surprise*). Sir, he's very right, and it's my way too.

HARDCASTLE. Sir, you have a right to command here. Here, Roger, bring us the bill of fare for tonight's supper. I believe it's drawn out. Your manner, Mr. Hastings, puts me in mind of my uncle, Colonel Wallop. It was a saying of his, that no man was sure of his supper till he had eaten it.

HASTINGS (*aside*). All upon the high ropes! His uncle a Colonel! We shall soon hear of his mother being a justice of peace. But let's hear the bill of fare.

MARLOW (*perusing*). What's here? For the first course; for the second course; for the dessert. The devil, sir, do you think we have brought down the whole Joiners Company, or the Corporation of Bedford, to eat up such a supper? Two or three little things, clean and comfortable, will do.

HASTINGS. But, let's hear it.

MARLOW (*reading*). For the first course, at the top, a pig and prune sauce.

HASTINGS. Damn your pig, I say.

MARLOW. And damn your prune sauce, say I.

HARDCASTLE. And yet, gentlemen, to men that are hungry, pig with prune sauce is very good eating.

MARLOW. At the bottom, a calve's tongue and brains.

HASTINGS. Let your brains be knocked out, my good sir; I don't like them.

MARLOW. Or you may clap them on a plate by themselves, I do.

HARDCASTLE (*aside*). Their impudence confounds me. (*To them.*) Gentlemen, you are my guests; make what alterations you please. Is there any thing else you wish to retrench or alter, gentlemen?

MARLOW. Item: A pork pie, a boiled rabbit and sausages, a florentine, a shaking pudding, and a dish of tiff—taff— taffety cream!

HASTINGS. Confound your made dishes,[8] I shall be as much at a loss in this house as at a green and yellow dinner at the French ambassador's table.[9] I'm for plain eating.

HARDCASTLE. I'm sorry, gentlemen, that I have nothing you like, but if there be any thing you have a particular fancy to—

MARLOW. Why, really, sir, your bill of fare is so exquisite that any one part of it is full as good as another. Send us what you please. So much for supper. And now to see that our beds are aired, and properly taken care of.

HARDCASTLE. I entreat you'll leave all that to me. You shall not stir a step.

MARLOW. Leave that to you! I protest, sir, you must excuse me, I always look to these things myself.

HARDCASTLE. I must insist, sir, you'll make yourself easy on that head.

MARLOW. You see I'm resolved on it. *(Aside.)* A very troublesome fellow this, as ever I met with.

HARDCASTLE. Well, sir, I'm resolved at least to attend you. *(Aside.)* This may be modern modesty, but I never saw anything look so like old-fashioned impudence.

(Exeunt MARLOW *and* HARDCASTLE.*)*

HASTINGS. So I find this fellow's civilities begin to grow troublesome. But who can be angry at those assiduities[10] which are meant to please him? Ha! what do I see? Miss Neville, by all that's happy!

(Enter MISS NEVILLE.*)*

MISS NEVILLE. My dear Hastings! To what unexpected good fortune, to what accident am I to ascribe this happy meeting?

[8]*made dishes:* food dishes made of several ingredients
[9]*green and yellow dinner . . . table:* a dig at the extravagant style and disappointing substance of French diplomatic dinners
[10]*assiduities:* persistent personal attentions

HASTINGS.   Rather let me ask the same question, as I could never have hoped to meet my dearest Constance at an inn.

MISS NEVILLE.   An inn! sure you mistake! my aunt, my guardian, lives here. What could induce you to think this house an inn?

HASTINGS.   My friend, Mr. Marlow, with whom I came down, and I, have been sent here as to an inn, I assure you. A young fellow whom we accidentally met at a house hard by directed us hither.

MISS NEVILLE.   Certainly it must be one of my hopeful cousin's tricks, of whom you have heard me talk so often, ha! ha! ha!

HASTINGS.   He whom your aunt intends for you? He of whom I have such just apprehensions?

MISS NEVILLE.   You have nothing to fear from him, I assure you. You'd adore him if you knew how heartily he despises me. My aunt knows it too, and has undertaken to court me for him, and actually begins to think she has made a conquest.

HASTINGS.   Thou dear dissembler![11] You must know, my Constance, I have just seized this happy opportunity of my friend's visit here to get admittance into the family. The horses that carried us down are now fatigued with their journey, but they'll soon be refreshed; and then, if my dearest girl will trust in her faithful Hastings, we shall soon be landed in France, where even among slaves the laws of marriage are respected.[12]

MISS NEVILLE.   I have often told you, that though ready to obey you, I yet should leave my little fortune behind with reluctance. The greatest part of it was left me by my uncle, the India director,[13] and chiefly consists in jewels. I have been for some time persuading my aunt to let me wear them. I fancy I'm very near succeeding. The instant they are put into my possession you shall find me ready to make them and myself yours.

[11]*dissembler:* one who conceals his true feelings by pretense
[12]*France, . . . respected:* a dig at the restrictive Royal Marriage Act of 1772
[13]*India director:* director of the East India Company

HASTINGS.   Perish the baubles! Your person is all I desire. In the meantime, my friend Marlow must not be let into his mistake. I know the strange reserve of his temper is such that if abruptly informed of it, he would instantly quit the house before our plan was ripe for execution.

MISS NEVILLE.   But how shall we keep him in the deception? Miss Hardcastle is just returned from walking; what if we still continue to deceive him?—This, this way—

(They confer.)

(Enter MARLOW.*)*

MARLOW.   The assiduities of these good people tease me beyond bearing. My host seems to think it ill manners to leave me alone and so he claps not only himself but his old-fashioned wife on my back. They talk of coming to sup with us too; and then, I suppose, we are to run the gauntlet through all the rest of the family.—What have we got here!—

HASTINGS.   My dear Charles! Let me congratulate you!— The most fortunate accident!—Who do you think is just alighted?

MARLOW.   Cannot guess.

HASTINGS.   Our mistresses, boy, Miss Hardcastle and Miss Neville. Give me leave to introduce Miss Constance Neville to your acquaintance. Happening to dine in the neighborhood, they called, on their return, to take fresh horses, here. Miss Hardcastle has just stepped into the next room and will be back in an instant. Wasn't it lucky? eh!

MARLOW *(aside).*   I have just been mortified enough of all conscience; and here comes something to complete my embarrassment.

HASTINGS.   Well! but wasn't it the most fortunate thing in the world?

MARLOW.   Oh! yes. Very fortunate—a most joyful encounter —But our dresses, George, you know, are in disorder— What if we should postpone the happiness 'till tomorrow? —tomorrow at her own house—It will be every bit as convenient—And rather more respectful—Tomorrow let it be. *(Offering to go.)*

MISS NEVILLE. By no means, sir. Your ceremony will displease her. The disorder of your dress will show the ardor of your impatience. Besides, she knows you are in the house and will permit you to see her.

MARLOW. Oh! the devil! how shall I support[14] it? Hem! hem! Hastings, you must not go. You are to assist me, you know. I shall be confoundly ridiculous. Yet, hang it! I'll take courage. Hem!

HASTINGS. Pshaw, man! it's but the first plunge, and all's over. She's but a woman, you know.

MARLOW. And of all women, she that I dread most to encounter!

(Enter MISS HARDCASTLE *as returned from walking, with a bonnet, etc.)*

HASTINGS *(introducing them).* Miss Hardcastle, Mr. Marlow; I'm proud of bringing two persons of such merit together, that only want to know, to esteem each other.

MISS HARDCASTLE *(aside).* Now, for meeting my modest gentleman with a demure face and quite in his own manner. *(After a pause in which he appears very uneasy and disconcerted.)* I'm glad of your safe arrival, si—I'm told you had some accidents by the way.

MARLOW. Only a few, madam. Yes, we had some. Yes, madam, a good many accidents, but should be sorry—madam—or rather glad of any accidents—that are so agreeably concluded. Hem!

HASTINGS *(to him).* You never spoke better in your whole life. Keep it up, and I'll insure you the victory.

MISS HARDCASTLE. I'm afraid you flatter, sir. You that have seen so much of the finest company can find little entertainment in an obscure corner of the country.

MARLOW *(gathering courage).* I have lived, indeed, in the

---

[14]*support:* endure

world, madam; but I have kept very little company. I
have been but an observer upon life, madam, while
others were enjoying it.

MISS NEVILLE.   But that, I am told, is the way to enjoy it at
last.

HASTINGS *(to him).*   Cicero never spoke better. Once more,
and you are confirmed in assurance for ever.

MARLOW *(to him).*   Hem! Stand by me then, and when I'm
down, throw in a word or two to set me up again.

MISS HARDCASTLE.   An observer, like you, upon life were,
I fear, disagreeably employed, since you must have had
much more to censure than to approve.

MARLOW.   Pardon me, madam. I was always willing to be
amused. The folly of most people is rather an object of
mirth than uneasiness.

HASTINGS *(to him).*   Bravo, bravo! Never spoke so well in
your whole life. Well! Miss Hardcastle, I see that you and
Mr. Marlow are going to be very good company. I believe
our being here will but embarrass the interview.

MARLOW.   Not in the least, Mr. Hastings. We like your company of all things. *(To him.)* Zounds! George, sure you
won't go? How can you leave us?

HASTINGS.   Our presence will but spoil conversation, so
we'll retire to the next room. *(To him.)* You don't consider,
man, that we are to manage a little *tête-à-tête* of our own.
(Exeunt.)

MISS HARDCASTLE *(after a pause).*   But you have not been
wholly an observer, I presume, sir: The ladies I should
hope have employed some part of your addresses.

MARLOW *(relapsing into timidity).*   Pardon me, madam, I—
I—I—as yet have studied—only—to—deserve them.

MISS HARDCASTLE.   And that, some say, is the very worst
way to obtain them.

MARLOW.   Perhaps so, madam. But I love to converse only
with the more grave and sensible part of the sex.—But
I'm afraid I grow tiresome.

MISS HARDCASTLE.   Not at all, sir; there is nothing I like so
much as grave conversation myself; I could hear it for

ever. Indeed I have often been surprised how a man of *sentiment*[15] could ever admire those light, airy pleasures, where nothing reaches the heart.

MARLOW. It's—a disease—of the mind, Madam. In the variety of tastes there must be some who, wanting a relish—for—um—a—um.

MISS HARDCASTLE. I understand you, sir. There must be some, who, wanting a relish for refined pleasures, pretend to despise what they are incapable of tasting.

MARLOW. My meaning, madam, but infinitely better expressed. And I can't help observing—a—

MISS HARDCASTLE *(aside)*. Who could ever suppose this fellow impudent upon some occasions. *(To him.)* You were going to observe, sir—

MARLOW. I was observing, madam—I protest, madam, I forget what I was going to observe.

MISS HARDCASTLE *(aside)*. I vow and so do I. *(To him.)* You were observing, sir, that in this age of hypocrisy—something about hypocrisy, sir.

MARLOW. Yes, madam. In this age of hypocrisy there are few who upon strict enquiry do not—a—a—a—

MISS HARDCASTLE. I understand you perfectly, sir.

MARLOW *(aside)*. Egad! and that's more than I do myself.

MISS HARDCASTLE. You mean that in this hypocritical age there are few that do not condemn in public what they practise in private and think they pay every debt to virtue when they praise it.

MARLOW. True, madam; those who have most virtue in their mouths, have least of it in their bosoms. But I'm sure I tire you, Madam.

MISS HARDCASTLE. Not in the least, sir; there's something so agreeable and spirited in your manner, such life and force—pray, sir, go on.

MARLOW. Yes, madam. I was saying—that there are some occasions—when a total want of courage, madam, destroys all the—and puts us—upon a—a—a—

MISS HARDCASTLE. I agree with you entirely: a want of

---

[15]*sentiment:* genuine feeling

courage upon some occasions assumes the appearance of ignorance and betrays us when we most want to excel. I beg you'll proceed.

MARLOW. Yes, madam. Morally speaking, madam — But I see Miss Neville expecting us in the next room. I would not intrude for the world.

MISS HARDCASTLE. I protest, sir, I never was more agreeably entertained in all my life. Pray go on.

MARLOW. Yes, madam. I was — But she beckons us to join her. Madam, shall I do myself the honor to attend you?

MISS HARDCASTLE. Well then, I'll follow.

MARLOW *(aside).* This pretty, smooth dialogue has done for me. *(Exit.)*

MISS HARDCASTLE. Ha! ha! ha! Was there ever such a sober, sentimental interview? I'm certain he scarce looked in my face the whole time. Yet the fellow, but for his unaccountable bashfulness, is pretty well, too. He has good sense, but then so buried in his fears that it fatigues one more than ignorance. If I could teach him a little confidence, it would be doing somebody that I know of a piece of service. But who is that somebody? — that, faith, is a question I can scarce answer. *(Exit.)*

(Enter TONY *and* MISS NEVILLE, *followed by* MRS. HARDCASTLE *and* HASTINGS.*)*

TONY. What do you follow me for, cousin Con? I wonder you're not ashamed to be so very engaging.

MISS NEVILLE. I hope, cousin, one may speak to one's own relations and not be to blame.

TONY. Ay, but I know what sort of a relation you want to make me though; but it won't do. I tell you, cousin Con, it won't do; so I beg you'll keep your distance. I want no nearer relationship. *(She follows coquetting him to the back scene.)*

MRS. HARDCASTLE. Well! I vow Mr. Hastings, you are very entertaining. There's nothing in the world I love to talk of so much as London and the fashions, though I was never there myself.

HASTINGS.　Never there! You amaze me! From your air and
manner, I concluded you had been bred all your life
either at Ranelagh, St. James's, or Tower Wharf.[16]

MRS. HARDCASTLE.　O! Sir, you're only pleased to say so. We
country persons can have no manner at all. I'm in love
with the town and that serves to raise me above some of
our neighbouring rustics; but who can have a manner
that has never seen the Pantheon, the Grotto Gardens,
the Borough, and such places where the nobility chiefly
resort? All I can do is to enjoy London at second-hand.
I take care to know every *tête-à-tête* from the *Scandalous
Magazine,*[17] and have all the fashions, as they come out,
in a letter from the two Miss Rickets of Crooked Lane.
Pray how do you like this head, Mr. Hastings?

HASTINGS.　Extremely elegant and *dégagée*[18] upon my word,
Madam. Your *friseur*[19] is a Frenchman, I suppose?

MRS. HARDCASTLE.　I protest. I dressed it myself from a
print in the *Ladies Memorandum Book* for the last year.

HASTINGS.　Indeed. Such a head in a side-box, at the Play-
house, would draw as many gazers as my Lady May'ress
at a City Ball.

MRS. HARDCASTLE.　I vow, since inoculation[20] began, there
is no such thing to be seen as a plain woman; so one must
dress a little particular or one may escape in the crowd.

HASTINGS.　But that can never be your case madam, in any
dress. *(Bowing.)*

MRS. HARDCASTLE.　Yet, what signifies *my* dressing when I
have such a piece of antiquity by my side as Mr. Hardcastle. All I can say will never argue down a single button
from his clothes. I have often wanted him to throw off his

[16]*Ranelagh . . . Wharf:* The first two are fashionable parks, the latter is a
slum. Mrs. Hardcastle does not know the difference. Later, she mingles a
fashionable resort, the Pantheon, with the vulgar Grotto Gardens and Borough (of Southwark).
[17]*tête-à-tête . . . Magazine:* refers to *Town and Country Magazine,* notorious for its "Tête-à-Tête" sketches of society scandals
[18]*dégagée:* graceful, casual
[19]*friseur:* hairdresser
[20]*inoculation:* against smallpox, begun in England in 1718

great flaxen wig, and where he was bald, to plaster it over like my Lord Pately, with powder.

HASTINGS.   You are right, Madam; for, as among the ladies, there are none ugly, so among the men there are none old.

MRS. HARDCASTLE.   But what do you think his answer was? Why, with his usual Gothic[21] vivacity, he said I only wanted him to throw off his wig to convert it into a *tête*[22] for my own wearing.

HASTINGS.   Intolerable! At your age you may wear what you please, and it must become you.

MRS. HARDCASTLE.   Pray, Mr. Hastings, what do you take to be the most fashionable age about town?

HASTINGS.   Some time ago, forty was all the mode; but I'm told the ladies intend to bring up fifty for the ensuing winter.

MRS. HARDCASTLE.   Seriously? Then I shall be too young for the fashion.

HASTINGS.   No lady begins now to put on jewels 'till she's past forty. For instance, Miss there, in a polite circle, would be considered as a child, as a mere maker of samplers.

MRS. HARDCASTLE.   And yet Mrs.[23] Niece thinks herself as much a woman and is as fond of jewels as the oldest of us all.

HASTINGS.   Your niece, is she? And that young gentleman, —a brother of yours, I should presume?

MRS. HARDCASTLE.   My son, sir. They are contracted to each other. Observe their little sports. They fall in and out ten times a day, as if they were man and wife already. *(To them.)* Well, Tony, child, what soft things are you saying to your cousin Constance this evening?

TONY.   I have been saying no soft things; but that it's very hard to be followed about so. Ecod! I've not a place in the house now that's left to myself but the stable.

---

[21]*Gothic:* crude

[22]*tête:* fashionable lady's wig

[23]*Mrs.:* could also be applied to any unmarried woman in authority over servants or children

MRS. HARDCASTLE.   Never mind him, Con, my dear. He's in another story behind your back.

MISS NEVILLE.   There's something generous in my cousin's manner. He falls out before faces to be forgiven in private.

TONY.   That's a damned confounded — crack.[24]

MRS. HARDCASTLE.   Ah! he's a sly one. Don't you think they're like each other about the mouth, Mr. Hastings? The Blenkinsop mouth to a T. They're of a size too. Back to back, my pretties, that Mr. Hastings may see you. Come Tony.

TONY.   You had as good not make me, I tell you. *(Measuring.)*

MISS NEVILLE.   O lud! he has almost cracked my head.

MRS. HARDCASTLE.   O the monster! For shame, Tony. You a man, and behave so!

TONY.   If I'm a man, let me have my fortin. Ecod! I'll not be made a fool of no longer.

MRS. HARDCASTLE.   Is this, ungrateful boy, all that I'm to get for the pains I have taken in your education? I that have rocked you in your cradle, and fed that pretty mouth with a spoon! Did not I work that waistcoat to make you genteel? Did not I prescribe for you every day and weep while the receipt[25] was operating?

TONY.   Ecod! you had reason to weep, for you have been dosing me ever since I was born. I have gone through every receipt in *The Complete Huswife*[26] ten times over; and you have thoughts of coursing me through *Quincy*[27] next spring. But, ecod! I tell you, I'll not be made a fool of no longer.

MRS. HARDCASTLE.   Wasn't it all for your good, viper? Wasn't it all for your good?

TONY.   I wish you'd let me and my good alone then. Snubbing this way when I'm in spirits. If I'm to have any good, let it come of itself; not to keep dinging it, dinging it into one so.

[24]*crack:* lie

[25]*receipt:* medical prescription

[26]*The Complete Huswife: The Compleat Housewife,* a popular cookbook of the period

[27]*Quincy:* Dr. John Quincy's *Compleat English Dispensatory,* a book of medical formulas and prescriptions

MRS. HARDCASTLE.   That's false; I never see you when you're in spirits. No, Tony, you then go to the alehouse or kennel. I'm never to be delighted with your agreeable, wild notes, unfeeling monster!

TONY.   Ecod! Mamma, your own notes are the wildest of the two.

MRS. HARDCASTLE.   Was ever the like? But I see he wants to break my heart, I see he does.

HASTINGS.   Dear Madam, permit me to lecture the young gentleman a little. I'm certain I can persuade him to his duty.

MRS. HARDCASTLE.   Well! I must retire. Come, Constance, my love. You see, Mr. Hastings, the wretchedness of my situation: Was ever poor woman so plagued with a dear, sweet, pretty, provoking, undutiful boy.

(*Exeunt* MRS. HARDCASTLE *and* MISS NEVILLE.)

TONY (*singing*).   *There was a young man riding by, and fain would have his will. Rang do didlo dee.* Don't mind her. Let her cry. It's the comfort of her heart. I have seen her and sister cry over a book for an hour together, and they said, they liked the book the better the more it made them cry.

HASTINGS.   Then you're no friend to the ladies, I find, my pretty young gentleman?

TONY.   That's as I find 'um.

HASTINGS.   Not to her of your mother's choosing, I dare answer? And yet she appears to me a pretty, well-tempered girl.

TONY.   That's because you don't know her as well as I. Ecod! I know every inch about her; and there's not a more bitter, cantankerous toad in all Christendom.

HASTINGS (*aside*).   Pretty encouragement this for a lover!

TONY.   I have seen her since the height of that. She has as many tricks as a hare in a thicket, or a colt the first day's breaking.

HASTINGS.   To me she appears sensible and silent!

TONY.   Ay, before company. But when she's with her playmates, she's as loud as a hog in a gate.

HASTINGS. But there is a meek modesty about her that charms me.

TONY. Yes, but curb her never so little, she kicks up, and you're flung in a ditch.

HASTINGS. Well, but you must allow her a little beauty. Yes, you must allow her some beauty.

TONY. Bandbox! She's all a made up thing, mun. Ah! could you but see Bet Bouncer of these parts, you might then talk of beauty. Ecod, she has two eyes as black as sloes, and cheeks as broad and red as a pulpit cushion. She'd make two of she.

HASTINGS. Well, what say you to a friend that would take this bitter bargain off your hands?

TONY. Anon![28]

HASTINGS. Would you thank him that would take Miss Neville and leave you to happiness and your dear Betsy?

TONY. Ay; but where is there such a friend, for who would take *her?*

HASTINGS. I am he. If you but assist me, I'll engage to whip her off to France and you shall never hear more of her.

TONY. Assist you! Ecod, I will, to the last drop of my blood. I'll clap a pair of horses to your chaise that shall trundle you off in a twinkling, and maybe get you a part of her fortin beside, in jewels, that you little dream of.

HASTINGS. My dear squire, this looks like a lad of spirit.

TONY. Come along then, and you shall see more of my spirit before you have done with me. *(Singing.)*

> *We are the boys*
> *That fears no noise*
> *Where the thundering cannons roar.*

(Exeunt.)

[28]*Anon!*: How? What do you say?

Act III

The house. Enter HARDCASTLE *alone.*

HARDCASTLE.   What could my old friend Sir Charles mean by recommending his son as the modestest young man in town? To me he appears the most impudent piece of brass that ever spoke with a tongue. He has taken possession of the easy chair by the fire-side already. He took off his boots in the parlor, and desired me to see them taken care of. I'm desirous to know how his impudence affects my daughter. — She will certainly be shocked at it.

(Enter MISS HARDCASTLE, *plainly dressed.)*

HARDCASTLE.   Well, my Kate, I see you have changed your dress as I bid you; and yet, I believe, there was no great occasion.

MISS HARDCASTLE.   I find such a pleasure, sir, in obeying your commands, that I take care to observe them without ever debating their propriety.

HARDCASTLE.   And yet, Kate, I sometimes give you some cause, particularly when I recommended my *modest* gentleman to you as a lover today.

MISS HARDCASTLE.   You taught me to expect something extraordinary, and I find the original exceeds the description.

HARDCASTLE.   I was never so surprised in my life! He has quite confounded all my faculties!

MISS HARDCASTLE.   I never saw anything like it. And a man of the world too!

HARDCASTLE.   Ay, he learned it all abroad, — what a fool was I, to think a young man could learn modesty by travelling. He might as soon learn wit at a masquerade.

MISS HARDCASTLE.   It seems all natural to him.

HARDCASTLE.   A good deal assisted by bad company and a French dancing-master.

MISS HARDCASTLE.   Sure you mistake, papa! a French

dancing-master could never have taught him that timid look,—that awkward address,—that bashful manner—

HARDCASTLE.   Whose look? whose manner? child!

MISS HARDCASTLE.   Mr. Marlow's: his *mauvaise honte*,[1] his *timidity*, struck me at the first sight.

HARDCASTLE.   Then your first sight deceived you; for I think him one of the most brazen first sights that ever astonished my senses.

MISS HARDCASTLE.   Sure, sir, you rally![2] I never saw any one so modest.

HARDCASTLE.   And can you be serious! I never saw such a bouncing, swaggering puppy since I was born. Bully Dawson[3] was but a fool to him.

MISS HARDCASTLE.   Surprising! He met me with a respectful bow, a stammering voice, and a look fixed on the ground.

HARDCASTLE.   He met me with a loud voice, a lordly air, and a familiarity that made my blood freeze again.

MISS HARDCASTLE.   He treated me with diffidence and respect; censured the manners of the age; admired the prudence of girls that never laughed; tired me with apologies for being tiresome; then left the room with a bow, and, "madam, I would not for the world detain you."

HARDCASTLE.   He spoke to me as if he knew me all his life before. Asked twenty questions, and never waited for an answer. Interrupted my best remarks with some silly pun, and when I was in my best story of the Duke of Marlborough and Prince Eugene, he asked if I had not a good hand at making punch. Yes, Kate, he ask'd your father if he was a maker of punch!

MISS HARDCASTLE.   One of us must certainly be mistaken.

HARDCASTLE.   If he be what he has shown himself, I'm determined he shall never have my consent.

MISS HARDCASTLE.   And if he be the sullen thing I take him, he shall never have mine.

HARDCASTLE.   In one thing then we are agreed—to reject him.

[1]*mauvaise honte:* self-consciousness (French)
[2]*rally:* tease, joke
[3]*Bully Dawson:* a notorious London gambler and ruffian

MISS HARDCASTLE. Yes. But upon conditions. For if you should find him less impudent, and I more presuming; if you find him more respectful, and I more importunate— I don't know—the fellow is well enough for a man— Certainly we don't meet many such at a horse race in the country.

HARDCASTLE. If we should find him so—But that's impossible. The first appearance has done my business. I'm seldom deceived in that.

MISS HARDCASTLE. And yet there may be many good qualities under that first appearance.

HARDCASTLE. Ay, when a girl finds a fellow's outside to her taste, she then sets about guessing the rest of his furniture. With her, a smooth face stands for good sense, and a genteel figure for every virtue.

MISS HARDCASTLE. I hope, sir, a conversation begun with a compliment to my good sense won't end with a sneer at my understanding?

HARDCASTLE. Pardon me, Kate. But if young Mr. Brazen can find the art of reconciling contradictions, he may please us both, perhaps.

MISS HARDCASTLE. And as one of us must be mistaken, what if we go to make further discoveries?

HARDCASTLE. Agreed. But depend on't I'm in the right.

MISS HARDCASTLE. And depend on't I'm not much in the wrong. (*Exeunt.*)

(*Enter* TONY, *running in with a casket.*)

TONY. Ecod! I have got them. Here they are. My Cousin Con's necklaces, bobs[4] and all. My mother shan't cheat the poor souls out of their fortin neither. O! my genius, is that you?

(*Enter* HASTINGS.)

HASTINGS. My dear friend, how have you managed with your mother? I hope you have amused her with pretend-

[4]*bobs:* pendants

ing love for your cousin, and that you are willing to be
reconciled at last? Our horses will be refreshed in a short
time, and we shall soon be ready to set off.

TONY.   And here's something to bear your charges by the
way. (*Giving the casket.*) Your sweetheart's jewels. Keep
them, and hang those, I say, that would rob you of one of
them.

HASTINGS.   But how have you procured them from your
mother?

TONY.   Ask me no questions, and I'll tell you no fibs. I procured them by the rule of thumb. If I had not a key to
every draw in mother's bureau, how could I go to the ale-
house so often as I do? An honest man may rob himself of
his own at any time.

HASTINGS.   Thousands do it every day. But to be plain with
you; Miss Neville is endeavoring to procure them from
her aunt this very instant. If she succeeds, it will be the
most delicate way at least of obtaining them.

TONY.   Well, keep them, till you know how it will be. But I
know how it will be well enough; she'd as soon part with
the only sound tooth in her head.

HASTINGS.   But I dread the effects of her resentment, when
she finds she has lost them.

TONY.   Never you mind her resentment; leave *me* to manage
that. I don't value her resentment the bounce of a cracker.
Zounds! here they are. Morrice![5] Prance! (*Exit* HASTINGS.)

MRS. HARDCASTLE.   Indeed, Constance, you amaze me. Such
a girl as you want jewels? It will be time enough for
jewels, my dear, twenty years hence, when your beauty
begins to want repairs.

MISS NEVILLE.   But what will repair beauty at forty, will
certainly improve it at twenty, madam.

MRS. HARDCASTLE.   Yours, my dear, can admit of none. That
natural blush is beyond a thousand ornaments. Besides,
child, jewels are quite out at present. Don't you see half
the ladies of our acquaintance, my Lady Kill-day-light,
and Mrs. Crump, and the rest of them, carry their jewels

[5]*Morrice:* Dash off!

to town, and bring nothing but paste and marcasites[6] back?

MISS NEVILLE.   But who knows, madam, but somebody that shall be nameless would like me best with all my little finery about me?

MRS. HARDCASTLE.   Consult your glass, my dear, and then see if with such a pair of eyes you want any better sparklers. What do you think, Tony, my dear, does your Cousin Con want any jewels, in your eyes, to set off her beauty?

TONY.   That's as thereafter may be.

MISS NEVILLE.   My dear aunt, if you knew how it would oblige me.

MRS. HARDCASTLE.   A parcel of old-fashioned rose and table-cut things.[7] They would make you look like the court of King Solomon at a puppet-show. Besides, I believe I can't readily come at them. They may be missing, for aught I know to the contrary.

TONY *(apart to* MRS. HARDCASTLE*)*.   Then why don't you tell her so at once, as she's so longing for them. Tell her they're lost. It's the only way to quiet her. Say they're lost, and call me to bear witness.

MRS. HARDCASTLE *(apart to* TONY*)*.   You know, my dear, I'm only keeping them for you. So if I say they're gone, you'll bear me witness, will you? He! he! he!

TONY.   Never fear me. Ecod! I'll say I saw them taken out with my own eyes.

MISS NEVILLE.   I desire them but for a day, madam. Just to be permitted to show them as relics, and then they may be locked up again.

MRS. HARDCASTLE.   To be plain with you, my dear Constance, If I could find them, you should have them. They're missing, I assure you. Lost, for aught I know; but we must have patience wherever they are.

MISS NEVILLE.   I'll not believe it; this is but a shallow pre-

---

[6]*paste and marcasites:* common glass and mineral ornaments

[7]*rose . . . things:* jewelry with stones cut into many facets, somewhat resembling a rose, and with stones cut flat like a table surface

tence to deny me. I know they're too valuable to be so slightly kept, and as you are to answer for the loss.

MRS. HARDCASTLE. Don't be alarmed, Constance. If they be lost, I must restore an equivalent. But my son knows they are missing, and not to be found.

TONY. That I can bear witness to. They are missing and not to be found, I'll take my oath on't.

MRS. HARDCASTLE. You must learn resignation, my dear; for though we lose our fortune, yet we should not lose our patience. See me, how calm I am.

MISS NEVILLE. Ay, people are generally calm at the misfortunes of others.

MRS. HARDCASTLE. Now, I wonder a girl of your good sense should waste a thought upon such trumpery.[8] We shall soon find them; and, in the meantime, you shall make use of my garnets till your jewels be found.

MISS NEVILLE. I detest garnets.

MRS. HARDCASTLE. The most becoming things in the world to set off a clear complexion. You have often seen how well they look upon me. You *shall* have them. (*Exit.*)

MISS NEVILLE. I dislike them of all things. You shan't stir. —Was ever anything so provoking—to mislay my own jewels and force me to wear her trumpery.[9]

TONY. Don't be a fool. If she gives you the garnets, take what you can get. The jewels are your own already. I have stolen them out of her bureau and she does not know it. Fly to your spark;[10] he'll tell you more of the matter. Leave me to manager *her*.

MISS NEVILLE. My dear cousin!

TONY. Vanish. She's here and has missed them already. (*Exit* MISS NEVILLE.) Zounds! how she fidgets and spits about like a Catherine wheel.[11]

(*Enter* MRS. HARDCASTLE.)

[8]*trumpery:* nonsense
[9]*trumpery:* something showy but worthless
[10]*spark:* beau, sweetheart
[11]*Catherine wheel:* pinwheel type of fireworks

MRS. HARDCASTLE. Confusion! thieves! robbers! We are cheated, plundered, broke open, undone.

TONY. What's the matter, what's the matter, mamma? I hope nothing has happened to any of the good family!

MRS. HARDCASTLE. We are robbed. My bureau has been broke open, the jewels taken out, and I'm undone.

TONY. Oh, is that all? Ha! ha! ha! By the laws I never saw it better acted in my life. Ecod, I thought you was ruined in earnest, ha, ha, ha!

MRS. HARDCASTLE. Why boy, I *am* ruined in earnest. My bureau has been broken open, and all taken away.

TONY. Stick to that; ha, ha, ha! stick to that. I'll bear witness, you know, call me to bear witness.

MRS. HARDCASTLE. I tell you, Tony, by all that's precious, the jewels are gone, and I shall be ruined for ever.

TONY. Sure I know they're gone, and I am to say so.

MRS. HARDCASTLE. My dearest Tony, but hear me. They're gone, I say.

TONY. By the laws, mamma, you make me for to laugh, ha! ha! I know who took them well enough, ha! ha! ha!

MRS. HARDCASTLE. Was there ever such a blockhead, that can't tell the difference between jest and earnest. I tell you I'm not in jest, booby.

TONY. That's right, that's right. You must be in a bitter passion, and then nobody will suspect either of us. I'll bear witness that they are gone.

MRS. HARDCASTLE. Was there ever such a cross-grained brute, that won't hear me! Can you bear witness that you're no better than a fool? Was ever poor woman so beset with fools on one hand, and thieves on the other?

TONY. I can bear witness to that.

MRS. HARDCASTLE. Bear witness again, you blockhead you, and I'll turn you out of the room directly. My poor niece, what will become of *her!* Do you laugh, you unfeeling brute, as if you enjoyed my distress?

TONY. I can bear witness to that.

MRS. HARDCASTLE. Do you insult me, monster? I'll teach you to vex your mother, I will.

TONY. I can bear witness to that. *(He runs off, she follows him.)*

(Enter MISS HARDCASTLE *and Maid.)*

MISS HARDCASTLE. What an unaccountable creature is that brother of mine to send them to the house as an inn, ha! ha! I don't wonder at his impudence.

MAID. But what is more, madam, the young gentleman as you passed by in your present dress, asked me if you were the barmaid. He mistook you for the barmaid, Madam.

MISS HARDCASTLE. Did he? Then as I live, I'm resolved to keep up the delusion. Tell me, Pimple, how do you like my present dress? Don't you think I look something like Cherry[12] in *The Beaux' Stratagem?*

MAID. It's the dress, madam, that every lady wears in the country, but when she visits, or receives company.

MISS HARDCASTLE. And are you sure he does not remember my face or person?

MAID. Certain of it.

MISS HARDCASTLE. I vow, I thought so; for though we spoke for some time together, yet his fears were such that he never once looked up during the interview. Indeed, if he had, my bonnet would have kept him from seeing me.

MAID. But what do you hope from keeping him in his mistake?

MISS HARDCASTLE. In the first place, I shall be *seen,* and that is no small advantage to a girl who brings her face to market. Then I shall perhaps make an acquaintance, and that's no small victory gained over one who never addresses any but the wildest of her sex. But my chief aim is to take my gentleman off his guard, and, like an invisible champion of romance, examine the giant's force before I offer to combat.

MAID. But are you sure you can act your part and disguise your voice, so that he may mistake that, as he has already mistaken your person?

[12]*Cherry:* the landlord's daughter in this comedy by Farquhar

MISS HARDCASTLE. Never fear me. I think I have got the true bar-cant.—Did your honor call?—Attend the Lion there.—Pipes and tobacco for the Angel.—The Lamb has been outrageous this half hour.[13]

MAID. It will do, madam. But he's here. *(Exit.)*

(Enter MARLOW.*)*

MARLOW. What a bawling in every part of the house. I have scarce a moment's repose. If I go to the best room, there I find my host and his story. If I fly to the gallery there we have my hostess with her curtsy down to the ground. I have at last got a moment to myself, and now for recollection. *(Walks and muses.)*

MISS HARDCASTLE. Did you call sir? Did your honor call?

MARLOW *(musing).* As for Miss Hardcastle, she's too grave and sentimental for me.

MISS HARDCASTLE. Did your honor call? *(She still places herself before him, he turning away.)*

MARLOW. No, child. *(Musing.)* Besides, from the glimpse I had of her, I think she squints.

MISS HARDCASTLE. I'm sure, sir, I heard the bell ring.

MARLOW. No, no. *(Musing.)* I have pleased my father, however, by coming down, and I'll tomorrow please myself by returning. *(Taking out his tablets,[14] and perusing.)*

MISS HARDCASTLE. Perhaps the other gentleman called, sir?

MARLOW. I tell you, no.

MISS HARDCASTLE. I should be glad to know, sir. We have such a parcel of servants.

MARLOW. No, no, I tell you. *(Looks full in her face.)* Yes, child, I think I did call. I wanted—I wanted—I vow, child, you are vastly handsome.

MISS HARDCASTLE. O la, sir, you'll make one ashamed.

MARLOW. Never saw a more sprightly, malicious eye. Yes, yes, my dear, I did call. Have you got any of your—a— what d'ye call it in the house?

---

[13]*Lion . . . Angel . . . Lamb:* names of inn-rooms
[14]*tablets:* a pocket notebook

MISS HARDCASTLE. No, sir, we have been out of that these ten days.

MARLOW. One may call in this house, I find, to very little purpose. Suppose I should call for a taste, just by way of trial, of the nectar of your lips; perhaps I might be disappointed in that too.

MISS HARDCASTLE. Nectar! nectar! That's a liquor there's no call for in these parts. French, I suppose. We keep no French wines here, sir.

MARLOW. Of true English growth, I assure you.

MISS HARDCASTLE. Then it's odd I should not know it. We brew all sorts of wines in this house, and I have lived here these eighteen years.

MARLOW. Eighteen years! Why one would think, child, you kept the bar before you were born. How old are you?

MISS HARDCASTLE. O! Sir, I must not tell my age. They say women and music should never be dated.

MARLOW. To guess at this distance, you can't be much above forty. *(Approaching.)* Yet nearer, I don't think so much. *(Approaching.)* By coming close to some women, they look younger still; but when we come very close indeed— *(Attempting to kiss her.)*

MISS HARDCASTLE. Pray, sir, keep your distance. One would think you wanted to know one's age as they do horses, by mark of mouth.

MARLOW. I protest, child, you use me extremely ill. If you keep me at this distance how is it possible you and I can be ever acquainted?

MISS HARDCASTLE. And who wants to be acquainted with you? I want no such acquaintance, not I. I'm sure you did not treat Miss Hardcastle that was here awhile ago in this obstropalous[15] manner. I'll warrant me, before her you looked dashed,[16] and kept bowing to the ground, and talked for all the world as if you was before a justice of peace.

MARLOW *(aside).* Egad! she has hit it, sure enough. *(To her.)* In awe of her, child? Ha! ha! ha! A mere, awkward, squint-

---

[15]*obstropalous:* (obstreperous) unruly
[16]*dashed:* self-conscious and embarrassed

ing thing? no, no! I find you don't know me. I laughed and rallied her a little; but I was unwilling to be too severe. No, I could not be too severe, curse me!

MISS HARDCASTLE. Oh! then, sir, you are a favorite, I find, among the ladies?

MARLOW. Yes, my dear, a great favorite. And yet, hang me, I don't see what they find in me to follow. At the Ladies Club in town, I'm called their agreeable Rattle. Rattle, child, is not my real name, but one I'm known by. My name is Solomons. Mr. Solomons, my dear, at your service. *(Offering to salute her.)*

MISS HARDCASTLE. Hold, sir; you are introducing me to your club, not to yourself. And you're so great a favorite there, you say?

MARLOW. Yes, my dear. There's Mrs. Mantrap, Lady Betty Blackleg, the Countess of Sligo, Mrs. Langhorns, old Miss Biddy Buckskin, and your humble servant, keep up the spirit of the place.

MISS HARDCASTLE. Then it's a very merry place, I suppose?

MARLOW. Yes, as merry as cards, suppers, wine, and old women can make us.

MISS HARDCASTLE. And their agreeable Rattle, ha! ha! ha!

MARLOW. *(aside).* Egad! I don't quite like this chit. She looks knowing, methinks. You laugh, child!

MISS HARDCASTLE. I can't but laugh to think what time they all have for minding their work or their family.

MARLOW *(aside).* All's well; she don't laugh at me. *(To her.)* Do *you* ever work, child?

MISS HARDCASTLE. Ay, sure. There's not a screen or a quilt in the whole house but what can bear witness to that.

MARLOW. Odso! Then you must show me your embroidery. I embroider and draw patterns myself a little. If you want a judge of your work you must apply to me. *(Seizing her hand.)*

(Enter HARDCASTLE, *who stands in surprise.)*

MISS HARDCASTLE. Ay, but the colors don't look well by candlelight. You shall see all in the morning. *(Struggling.)*

MARLOW.   And why not now, my angel? Such beauty fires
beyond the power of resistance. — Pshaw! The father here!
My old luck: I never nicked seven that I did not throw
amesace[17] three times following. *(Exit.)*

HARDCASTLE.   So, madam. So I find *this* your *modest* lover.
This is your humble admirer that kept his eyes fixed on
the ground, and only adored at humble distance. Kate,
Kate, art thou not ashamed to deceive your father so?

MISS HARDCASTLE.   Never trust me, dear papa, but he's still
the modest man I first took him for; you'll be convinced
of it as well as I.

HARDCASTLE.   By the hand of my body, I believe his impudence is infectious! Didn't I see him seize your hand?
Didn't I see him haul you about like a milkmaid? and now
you talk of his respect and his modesty, forsooth!

MISS HARDCASTLE.   But if I shortly convince you of his modesty, that he has only the faults that will pass off with
time, and the virtues that will improve with age, I hope
you'll forgive him.

HARDCASTLE.   The girl would actually make one run mad! I
tell you I'll not be convinced. I am convinced. He has
scarcely been three hours in the house, and he has already
encroached on all my prerogatives. You may like his impudence, and call it modesty. But my son-in-law, madam,
must have very different qualifications.

MISS HARDCASTLE.   Sir, I ask but this night to convince you.

HARDCASTLE.   You shall not have half the time, for I have
thoughts of turning him out this very hour.

MISS HARDCASTLE.   Give me that hour then, and I hope to
satisfy you.

HARDCASTLE.   Well, an hour let it be then. But I'll have no
trifling with your father. All fair and open, do you mind
me?

MISS HARDCASTLE.   I hope, sir, you have ever found that I
considered your commands as my pride; for your kindness
is such that my duty as yet has been inclination. *(Exeunt.)*

---

[17]*seven . . . amesace:* the highest and lowest scores possible in throwing
dice

Act IV

The house. Enter HASTINGS *and* MISS NEVILLE.

HASTINGS.   You surprise me! Sir Charles Marlow expected
here this night? Where have you had your information?

MISS NEVILLE.   You may depend upon it. I just saw his letter
to Mr. Hardcastle, in which he tells him he intends setting
out a few hours after his son.

HASTINGS.   Then, my Constance, all must be completed before he arrives. He knows me; and should he find me here,
would discover[1] my name and perhaps my designs to the
rest of the family.

MISS NEVILLE.   The jewels, I hope, are safe.

HASTINGS.   Yes, yes. I have sent them to Marlow, who keeps
the keys of our baggage. In the meantime, I'll go to prepare matters for our elopement. I have had the squire's
promise of a fresh pair of horses; and, if I should not see
him again will write him further directions. *(Exit.)*

MISS NEVILLE.   Well! success attend you. In the meantime,
I'll go amuse my aunt with the old pretence of a violent
passion for my cousin. *(Exit.)*

(Enter MARLOW, *followed by a* SERVANT.)

MARLOW.   I wonder what Hastings could mean by sending
me so valuable a thing as a casket to keep for him, when
he knows the only place I have is the seat of a post-coach
at an inn door. Have you deposited the casket with the
landlady, as I ordered you? Have you put it into her own
hands?

SERVANT.   Yes, your honor.

MARLOW.   She said she'd keep it safe, did she?

SERVANT.   Yes, she said she'd keep it safe enough; she asked
me how I came by it? and she said she had a great mind
to make me give an account of myself. *(Exit.)*

[1]*discover:* reveal

MARLOW.   Ha! ha! ha! They're safe, however. What an unaccountable set of beings have we got amongst! This little
barmaid, though, runs in my head most strangely and
drives out the absurdities of all the rest of the family. She's
mine, she must be mine, or I'm greatly mistaken.

(*Enter* HASTINGS.)

HASTINGS.   Bless me! I quite forgot to tell her that I intended
to prepare at the bottom of the garden. Marlow here, and
in spirits too!

MARLOW.   Give me joy, George! Crown me, shadow me with
laurels! Well, George, after all, we modest fellows don't
want for success among the women.

HASTINGS.   Some women, you mean. But what success has
your honor's modesty been crowned with now, that it
grows so insolent upon us?

MARLOW.   Didn't you see the tempting, brisk, lovely, little
thing that runs about the house with a bunch of keys to
its girdle?

HASTINGS.   Well! and what then?

MARLOW.   She's mine, you rogue you. Such fire, such motion, such eyes, such lips—but, egad! she would not let
me kiss them, though.

HASTINGS.   But are you so sure, so very sure of her?

MARLOW.   Why man, she talked of showing me her work
above-stairs, and I am to improve the pattern.

HASTINGS.   But how can *you*, Charles, go about to rob a
woman of her honor?

MARLOW.   Pshaw! pshaw! we all know the honor of the barmaid of an inn. I don't intend to *rob* her, take my word for
it; there's nothing in this house I shan't honestly *pay* for.

HASTINGS.   I believe the girl has virtue.

MARLOW.   And if she has, I should be the last man in the
world that would attempt to corrupt it.

HASTINGS.   You have taken care, I hope, of the casket I sent
you to lock up? It's in safety?

MARLOW.   Yes, yes. It's safe enough. I have taken care of it.
But how could you think the seat of a post-coach at an inn

door a place of safety? Ah! numbskull! I have taken better precautions for you then you did for yourself. — I have —

HASTINGS. What!

MARLOW. I have sent it to the landlady to keep for you.

HASTINGS. To the landlady!

MARLOW. The landlady.

HASTINGS. You did!

MARLOW. I did. She's to be answerable for its forthcoming, you know.

HASTINGS. Yes, she'll bring it forth, with a witness.

MARLOW. Wasn't I right? I believe you'll allow that I acted prudently upon this occasion?

HASTINGS (*aside*). He must not see my uneasiness.

MARLOW. You seem a little disconcerted though, methinks. Sure nothing has happened?

HASTINGS. No, nothing. Never was in better spirits in all my life. And so you left it with the landlady, who, no doubt, very readily undertook the charge?

MARLOW. Rather too readily. For she not only kept the casket; but, through her great precaution, was going to keep the messanger too. Ha! ha! ha!

HASTINGS. He! he! he! They're safe, however.

MARLOW. As a guinea in a miser's purse.

HASTINGS (*aside*). So now all hopes of fortune are at an end, and we must set off without it. (*To him.*) Well, Charles, I'll leave you to your meditations on the pretty barmaid, and, he! he! he! may you be as successful for yourself as you have been for me. (*Exit.*)

MARLOW. Thank ye, George! I ask no more! Ha! ha! ha!

(*Enter* HARDCASTLE.)

HARDCASTLE. I no longer know my own house. It's turned all topsey-turvey. His servants have got drunk already. I'll bear it no longer, and yet, from my respect for his father, I'll be calm. (*To him.*) Mr. Marlow, your servant. I'm your very humble servant. (*Bowing low.*)

MARLOW. Sir, your humble servant. (*Aside.*) What's to be the wonder now?

HARDCASTLE. I believe, sir, you must be sensible, sir, that no man alive ought to be more welcome than your father's son, sir. I hope you think so?

MARLOW. I do from my soul, sir. I don't want much intreaty. I generally make my father's son welcome wherever he goes.

HARDCASTLE. I believe you do, from my soul, sir. But though I say nothing to your own conduct, that of your servants is insufferable. Their manner of drinking is setting a very bad example in this house, I assure you.

MARLOW. I protest, my very good sir, that's no fault of mine. If they don't drink as they ought *they* are to blame. I ordered them not to spare the cellar. I did, I assure you. *(To the side scene.[2])* Here, let one of my servants come up. *(To him.)* My positive directions were, that as I did not drink myself, they should make up for my deficiencies below.

HARDCASTLE. Then they had your orders for what they do! I'm satisfied!

MARLOW. They had, I assure you. You shall hear from one of themselves.

(Enter SERVANT, *drunk.)*

MARLOW. You, Jeremy! Come forward, sirrah! What were my orders? Were you not told to drink freely, and call for what you thought fit, for the good of the house?

HARDCASTLE *(aside).* I begin to lose my patience.

JEREMY. Please your honor, liberty and Fleet Street[3] for ever! Though I'm but a servant, I'm as good as another man. I'll drink for no man before supper, sir, dammy! Good liquor will sit upon a good supper, but a good supper will not sit upon—*hiccup*—upon my conscience, sir. *(Exit.)*

MARLOW. You see, my old friend, the fellow is as drunk as he can possibly be. I don't know what you'd have more, unless you'd have the poor devil soused in a beer-barrel.

[2]*side scene:* stage wing
[3]*Fleet Street:* known for its convivial taverns

HARDCASTLE.   Zounds! He'll drive me distracted if I contain myself any longer.—Mr. Marlow, sir; I have submitted to your insolence for more than four hours, and I see no likelihood of its coming to an end. I'm now resolved to be master here, sir, and I desire that you and your drunken pack may leave my house directly.

MARLOW.   Leave your house!—Sure you jest, my good friend! What, when I'm doing what I can to please you!

HARDCASTLE.   I tell you, sir, you don't please me; so I desire you'll leave my house.

MARLOW.   Sure you cannot be serious? At this time o'night, and such a night? You only mean to banter me?

HARDCASTLE.   I tell you, sir, I'm serious; and, now that my passions are roused, I say this house is mine, sir; this house is mine, and I command you to leave it directly.

MARLOW.   Ha! ha! ha! A puddle in a storm. I shan't stir a step, I assure you. *(In a serious tone.)* This, your house, fellow! It's my house. This is my house. Mine, while I choose to stay. What right have you to bid me leave this house, sir? I never met with such impudence, curse me, never in my whole life before.

HARDCASTLE.   Nor I, confound me if ever I did. To come to my house, to call for what he likes, to turn me out of my own chair, to insult the family, to order his servants to get drunk, and then to tell me *This house is mine, sir.* By all that's impudent, it makes me laugh. Ha! ha! ha! Pray, sir, *(bantering)* as you take the house, what think you of taking the rest of the furniture? There's a pair of silver candlesticks, and there's a fire-screen, and here's a pair of brazen-nosed bellows, perhaps you may take a fancy to them?

MARLOW.   Bring me your bill, sir, bring me your bill, and let's make no more words about it.

HARDCASTLE.   There are a set of prints too. What think you of *The Rake's Progress*[4] for your own apartment?

MARLOW.   Bring me your bill, I say; and I'll leave you and your infernal house directly.

---

[4]*The Rake's Progress:* Series of engravings by William Hogarth (1735)

HARDCASTLE.   Then there's mahogany table, that you may see your own face in.

MARLOW.   My bill, I say.

HARDCASTLE.   I had forgot the great chair, for your own particular slumbers after a hearty meal.

MARLOW.   Zounds! bring me my bill, I say, and let's hear no more on't.

HARDCASTLE.   Young man, young man, from your father's letter to me, I was taught to expect a well-bred, modest man, as a vistor here, but now I find him no better than a coxcomb[5] and a bully; but he will be down here presently, and shall hear more of it. *(Exit.)*

MARLOW.   How's this! Sure I have not mistaken the house? Everything looks like an inn. The servants cry, *Coming.* The attendance is awkward; the barmaid, too, to attend us. But she's here, and will further inform me. Whither so fast, child? A word with you.

(Enter MISS HARDCASTLE.)

MISS HARDCASTLE.   Let it be short then. I'm in a hurry. *(Aside.)* I believe he begins to find out his mistake, but it's too soon quite to undeceive him.

MARLOW.   Pray, child, answer me one question. What are you, and what may your business in this house be?

MISS HARDCASTLE.   A relation of the family, sir.

MARLOW.   What! A poor relation?

MISS HARDCASTLE.   Yes, sir. A poor relation appointed to keep the keys, and to see that the guests want nothing in my power to give them.

MARLOW.   That is, you act as the barmaid of this inn.

MISS HARDCASTLE.   Inn! O law—what brought that in your head? One of the best families in the county keep an inn! Ha, ha, ha, old Mr. Hardcastle's house an inn?

MARLOW.   Mr. Hardcastle's house? Is this house Mr. Hardcastle's house, child?

MISS HARDCASTLE.   Ay, sure. Whose else should it be?

---

[5]*coxcomb:* a silly, vain, affected fellow; a fop or dandy

MARLOW. So then all's out, and I have been damnably imposed on. Oh, confound my stupid head, I shall be
laughed at over the whole town. I shall be struck up in
caricatura in all the printshops. The Dullissimo Macaroni.[6] To mistake this house of all others for an inn, and
my father's old friend for an inn-keeper. What a swaggering puppy must he take me for. What a silly puppy do I
find myself. There again, may I be hanged, my dear, but
I mistook you for the barmaid.

MISS HARDCASTLE. Dear me! dear me! I'm sure there's nothing in my *behavior* to put me upon a level with one of that
stamp.

MARLOW. Nothing, my dear, nothing. But I was in for a list
of blunders, and could not help making you a subscriber.
My stupidity saw everything the wrong way. I mistook
your assiduity for assurance and your simplicity for al-
lurement. But it's over—This house I no more show *my*
face in.

MISS HARDCASTLE. I hope, sir, I have done nothing to dis-
oblige you. I'm sure I should be sorry to affront any
gentleman, who has been so polite, and said so many civil
things to me. I'm sure I should be sorry (*pretending to
cry*) if he left the family upon my account. I'm sure I
should be sorry people said anything amiss, since I have
no fortune but my character.

MARLOW (*aside*). By heaven, she weeps. This is the first
mark of tenderness I ever had from a modest woman, and
it touches me. (*To her.*) Excuse me, my lovely girl, you
are the only part of the family I leave with reluctance. But
to be plain with you, the difference of our birth, fortune,
and education make an honorable connection impossible;
and I can never harbor a thought of seducing simplicity
that trusted in my honor, or bringing ruin upon one,
whose only fault was being too lovely.

MISS HARDCASTLE (*aside*). Generous man! I now begin to
admire him. (*To him.*) But I'm sure my family is as good
as Miss Hardcastle's, and though I'm poor, that's no great

---

[6]*Dullissimo Macaroni:* dullest dandy

misfortune to a contented mind, and, until this moment, I never thought that it was bad to want fortune.

MARLOW.   And why now, my pretty simplicity?

MISS HARDCASTLE.   Because it puts me at a distance from one that if I had a thousand pound I would give it all to.

MARLOW *(aside)*.   This simplicity bewitches me, so that if I stay I'm undone. I must make one bold effort, and leave her. *(To her.)* Your partiality in my favor, my dear, touches me most sensibly,[7] and were I to live for myself alone, I could easily fix my choice. But I owe too much to the opinion of the world, too much to the authority of a father, so that — I can scarcely speak it — it affects me. Farewell. *(Exit.)*

MISS HARDCASTLE.   I never knew half his merit till now. He shall not go, if I have power or art to detain him. I'll still preserve the character in which I stooped to conquer, but will undeceive my papa, who, perhaps, may laugh him out of his resolution *(Exit.)*

(Enter TONY, MISS NEVILLE.*)*

TONY.   Ay, you may steal for yourselves the next time. I have done my duty. She has got the jewels again, that's a sure thing; but she believes it was all a mistake of the servants.

MISS NEVILLE.   But, my dear cousin, sure you won't forsake us in this distress. If she in the least suspects that I am going off, I shall certainly be locked up or sent to my Aunt Pedigree's, which is ten times worse.

TONY.   To be sure, aunts of all kinds are damned bad things. But what can I do? I have got you a pair of horses that will fly like Whistlejacket[8] and I'm sure you can't say but I have courted you nicely before her face. Here she comes; we must court a bit or two more, for fear she should suspect us. *(They retire, and seem to fondle.)*

(Enter MRS. HARDCASTLE.*)*

MRS. HARDCASTLE.   Well, I was greatly fluttered, to be sure. But my son tells me it was all a mistake of the servants.

[7]*sensibly:* noticeably
[8]*Whistlejacket:* a famous race horse

I shan't be easy, however, until they are fairly married, and then let her keep her own fortune. But what do I see! Fondling together, as I'm alive. I never saw Tony so sprightly before. Ah! have I caught you, my pretty doves? What, billing, exchanging stolen glances, and broken murmurs. Ah!

TONY.   As for murmurs, mother, we grumble a little now and then, to be sure. But there's no love lost between us.

MRS. HARDCASTLE.   A mere sprinkling, Tony, upon the flame, only to make it burn brighter.

MISS NEVILLE.   Cousin Tony promises to give us more of his company at home. Indeed, he shan't leave us any more. It won't leave us, cousin Tony, will it?

TONY.   Oh! it's a pretty creature. No. I'd sooner leave my horse in a pound, than leave you when you smile upon one so. Your laugh makes you so becoming.

MISS NEVILLE.   Agreeable cousin! Who can help admiring that natural humor, that pleasant, broad, red, thoughtless *(patting his cheek)* ah! it's a bold face.

MRS. HARDCASTLE.   Pretty innocence!

TONY.   I'm sure I always loved cousin Con's hazel eyes, and her pretty long fingers, that she twists this way and that over the haspicholls,[9] like a parcel of bobbins.

MRS. HARDCASTLE.   Ah, he would charm the bird from the tree. I was never so happy before. My boy takes after his father, poor Mr. Lumpkin, exactly. The jewels, my dear Con, shall be yours incontinently.[10] You shall have them. Isn't he a sweet boy, my dear? You shall be married to-morrow, and we'll put off the rest of his education, like Dr. Drowsy's sermons, to a fitter opportunity.

(Enter DIGGORY.*)*

DIGGORY.   Where's the squire? I have got a letter for your worship.

TONY.   Give it to my mamma. She reads all my letters first.

DIGGORY.   I had orders to deliver it into your own hands.

TONY.   Who does it come from?

[9]*haspicholls:* harpsichord
[10]*incontinently:* immediately

DIGGORY. Your worship must ask that o' the letter itself. *(Exit.)*

TONY.   I could wish to know, though. *(Turning the letter, and gazing on it.)*

MISS NEVILLE *(aside).*   Undone, undone. A letter to him from Hastings. I know the hand. If my aunt sees it, we are ruined for ever. I'll keep her employed a little if I can. *(To MRS. HARDCASTLE.)* But I have not told you, Madam, of my cousin's smart answer just now to Mr. Marlow. We so laughed—You must know, Madam—this way a little, for he must not hear us. *(They confer.)*

TONY *(still gazing).*   A damned cramp piece of penmanship, as ever I saw in my life. I can read your print-hand very well. But here there are such handles, and shanks, and dashes, that one can scarce tell the head from the tail. *To Anthony Lumpkin, Esquire.* It's very odd, I can read the outside of my letters, where my own name is, well enough. But when I come to open it, it's all—buzz. That's hard, very hard; for the inside of the letter is always the cream of the correspondence.

MRS. HARDCASTLE.   Ha! ha! ha! Very well, very well! And so my son was too hard for the philosopher.

MISS NEVILLE.   Yes, madam; but you must hear the rest, madam. A little more this way, or he may hear us. You'll hear how he puzzled him again.

MRS. HARDCASTLE.   He seems strangely puzzled now himself, methinks.

TONY *(still gazing).*   A damned up-and-down hand, as if it was disguised in liquor. *(Reading.)* Dear Sir. Ay, that's that. Then there's an *M*, and a *T*, and an *S*, but whether the next be an *izzard*[11] or an *R*, confound me, I cannot tell.

MRS. HARDCASTLE.   What's that, my dear? Can I give you any assistance?

MISS NEVILLE.   Pray, aunt, let me read it. Nobody reads a cramp hand better than I. *(Twitching the letter from her.)* Do you know who it is from?

TONY.   Can't tell, except from Dick Ginger the feeder.[12]

[11]*izzard:* the letter *z*
[12]*feeder:* trainer of game-cocks

MISS NEVILLE.   Ay, so it is. *(Pretending to read.)* Dear Squire,
Hoping that you're in health, as I am at this present. The
gentlemen of the Shake-bag[13] club has cut the gentlemen
of Goose-green quite out of feather. The odds—um—odd
battle—um—long fighting—um, here, here, it's all about
cocks, and fighting; it's of no consquence; here, put it up,
put it up. *(Thrusting the crumpled letter upon him.)*

TONY.   But I tell you, miss, it's of all the consequence in
the world. I would not lose the rest of it for a guinea. Here,
mother, do you make it out. Of no consequence! *(Giving*
MRS. HARDCASTLE *the letter.)*

MRS. HARDCASTLE.   How's this! *(Reads.)* "Dear Squire. I'm
now waiting for Miss Neville with a post-chaise and pair
at the bottom of the garden, but I find my horses yet unable to perform the journey. I expect you'll assist us with
a pair of fresh horses, as you promised. Dispatch is necessary, as the *hag*, (ay, the hag) your mother, will otherwise
suspect us. Yours, Hastings." Grant me patience. I shall
run distracted! My rage chokes me!

MISS NEVILLE.   I hope, madam, you'll suspend your resentment for a few moments, and not impute to me any impertinence, or sinister design that belongs to another.

MRS. HARDCASTLE *(curtsying very low).*   Fine spoken, madam; you are most miraculously polite and engaging and
quite the very pink of courtesy and circumspection,
madam. *(Changing her tone.)* And you, you great ill-
fashioned oaf, with scarce sense enough to keep your
mouth shut. Were you too joined against me? But I'll defeat all your plots in a moment. As for you, madam, since
you have got a pair of fresh horses ready, it would be
cruel to disappoint them. So, if you please, instead of
running away with your spark, prepare, this very moment,
to run off with *me*. Your old Aunt Pedigree will keep you
secure, I'll warrant me. You too, sir, may mount your
horse, and guard us upon the way. Here, Thomas, Roger,
Diggory! I'll show you, that I wish you better than you
do yourselves. *(Exit.)*

MISS NEVILLE.   So, now I'm completely ruined.

---

[13]*Shake-bag:* a large game-cock

TONY. Ay, that's a sure thing.

MISS NEVILLE. What better could be expected from being connected with such a stupid fool, and after all the nods and signs I made him.

TONY. By the laws, miss, it was your own cleverness and not my stupidity that did your business. You were so nice and so busy with your Shake-bags and Goose-greens, that I thought you could never be making believe.

(Enter HASTINGS.*)*

HASTINGS. So, sir, I find by my servant, that you have shown my letter, and betrayed us. Was this well done, young gentleman?

TONY. Here's another. Ask miss there who betrayed you. Ecod, it was her doing, not mine.

(Enter MARLOW.*)*

MARLOW. So I have been finely used here among you. Rendered contemptible, driven into ill manners, despised, insulted, laughed at.

TONY. Here's another. We shall have old Bedlam[14] broke loose presently.

MISS NEVILLE. And there, sir, is the gentlemen to whom we all owe every obligation.

MARLOW. What can I say to him, a mere boy, an idiot, whose ignorance and age are a protection.

HASTINGS. A poor contemptible booby that would but disgrace correction.

MISS NEVILLE. Yet with cunning and malice enough to make himself merry with all our embarrassments.

HASTINGS. An insensible cub.

MARLOW. Replete with tricks and mischief.

TONY. Baw! damme, but I'll fight you both one after the other,—with baskets.[15]

---

[14]*Bedlam:* insane asylum in London
[15]*baskets:* fencing swords having hilts with a basketlike guard for the hand

MARLOW. As for him, he's below resentment. But your conduct, Mr. Hastings, requires an explanation. You knew of
my mistakes, yet would not undeceive me.

HASTINGS. Tortured as I am with my own disappointments,
is this a time for explanations? It is not friendly, Mr.
Marlow.

MARLOW. But, sir—

MISS NEVILLE. Mr. Marlow, we never kept on your mistake,
till it was too late to undeceive you. Be pacified.

(Enter SERVANT.)

SERVANT. My mistress desires you'll get ready immediately,
madam. The horses are putting to. Your hat and things are
in the next room. We are to go thirty miles before morning.
(Exit.)

MISS NEVILLE. Well, well; I'll come presently.

MARLOW *(To* HASTINGS*)*. Was it well done, sir, to assist in
rendering me ridiculous? To hang me out for the scorn
of all my acquaintance? Depend upon it, sir, I shall expect
an explanation.

HASTINGS. Was it well done, sir, if you're upon that subject
to deliver what I entrusted to yourself to the care of another, sir?

MISS NEVILLE. Mr. Hastings! Mr. Marlow! Why will you increase my distress by this groundless dispute? I implore,
I intreat you—

(Enter SERVANT.)

SERVANT. Your cloak, madam. My mistress is impatient.

MISS NEVILLE. I come. *(Exit* SERVANT.)* Pray be pacified.
If I leave you thus, I shall die with apprehension.

(Enter SERVANT.)

SERVANT. Your fan, muff, and gloves, madam. The horses
are waiting.

MISS NEVILLE.   Oh, Mr. Marlow! if you knew what a scene of constraint and ill-nature lies before me, I'm sure it would convert your resentment into pity.

MARLOW.   I'm so distracted with a variety of passions that I don't know what I do. Forgive me, madam. George, forgive me. You know my hasty temper, and should not exasperate it.

HASTINGS.   The torture of my situation is my only excuse.

MISS NEVILLE.   Well, my dear Hastings, if you have that esteem for me that I think, that I am sure you have, your constancy for three years will but increase the happiness of our future connection. If—

MRS. HARDCASTLE *(within).*   Miss Neville! Constance, why Constance, I say!

MISS NEVILLE.   I'm coming. Well, constancy. Remember, constancy is the word. *(Exit.)*

HASTINGS.   My heart! How can I support this. To be so near happiness, and such happiness.

MARLOW *(to* TONY*).*   You see now, young gentleman, the effects of your folly. What might be amusement to you, is here disappointment, and even distress.

TONY *(from a reverie).*   Ecod, I have hit it. It's here. Your hands. Yours and yours, my poor Sulky. My boots there, ho! Meet me two hours hence at the bottom of the garden; and if you don't find Tony Lumpkin a more good-natured fellow than you thought for, I'll give you leave to take my best horse and Bet Bouncer into the bargain. Come along. My boots, ho! *(Exeunt.)*

Act V   SCENE 1

The house. Enter HASTINGS *and* SERVANT.

HASTINGS.   You saw the old lady and Miss Neville drive off, you say?

SERVANT.   Yes, your honor. They went off in a post coach,

and the young 'Squire went on horseback. They're thirty miles off by this time.

HASTINGS.   Then all my hopes are over.

SERVANT.   Yes, sir. Old Sir Charles is arrived. He and the old gentleman of the house have been laughing at Mr. Marlow's mistake this half hour. They are coming this way.

HASTINGS.   Then I must not be seen. So now to my fruitless appointment at the bottom of the garden. This is about the time. *(Exit.)*

(Enter SIR CHARLES *and* HARDCASTLE.*)*

HARDCASTLE.   Ha! ha! ha! The peremptory tone in which he sent forth his sublime commands.

SIR CHARLES.   And the reserve with which I suppose he treated all your advances.

HARDCASTLE.   And yet he might have seen something in me above a common inn-keeper, too.

SIR CHARLES.   Yes, Dick, but he mistook you for an uncommon inn-keeper, ha! ha! ha!

HARDCASTLE.   Well, I'm in too good spirits to think of any thing but joy. Yes, my dear friend, this union of our families will make our personal friendships hereditary; and though my daughter's fortune is but small—

SIR CHARLES.   Why, Dick, will you talk of fortune to *me*. My son is possessed of more than a competence already, and can want nothing but a good and virtuous girl to share his happiness and increase it. If they like each other as you say they do—

HARDCASTLE.   *If,* man! I tell you they *do* like each other. My daughter as good as told me so.

SIR CHARLES.   But girls are apt to flatter themselves, you know.

HARDCASTLE.   I saw him grasp her hand in the warmest manner myself; and here he comes to put you out of your *ifs*, I warrant him.

(Enter MARLOW.*)*

MARLOW.   I come, sir, once more, to ask your pardon for my strange conduct. I can scarce reflect on my insolence without confusion.

HARDCASTLE.   Tut, boy, a trifle. You take it too gravely. An hour or two's laughing with my daughter will set all to rights again. She'll never like you the worse for it.

MARLOW.   Sir, I shall be always proud of her approbation.[1]

HARDCASTLE.   Approbation is but a cold word, Mr. Marlow; if I am not deceived, you have something more than approbation thereabouts. You take me.

MARLOW.   Really, sir, I have not that happiness.

HARDCASTLE.   Come, boy, I'm an old fellow, and know what's what, as well as you that are younger. I know what has passed between you; but mum.

MARLOW.   Sure, sir, nothing has passed between us but the most profound respect on my side, and the most distant reserve on hers. You don't think, sir, that my impudence has been passed upon all the rest of the family?

HARDCASTLE.   Impudence! No, I don't say that—Not quite impudence—Though girls like to be played with, and rumpled a little, too, sometimes. But she has told no tales, I assure you.

MARLOW.   I never gave her the slightest cause.

HARDCASTLE.   Well, well, I like modesty in its place well enough. But this is over-acting, young gentleman. You may be open. Your father and I will like you the better for it.

MARLOW.   May I die, sir, if I ever—

HARDCASTLE.   I tell you, she don't dislike you; and as I'm sure you like her—

MARLOW.   Dear sir—I protest, sir,—

HARDCASTLE.   I see no reason why you should not be joined as fast as the parson can tie you.

MARLOW.   But hear me, sir—

HARDCASTLE.   Your father approves the match, I admire it, every moment's delay will be doing mischief, so—

MARLOW.   But why won't you hear me? By all that's just and

[1]*approbation:* approval

true, I never gave Miss Hardcastle the slightest mark of my attachment, or even the most distant hint to suspect me of affection. We had but one interview, and that was formal, modest and uninteresting.

HARDCASTLE *(aside)*. This fellow's formal, modest impudence is beyond bearing.

SIR CHARLES. And you never grasped her hand, or made any protestations!

MARLOW. As heaven is my witness, I came down in obedience to your commands. I saw the lady without emotion, and parted without reluctance. I hope you'll exact no further proofs of my duty, nor prevent me from leaving a house in which I suffer so many mortifications. *(Exit.)*

SIR CHARLES. I'm astonished at the air of sincerity with which he parted.

HARDCASTLE. And I'm astonished at the deliberate intrepidity[2] of his assurance.

SIR CHARLES. I dare pledge my life and honor upon his truth.

HARDCASTLE. Here comes my daughter, and I would stake my happiness upon her veracity.[3]

(Enter MISS HARDCASTLE.*)*

HARDCASTLE. Kate, come hither, child. Answer us sincerely, and without reserve; has Mr. Marlow made you any professions of love and affection?

MISS HARDCASTLE. The question is very abrupt, sir! But since you require unreserved sincerity, I think he has.

HARDCASTLE *(to* SIR CHARLES*)*. You see.

SIR CHARLES. And pray, madam, have you and my son had more than one interview?

MISS HARDCASTLE. Yes, sir, several.

HARDCASTLE *(to* SIR CHARLES*)*. You see.

SIR CHARLES. But did he profess any attachment?

MISS HARDCASTLE. A lasting one.

SIR CHARLES. Did he talk of love?

[2]*intrepidity:* boldness
[3]*veracity:* habitual truthfulness

MISS HARDCASTLE. Much, sir.

SIR CHARLES. Amazing! And all this formally?

MISS HARDCASTLE. Formally.

HARDCASTLE. Now, my friend, I hope you are satisfied.

SIR CHARLES. And how did he behave, Madam?

MISS HARDCASTLE. As most professed admirers do. Said some civil things of my face, talked much of his want of merit, and the greatness of mine; mentioned his heart, and gave a short tragedy speech, and ended with pretended rapture.

SIR CHARLES. Now I'm perfectly convinced, indeed. I know his conversation among women to be modest and submissive. This forward, canting, ranting manner by no means describes him, and I am confident, he never sat for the picture.

MISS HARDCASTLE. Then what, sir, if I should convince you to your face of my sincerity? If you and my papa, in about half an hour, will place yourselves behind that screen, you shall hear him declare his passion to me in person.

SIR CHARLES. Agreed. And if I find him what you describe, all my happiness in him must have an end. *(Exit.)*

MISS HARDCASTLE. And if you don't find him what I describe —I fear my happiness must never have a beginning. *(Exeunt.)*

Act V SCENE 2

The back of the garden. Enter HASTINGS.

HASTINGS. What an idiot am I, to wait here for a fellow, who probably takes delight in mortifying me. He never intended to be punctual, and I'll wait no longer. What do I see! It is he, and perhaps with news of my Constance.

(Enter TONY, *booted and spattered.)*

HASTINGS. My honest squire! I now find you a man of your word. This looks like friendship.

TONY. Ay, I'm your friend, and the best friend you have in the world, if you knew but all. This riding by night, by the bye, is cursedly tiresome. It has shook me worse than the basket of a stage-coach.

HASTINGS. But how? Where did you leave your fellow travellers? Are they in safety? Are they housed?

TONY. Five and twenty miles in two hours and a half is no such bad driving. The poor beasts have smoked for it: Rabbit me, but I'd rather ride forty miles after a fox, than ten with such *varment*.

HASTINGS. Well, but where have you left the ladies? I die with impatience.

TONY. Left them? Why, where should I leave them, but where I found them?

HASTINGS. This is a riddle.

TONY. Riddle me this then. What's that goes round the house, and round the house, and never touches the house?

HASTINGS. I'm still astray.

TONY. Why that's it, mon. I have led them astray. By jingo, there's not a pond or slough within five miles of the place but they can tell the taste of.

HASTINGS. Ha, ha, ha, I understand; you took them in a round, while they supposed themselves going forward. And so you have at last brought them home again.

TONY. You shall hear. I first took them down Feather-bed-lane, where we stuck fast in the mud. I then rattled them crack over the stones of Up-and-down Hill—I then introduced them to the gibbet[1] on Heavy-tree Heath, and from that, with a circumbendibus,[2] I fairly lodged them in the horse-pond at the bottom of the garden.

HASTINGS. But no accident, I hope.

TONY. No, no! Only mother is confoundedly frightened. She thinks herself forty miles off. She's sick of the journey,

[1] *gibbet:* gallows
[2] *circumbendibus:* roundabout route

and the cattle can scarce crawl. So if your own horses be ready, you may whip off with cousin, and I'll be bound that no soul here can budge a foot to follow you.

HASTINGS.   My dear friend, how can I be grateful?

TONY.   Ay, now it's "dear friend," noble squire." Just now, it was all "idiot," "cub," and "run me through the guts." Damn *your* way of fighting, I say. After we take a knock in this part of the country, we kiss and be friends. But if you had run me through the guts, then I should be dead, and you might go kiss the hangman.

HASTINGS.   The rebuke is just. But I must hasten to relieve Miss Neville; if you keep the old lady employed, I promise to take care of the young one. *(Exit.)*

TONY.   Never fear me. Here she comes. Vanish. She's got from the pond, and draggled up to the waist like a mermaid.

(Enter MRS. HARDCASTLE.*)*

MRS. HARDCASTLE.   Oh, Tony, I'm killed! Shook! Battered to death! I shall never survive it. That last jolt that laid us against the quickset hedge has done my business.

TONY.   Alack, mama, it was all your own fault. You would be for running away by night, without knowing one inch of the way.

MRS. HARDCASTLE.   I wish we were at home again. I never met so many accidents in so short a journey. Drenched in the mud, overturned in a ditch, stuck fast in a slough, jolted to a jelly, and at last to lose our way. Whereabouts do you think we are, Tony?

TONY.   By my guess we should be upon Crackskull Common, about forty miles from home.

MRS. HARDCASTLE.   O lud! O lud! the most notorious spot in all the country. We only want a robbery to make a complete night on't.

TONY.   Don't be afraid, mama, don't be afraid. Two of the five that kept[3] here are hanged, and the other three may

---

[3]*kept:* lived

not find us. Don't be afraid. Is that a man that's galloping behind us? No; it's only a tree. Don't be afraid.

MRS. HARDCASTLE. The fright will certainly kill me.

TONY. Do you see anything like a black hat moving behind the thicket?

MRS. HARDCASTLE. O death!

TONY. No, it's only a cow. Don't be afraid, mama; don't be afraid!

MRS. HARDCASTLE. As I'm alive, Tony, I see a man coming towards us. Ah! I'm sure on't. If he perceives us, we are undone.

TONY *(aside)*. Father-in-law, by all that's unlucky, come to take one of his night walks. *(To her.)* Ah, it's a highwayman, with pistols as long as my arm. A damned ill-looking fellow.

MRS. HARDCASTLE. Good heaven defend us! He approaches!

TONY. Do you hide yourself in that thicket, and leave me to manage him. If there be danger, I'll cough, and cry hem. When I cough be sure to keep close.

(MRS. HARDCASTLE *hides behind a tree in the back scene. Enter* HARDCASTLE.)

HARDCASTLE. I'm mistaken, or I heard voices of people in want of help. Oh, Tony, is that you? I did not expect you so soon back. Are your mother and her charge in safety?

TONY. Very safe, sir, at my Aunt Pedigree's. Hem.

MRS. HARDCASTLE *(from behind)*. Ah death! I find there's danger.

HARDCASTLE. Forty miles in three hours; sure, that's too much, my youngster.

TONY. Stout horses and willing minds make short journeys, as they say. Hem.

MRS. HARDCASTLE *(from behind)*. Sure he'll do the dear boy no harm.

HARDCASTLE. But I heard a voice here; I should be glad to know from whence it came?

TONY. It was I, sir, talking to myself, sir. I was saving that forty miles in four hours was very good going. Hem! As to be sure it was. Hem! I have got a sort of cold by being out in the air. We'll go in, if you please. Hem!

HARDCASTLE. But if you talk'd to yourself, you did not answer yourself. I am certain I heard two voices, and am resolved *(raising his voice)* to find the other out.

MRS. HARDCASTLE *(from behind).* Oh! he's coming to find me out, Oh!

TONY. What need you go, sir, if I tell you? Hem. I'll lay down my life for the truth—hem—I'll tell you all, sir. *(Detaining him.)*

HARDCASTLE. I tell you, I will not be detained. I insist on seeing. It's in vain to expect I'll believe you.

MRS. HARDCASTLE *(running forward from behind).* O lud, he'll murder my poor boy, my darling. Here, good gentlemen, whet your rage upon me. Take my money, my life, but spare that young gentleman, spare my child, if you have any mercy!

HARDCASTLE. My wife! as I'm a Christian. From whence can she come, or what does she mean?

MRS. HARDCASTLE *(kneeling).* Take compassion on us, good Mr. Highwayman. Take our money, our watches, all we have, but spare our lives. We will never bring you to justice, indeed we won't, good Mr. Highwayman.

HARDCASTLE. I believe the woman's out of her senses. What, Dorothy, don't you know *me?*

MRS. HARDCASTLE. Mr. Hardcastle, as I'm alive! My fears blinded me. But who, my dear, could have expected to meet you here, in this frightful place, so far from home? What has brought you to follow us?

HARDCASTLE. Sure, Dorothy, you have not lost your wits. So far from home, when you are within forty yards of your own door. *(To him.)* This is one of your old tricks, you graceless rogue you. *(To her.)* Don't you know the gate, and the mulberry-tree; and don't you remember the horse-pond, my dear?

MRS. HARDCASTLE. Yes, I shall remember the horse-pond as long as I live; I have caught my death in it. *(To* TONY.*)* And is it to you, you graceless varlet, I owe all this? I'll teach you to abuse your mother, I will.

TONY. Ecod, mother, all the parish says you have spoiled me, and so you may take the fruits on't.

MRS. HARDCASTLE. I'll spoil you. I will. *(Follows him off stage. Exit.)*

HARDCASTLE. There's morality, however, in his reply. *(Exit.)*

(Enter HASTINGS *and* NEVILLE.*)*

HASTINGS. My dear Constance, why will you deliberate thus? If we delay a moment, all is lost for ever. Pluck up a little resolution, and we shall soon be out of reach of her malignity.

MISS NEVILLE. I find it impossible. My spirits are so sunk with the agitations I have suffered, that I am unable to face any new danger. Two or three years patience will at last crown us with happiness.

HASTINGS. Such a tedious delay is worse than inconstancy. Let us fly, my charmer. Let us date our happiness from this very moment. Perish fortune. Love and content will increase what we possess beyond a monarch's revenue. Let me prevail.

MISS NEVILLE. No, Mr. Hastings; no. Prudence once more comes to my relief, and I will obey its dictates. In the moment of passion, fortune may be despised, but it produces a lasting repentance. I'm resolved to apply to Mr. Hardcastle's compassion and justice for redress.

HASTINGS. But though he has the will, he has not the power to relieve you.

MISS NEVILLE. But he has influence, and upon that I am resolved to rely.

HASTINGS. I have no hopes. But since you persist, I must reluctantly obey you.   *(Exeunt.)*

Act V SCENE 3

The parlor. Enter SIR CHARLES *and* MISS HARDCASTLE.

SIR CHARLES. What a situation am I in. If what you say appears, I shall then find a guilty son. If what he says be true, I shall then lose one that, of all others, I most wished for a daughter.

MISS HARDCASTLE. I am proud of your approbation, and to show I merit it, if you place yourselves as I directed, you shall hear his explicit declaration. But he comes.

SIR CHARLES. I'll to your father, and keep him to the appointment. *(Exit.)*

(Enter MARLOW.)

MARLOW. Though prepared for setting out, I come once more to take leave, nor did I, till this moment, know the pain I feel in the separation.

MISS HARDCASTLE *(in her own natural manner).* I believe these sufferings cannot be very great, sir, which you can so easily remove. A day or two longer, perhaps, might lessen your uneasiness, by showing the little value of what you now think proper to regret.

MARLOW *(aside).* This girl every moment improves upon me. *(To her.)* It must not be, madam. I have already trifled too long with my heart. My very pride begins to submit to my passion. The disparity[1] of education and fortune, the anger of a parent, and the contempt of my equals, begin to lose their weight; and nothing can restore me to myself but this painful effort of resolution.

MISS HARDCASTLE. Then go, sir. I'll urge nothing more to detain you. Though my family be as good as hers you came down to visit, and my education, I hope, not inferior, what are these advantages without equal affluence?[2] I must remain contented with the slight approbation of

[1] *disparity*: difference
[2] *affluence*: wealth

imputed merit; I must have only the mockery of your addresses, while all your serious aims are fixed on fortune.

(Enter HARDCASTLE *and* SIR CHARLES *from behind.)*

SIR CHARLES.   Here, behind this screen.

HARDCASTLE.   Ay, ay, make no noise. I'll engage³ my Kate
covers him with confusion at last.

MARLOW.   By heavens, madam, fortune was ever my smallest consideration. Your beauty at first caught my eye; for
who could see that without emotion? But every moment
that I converse with you steals in some new grace, height-
ens the picture and gives it stronger expression. What at
first seemed rustic plainness, now appears refined simplicity. What seemed forward assurance, now strikes me
as the result of courageous innocence, and conscious
virtue.

SIR CHARLES.   What can it mean! He amazes me!

HARDCASTLE.   I told you how it would be. Hush!

MARLOW.   I am now determined to stay, madam, and I have
too good an opinion of my father's discernment, when he
sees you, to doubt his approbation.

MISS HARDCASTLE.   No, Mr. Marlow, I will not, cannot detain you. Do you think I could suffer a connection, in
which there is the smallest room for repentance? Do you
think I would take the mean advantage of a transient passion, to load you with confusion? Do you think I could
ever relish that happiness, which was acquired by lessen-
ing yours?

MARLOW.   By all that's good, I can have no happiness but
what's in your power to grant me. Nor shall I ever feel
repentance, but in not having seen your merits before. I
will stay, even contrary to your wishes; and though you
should persist to shun me, I will make my respectful assiduities atone for the levity⁴ of my past conduct.

MISS HARDCASTLE.   Sir, I must entreat you'll desist. As our
acquaintance began, so let it end, in indifference. I might

³*engage:* promise, guarantee
⁴*levity:* lack of seriousness

have given an hour or two to levity; but seriously, Mr. Marlow, do you think I could ever submit to a connection, where *I* must appear mercenary, and *you* imprudent? Do you think I could ever catch at the confident addresses of a secure[5] admirer?

MARLOW *(kneeling).* Does this look like security? Does this look like confidence? No, madam, every moment that shows me your merit, only serves to increase my diffidence[6] and confusion. Here let me continue—

SIR CHARLES. I can hold it no longer! Charles, Charles, how hast thou deceived me! Is this your indifference, your uninteresting conversation?

HARDCASTLE. Your cold contempt; your formal interview! What have you to say now?

MARLOW. That I'm all amazement. What can it mean!

HARDCASTLE. It means that you can say and unsay things at pleasure. That you can address a lady in private, and deny it in public; that you have one story for us, and another for my daughter.

MARLOW. Daughter!—this lady your daughter!

HARDCASTLE. Yes, sir, my only daughter. My Kate, whose else should she be?

MARLOW. Oh, the devil!

MISS HARDCASTLE. Yes, sir, that very identical tall, squinting lady you were pleased to take me for. *(Curtsying.)* She that you addressed as the mild, modest, sentimental man of gravity, and the bold, forward, agreeable Rattle of the Ladies Club; ha, ha, ha.

MARLOW. Zounds, there's no bearing this; it's worse than death.

MISS HARDCASTLE. In which of your characters, Sir, will you give us to leave to address you? As the faltering gentleman, with looks on the ground, that speaks just to be heard, and hates hypocrisy; or the loud, confident creature, that keeps it up with Mrs. Mantrap, and old Miss Biddy Buckskin, till three in the morning; ha, ha, ha!

MARLOW. Oh, curse on my noisy head. I never attempted

[5]*secure:* overconfident, careless
[6]*diffidence:* shyness, lack of confidence

to be impudent yet, that I was not taken down. I must be gone.

HARDCASTLE. By the hand of my body, but you shall not. I see it was all a mistake, and I am rejoiced to find it. You shall not, sir, I tell you. I know she'll forgive you. Won't you forgive him, Kate? We'll all forgive you. Take courage, man. *(They retire, she tormenting him, to the back scene.)*

(Enter MRS. HARDCASTLE, TONY.*)*

MRS. HARDCASTLE. So, so they're gone off. Let them go, I care not.

HARDCASTLE. Who gone?

MRS. HARDCASTLE. My dutiful niece and her gentleman, Mr. Hastings, from town. He who came down with our modest visitor here.

SIR CHARLES. Who, my honest George Hastings? As worthy a fellow as lives, and the girl could not have made a more prudent choice.

HARDCASTLE. Then, by the hand of my body, I'm proud of the connection.

MRS. HARDCASTLE. Well, if he has taken away the lady, he has not taken her fortune; that remains in this family to console us for her loss.

HARDCASTLE. Sure, Dorothy, you would not be so mercenary?

MRS. HARDCASTLE. Ay, that's my affair, not yours.

HARDCASTLE. But you know if your son, when of age, refuses to marry his cousin, her whole fortune is then at her own disposal.

MRS. HARDCASTLE. Ay, but he's not of age, and she has not thought proper to wait for his refusal.

(Enter HASTINGS *and* MISS NEVILLE.*)*

MRS. HARDCASTLE *(aside).* What! returned so soon? I begin not to like it.

HASTINGS *(to* HARDCASTLE*).* For my late attempt to fly off with your niece, let my present confusion be my punishment. We are now come back, to appeal from your justice to your humanity. By her father's consent, I first paid her my addresses, and our passions were first founded in duty.

MISS NEVILLE.　Since his death, I have been obliged to stoop to dissimulation to avoid oppression. In an hour of levity, I was ready even to give up my fortune to secure my choice. But I'm now recovered from the delusion, and hope from your tenderness what is denied me from a nearer connection.

MRS. HARDCASTLE.　Pshaw, pshaw, this is all but the whining end of a modern novel.

HARDCASTLE.　Be it what it will, I'm glad they're come back to reclaim their due. Come hither, Tony boy. Do you refuse this lady's hand whom I now offer you?

TONY.　What signifies my refusing? You know I can't refuse her till I'm of age, father.

HARDCASTLE.　While I thought concealing your age, boy, was likely to conduce to your improvement, I concurred with your mother's desire to keep it secret. But since I find she turns it to a wrong use, I must now declare, you have been of age these three months.

TONY.　Of age! Am I of age, father?

HARDCASTLE.　Above three months.

TONY.　Then you'll see the first use I'll make of my liberty. (*Taking* MISS NEVILLE'S *hand.*) Witness all men by these presents, that I, Anthony Lumpkin, Esquire, of Blank place, refuse you, Constantia Neville, spinster, of no place at all, for my true and lawful wife. So Constance Neville may marry whom she pleases, and Tony Lumpkin is his own man again!

SIR CHARLES.　O brave squire!

HASTINGS.　My worthy friend!

MRS. HARDCASTLE.　My undutiful offspring!

MARLOW.　Joy, my dear George, I give you joy sincerely. And could I prevail upon my little tyrant here to be less arbitrary, I should be the happiest man alive, if you would return me the favor.

HASTINGS (*to* HARDCASTLE).　Come, madam, you are now driven to the very last scene of all your contrivances. I know you like him, I'm sure he loves you, and you must and shall have him.

HARDCASTLE *(joining their hands).* And I say so too. And Mr. Marlow, if she makes as good a wife as she has a daughter. I don't believe you'll ever repent your bargain. So now to supper; tomorrow we shall gather all the poor of the parish about us, and the Mistakes of the Night shall be crowned with a merry morning; so boy, take her; and as you have been mistaken in the mistress, my wish is, that you may never be mistaken in the wife. *(Exeunt.)*

FOR DISCUSSION

Act I SCENE 1

1. Like much of eighteenth-century writing, this play reflects a certain amount of tension between city life and country life. How do Mr. and Mrs. Hardcastle differ in their attitudes? What do they reveal about their characters through their differences of opinion? How does Mr. Hardcastle's attitude toward city life directly affect his daughter Kate?

2. During their opening conversation Mr. and Mrs. Hardcastle naturally and casually provide information that will become important later in the play. How does Mrs. Hardcastle describe the appearance of the house? What are you led to suspect by their comments on the ages of Mrs. Hardcastle and Tony?

3. Mr. and Mrs. Hardcastle seem to have very different opinions of Tony. Which appraisal is more accurate? Explain. What do Mr. Hardcastle's ironical comments reveal about Mrs. Hardcastle's relationship with her son? How would you characterize Tony's attitude toward his mother?

4. Who is Young Marlow? How does Mr. Hardcastle describe him to his daughter? What further information about his behavior is revealed to Kate by her cousin Constance Neville? What coincidence involving Hastings does she also reveal?

5. What further information about Mrs. Hardcastle and Tony does Kate provide? How does she explain Mrs. Hardcastle's behavior? What sentiments do the two girls have concerning Tony?

6. In a well-written play most of the necessary *exposition* (see Glos-

sary) is provided early in the drama. Is this true of *She Stoops to Conquer?* Which characters provide most of the background information for the play? Do they introduce the information naturally, or does the dialogue seem contrived? Explain. How does Goldsmith let you know who each character is as soon as he or she steps on stage?

Act I   SCENE 2

1. How is Tony's behavior in this scene consistent with what you learned of him in Scene 1? What is his attitude toward his stepfather?
2. What joke does Tony play on Marlow and Hastings? How does he prepare them in advance for any "un-landlord-like" behavior on the part of his stepfather?
3. What motivation do you find for Tony's behavior?

Act II

1. How does Marlow view the prospect of meeting Kate Hardcastle? Is his attitude consistent with what you have already learned about him? Why? What is his main reason for coming to meet her?
2. The conversation between Marlow and Hastings introduces the *subplot* (see Glossary) involving Hastings and Constance Neville. How were you prepared for the subplot in the first scene of the play? How do matters stand between Constance and Hastings?
3. The initial meeting of Marlow and Hastings and Hardcastle provides Goldsmith with an excellent opportunity for *dramatic irony* (see Glossary). Do any of the men have full knowledge of the situation? What is the function of the frequent *asides* (see Glossary) during the conversation? What is Hardcastle's opinion of the two young men? What is their impression of him?
4. Constance Neville reveals Tony's deception to Hastings. Why do they decide to keep Marlow in ignorance of the situation? How do they maintain the deception?
5. In eighteenth-century sentimental comedy, the young man was usually very worldly-wise and the young woman was shy and sensitive. How does Goldsmith ridicule this notion with the first meeting between Kate and Marlow? At what points does

Kate's conversation attack the gentility and sentimentality of the times?

6. Why is Constance reluctant to elope to France with Hastings? At the end of the act, what steps does Hastings take to make an elopement possible?

Act III

1. Both Mr. Hardcastle and Kate have met Marlow at this point. What dramatic contrast is presented by their differing conceptions of his character? Why is the contrast ironical (see Glossary, *irony*)? How do they decide to reconcile their contradictory opinions?

2. What is the dramatic purpose of the brief encounter between Tony and Hastings at the beginning of Act III? How is the subsequent discussion of the jewels by Mrs. Hardcastle, Constance, and Tony another example of Goldsmith's use of *dramatic irony*?

3. After Kate discovers Tony's practical joke, why does she decide to keep Marlow uninformed of the situation? How is it possible for her to deceive him about her identity in a perfectly natural manner?

4. What is Marlow's impression of Kate after their first meeting? How are their manners and attitudes toward each other altogether different during their second encounter? In what sense has Kate "stooped to conquer"?

5. What complication arises for Kate at the end of the act with the inopportune entrance of her father? What is the dramatic effect of this complication on the audience or reader?

Act IV

1. How does Marlow unwittingly complicate the matter of Constance's jewels?

2. What conflict arises in the main plot because of the behavior of Marlow's servants? How does this conflict lead Marlow to the discovery that he is being deceived? How does Kate manage to keep him partially deceived about her own position for a while longer? Why does she continue her deception? What are Marlow's feelings toward Kate at this point?

3. What oversight does Hastings mention at the beginning of the act? How does his attempt to remedy his oversight bring an end to his plans for elopement?

4. What is the significance of Tony's final words? What is their dramatic effect in terms of the audience or reader?
5. Goldsmith builds complication upon complication in Acts II, III, and IV. At what point in Act IV does the *rising action* (see Glossary) of the main plot reach a *climax* (see Glossary)? Is this the point of greatest dramatic intensity? Explain. What happens to the intensity of the action following this climax? Where does the climax of the subplot occur? Are you able to guess the outcome of the situation at this point?

Act V SCENE 1

1. What final complication in the main plot occurs in this scene? How does Kate propose to clear up everything?
2. Why do you think Goldsmith added this final complication to the main plot so late in the play?

Act V SCENE 2

1. What are the results of the carriage ride "to Aunt Pedigree's"?
2. Why do you suppose Goldsmith ignored the opportunity of bringing the subplot to a conclusion at this point?
3. How do you interpret Mr. Hardcastle's final remark?

Act V SCENE 3

1. Does the revelation of Tony's correct age come as a surprise to you? Why?
2. How does Goldsmith tidily resolve both the main plot and the subplot in this final scene? In what sense has Constance also "stooped to conquer"?

ON THE PLAY AS A WHOLE

1. Goldsmith's primary objective as a playwright was to provide amusement. He intended to counter the tearful sentimentality of his time with gay, rollicking humor. How successful do you think he was in achieving his objective? The scene in Act II

where Hardcastle instructs his servants is an example of *farce* (see Glossary). In what other scenes does Goldsmith use farce to add merriment to the plot? Do these situations seem to arise naturally from the main action, or do they seem contrived? Explain.

2. In viewing the main plot and the subplot as separate but related stories, which story do you find more interesting? Why? In what ways is the main plot more contrived than the subplot? Does this add to your interest or detract from it?

3. Even though the climax of both the plot and the subplot occurs in Act IV, Goldsmith is able to maintain interest throughout the *denouement* (see Glossary) in Act V. What means does he use to prevent the action from dragging during these final scenes?

4. In viewing Goldsmith's characterizations as a whole, do you find his characters believable? Explain. Are they fully developed? Which seem to be stock types? Which of them seem to be reactions against the sentimental drama of the time? Explain.

5. What is your opinion of Tony? Is your attitude toward him at the end of the play different from that at the end of Act I? If so, in what ways? One of the *stock characters* (see Glossary) of eighteenth-century sentimental comedy was the upright, obedient son. In what ways is Tony an amusing reaction against this stock role?

6. Mr. Hardcastle tells his wife, "In my time the follies of the town crept slowly among us, but now they travel faster than a stage-coach." In what ways is Mrs. Hardcastle a victim of the "follies of the town"? How does Goldsmith use certain of her weaknesses as the basis for complications in the plot?

7. Goldsmith directs a gentle *satire* (see Glossary) at some of the foibles and excesses of eighteenth-century society. Tony, for example, comments that "they liked the book better the more it made them cry." What characteristic of the society is Tony ridiculing? What other manners, customs, or conventions does Goldsmith satirize in the dialogue and in the situations he has created?

8. *She Stoops to Conquer* has been revived again and again, both in England and in the United States, and it has always played successfully. How do you account for its continuing popularity in light of the fact that most eighteenth-century drama has been long forgotten or ignored?

FOR COMPOSITION

1. In eighteenth-century sentimental drama, the heroine was usually timid, tenderhearted, and often tearful. Write a brief essay
   discussing Kate Hardcastle as Goldsmith's way of poking fun at
   the typical sentimental heroine. Use specific examples of her
   speech and behavior in your composition.
2. Imagine that you are a member of eighteenth-century London
   society and that you are paying your first visit to the Hardcastles.
   From what you have learned in the play about the "rivalry" between city and country, write a letter to a friend back in London
   in which you describe your impressions of either Mrs. Hardcastle
   or Mr. Hardcastle.
3. Kate remarks to Marlow that "in this hypocritical age there are
   few who do not condemn in public what they practice in private."
   In a well-organized essay, explain her statement and tell why you
   do or do not think that it is just as true of society today as it was
   of eighteenth-century society. Give examples from the play and
   from your own experience to illustrate your view.
4. Write a character sketch for one of the following: Kate Hardcastle, Marlow, Constance Neville, Hastings, or Tony Lumpkin.
   Include in your sketch the character's outstanding traits, his
   motives, his beliefs and opinions, and his importance to the play.
   Refer to specific incidents and speeches in the play to support
   your ideas.
5. Mrs. Hardcastle was hoping to keep Constance Neville's jewels
   in the family by having Tony marry her. Using your imagination
   along with what you already know about Mrs. Hardcastle, write
   a brief composition, in the form of an interior monologue, in
   which you reveal her thoughts during the final scene of the play.

George Bernard Shaw

For more than half a century the most prolific, controversial, and successful dramatist of the modern British theater was George Bernard Shaw. He was, like most of the great playwrights since Shakespeare, a writer of comedy, and like them he drew his audiences by wit and held them by ideas. His talent lay in a special variety of comedy, one that satisfied the popular taste for witty and light entertainment at the same time that it allowed for the vivacious and clashing expression of ideas. Shaw believed that the modern theater should be an intellectual arena where ideas might be debated, and he was largely responsible for making it so. A superb craftsman, he knew how to animate ideas—to make them live. Most of all, he knew how to set them up one against another and thus bring into sharp and surprising contrast illusion and reality, romantic beliefs and unromantic facts, social and moral pretensions and what lay beneath them.

A fearless intellectual critic, Shaw used his remarkable gifts of inventiveness, wit, and humor to expose wrongs, attack shams, and destroy conventionality by ridiculing it. In *Arms and the Man* the target of his comic satire was the romantic concept of the military hero and the glories of war. This play was the first of four comedies which Shaw published in a volume titled *Pleasant Plays* when, early in his career, theater

189

producers refused him a hearing. ("He was the first dramatist to win fame in the library without a stage success to his name."[1]) Described by Shaw as "an anti-romantic comedy," *Arms and the Man* enjoyed a greater success in England than had the earlier social dramas, and when it was produced in America in the late 1890's, it became Shaw's first money-maker. The satire has since lost some of its sting, but the dialogue, characters, and incidents continue to delight readers and audiences alike. In 1909 the plot of the play was borrowed for the still popular operetta *The Chocolate Soldier*.

Before the close of the nineteenth century, Shaw had given ample proof of his versatility and talent as a playwright. In the years that followed, he revealed what seemed an inexhaustible fertility of invention and an unlimited fund of ideas in the rich critical entertainment he created for a steadily growing audience. "Many who by no means agreed with him found his wit and his capacity for creating absurd situations irresistibly amusing, and his intellectual liveliness and zest exhilarating."[2] Though England could boast of a number of distinguished playwrights, Shaw remained the unsurpassed leader of the new drama.

[1] Homer E. Woodbridge, *George Bernard Shaw: Creative Artist* (Carbondale: Southern Illinois University Press, 1963), p. 31.
[2] John Ball (ed.), *From Beowulf to Modern British Writers* (New York: The Odyssey Press, Inc., 1959), p. 1152.

Arms and the Man

CHARACTERS

MAJOR PAUL PETKOFF
CATHERINE, his wife
RAINA, his daughter
LOUKA, their maid
NICOLA, their manservant
MAJOR SERGIUS SARANOFF
CAPTAIN BLUNTSCHLI
An officer

Act I

Night. A lady's bedchamber in Bulgaria, in a small town near the Dragoman Pass. It is late in November in the year 1885, and through an open window with a little balcony on the left can be seen a peak of the Balkans, wonderfully white and beautiful in the starlit snow. The interior of the room is not like anything to be seen in the east of Europe. It is half rich Bulgarian, half cheap Viennese.

191

The counterpane and hangings of the bed, the window curtains, the little carpet, and all the ornamental textile fabrics in the room are oriental and gorgeous: the paper on the wall is occidental and paltry. Above the head of the bed, which stands against a little wall cutting off the right-hand corner of the room diagonally, is a painted wooden shrine, blue and gold, with an ivory image of Christ, and a light hanging before it in a pierced metal ball suspended by three chains. On the left, further forward, is an ottoman. The washstand, against the wall on the left, consists of an enamelled iron basin with a pail beneath it in a painted metal frame, and a single towel on the rail at the side. A chair near it is Austrian bent wood, with cane seat. The dressing table, between the bed and the window, is an ordinary pine table, covered with a cloth of many colors, but with an expensive toilet mirror on it. The door is on the right; and there is a chest of drawers between the door and the bed. This chest of drawers is also covered by a variegated native cloth, and on it there is a pile of paperbacked novels, a box of chocolate creams, and a miniature easel, on which is a large photograph of an extremely handsome officer, whose lofty bearing and magnetic glance can be felt even from the portrait. The room is lighted by a candle on the chest of drawers, and another on the dressing table, with a box of matches beside it.

The window is hinged doorwise and stands wide open, folding back to the left. Outside a pair of wooden shutters, opening outward, also stand open. On the balcony, a young lady, intensely conscious of the romantic beauty of the night, and of the fact that her own youth and beauty is a part of it, is gazing at the snowy Balkans. She is covered by a long mantle of furs, worth, on a moderate estimate, about three times the furniture of her room.

Her reverie is interrupted by her mother, CATHERINE PETKOFF, *a woman over forty, imperiously energetic, with magnificent black hair and eyes, who might be a very splendid specimen of the wife of a mountain farmer,*

*but is determined to be a Viennese lady, and to that end
wears a fashionable tea gown on all occasions.*

CATHERINE *(entering hastily, full of good news)*.   Raina—
   (she pronounces it Rah-eena, with the stress on the ee)
   Raina—*(she goes to the bed, expecting to find* RAINA
   there.) Why, where—*(*RAINA *looks into the room.)* Heavens! child, are you out in the night air instead of in your
   bed? You'll catch your death. Louka told me you were
   asleep.
RAINA *(coming in)*.   I sent her away. I wanted to be alone.
   The stars are so beautiful! What is the matter?
CATHERINE.   Such news. There has been a battle!
RAINA *(her eyes dilating)*.   Ah! *(She throws the cloak on the
   ottoman, and comes eagerly to* CATHERINE *in her nightgown, a pretty garment, but evidently the only one she
   has on.)*
CATHERINE.   A great battle at Slivnitza! A victory! And it
   was won by Sergius.
RAINA *(with a cry of delight)*.   Ah! *(Rapturously.)* Oh, mother!
   (then, with sudden anxiety.) Is father safe?
CATHERINE.   Of course: he sent me the news. Sergius is the
   hero of the hour, the idol of the regiment.
RAINA.   Tell me, tell me. How was it! *(Ecstatically.)* Oh,
   mother, mother, mother! *(*RAINA *pulls her mother down
   on the ottoman; and they kiss one another frantically.)*
CATHERINE *(with surging enthusiasm)*.   You can't guess how
   splendid it is. A cavalry charge—think of that! He defied
   our Russian commanders—acted without orders—led a
   charge on his own responsibility—headed it himself—
   was the first man to sweep through their guns. Can't you
   see it, Raina; our gallant splendid Bulgarians with their
   swords and eyes flashing, thundering down like an ava-
   lanche and scattering the wretched Servian dandies like
   chaff. And you—you kept Sergius waiting a year before
   you would be betrothed to him. Oh, if you have a drop of
   Bulgarian blood in your veins, you will worship him
   when he comes back.

RAINA. What will he care for my poor little worship after the acclamations of a whole army of heroes? But no matter: I am so happy—so proud! *(She rises and walks about excitedly.)* It proves that all our ideas were real after all.

CATHERINE *(indignantly).* Our ideas real! What do you mean?

RAINA. Our ideas of what Sergius would do—our patriotism —our heroic ideals. Oh, what faithless little creatures girls are!—I sometimes used to doubt whether they were anything but dreams. When I buckled on Sergius's sword he looked so noble: it was treason to think of disillusion or humiliation or failure. And yet—and yet— *(Quickly.)* Promise me you'll never tell him.

CATHERINE. Don't ask me for promises until I know what I am promising.

RAINA. Well, it came into my head just as he was holding me in his arms and looking into my eyes, that perhaps we only had our heroic ideas because we are so fond of reading Byron and Pushkin, and because we were so delighted with the opera that season at Bucharest. Real life is so seldom like that—indeed never, as far as I knew it then. *(Remorsefully.)* Only think mother, I doubted him: I wondered whether all his heroic qualities and his soldiership might not prove mere imagination when he went into a real battle. I had an uneasy fear that he might cut a poor figure there beside all those clever Russian officers.

CATHERINE. A poor figure! Shame on you! The Servians have Austrian officers who are just as clever as our Russians; but we have beaten them in every battle for all that.

RAINA *(laughing and sitting down again).* Yes, I was only a prosaic little coward. Oh, to think that it was all true—that Sergius is just as splendid and noble as he looks—that the world is really a glorious world for women who can see its glory and men who can act its romance! What happiness! what unspeakable fulfilment! Ah!

(She throws herself on her knees beside her mother and flings her arms passionately round her. They are interrupted by the entry of LOUKA, *a handsome, proud girl in*

*a pretty Bulgarian peasant's dress with double apron, so
defiant that her servility to* RAINA *is almost insolent. She
is afraid of* CATHERINE, *but even with her goes as far as
she dares. She is just now excited like the others; but she
has no sympathy for* RAINA'S *raptures and looks contemptuously at the ecstasies of the two before she addresses them.)*

LOUKA. If you please, madam, all the windows are to be
closed and the shutters made fast. They say there may be
shooting in the streets. (RAINA *and* CATHERINE *rise together, alarmed.)* The Servians are being chased right
back through the pass; and they say they may run into the
town. Our cavalry will be after them; and our people will
be ready for them you may be sure, now that they are
running away. (*She goes out on the balcony and pulls the
outside shutters to; then steps back into the room.*)

RAINA. I wish our people were not so cruel. What glory is
there in killing wretched fugitives?

CATHERINE (*businesslike, her housekeeping instincts aroused*).
I must see that everything is made safe downstairs.

RAINA (*to* LOUKA). Leave the shutters so that I can just close
them if I hear any noise.

CATHERINE (*authoritatively, turning on her way to the door*).
Oh, no, dear, you must keep them fastened. You would be
sure to drop off to sleep and leave them open. Make them
fast, Louka.

LOUKA. Yes, madam. (*She fastens them.*)

RAINA. Don't be anxious about me. The moment I hear a
shot, I shall blow out the candles and roll myself up in
bed with my ears well covered.

CATHERINE. Quite the wisest thing you can do, my love.
Good night.

RAINA. Good night. (*They kiss one another, and* RAINA'S
emotions comes back for a moment.) Wish me joy of the
happiest night of my life—if only there are no fugitives.

CATHERINE. Go to bed, dear; and don't think of them. (*She
goes out.*)

LOUKA (*secretly, to* RAINA). If you would like the shutters open, just give them a push like this. *(She pushes them: they open: she pulls them to again.)* One of them ought to be bolted at the bottom; but the bolt's gone.

RAINA *(with dignity, reproving her).* Thanks, Louka; but we must do what we are told. *(LOUKA makes a grimace.)* Good night.

LOUKA *(carelessly).* Good night. *(She goes out, swaggering.)* *(RAINA, left alone, goes to the chest of drawers, and adores the portrait there with feelings that are beyond all expression. She does not kiss it or press it to her breast, or show it any mark of bodily affection; but she takes it in her hands and elevates it like a priestess.)*

RAINA *(looking up at the picture with worship).* Oh, I shall never be unworthy of you any more, my hero—never, never, never. *(She replaces it reverently, and selects a novel from the little pile of books. She turns over the leaves dreamily; find her page; turns the book inside out at it; and then, with a happy sigh, gets into bed and prepares to read herself to sleep. But before abandoning herself to fiction, she raises her eyes once more, thinking of the blessed reality and murmurs:)* My hero! my hero!

(A distant shot breaks the quiet of the night outside. She starts, listening; and two more shots, much nearer, follow, startling her so that she scrambles out of bed, and hastily blows out the candle on the chest of drawers. Then, putting her fingers in her ears, she runs to the dressing table and blows out the light there, and hurries back to bed. The room is now in darkness: nothing is visible but the glimmer of the light in the pierced ball before the image, and the starlight seen through the slits at the top of the shutters. The firing breaks out again: there is a startling fusillade quite close at hand. While it is still echoing, the shutters disappear, pulled open from without, and for an instant the rectangle of snowy starlight flashes out with the figure of a man in black upon it. The shutters close immediately and the room is dark again. But the silence

*is now broken by the sound of panting. Then there is a
scrape; and the flame of a match is seen in the middle of
the room.)*

RAINA *(crouching on the bed).* Who's there? *(The match is
out instantly.)* Who's there? Who is that?

A MAN'S VOICE *(in the darkness, subduedly, but threateningly).*
Sh—sh! Don't call out or you'll be shot. Be good; and no
harm will happen to you. *(She is heard leaving her bed,
and making for the door.)* Take care, there's no use in
trying to run away. Remember, if you raise your voice my
pistol will go off. *(Commandingly.)* Strike a light and let
me see you. Do you hear? *(Another moment of silence and
darkness. Then she is heard retreating to the dressing
table. She lights a candle, and the mystery is at an end.
A man of about 35, in a deplorable plight, bespattered
with mud and blood and snow, his belt and the strap of
his revolver case keeping together the torn ruins of the
blue coat of a Servian artillery officer. As far as the candlelight and his unwashed, unkempt condition make it possible to judge, he is a man of middling stature and undis-
tinguished appearance, with strong neck and shoulders,
a roundish, obstinate-looking head covered with short
crisp bronze curls, clear quick blue eyes and good brows
and mouth, a hopelessly prosaic nose like that of a strong-
minded baby, trim soldierlike carriage and energetic manner, and with all his wits about him in spite of his desperate predicament—even with a sense of humor of it, without, however, the least intention of trifling with it or
throwing away a chance. He reckons up what he can
guess about* RAINA—*her age, her social position, her
character, the extent to which she is frightened—at a
glance, and continues, more politely but still most determinedly:)* Excuse my disturbing you; but you recognize
my uniform—Servian. If I'm caught I shall be killed.
(Determinedly.) Do you understand that?

RAINA. Yes

MAN. Well, I don't intend to get killed if I can help it. *(Still* *more determinedly.)* Do you understand t h a t?* *(He locks the door with a snap.)*

RAINA *(disdainfully).* I suppose not. *(She draws herself up superbly, and looks him straight in the face, saying with emphasis:)* S o m e soldiers, I know, are a f r a i d of death.

MAN *(with grim goodhumor).* All of them, dear lady, all of them, believe me. It is our duty to live as long as we can, and kill as many of the enemy as we can. Now if you raise an alarm—

RAINA *(cutting him short).* You will shoot me. How do you know that I am afraid to die?

MAN *(cunningly).* Ah; but suppose I don't shoot you, what will happen then? Why, a lot of your cavalry—the greatest black-guards in your army—will burst into this pretty room of yours and slaughter me here like a pig; for I'll fight like a demon: they shan't get m e into the street to amuse themselves with: I know what they are. Are you prepared to receive that sort of company in your present undress? *(RAINA, suddenly conscious of her nightgown, instinctively shrinks and gathers it more closely about her. He watches her, and adds, pitilessly:)* It's rather scanty, eh? *(She turns to the ottoman. He raises his pistol instantly, and cries:)* Stop! *(She stops.)* Where are you going?

RAINA *(with dignified patience).* Only to get my cloak.

MAN *(darting to the ottoman and snatching the cloak)* A good idea. No: I'll keep the cloak: and you will take care that nobody comes in and sees you without it. This is a better weapon than the pistol. *(He throws the pistol down on the ottoman.)*

RAINA *(revolted)* It is not the weapon of a gentleman!

MAN. It's good enough for a man with only you to stand between him and death. *(As they look at one another for a moment, RAINA hardly able to believe that even a Servian officer can be so cynically and selfishly unchivalrous, they are startled by a sharp fusillade in the street. The chill of*

---

* All words which Shaw wanted to emphasize are printed with the letters spaced out in this manner.

imminent death hushes the man's voice as he adds:) Do
you hear? If you are going to bring those scoundrels in
on me you shall receive them as you are. (RAINA *meets his
eye with unflinching scorn. Suddenly he starts, listening.
There is a step outside. Someone tries the door, and then
knocks hurriedly and urgently at it.* RAINA *looks at the
man, breathless. He throws up his head with the gesture
of a man who sees that it is all over with him, and, dropping the manner which he has been assuming to intimidate her, flings the cloak to her, exclaiming, sincerely and
kindly:)* No use: I'm done for. Quick! wrap yourself up:
they're coming!

RAINA *(catching the cloak eagerly)*. Oh, thank you. *(She
wraps herself up with great relief. He draws his sabre and
turns to the door, waiting.)*

LOUKA *(outside, knocking)*. My lady, my lady! Get up, quick,
and open the door.

RAINA *(anxiously)*. What will you do?

MAN *(grimly)*. Never mind. Keep out of the way. It will not
last long.

RAINA *(impulsively)*. I'll help you. Hide yourself, oh, hide
yourself, quick, behind the curtain. *(She seizes him by a
torn strip of his sleeve, and pulls him towards the window.)*

MAN *(yielding to her)*. There is just half a chance, if you keep
your head. Remember: nine soldiers out of ten are born
fools. *(He hides behind the curtain, looking out for a
moment to say, finally:)* If they find me, I promise you a
fight—a devil of a fight!

(He disappears. RAINA *takes off the cloak and throws it
across the foot of the bed. Then with a sleepy, disturbed
air, she opens the door.* LOUKA *enters excitedly.)*

LOUKA. A man has been seen climbing up the water-pipe to
your balcony—a Servian. The soldiers want to search for
him; and they are so wild and drunk and furious. My lady
says you are to dress at once.

RAINA *(as if annoyed at being disturbed)*. They shall not
search here. Why have they been let in?

CATHERINE *(coming in hastily).* Raina, darling, are you safe? Have you seen anyone or heard anything?

RAINA. I heard the shooting. Surely the soldiers will not dare come in here?

CATHERINE. I have found a Russian officer, thank Heaven: he knows Sergius. *(Speaking through the door to someone outside.)* Sir, will you come in now! My daughter is ready.

(A young Russian Officer, in Bulgarian uniform, enters, sword in hand.)

THE OFFICER *(with soft, feline politeness and stiff military carriage).* Good evening, gracious lady; I am sorry to intrude, but there is a fugitive hiding on the balcony. Will you and the gracious lady your mother please to withdraw while we search?

RAINA *(petulantly).* Nonsense, sir, you can see that there is no one on the balcony.

(She throws the shutters wide open and stands with her back to the curtain where the man is hidden, pointing to the moonlit balcony. A couple of shots are fired right under the window, and a bullet shatters the glass opposite RAINA, who winks and gasps, but stands her ground, while CATHERINE screams, and the Officer rushes to the balcony.)

THE OFFICER *(on the balcony, shouting savagely down to the street).* Cease firing there, you fools: do you hear? Cease firing, damn you. *(He glares down for a moment; then turns to RAINA, trying to resume his polite manner.)* Could anyone have got in without your knowledge? Were you asleep?

RAINA. No, I have not been to bed.

THE OFFICER *(impatiently, coming back into the room).* Your neighbours have their heads so full of runaway Servians that they see them everywhere. *(Politely.)* Gracious lady, a thousand pardons. Good night.

(Military bow, which RAINA *returns coldly. Another to* CATHERINE, *who follows him out.* RAINA *closes the shutters. She turns and see* LOUKA, *who has been watching the scene curiously.)*

RAINA. Don't leave my mother, Louka, while the soldiers are here.

(LOUKA *glances at* RAINA, *at the ottoman, at the curtain; then purses her lips secretively, laughs to herself, and goes out.* RAINA *follows her to the door, shuts it behind her with a slam, and locks it violently. The man immediately steps from behind the curtain, sheathing his sabre, and dismissing the danger from his mind in a businesslike way.)*

MAN. A narrow shave; but a miss is as good as a mile. Dear young lady, your servant until death. I wish for your sake I had joined the Bulgarian army instead of the Servian. I am not a native Servian.

RAINA *(haughtily).* No, you are one of the Austrians who set the Servians on to rob us of our national liberty, and who officer their army for them. We hate them!

MAN. Austrian! not I. Don't hate me, dear young lady. I am only a Swiss, fighting merely as a professional soldier. I joined Servia because it was nearest to me. Be generous: you've beaten us hollow.

RAINA. Have I not been generous?

MAN. Noble!—heroic! But I'm not saved yet. This particular rush will soon pass through; but the pursuit will go on all night by fits and starts. I must take my chance to get off during a quiet interval. You don't mind my waiting just a minute or two, do you?

RAINA. Oh, no: I am sorry you will have to go into danger again. *(Motioning towards ottoman.)* Won't you sit—*(She breaks off with an irrepressible cry of alarm as she catches sight of the pistol. The man, all nerves, shies like a frightened horse.)*

MAN *(irritably).* Don't frighten me like that. What is it?

RAINA. Your pistol! It was staring that officer in the face all the time. What an escape!

MAN (*vexed at being unnecessarily terrified*). Oh, is that all?

RAINA (*staring at him rather superciliously, conceiving a poorer and poorer opinion of him, and feeling proportionately more and more at her ease with him*). I am sorry I frightened you. (*She takes up the pistol and hands it to him.*) Pray take it to protect yourself against me.

MAN (*grinning wearily at the sarcasm as he takes the pistol*). No use, dear young lady: there's nothing in it. It's not loaded. (*He makes a grimace at it, and drops it disparagingly into his revolver case.*)

RAINA. Load it by all means.

MAN. I've no ammunition. What use are cartridges in battle? I always carry chocolate instead; and I finished the last cake of that yesterday.

RAINA (*outraged in her most cherished ideals of manhood*). Chocolate! Do you stuff your pockets with s w e e t s — like a schoolboy — even in the field?

MAN. Yes. Isn't it contemptible?

(RAINA *stares at him, unable to utter her feelings. Then she sails away scornfully to the chest of drawers, and returns with the box of confectionery in her hand.*)

RAINA. Allow me. I am sorry I have eaten them all except these. (*She offers him the box.*)

MAN (*ravenously*). You're an angel! (*He gobbles the comfits.*) Creams! Delicious! (*He looks anxiously to see whether there are any more. There are none. He accepts the inevitable with pathetic goodhumor, and says, with grateful emotion:*) Bless you, dear lady. You can always tell an old soldier by the inside of his holsters and cartridge boxes. The young ones carry pistols and cartridges; the old ones, grub. Thank you. (*He hands back the box. She snatches it contemptuously from him and throws it away. This impatient action is so sudden that he shies again.*) Ugh! Don't do things so suddenly, gracious lady. Don't revenge yourself because I frightened you just now.

RAINA (*superbly*). Frighten m e! Do you know, sir, that
    though I am only a woman, I think I am at heart as brave
    as you.
MAN. I should think so. You haven't been under fire for three
    days as I have. I can stand two days without showing it
    much; but no man can stand three days: I'm as nervous
    as a mouse. (*He sits down on the ottoman, and takes his
    head in his hands.*) Would you like to see me cry?
RAINA (*quickly*). No.
MAN. If you would, all you have to do is to scold me just as if
    I were a little boy and you my nurse. If I were in camp
    now they'd play all sorts of tricks on me.
RAINA (*a little moved*).   I'm sorry. I won't scold you. (*Touched
    by the sympathy in her voice, he raises his head and looks
    gratefully at her: she immediately draws back and says
    stiffly:*) You must excuse me: o u r soldiers are not like
    that. (*She moves away from the ottoman.*)
MAN.   Oh, yes, they are. There are only two sorts of soldiers:
    old ones and young ones. I've served fourteen years: half
    of your fellows never smelt powder before. Why, how is it
    that you've just beaten us? Sheer ignorance of the art of
    war, nothing else. (*Indignantly.*) I never saw anything so
    unprofessional.
RAINA (*ironically*). Oh, was it unprofessional to beat you?
MAN. Well, come, is it professional to throw a regiment of
    cavalry on a battery of machine guns, with the dead cer-
    tainty that if the guns go off not a horse or man will ever
    get within fifty yards of the fire? I couldn't believe my
    eyes when I saw it.
RAINA (*eagerly turning to him, as all her enthusiasm and her
    dream of glory rush back on her*). Did you see the great
    cavalry charge? Oh, tell me about it. Describe it to me.
MAN. You never saw a cavalry charge, did you?
RAINA. How could I?
MAN. Ah, perhaps not—of course. Well, it's a funny sight. It's
    like slinging a handful of peas against a window pane:
    first one comes; then two or three close behind him; and
    then all the rest in a lump.
RAINA (*her eyes dilating as she raises her clasped hands ec-*

statically). Yes, first One!—the bravest of the brave!

MAN *(prosaically).* Hm! you should see the poor devil pulling at his horse.

RAINA. Why should he pull at his horse?

MAN *(impatient of so stupid a question).* It's running away with him, of course: do you suppose the fellow wants to get there before the others and be killed? Then they all come. You can tell the young ones by their wildness and their slashing. The old ones come bunched up under the number one guard: t h e y know that they are mere projectiles, and that it's no use trying to fight. The wounds are mostly broken knees, from the horses cannoning together.

RAINA. Ugh! But I don't believe the first man is a coward. I believe he is a hero!

MAN *(goodhumoredly).* That's what you'd have said if you'd seen the first man in the charge today.

RAINA *(breathless).* Ah, I knew it! Tell me—tell me about h i m.

MAN. He did it like an operatic tenor—a regular handsome fellow, with flashing eyes and lovely moustache, shouting a war-cry and charging like Don Quixote at the windmills. We nearly burst with laughter at him; but when the sergeant ran up as white as a sheet, and told us they'd sent us the wrong cartridges, and that we couldn't fire a shot for the next ten minutes, we laughed at the other side of our mouths. I never felt so sick in my life, though I've been in one or two very tight places. And I hadn't even a revolver cartridge—nothing but chocolate. We'd no bayonets—nothing. Of course, they just cut us to bits. And there was Don Quixote flourishing like a drum major, thinking he'd done the cleverest thing ever known, whereas he ought to be courtmartialled for it. Of all the fools ever let loose on a field of battle, that man must be the very maddest. He and his regiment simply committed suicide—only the pistol missed fire, that's all.

RAINA *(deeply wounded, but steadfastly loyal to her ideals).* Indeed! Would you know him again if you saw him?

MAN. Shall I ever forget him.

(She again goes to the chest of drawers. He watches her with a vague hope that she may have something else for him to eat. She takes the portrait from its stand and brings it to him.)

RAINA. That is a photograph of the gentleman—the patriot and hero—to whom I am betrothed.

MAN *(looking at it).* I'm really very sorry. *(Looking at her.)* Was it fair to lead me on? *(He looks at the portrait again.)* Yes: that's him: not a doubt of it. *(He stifles a laugh.)*

RAINA *(quickly).* Why do you laugh?

MAN *(shamefacedly, but still greatly tickled).* I didn't laugh, I assure you. At least I didn't mean to. But when I think of him charging the windmills and thinking he was doing the finest thing—*(chokes with suppressed laughter).*

RAINA *(sternly).* Give me back the portrait, sir.

MAN *(with sincere remorse).* Of course. Certainly. I'm really very sorry. *(She deliberately kisses it, and looks him straight in the face, before returning to the chest of drawers to replace it. He follows her, apologizing.)* Perhaps I'm quite wrong, you know: no doubt I am. Most likely he had got wind of the cartridge business somehow, and knew it was a safe job.

RAINA. That is to say, he was a pretender and a coward! You did not dare say that before.

MAN *(with a comic gesture of despair).* It's no use, dear lady: I can't make you see it from the professional point of view. *(As he turns away to get back to the ottoman, the firing begins again in the distance.)*

RAINA *(sternly, as she sees him listening to the shots).* So much the better for you.

MAN *(turning).* How?

RAINA. You are my enemy; and you are at my mercy. What would I do if I were a professional soldier?

MAN. Ah, true, dear young lady: you're always right. I know how good you have been to me: to my last hour I shall remember those three chocolate creams. It was unsoldierly; but it was angelic.

RAINA *(coldly).* Thank you. And now I will do a soldierly

thing. You cannot stay here after what you have just said about my future husband; but I will go out on the balcony and see whether it is safe for you to climb down into the street. *(She turns to the window.)*

MAN *(changing countenance).* Down that water pipe! Stop! Wait! I can't! I daren't! The very thought of it makes me giddy. I came up it fast enough with death behind me. But to face it now in cold blood!—*(He sinks on the ottoman.)* It's no use: I give up: I'm beaten. Give the alarm. *(He drops his head in his hands in the deepest dejection.)*

RAINA *(disarmed by pity).* Come, don't be disheartened. *(She stoops over him almost maternally: he shakes his head.)* Oh, you are a very poor soldier—a chocolate cream soldier. Come, cheer up: it takes less courage to climb down than to face capture—remember that.

MAN *(dreamily, lulled by her voice).* No, capture only means death; and death is sleep—oh, sleep, sleep, sleep, undisturbed sleep! Climbing down the pipe means doing something—exerting myself—thinking! Death ten times over first.

RAINA *(softly and wonderingly, catching the rhythm of his weariness).* Are you so sleepy as that?

MAN. I've not had two hours undisturbed sleep since the war began. I'm on the staff: you don't know what that means. I haven't closed my eyes for thirty-six hours.

RAINA *(desperately).* But what am I to do with you.

MAN *(staggering up).* Of course I must do something. *(He shakes himself; pulls himself together; and speaks with rallied vigour and courage.)* You see, sleep or no sleep, hunger or no hunger, tired or not tired, you can always do a thing when you know it must be done. Well, that pipe m u s t be got down—*(He hits himself on the chest, and adds:)*—Do you hear that, you chocolate cream soldier? *(He turns to the window.)*

RAINA *(anxiously).* But if you fall?

MAN. I shall sleep as if the stones were a feather bed. Goodbye. *(He makes boldly for the window, and his hand is on the shutter when there is a terrible burst of firing in the street beneath.)*

RAINA *(rushing to him).* Stop! *(She catches him by the shoulder, and turns him quite round.)* They'll kill you.

MAN *(coolly, but attentively).* Never mind: this sort of thing is all in my day's work. I'm bound to take my chance. *(Decisively.)* Now do what I tell you. Put out the candles, so that they shan't see the light when I open the shutters. And keep away from the window, whatever you do. If they see me, they're sure to have a shot at me.

RAINA *(clinging to him).* They're sure to see you: it's bright moonlight. I'll save you—oh, how can you be so indifferent? You want me to save you, don't you?

MAN. I really don't want to be troublesome. *(She shakes him in her impatience.)* I am not indifferent, dear young lady, I assure you. But how is it to be done?

RAINA. Come away from the window—please. *(She coaxes him back to the middle of the room. He submits humbly. She releases him, and addresses him patronizingly.)* Now listen. You must trust to our hospitality. You do not yet know in whose house you are. I am a Petkoff.

MAN. What's that?

RAINA *(rather indignantly).* I mean that I belong to the family of the Petkoffs, the richest and best known in our country.

MAN. Oh, yes, of course. I beg your pardon. The Petkoffs, to be sure. How stupid of me!

RAINA. You know you never heard of them until this minute. How can you stoop to pretend?

MAN. Forgive me: I'm too tired to think; and the change of subject was too much for me. Don't scold me.

RAINA. I forgot. It might make you cry. *(He nods, quite seriously. She pouts and then resumes her patronizing tone.)* I must tell you that my father holds the highest command of any Bulgarian in our army. He is *(proudly)* a Major.

MAN *(pretending to be deeply impressed).* A Major! Bless me! Think of that!

RAINA. You showed great ignorance in thinking that it was necessary to climb up to the balcony, because ours is the only private house that has two rows of windows. There is a flight of stairs inside to get up and down by.

MAN.   Stairs! How grand! You live in great luxury indeed, dear young lady.

RAINA.   Do you know what a library is?

MAN.   A library? A roomful of books.

RAINA.   Yes, we have one, the only one in Bulgaria.

MAN.   Actually a real library! I should like to see that.

RAINA *(affectedly)*.   I tell you these things to show you that you are not in the house of ignorant country folk who would kill you the moment they saw your Servian uniform, but among civilized people. We go to Bucharest every year for the opera season; and I have spent a whole month in Vienna.

MAN.   I saw that, dear young lady. I saw at once that you knew the world.

RAINA.   Have you ever seen the opera of Ernani?

MAN.   Is that the one with the devil in it in red velvet, and a soldier's chorus?

RAINA *(contemptuously)*.   No!

MAN *(stifling a heavy sigh of weariness)*.   Then I don't know it.

RAINA.   I thought you might have remembered the great scene where Ernani, flying from his foes just as you are tonight, takes refuge in the castle of his bitterest enemy, an old Castilian noble. The noble refuses to give him up. His guest is sacred to him.

MAN *(quickly waking up a little)*.   Have your people got that notion?

RAINA *(with dignity)*.   My mother and I can understand that notion, as you call it. And if instead of threatening me with your pistol as you did, you had simply thrown yourself as a fugitive on our hospitality, you would have been as safe as in your father's house.

MAN.   Quite sure?

RAINA *(turning her back on him in disgust)*.   Oh, it is useless to try and make y o u understand.

MAN.   Don't be angry: you see how awkward it would be for me if there was any mistake. My father is a very hospitable man: he keeps six hotels; but I couldn't trust him as far as that. What about y o u r father?

RAINA. He is away at Slivnitza fighting for his country. I answer for your safety. There is my hand in pledge of it. Will that reassure you? *(She offers him her hand.)*

MAN *(looking dubiously at his own hand).* Better not touch my hand, dear young lady. I must have a wash first.

RAINA *(touched).* That is very nice of you. I see that you are a gentleman.

MAN *(puzzled).* Eh?

RAINA. You must not think I am surprised. Bulgarians of really good standing—people in o u r position—wash their hands nearly every day. But I appreciate your delicacy. You may take my hand. *(She offers it again.)*

MAN *(kissing it with his hands behind his back).* Thanks, gracious young lady: I feel safe at last. And now would you mind breaking the news to your mother? I had better not stay here secretly longer than is necessary.

RAINA. If you will be so good as to keep perfectly still while I am away.

MAN. Certainly. *(He sits down on the ottoman.)*

(RAINA goes to the bed and wraps herself in the fur cloak. His eyes close. She goes to the door, but on turning for a last look at him, sees that he is dropping off to sleep.)

RAINA *(at the door).* You are not going asleep, are you? *(He murmurs inarticulately: she runs to him and shakes him.)* Do you hear? Wake up: you are falling asleep.

MAN. Eh! Falling aslee—? Oh, no, not the least in the world: I was only thinking. It's all right: I'm wide awake.

RAINA *(severely).* Will you please stand up while I am away. *(He rises reluctantly.)* All the time, mind.

MAN *(standing unsteadily).* Certainly—certainly: you may depend on me.

(RAINA looks doubtfully at him. He smiles foolishly. She goes reluctantly, turning again at the door and almost catching him in the act of yawning. She goes out.)

MAN *(drowsily).* Sleep, sleep, sleep, sleep, slee—*(The words trail off into a murmur. He wakes again with a shock on the point of falling.)* Where am I? That's what I want to know: where am I? Must keep awake. Nothing keeps me awake except danger—remember that—*(intently)* danger, danger, danger, dan— Where's danger? Must find it. *(He starts off vaguely around the room in search of it.)* What am I looking for? Sleep—danger—don't know. *(He stumbles against the bed.)* Ah, yes: now I know. All right now. I'm to go to bed, but not to sleep—be sure not to sleep— because of danger. Not to lie down, either, only sit down. *(He sits on the bed. A blissful expression comes into his face.)* Ah! *(With a happy sigh he sinks back at full length; lifts his boots into the bed with a final effort and falls fast asleep instantly.)*

(CATHERINE comes in, followed by RAINA.)

RAINA *(looking at the ottoman).*   He's gone! I left him here.

CATHERINE.   Here! Then he must have climbed down from the—

RAINA *(seeing him).*   Oh! *(She points.)*

CATHERINE *(scandalized).*   Well! *(She strides to the left side of the bed,* RAINA *following and standing opposite her on the right.)* He's fast asleep. The brute!

RAINA *(anxiously).*   Sh!

CATHERINE *(shaking him).*   Sir! *(Shaking him again, harder.)* Sir!! *(Vehemently shaking very hard.)* Sir!!!

RAINA *(catching her arm).*   Don't, mamma: the poor dear is worn out. Let him sleep.

CATHERINE *(letting him go and turning amazed to* RAINA*).* The poor dear! Raina!!!

(She looks sternly at her daughter. The man sleeps profoundly. Curtain.)

Act II

The sixth of March, 1886. In the garden of MAJOR PET-
KOFF'S *house. It is a fine spring morning; and the garden
looks fresh and pretty. Beyond the paling the tops of a
couple of minarets can be seen, showing that there is a
valley there, with the little town in it. A few miles further
the Balkan mountains rise and shut in the view. Within
the garden the side of the house is seen on the right, with
a garden door reached by a little flight of steps. On the
left the stable yard, with its gateway, encroaches on the
garden. There are fruit bushes along the paling and house,
covered with washing hung out to dry. A path runs by the
house, and rises by two steps at the corner where it turns
out of sight along the front. In the middle a small table,
with two bent wood chairs at it, is laid for breakfast with
Turkish coffeepot, cups, rolls, etc.; but the cups have been
used and the bread broken. There is a wooden garden seat
against the wall on the left.*

*LOUKA, smoking a cigaret, is standing between the
table and the house, turning her back with angry disdain
on a manservant who is lecturing her. He is a middle-aged
man of cool temperament and low but clear and keen
intelligence, with the complacency of the servant who
values himself on his rank in servility, and the imper-
turbability of the accurate calculator who has no illusions. He wears a white Bulgarian costume jacket with
decorated border, sash, wide knickerbockers, and decorated gaiters. His head is shaved up to the crown, giving
him a high Japanese forehead. His name is* NICOLA.

NICOLA.   Be warned in time, Louka; mend your manners.
   I know the mistress. She is so grand that she never dreams
   that any servant could dare to be disrespectful to her; but
   if she once suspects that you are defying her, out you go.
LOUKA.   I do defy her. I will defy her. What do I care for her?

NICOLA. If you quarrel with the family, I never can marry you. It's the same as if you quarrelled with me!

LOUKA. You take her part against me, do you?

NICOLA *(sedately)*. I shall always be dependent on the good will of the family. When I leave their service and start a shop in Sofia, their custom will be half my capital: their bad word would ruin me.

LOUKA. You have no spirit. I should like to see them dare say a word against me!

NICOLA *(pityingly)*. I should have expected more sense from you, Louka. But you're young, you're young!

LOUKA. Yes; and you like me the better for it, don't you? But I know some family secrets they wouldn't care to have told, young as I am. Let them quarrel with me if they dare!

NICOLA *(with compassionate superiority)*. Do you know what they would do if they heard you talk like that?

LOUKA. What could they do?

NICOLA. Discharge you for untruthfulness. Who would believe any stories you told after that? Who would give you another situation? Who in this house would dare be seen speaking to you ever again? How long would your father be left on his little farm? *(She impatiently throws away the end of her cigaret, and stamps on it.)* Child, you don't know the power such high people have over the likes of you and me when we try to rise out of our poverty against them. *(He goes close to her and lowers his voice.)* Look at me, ten years in their service. Do you think I know no secrets? I know things about the mistress that she wouldn't have the master know for a thousand levas. I know things about him that she wouldn't let him hear the last of for six months if I blabbed them to her. I know things about Raina that would break off her match with Sergius if—

LOUKA *(turning on him quickly)*. How do you know? I never told you!

NICOLA *(opening his eyes cunningly)*. So that's your little secret, is it? I thought it might be something like that. Well, you take my advice, and be respectful; and make the mistress feel that no matter what you know or don't know, they can depend on you to hold your tongue and serve

the family faithfully. That's what they like; and that's how
you'll make most out of them.

LOUKA *(with searching scorn)*.   You have the soul of a servant,
Nicola.

NICOLA *(complacently)*.   Yes: that's the secret of success in
service.

*(A loud knocking with a whip handle on a wooden door,
outside on the left, is heard.)*

MALE VOICE OUTSIDE.   Hollo! Hollo there! Nicola!

LOUKA.   Master! back from the war!

NICOLA *(quickly)*.   My word for it, Louka, the war's over. Off
with you and get some fresh coffee. *(He runs out into the
stable yard.)*

LOUKA *(as she puts the coffeepot and the cups upon the tray,
and carries it into the house)*.   You'll never put the soul
of a servant into me.

*(*MAJOR PETKOFF *comes from the stable yard, followed by*
NICOLA. *He is a cheerful, excitable, insignificant, un-
polished man of about 50, naturally unambitious except
as to his income and his importance in local society, but
just now greatly pleased with the military rank which the
war has thrust on him as a man of consequence in his
town. The fever of plucky patriotism which the Servian
attack roused in all the Bulgarians has pulled him
through the war; but he is obviously glad to be home
again.)*

PETKOFF *(pointing to the table with his whip)*.   Breakfast out
here, eh?

NICOLA.   Yes, sir. The mistress and Miss Raina have just gone
in.

PETKOFF *(sitting down and taking a roll)*.   Go in and say I've
come; and get me some fresh coffee.

NICOLA.   It's coming, sir. *(He goes to the house door.* LOUKA,
*with fresh coffee, a clean cup, and a brandy bottle on her
tray, meets him.)* Have you told the mistress?

LOUKA.   Yes: she's coming.

(NICOLA *goes into the house.* LOUKA *brings the coffee to the table.)*

PETKOFF.   Well, the Servians haven't run away with you, have they?

LOUKA.   No, sir.

PETKOFF.   That's right. Have you brought me some cognac?

LOUKA *(putting the bottle on the table).*   Here, sir.

PETKOFF.   T h a t ' s right. *(He pours some into his coffee.)*

(CATHERINE, *who has at this early hour made only a very perfunctory toilet, and wears a Bulgarian apron over a once brilliant but now half worn out red dressing gown, and a colored handkerchief tied over her thick black hair, with Turkish slippers on her bare feet, comes from the house, looking astonishingly handsome and stately under all the circumstances.* LOUKA *goes into the house.)*

CATHERINE.   My dear Paul, what a surprise for us. *(She stoops over the back of his chair to kiss him.)* Have they brought you fresh coffee?

PETKOFF.   Yes, Louka's been looking after me. The war's over. The treaty was signed three days ago at Bucharest; and the decree for our army to demobilize was issued yesterday.

CATHERINE *(springing erect, with flashing eyes).*   The war over! Paul: have you let the Austrians force you to make peace?

PETKOFF *(submissively).*   My dear: they didn't consult me. What could I do? *(She sits down and turns away from him.)* But of course we saw to it that the treaty was an honorable one. It declares peace —

CATHERINE *(outraged).*   Peace!

PETKOFF *(appeasing her).*   —but not friendly relations: remember that. They wanted to put that in; but I insisted on its being struck out. What more could I do?

CATHERINE.   You could have annexed Servia and made Prince Alexander Emperor of the Balkans. That's what I would have done.

PETKOFF.   I don't doubt it in the least, my dear. But I should have had to subdue the whole Austrian Empire first; and that would have kept me too long away from you. I missed you greatly.

CATHERINE *(relenting)*. Ah! *(Stretches her hand affectionately across the table to squeeze his.)*

PETKOFF. And how have you been, my dear?

CATHERINE. Oh, my usual sore throats, that's all.

PETKOFF *(with conviction)*. That comes from washing your neck every day. I've often told you so.

CATHERINE. Nonsense, Paul!

PETKOFF *(over his coffee and cigaret)*. I don't believe in going too far with these modern customs. All this washing can't be good for the health: it's not natural. There was an Englishman at Phillipopolis who used to wet himself all over with cold water every morning when he got up. Disgusting! It all comes from the English: their climate makes them so dirty that they have to be perpetually washing themselves. Look at my father: he never had a bath in his life; and he lived to be ninety-eight, the healthiest man in Bulgaria. I don't mind a good wash once a week to keep up my position; but once a day is carrying the thing to a ridiculous extreme.

CATHERINE. You are a barbarian at heart still, Paul. I hope you behaved yourself before all those Russian officers.

PETKOFF. I did my best. I took care to let them know that we had a library.

CATHERINE. Ah; but you didn't tell them that we have an electric bell in it? I have had one put up.

PETKOFF. What's an electric bell?

CATHERINE. You touch a button; something tinkles in the kitchen; and then Nicola comes up.

PETKOFF. Why not shout for him?

CATHERINE. Civilized people never shout for their servants. I've learnt that while you were away.

PETKOFF. Well, I'll tell you something I've learnt, too. Civilized people don't hang out their washing to dry where visitors can see it; so you'd better have all that *(indicating the clothes on the bushes)* put somewhere else.

CATHERINE. Oh, that's absurd, Paul: I don't believe really refined people notice such things.

(Someone is heard knocking at the stable gates.)

PETKOFF.   There's Sergius. *(Shouting.)* Hollo, Nicola!

CATHERINE.   Oh, don't shout, Paul: it really isn't nice.

PETKOFF.   Bosh! *(He shouts louder than before.)* Nicola!

NICOLA *(appearing at the house door)*.   Yes, sir.

PETKOFF.   If that is Major Saranoff, bring him round this way. *(He pronounces the name with the stress on the second syllable—Sarahnoff.)*

NICOLA.   Yes, sir. *(He goes into the stable yard.)*

PETKOFF.   You must talk to him, my dear, until Raina takes him off our hands. He bores my life out about our not promoting him—over m y head, mind you.

CATHERINE.   He certainly ought to be promoted when he marries Raina. Besides, the country should insist on having at least one native general.

PETKOFF.   Yes, so that he could throw away whole brigades instead of regiments. It's no use, my dear: he has not the slightest chance of promotion until we are quite sure that the peace will be a lasting one.

NICOLA *(at the gate, announcing)*.   Major Serguis Saranoff! *(He goes into the house and returns presently with a third chair, which he places at the table. He then withdraws.)*

(MAJOR SERGIUS SARANOFF, the original of the portrait in RAINA'S room, is a tall, romantically handsome man, with the physical hardihood, the high spirit, and the susceptible imagination of an untamed mountaineer chieftain. But his remarkable personal distinction is of a characteristically civilized type. The ridges of his eyebrows, curving with a ram's-horn twist round the marked projections at the outer corners, his jealously observant eye, his nose, thin, keen, and apprehensive in spite of the pugnacious high bridge and large nostril, his assertive chin, would not be out of place in a Paris salon. In short, the clever, imaginative barbarian has an acute critical faculty which has been thrown into intense activity by the arrival of western civilization in the Balkans; and the result is precisely what the advent of nineteenth-century thought

*first produced in England: to wit, Byronism. By his brood-
ing on the perpetual failure, not only of others, but of
himself, to live up to his imaginative ideals, his conse-
quent cynical scorn for humanity, the jejune credulity
as to the absolute validity of his ideals and the unworth-
iness of the world in disregarding them, his wincings and
mockeries under the sting of the petty disillusions which
every hour spent among men brings to his infallibly quick
observation, he has acquired the half tragic, half ironic
air, the mysterious moodiness, the suggestion of a strange
and terrible history that has left him nothing but undying
remorse, by which* Childe Harold[1] *fascinated the grandmothers of his Engdish contemporaries. Altogether it is
clear that here or nowhere is* RAINA'S *ideal hero.* CATH-
ERINE *is hardly less enthusiastic, and much less reserved
in showing her enthusiasm. As he enters from the stable
gate, she rises effusively to greet him.* PETKOFF *is dis-
tinctly less disposed to make a fuss about him.)*

PETKOFF. Here already, Sergius. Glad to see you!
CATHERINE. My dear Sergius! (*She holds out both her
hands.*)
SERGIUS (*kissing them with scrupulous gallantry*). My dear
mother, if I may call you so.
PETKOFF (*drily*). Mother-in-law, Sergius; mother-in-law! Sit
down, and have some coffee.
SERGIUS. Thank you, none for me. (*He gets away from the
table with a certain distaste for* PETKOFF'S *enjoyment of
it, and posts himself with conscious grace against the rail
of the steps leading to the house.*)
CATHERINE. You look superb—splendid. The campaign has
improved you. Everybody here is mad about you. We
were all wild with enthusiasm about that magnificent
cavalry charge.
SERGIUS (*with grave irony*). Madam: it was the cradle and
the grave of my military reputation.
CATHERINE. How so?

[1]*Childe Harold:* romantic hero of a poem by Byron

SERGIUS. I won the battle the wrong way when our worthy Russian generals were losing it the right way. That upset their plans, and wounded their self-esteem. Two of their colonels got their regiments driven back on the correct principles of scientific warfare. Two major-generals got killed strictly according to military etiquette. Those two colonels are now major-generals; and I am still a simple major.

CATHERINE. You shall not remain so, Sergius. The women are on your side; and they will see that justice is done you.

SERGIUS. It is too late. I have only waited for the peace to send in my resignation.

PETKOFF (*dropping his cup in his amazement*). Your resignation!

CATHERINE. Oh, you must withdraw it!

SERGIUS (*with resolute, measured emphasis, folding his arms*). I never withdraw!

PETKOFF (*vexed*). Now who could have supposed you were going to do such a thing?

SERGIUS (*with fire*). Everyone that knew me. But enough of myself and my affairs. How is Raina; and where is Raina?

RAINA (*suddenly coming round the corner of the house and standing at the top of the steps in the path*). Raina is here.

(*She makes a charming picture as they all turn to look at her. She wears an underdress of pale green silk, draped with an overdress of thin ecru canvas embroidered with gold. On her head she wears a pretty Phrygian cap of gold tinsel.* SERGIUS, *with an exclamation of pleasure, goes impulsively to meet her. She stretches out her hand: he drops chivalrously on one knee and kisses it.*)

PETKOFF (*aside to* CATHERINE, *beaming with parental pride*). Pretty, isn't it? She always appears at the right moment.

CATHERINE (*impatiently*). Yes: she listens for it. It is an abominable habit.

(SERGIUS *leads* RAINA *forward with splendid gallantry, as if she were a queen. When they come to the table, she turns to him with a bend of the head; he bows; and thus they separate, he coming to his place, and she going behind her father's chair.)*

RAINA *(stooping and kissing her father)*.   Dear father! Welcome home!

PETKOFF *(patting her cheek)*.   My little pet girl. *(He kisses her; she goes to the chair left by* NICOLA *for* SERGIUS, *and sits down.)*

CATHERINE.   And so you're no longer a soldier, Sergius.

SERGIUS.   I am no longer a soldier. Soldiering, my dear madam, is the coward's art of attacking mercilessly when you are strong, and keeping out of harm's way when you are weak. That is the whole secret of successful fighting. Get your enemy at a disadvantage; and never, on any account, fight him on equal terms. Eh, Major!

PETKOFF.   They wouldn't let us make a fair stand-up fight of it. However, I suppose soldiering has to be a trade like any other trade.

SERGIUS.   Precisely. But I have no ambition to succeed as a tradesman; so I have taken the advice of that bagman of a captain that settled the exchange of prisoners with us at Peerot, and given it up.

PETKOFF.   What, that Swiss fellow? Sergius: I've often thought of that exchange since. He overreached us about those horses.

SERGIUS.   Of course he overreached us. His father was a hotel and livery stable keeper; and he owed his first step to his knowledge of horse-dealing. *(With mock enthusiasm.)* Ah, he was a soldier—every inch a soldier! If only I had bought the horses for my regiment instead of foolishly leading it into danger, I should have been a field-marshal now!

CATHERINE.   A Swiss? What was he doing in the Servian army?

PETKOFF.   A volunteer of course—keen on picking up his profession. *(Chuckling)*. We shouldn't have been able to begin fighting if these foreigners hadn't shown us how to do it: we knew nothing about it; and neither did the Servians. Egad, there'd have been no war without them.

RAINA. Are there many Swiss officers in the Servian Army?

PETKOFF. No—all Austrians, just as our officers were all Russians. This was the only Swiss I came across. I'll never trust a Swiss again. He cheated us—humbugged us into giving him fifty able-bodied men for two hundred confounded worn-out chargers. They weren't even eatable!

SERGIUS. We were two children in the hands of that consummate soldier, Major: simply two innocent little children.

RAINA. What was he like?

CATHERINE. Oh, Raina, what a silly question!

SERGIUS. He was like a commercial traveller in uniform. Bourgeois to his boots.

PETKOFF (*grinning*). Sergius: tell Catherine that queer story his friend told us about him—how he escaped after Slivnitza. You remember?—about his being hid by two women.

SERGIUS (*with bitter irony*). Oh, yes, quite a romance. He was serving in the very battery I so unprofessionally charged. Being a thorough soldier, he ran away like the rest of them, with our cavalry at his heels. To escape their attentions, he had the good taste to take refuge in the chamber of some patriotic young Bulgarian lady. The young lady was enchanted by his persuasive commercial traveller's manners. She very modestly entertained him for an hour or so and then called in her mother lest her conduct should appear unmaidenly. The old lady was equally fascinated; and the fugitive was sent on his way in the morning, disguised in an old coat belonging to the master of the house, who was away at the war.

RAINA (*rising with marked stateliness*). Your life in the camp has made you coarse, Sergius. I did not think you would have repeated such a story before me. (*She turns away coldly.*)

CATHERINE (*also rising*). She is right, Sergius. If such women exist, we should be spared the knowledge of them.

PETKOFF. Pooh! nonsense! what does it matter?

SERGIUS (*ashamed*). No, Petkoff: I was wrong. (*To* RAINA, *with earnest humility.*) I beg your pardon. I have behaved abominably. Forgive me, Raina. (*She bows reservedly.*)

And you, too, madam. (CATHERINE *bows graciously and sits down. He proceeds solemnly, again addressing* RAINA.) The glimpses I have had of the seamy side of life during the last few months have made me cynical; but I should not have brought my cynicism here—least of all into your presence, Raina. I—(*Here, turning to the others, he is evidently about to begin a long speech when the* MAJOR *interrupts him.*)

PETKOFF.   Stuff and nonsense, Sergius. That's quite enough fuss about nothing: a soldier's daughter should be able to stand up without flinching to a little strong conversation. (*He rises.*) Come: it's time for us to get to business. We have to make up our minds how those three regiments are to get back to Phillipopolis:—there's no forage for them on the Sofia route. (*He goes towards the house.*) Come along. (SERGIUS *is about to follow him when* CATHERINE *rises and intervenes.*)

CATHERINE.   Oh, Paul, can't you spare Sergius for a few moments? Raina has hardly seen him yet. Perhaps I can help you to settle about the regiments.

SERGIUS (*protesting*).   My dear madam, impossible: you—

CATHERINE (*stopping him playfully*).   You stay here, my dear Sergius: there's no hurry. I have a word or two to say to Paul. (SERGIUS *instantly bows and steps back.*) Now, dear (*taking* PETKOFF'S *arm*), come and see the electric bell.

PETKOFF.   Oh, very well, very well.

(*They go into the house together affectionately.* SERGIUS, *left alone with* RAINA, *looks anxiously at her, fearing that she may be still offended. She smiles, and stretches out her arms to him.*)

SERGIUS (*hastening to her, but refraining from touching her without express permission*). Am I forgiven?

RAINA (*placing her hands on his shoulder as she looks up at him with admiration and worship.*)   My hero! My king!

SERGIUS.   My queen! (*He kisses her on the forehead with holy awe.*)

RAINA.   How I have envied you, Sergius! You have been out

in the world, on the field of battle, able to prove yourself
there worthy of any woman in the world; while I have had
to sit at home inactive—dreaming—useless—doing nothing that could give me the right to call myself worthy of
any man.

SERGIUS. Dearest, all my deeds have been yours. You in-
spired me. I have gone through the war like a knight in a
tournament with his lady looking on at him!

RAINA. And you have never been absent from my thoughts
for a moment. *(Very solemnly.)* Sergius: I think we two
have found the higher love. When I think of you, I feel
that I could never do a base deed, or think an ignoble
thought.

SERGIUS. My lady, and my saint! *(Clasping her reverently.)*

RAINA *(returning his embrace)*. My Lord and my g—

SERGIUS. Sh—sh! Let m e be the worshipper, dear. You little
know how unworthy even the best man is of a girl's pure
passion!

RAINA. I trust you. I love you. You will never disappoint me,
Sergius. *(LOUKA is heard singing within the house. They
quickly release each other.)* Hush! I can't pretend to talk
indifferently before her: my heart is too full. *(LOUKA
comes from the house with her tray. She goes to the table,
and begins to clear it, with her back turned to them.)* I
will go and get my hat; and then we can go out until lunch
time. Wouldn't you like that?

SERGIUS. Be quick. If you are away five minutes, it will seem
five hours. *(RAINA runs to the top of the steps and turns
there to exchange a look with him and wave him a kiss
with both hands. He looks after her with emotion for a
moment, then turns slowly away, his face radiant with
the exultation of the scene which has just passed. The
movement shifts his field of vision, into the corner of
which there now comes the tail of LOUKA'S double apron.
His eye gleams at once. He takes a stealthy look at her,
and begins to twirl his moustache nervously, with his left
hand akimbo on his hip. Finally, striking the ground with
his heels in something of a cavalry swagger, he strolls
over to the left of the table, opposite her, and says:)*
Louka: do you know what the higher love is?

LOUKA *(astonished)*. No, sir.

SERGIUS. Very fatiguing thing to keep up for any length of time, Louka. One feels the need of some relief after it.

LOUKA *(innocently)*. Perhaps you would like some coffee, sir? *(She stretches her hand across the table for the coffee-pot.)*

SERGIUS *(taking her hand)*. Thank you, Louka.

LOUKA *(pretending to pull)*. Oh, sir, you know I didn't mean that, I'm surprised at you!

SERGIUS *(coming clear of the table and drawing her with him)*. I am surprised at myself, Louka. What would Sergius, the hero of Slivnitza, say if he saw me now? What would Sergius, the apostle of the higher love, say if he saw me now? What would the half dozen Sergiuses who keep popping in and out of this handsome figure of mine say if they caught us here? *(Letting go her hand and slipping his arm dexterously round her waist.)* Do you consider my figure handsome, Louka?

LOUKA. Let me go, sir. I shall be disgraced. *(She struggles: he holds her inexorably.)* Oh, w i l l you let go?

SERGIUS *(looking straight into her eyes)*. No.

LOUKA. Then stand back where we can't be seen. Have you no common sense?

SERGIUS. Ah, that's reasonable. *(He takes her into the stable-yard gateway, where they are hidden from the house.)*

LOUKA *(complaining)*. I may have been seen from the window: Miss Raina is sure to be spying about after you.

SERGIUS *(stung—letting her go)*. Take care, Louka. I may be worthless enough to betray the higher love; but do not you insult it.

LOUKA *(demurely)*. Not for the world, sir, I'm sure. May I go on with my work please, now?

SERGIUS *(again putting his arm round her)*. You are a provoking little witch, Louka. If you were in love with me, would you spy out of windows on me?

LOUKA. Well, you see, sir, since you say you are half a dozen different gentlemen all at once, I should have a great deal to look after.

SERGIUS *(charmed)*. Witty as well as pretty. *(He tries to kiss her.)*

LOUKA (*avoiding him*).   No, I don't want your kisses. Gentlefolk are all alike—you making love to me behind Miss Raina's back, and she doing the same behind yours.

SERGIUS (*recoiling a step*).   Louka!

LOUKA.   It shows how little you really care!

SERGIUS (*dropping his familiarity and speaking with freezing politeness*).   If our conversation is to continue, Louka, you will please remember that a gentleman does not discuss the conduct of the lady he is engaged to with her maid.

LOUKA.   It's so hard to know what a gentleman considers right. I thought from your trying to kiss me that you had given up being so particular.

SERGIUS (*turning from her and striking his forehead as he comes back into the garden from the gateway*). Devil! devil!

LOUKA.   Ha! ha! I expect one of the six of you is very like me, sir, though I am only Miss Raina's maid. (*She goes back to her work at the table, taking no further notice of him.*)

SERGIUS (*speaking to himself*).   Which of the six is the real man?—that's the question that torments me. One of them is a hero, another a buffoon, another a humbug, another perhaps a bit of a blackguard. (*He pauses and looks furtively at* LOUKA, *as he adds with deep bitterness:*) And one, at least, is a coward—jealous, like all cowards. (*He goes to the table.*) Louka.

LOUKA.   Yes?

SERGIUS.   Who is my rival?

LOUKA.   You shall never get that out of me, for love or money.

SERGIUS.   Why?

LOUKA.   Never mind why. Besides, you would tell that I told you; and I should lose my place.

SERGIUS (*holding out his right hand in affirmation*).   No; on the honor of a—(*he checks himself, and his hand drops nerveless as he concludes, sardonically:*)—of a man capable of behaving as I have been behaving for the last five minutes. Who is he?

LOUKA.   I don't know. I never saw him. I only heard his voice through the door of her room.

SERGIUS.   Damnation! How dare you?

LOUKA *(retreating)*.   Oh, I mean no harm: you've no right to take up my words like that. The mistress knows all about it. And I tell you that if that gentleman ever comes here again, Miss Raina will marry him, whether he likes it or not. I know the difference between the sort of manner you and she put on before one another and the real manner. *(SERGIUS shivers as if she had stabbed him. Then, setting his face like iron, he strides grimly to her, and grips her above the elbows with both hands.)*

SERGIUS.   Now listen you to me!

LOUKA *(wincing)*.   Not so tight: you're hurting me!

SERGIUS.   That doesn't matter. You have stained my honor by making me a party to your eavesdropping. And you have betrayed your mistress—

LOUKA *(writhing)*.   Please—

SERGIUS.   That shows that you are an abominable little clod of common clay, with the soul of a servant. *(He lets her go as if she were an unclean thing, and turns away, dusting his hands of her, to the bench by the wall, where he sits down with averted head, meditating gloomily.)*

LOUKA *(whimpering angrily with her hands up her sleeves, feeling her bruised arms)*.   You know how to hurt with your tongue as well as with your hands. But I don't care, now I've found out that whatever clay I'm made of, you're made of the same. As for her, she's a liar; and her fine airs are a cheat; and I'm worth six of her.

(She shakes the pain off hardily; tosses her head; and sets to work to put the things on the tray. He looks doubtfully at her once or twice. She finishes packing the tray, and laps the cloth over the edges, so as to carry all out together. As she stoops to lift it, he rises.)

SERGIUS.   Louka! *(She stops and looks defiantly at him with the tray in her hands.)* A gentleman has no right to hurt a woman under any circumstances. *(With profound humility, uncovering his head.)* I beg your pardon.

LOUKA. That sort of apology may satisfy a lady. Of what use is it to a servant?

SERGIUS *(thus rudely crossed in his chivalry, throws it off with a bitter laugh and says slightingly).* Oh, you wish to be paid for the hurt? *(He puts on his shako,[2] and takes some money from his pocket.)*

LOUKA *(her eyes filling with tears in spite of herself).* No, I want my hurt made well.

SERGIUS *(sobered by her tone).* How? *(She rolls up her left sleeve; clasps her arm with the thumb and fingers of her right hand; and looks down at the bruise. Then she raises her head and looks straight at him. Finally, with a superb gesture she presents her arm to be kissed. Amazed, he looks at her; at the arm; at her again; hesitates; and then, with shuddering intensity, exclaims:)* Never! *(and gets away as far as possible from her.)*

(Her arm drops. Without a word, and with unaffected dignity, she takes her tray, and is approaching the house when RAINA *returns wearing a hat and jacket in the height of the Vienna fashion of the previous year, 1885.* LOUKA *makes way proudly for her, and then goes into the house.)*

RAINA. I'm ready! What's the matter? *(Gaily.)* Have you been flirting with Louka?

SERGIUS *(hastily).* No, no. How can you think such a thing?

RAINA *(ashamed of herself).* Forgive me, dear: it was only a jest. I am so happy today.

(He goes quickly to her, and kisses her hand remorsefully. CATHERINE *comes out and calls to them from the top of the steps.)*

CATHERINE *(coming down to them).* I am sorry to disturb you, children; but Paul is distracted over those three regiments. He does not know how to get them to Phillipopolis; and he objects to every suggestion of mine. You must go and help him, Sergius. He is in the library.

[2]*shako:* military dress hat

RAINA *(disappointed).*   But we are just going out for a walk.
SERGIUS.   I shall not be long. Wait for me just five minutes.
(He runs up the steps to the door.)
RAINA *(following him to the foot of the steps and looking up at him with timid coquetry).*   I shall go round and wait in full view of the library windows. Be sure you draw father's attention to me. If you are a moment longer than five minutes, I shall go in and fetch you, regiments or no regiments.
SERGIUS *(laughing).*   Very well.

(He goes in. RAINA watches him until he is out of her sight. Then, with a perceptible relaxation of manner, she begins to pace up and down about the garden in a brown study[3].)

CATHERINE.   Imagine their meeting that Swiss and hearing the whole story! The very first thing your father asked for was the old coat we sent him off in. A nice mess you have got us into!
RAINA *(gazing thoughtfully at the gravel as she walks).*   The little beast!
CATHERINE.   Little beast! What little beast?
RAINA.   To go and tell! Oh, if I had him here, I'd stuff him with chocolate creams till he couldn't ever speak again!
CATHERINE.   Don't talk nonsense. Tell me the truth, Raina. How long was he in your room before you came to me?
RAINA *(whisking round and recommencing her march in the opposite direction).*   Oh, I forget.
CATHERINE.   You cannot forget! Did he really climb up after the soldiers were gone, or was he there when that officer searched the room?
RAINA.   No, Yes, I think he must have been there then.
CATHERINE.   You t h i n k ! Oh, Raina, Raina! Will anything ever make you straightforward? If Sergius finds out, it is all over between you.
RAINA *(with cool impertinence).*   Oh, I know Sergius is your pet. I sometimes wish you could marry him instead of me. You would just suit him. You would pet him, and spoil him, and mother him to perfection.

[3]*in a brown study:* deeply absorbed in thought

CATHERINE (*opening her eyes very widely indeed*). Well, upon my word!

RAINA (*capriciously — half to herself*). I always feel a longing to do or say something dreadful to him — to shock his propriety — to scandalize the five senses out of him! (*To* CATHERINE, *perversely.*) I don't care whether he finds out about the chocolate cream soldier or not. I half hope he may. (*She again turns flippantly away and strolls up the path to the corner of the house.*)

CATHERINE. And what should I be able to say to your father, pray?

RAINA (*over her shoulder, from the top of the two steps*). Oh, poor father! As if h e could help himself! (*She turns the corner and passes out of sight.*)

CATHERINE (*looking after her, her fingers itching*). Oh, if you were only ten years younger! (LOUKA *comes from the house with a salver,*[4] *which she carries hanging down by her side.*) Well?

LOUKA. There's a gentleman just called, madam — a Servian officer —

CATHERINE (*flaming*). A Servian! How dare he — (*Checking herself bitterly.*) Oh, I forgot. We are at peace now. I suppose we shall have them calling every day to pay their compliments. Well, if he is an officer why don't you tell your master? He is in the library with Major Saranoff. Why do you come to me?

LOUKA. But he asks for you, madam. And I don't think he knows who you are: he said the lady of the house. He gave me this little ticket for you. (*She takes a card out of her bosom; puts it on the salver and offers it to* CATHERINE.)

CATHERINE (*reading*). "Captain Bluntschli!" That's a German name.

LOUKA. Swiss, madam, I think.

CATHERINE (*with a bound that makes* LOUKA *jump back*). Swiss! What is he like?

LOUKA (*timidly*). He has a big carpetbag, madam.

CATHERINE. Oh, Heavens, he's come to return the coat! Send him away — say we're not at home — ask him to leave his address and I'll write to him — Oh, stop: that will never

do Wait! (*She throws herself into a chair to think it out.*
LOUKA *waits.*) The master and Major Saranoff are busy in
the library, aren't they?

LOUKA. Yes, madam.

CATHERINE (*decisively*). Bring the gentleman out here at
once. (*Imperatively.*) And be very polite to him. Don't
delay. Here (*impatiently snatching the salver from her*):
leave that here; and go straight back to him.

LOUKA. Yes, madam. (*Going.*)

CATHERINE. Louka!

LOUKA (*stopping*). Yes, madam.

CATHERINE. Is the library door shut?

LOUKA. I think so, madam.

CATHERINE. If not, shut it as you pass through.

LOUKA. Yes, madam. (*Going.*)

CATHERINE. Stop! (LOUKA *stops.*) He will have to go out that
way (*indicating the gate of the stable yard*). Tell Nicola
to bring his bag here after him. Don't forget.

LOUKA (*surprised*). His bag?

CATHERINE. Yes, here as soon as possible. (*Vehemently.*) Be
quick. (LOUKA *runs into the house.* CATHERINE *snatches
her apron off and throws it behind a bush. She then takes
up the salver and uses it as a mirror, with the result that
the handkerchief tied round her head follows the apron.
A touch to her hair and a shake to her dressing gown
makes her presentable.*) Oh, how—how—how can a
man be such a fool! Such a moment to select! (LOUKA
appears at the door of the house, announcing "Captain
Bluntschli"; *and standing aside at the top of the steps
to let him pass before she goes in again. He is the man of
the adventure in* RAINA'S *room. He is now clean, well
brushed, smartly uniformed, and out of trouble, but still
unmistakably the same man. The moment* LOUKA'S *back
is turned,* CATHERINE *swoops on him with hurried, urgent, coaxing appeal.*) Captain Bluntschli, I am v e r y
glad to see you; but you must leave this house at once.
(*He raises his eyebrows.*) My husband has just returned,
with my future son-in-law; and they know nothing. If they
did, the consequences would be terrible. You are a for-

eigner: you do not feel our national animosities as we do. We still hate the Servians: the only effect of the peace on my husband is to make him feel like a lion baulked of his prey. If he discovered our secret, he would never forgive me; and my daughter's life would hardly be safe. Will you, like the chivalrous gentleman and soldier you are, leave at once before he finds you here?

BLUNTSCHLI (*disappointed, but philosophical*). At once, gracious lady. I only came to thank you and return the coat you lent me. If you will allow me to take it out of my bag and leave it with your servant as I pass out, I need detain you no further. (*He turns to go into the house.*)

CATHERINE (*catching him by the sleeve*). Oh, you must not think of going back that way. (*Coaxing him across to the stable gates.*) This is the shortest way out. Many thanks. So glad to have been of service to you. G o o dbye.

BLUNTSCHLI. But my bag?

CATHERINE. It will be sent on. You will leave me your address.

BLUNTSCHLI. True. Allow me. (*He takes out his card-case, and stops to write his address, keeping* CATHERINE *in an agony of impatience. As he hands her the card,* PETKOFF, *hatless, rushes from the house in a fluster of hospitality, followed by* SERGIUS.)

PETKOFF (*as he hurries down the steps*). My dear Captain Bluntschli—

CATHERINE. Oh Heavens! (*She sinks on the seat against the wall.*)

PETKOFF (*too preoccupied to notice her as he shakes* BLUN-TSCHLI'S *hand heartily*). Those stupid people of mine thought I was out here, instead of in the—haw!—library. (*He cannot mention the library without betraying how proud he is of it.*) I saw you through the window. I was wondering why you didn't come in. Saranoff is with me: you remember him, don't you?

SERGIUS (*saluting humorously, and then offering his hand with great charm of manner*). Welcome, our friend the enemy.

PETKOFF. No longer the enemy, happily. (*Rather anxiously.*) I hope you've come as a friend, and not on business.

CATHERINE. Oh, quite as a friend, Paul. I was just asking Captain Bluntschli to stay to lunch; but he declares he must go at once.

SERGIUS *(sardonically)*. Impossible, Bluntschli. We want you here badly. We have to send on three cavalry regiments to Phillipopolis; and we don't in the least know how to do it.

BLUNTSCHLI *(suddenly attentive and businesslike)*. Phillipopolis! The forage[5] is the trouble, eh?

PETKOFF *(eagerly)*. Yes, that's it. *(To* SERGIUS.) He sees the whole thing at once.

BLUNTSCHLI. I think I can show you how to manage that.

SERGIUS. Invaluable man! Come along! *(Towering over* BLUNTSCHLI, *he puts his hand on his shoulder and takes him to the steps,* PETKOFF *following. As* BLUNTSCHLI *puts his foot on the first step,* RAINA *comes out of the house.)*

RAINA *(completely losing her presence of mind)*. Oh, the chocolate cream soldier!

*(*BLUNTSCHLI *stands rigid.* SERGIUS, *amazed, looks at* RAINA, *then at* PETKOFF, *who looks back at him and then at his wife.)*

CATHERINE *(with commanding presence of mind)*. My dear Raina, don't you see that we have a guest here—Captain Bluntschli, one of our new Servian friends?

*(*RAINA *bows;* BLUNTSCHLI *bows.)*

RAINA. How silly of me! *(She comes down into the center of the group, between* BLUNTSCHLI *and* PETKOFF.) I made a beautiful ornament this morning for the ice pudding; and that stupid Nicola has just put down a pile of plates on it and spoiled it. *(To* BLUNTSCHLI, *winningly.)* I hope you didn't think that y o u were the chocolate cream soldier, Captain Bluntschli.

BLUNTSCHLI *(laughing)*. I assure you I did. *(Stealing a whimsical glance at her.)* Your explanation was a relief.

[5]*forage:* a search for food or provisions

PETKOFF *(suspiciously, to* RAINA*).* And since when, pray, have y o u taken to cooking?

CATHERINE. Oh, while you were away. It is her latest fancy.

PETKOFF *(testily).* And has Nicola taken to drinking? He used to be careful enough. First he shows Captain Bluntschli out here when he knew quite well I was in the—hum!—library; and then he goes downstairs and breaks Raina's chocolate soldier. He must— *(At this moment* NICOLA *appears at the top of the steps right with a carpetbag. He descends; places it respectfully before* BLUNTSCHLI; *and waits for further orders. General amazement.* NICOLA, *unconscious of the effect he is producing, looks perfectly satisfied with himself. When* PETKOFF *recovers his power of speech, he breaks out at him with:)* Are you mad, Nicola?

NICOLA *(taken aback).* Sir?

PETKOFF. What have you brought that for?

NICOLA. My lady's orders, sir. Louka told me that—

CATHERINE *(interrupting him).* M y orders! Why should I order you to bring Captain Bluntschli's luggage out here? What are you thinking of, Nicola?

NICOLA *(after a moment's bewilderment, picking up the bag as he addresses* BLUNTSCHLI *with the very perfection of servile discretion).* I beg your pardon, sir, I am sure. *(To* CATHERINE.*)* My fault, madam! I hope you'll overlook it! *(He bows, and is going to the steps with the bag, when* PETKOFF *addresses him angrily.)*

PETKOFF. You'd better go and slam that bag, too, down on Miss Raina's ice pudding! *(This is too much for* NICOLA. *The bag drops from his hands on* PETKOFF'S *corns, eliciting a roar of anguish from him.)* Begone you butterfingered donkey.

NICOLA *(snatching up the bag, and escaping into the house).* Yes, sir.

CATHERINE. Oh, never mind, Paul, don't be angry!

PETKOFF *(muttering).* Scoundrel. He's got out of hand while I was away. I'll teach him. *(Recollecting his guest.)* Oh, well, never mind. Come, Bluntschli, let's have no more nonsense about your having to go away. You know very

well you're not going back to Switzerland yet. Until you
do go back you'll stay with us.

RAINA.   Oh, do, Captain Bluntschli.

PETKOFF *(to* CATHERINE*)*.   Now, Catherine, it's of you that
he's afraid. Press him and he'll stay.

CATHERINE.   Of course I shall be only too delighted if *(ap-
pealing)* Captain Bluntschli really wishes to stay. He
knows my wishes.

BLUNTSCHLI *(in his driest military manner)*.   I am at madame's orders.

SERGIUS *(cordially)*.   That settles it!

PETKOFF *(heartily)*.   Of course!

RAINA.   You see, you m u s t stay!

BLUNTSCHLI *(smiling)*.   Well, if I must, I must!

(Gesture of despair from CATHERINE. *Curtain.)*

Act III

*In the library after lunch. It is not much of a library, its
literary equipment consisting of a single fixed shelf
stocked with old paper-covered novels, broken-backed,
coffee-stained, torn and thumbed, and a couple of little
shelves with a few gift books on them, the rest of the wall
space being occupied by trophies of war and the chase.
But it is a most comfortable sitting room. A row of three
large windows in the front of the house show a mountain
panorama, which is just now seen in one of its softest
aspects in the mellowing afternoon light. In the left-hand
corner, a square earthenware stove, a perfect tower of
colored pottery, rises nearly to the ceiling and guarantees
plenty of warmth. The ottoman in the middle is a circular
bank of decorated cushions, and the window seats are
well-upholstered divans. Little Turkish tables, one of
them with an elaborate hookah¹ on it, and a screen to*

---

¹*hookah:* an Oriental pipe having a long flexible tube that is drawn through
a vase filled with water for cooling the smoke

match them, complete the handsome effect of the furnishing. There is one object, however, which is hopelessly out of keeping with its surroundings. This is a small kitchen table, much the worse for wear, fitted as a writing table with an old canister full of pens, an eggcup filled with ink, and a deplorable scrap of severely used pink blotting paper.

At the side of this table, which stands on the right, BLUNTSCHLI *is hard at work, with a couple of maps before him, writing orders. At the head of it sits* SERGIUS, *who is also supposed to be at work, but who is actually gnawing the feather of a pen, and contemplating* BLUNTSCHLI'S *quick, sure, businesslike progress with a mixture of envious irritation at his own incapacity, and awestuck wonder at an ability which seems to him almost miraculous, though its prosaic character forbids him to esteem it. The* MAJOR *is comfortably established on the ottoman, with a newspaper in his hand and the tube of the hookah within his reach.* CATHERINE *sits at the stove, with her back to them, embroidering.* RAINA, *reclining on the divan under the left-hand window, is gazing in a daydream out at the Balkan landscape, with a neglected novel in her lap.*

The door is on the left. The buttom of the electric bell is between the door and the fireplace.

PETKOFF (*looking up from his paper to watch how they are getting on at the table*). Are you sure I can't help you in any way, Bluntschli?

BLUNTSCHLI (*without interrupting his writing or looking up*). Quite sure, thank you. Saranoff and I will manage it.

SERGIUS (*grimly*). Yes: we'll manage it. He finds out what to do; draws up the orders; and I sign 'em. Division of labor, Major. (BLUNTSCHLI *passes him a paper.*) Another one? Thank you. (*He plants the papers squarely before him; sets his chair carefully parallel to them; and signs with the air of a man resolutely performing a difficult and dangerous feat.*) This hand is more accustomed to the sword than to the pen.

PETKOFF. It's very good of you, Bluntschli, it is indeed, to let yourself be put upon in this way. Now are you q u i t e sure I can do nothing?

CATHERINE (*in a low, warning tone*). You can stop interrupting, Paul.

PETKOFF (*starting and looking round at her*). Eh! Oh! Quite right, my love, quite right. (*He takes his newspaper up, but lets it drop again.*) Ah, you haven't been campaigning, Catherine: you don't know how pleasant it is for us to sit here, after a good lunch, with nothing to do but enjoy ourselves. There's only one thing I want to make me thoroughly comfortable.

CATHERINE. What is that?

PETKOFF. My old coat. I'm not at home in this one: I feel as if I were on parade.

CATHERINE. My dear Paul, how absurd you are about that old coat! It must be hanging in the blue closet where you left it.

PETKOFF. My dear Catherine, I tell you I've looked there. Am I to believe my own eyes or not? (CATHERINE *quietly rises and presses the button of the electric bell by the fireplace.*) What are you showing off that bell for? (*She looks at him majestically, and silently resumes her chair and her needlework.*) My dear: if you think the obstinacy of your sex can make a coat out of two old dressing gowns of Raina's, your waterproof, and my mackintosh, you're mistaken. That's exactly what the blue closet contains at present.

(NICOLA *presents himself.*)

CATHERINE (*unmoved by* PETKOFF'S *sally*). Nicola: go to the blue closet and bring your master's old coat here—the braided one he usually wears in the house.

NICOLA. Yes, madam. (*Nicola goes out.*)

PETKOFF. Catherine.

CATHERINE. Yes, Paul?

PETKOFF. I bet you any piece of jewellery you like to order from Sofia against a week's housekeeping money, that the coat isn't there.

CATHERINE. Done, Paul.

PETKOFF *(excited by the prospect of a gamble).* Come: here's an opportunity for some sport. Who'll bet on it? Bluntschli: I'll give you six to one.

BLUNTSCHLI *(imperturbably).* It would be robbing you, Major. Madame is sure to be right. *(Without looking up, he passes another batch of papers to* SERGIUS.*)*

SERGIUS *(also excited).* Bravo, Switzerland! Major: I bet my best charger against an Arab mare for Raina that Nicola finds the coat in the blue closet.

PETKOFF *(eagerly).* Your best char—

CATHERINE *(hastily interrupting him).* Don't be foolish, Paul. An Arabian mare will cost you 50,000 levas.[2]

RAINA *(suddenly coming out of her picturesque reverie).* Really, mother, if you are going to take the jewellery, I don't see why you should grudge me my Arab.

(Nicola comes back with the coat and brings it to PETKOFF, *who can hardly believe his eyes.)*

CATHERINE. Where was it, Nicola?

NICOLA. Hanging in the blue closet, madam.

PETKOFF. Well, I am d—

CATHERINE *(stopping him).* Paul!

PETKOFF. I could have sworn it wasn't there. Age is beginning to tell on me. I'm getting hallucinations. *(To* NICOLA.*)* Here: help me to change. Excuse me, Bluntschli. *(He begins changing coats,* NICOLA *acting as valet.)* Remember: I didn't take that bet of yours, Sergius. You'd better give Raina that Arab steed yourself, since you've roused her expectations. Eh, Raina? *(He looks round at her; but she is again rapt in the landscape. With a little gush of paternal affection and pride, he points her out to them and says:)* She's dreaming, as usual.

SERGIUS. Assuredly she shall not be the loser.

PETKOFF. So much the better for her. I shan't come off so

---

[2]*50,000 levas:* about 15,000 dollars

cheap, I expect. (*The change is now complete.* NICOLA *goes out with the discarded coat.*) Ah, now I feel at home at last. (*He sits down and takes his newspaper with a grunt of relief.*)

BLUNTSCHLI (*to* SERGIUS, *handing a paper*). That's the last order.

PETKOFF (*jumping up*). What! finished?

BLUNTSCHLI. Finished.

PETKOFF (*goes beside* SERGIUS; *looks curiously over his left shoulder as he signs; and says with childlike envy*). Haven't you anything for m e to sign?

BLUNTSCHLI. Not necessary. His signature will do.

PETKOFF. Ah, well, I think we've done a thundering good day's work. (*He goes away from the table.*) Can I do anything more?

BLUNTSCHLI. You had better both see the fellows that are to take these. (*To* SERGIUS.) Pack them off at once; and show them that I've marked on the orders the time they should hand them in by. Tell them that if they stop to drink or tell stories—if they're five minutes late, they'll have the skin taken off their backs.

SERGIUS (*rising indignantly*). I'll say so. And if one of them is man enough to spit in my face for insulting him, I'll buy his discharge and give him a pension. (*He strides out, his humanity deeply outraged.*)

BLUNTSCHLI (*confidentially*). Just see that he talks to them properly, Major, will you?

PETKOFF (*officiously*). Quite right, Bluntschli, quite right. I'll see to it. (*He gets to the door importantly, but hesitates on the threshold.*) By the bye, Catherine, you may as well come, too. They'll be far more frightened of you than of me.

CATHERINE (*putting down her embroidery*). I daresay I had better. You will only splutter at them. (*She goes out,* PETKOFF *holding the door for her and following her.*)

BLUNTSCHLI. What a country! They make cannons out of cherry trees; and the officers send for their wives to keep discipline!

(He begins to fold and docket[3] the papers. RAINA, *who has risen from the divan, strolls down the room with her hands clasped behind her, and looks mischievously at him.)*

RAINA. You look ever so much nicer than when we last met. *(He looks up, surprised.)* What have you done to yourself?

BLUNTSCHLI. Washed; brushed; good night's sleep and breakfast. That's all.

RAINA. Did you get back safely that morning?

BLUNTSCHLI. Quite, thanks.

RAINA. Were they angry with you for running away from Sergius's charge?

BLUNTSCHLI. No, they were glad; because they'd all just run away themselves.

RAINA *(going to the table, and leaning over it towards him).* It must have made a lovely story for them — all that about me and my room.

BLUNTSCHLI. Capital story. But I only told it to one of them — a particular friend.

RAINA. On whose discretion you could absolutely rely?

BLUNTSCHLI. Absolutely.

RAINA. Hm! He told it all to my father and Sergius the day you exchanged prisoners. *(She turns away and strolls carelessly across to the other side of the room.)*

BLUNTSCHLI *(deeply concerned and half incredulous).* No! you don't mean that, do you?

RAINA *(turning, with sudden earnestness).* I do indeed. But they don't know that it was in this house that you hid. If Sergius knew, he would challenge you and kill you in a duel.

BLUNTSCHLI. Bless me! then don't tell him.

RAINA *(full of reproach for his levity).* Can you realize what it is to me to deceive him? I want to be quite perfect with Sergius — no meanness, no smallness, no deceit. My relation to him is the one really beautiful and noble part of my life. I hope you can understand that.

[3]*docket:* label the outer cover of a document with an identification of its contents

BLUNTSCHLI *(sceptically).*   You mean that you wouldn't like him to find out that the story about the ice pudding was a—a—a—You know.

RAINA *(wincing).*   Ah, don't talk of it in that flippant way. I lied: I know it. But I did it to save your life. He would have killed you. That was the second time I ever uttered a falsehood. *(BLUNTSCHLI rises quickly and looks doubtfully and somewhat severely at her.)* Do you remember the first time?

BLUNTSCHLI.   I! No. Was I present?

RAINA.   Yes; and I told the officer who was searching for you that you were not present.

BLUNTSCHLI.   True. I should have remembered it.

RAINA *(greatly encouraged).*   Ah, it is natural that y o u should forget it first. It cost you nothing: it cost me a lie!—a lie!!

(She sits down on the ottoman, looking straight before her with her hands clasped on her knee. BLUNTSCHLI, quite touched, goes to the ottoman with a particularly reassuring and considerate air, and sits down beside her.)

BLUNTSCHLI.   My dear young lady, don't let this worry you. Remember: I'm a soldier. Now what are the two things that happen to a soldier so often that he comes to think nothing of them? One is hearing people tell lies *(RAINA recoils):* the other is getting his life saved in all sorts of ways by all sorts of people.

RAINA *(rising in indignant protest).*   And so he becomes a creature incapable of faith and of gratitude.

BLUNTSCHLI *(making a wry face).*   Do you like gratitude? I don't. If pity is akin to love, gratitude is akin to the other thing.

RAINA.   Gratitude! *(Turning on him.)* If you are incapable of gratitude you are incapable of any noble sentiment. Even animals are grateful. Oh, I see now exactly what you think of me! You were not surprised to hear me lie. To you it was something I probably did every day—every hour. That is how men think of women. *(She walks up the room melodramatically.)*

BLUNTSCHLI (*dubiously*).   There's reason in everything. You
said you'd told only two lies in your whole life. Dear
young lady: isn't that rather a short allowance? I'm quite
a straightforward man myself; but it wouldn't last me a
whole morning.

RAINA (*staring haughtily at him*).   Do you know, sir, that you
are insulting me?

BLUNTSCHLI.   I can't help it. When you get into that noble
attitude and speak in that thrilling[4] voice, I admire you;
but I find it impossible to believe a single word you say.

RAINA (*superbly*).   Captain Bluntschli!

BLUNTSCHLI (*unmoved*).   Yes?

RAINA (*coming a little toward him, as if she could not believe
her senses*).   Do you mean what you said just now? Do
you k n o w what you said just now?

BLUNTSCHLI.   I do.

RAINA (*gasping*).   I! I!!! (*She points to herself incredulously,
meaning "I, Raina Petkoff, tell lies!" He meets her gaze
unflinchingly. She suddenly sits down beside him, and
adds, with a complete change of manner from the heroic
to the familiar:*) How did you find me out?

BLUNTSCHLI (*promptly*).   Instinct, dear young lady. Instinct,
and experience of the world.

RAINA (*wonderingly*).   Do you know, you are the first man I
ever met who did not take me seriously?

BLUNTSCHLI.   You mean, don't you, that I am the first man
that has ever taken you quite seriously?

RAINA.   Yes, I suppose I d o mean that. (*Cosily, quite at her
ease with him.*) How strange it is to be talked to in such a
way! You know, I've always gone on like that—I mean the
noble attitude and the thrilling voice. I did it when I was
a tiny child to my nurse. S h e believed in it. I do it before
my parents. T h e y believe in it. I do it before Sergius. H e
believes in it.

BLUNTSCHLI.   Yes: he's a little in that line himself, isn't he?

RAINA.   I wonder—I w o n d e r is he? If I thought that—!

[4]*thrilling:* trembling

(*Discouraged.*) Ah, well, what does it matter? I suppose, now that you've found me out, you despise me.

BLUNTSCHLI (*warmly, rising*). No, my dear young lady, no, no, no a thousand times. It's part of your youth—part of your charm. I'm like all the rest of them—the nurse—your parents—Sergius: I'm your infatuated admirer.

RAINA (*pleased*). Really?

BLUNTSCHLI (*slapping his breast smartly with his hand, German fashion*). Hand aufs Herz![5] Really and truly.

RAINA (*very happy*). But what did you think of me for giving you my portrait?

BLUNTSCHLI (*astonished*). Your portrait! You never gave me your portrait.

RAINA (*quickly*). Do you mean to say you never got it?

BLUNTSCHLI. No. (*He sits down beside her, with renewed interest, and says, with some complacency.*) When did you send it to me?

RAINA (*indignantly*). I did not send it to you. (*She turns her head away, and adds, reluctantly.*) It was in the pocket of that coat.

BLUNTSCHLI (*pursing his lips and rounding his eyes*). Oh-o-oh! I never found it. It must be there still.

RAINA (*springing up*). There still!—for my father to find the first time he puts his hand in his pocket! Oh, how could you be so stupid?

BLUNTSCHLI (*rising also.*) It doesn't matter: it's only a photograph: how can he tell who it was intended for? Tell him he put it there himself.

RAINA (*impatiently*). Yes, that is so clever—s o clever! What shall I do?

BLUNTSCHLI. Ah, I see. You wrote something on it. That was rash!

RAINA (*annoyed almost to tears*). Oh, to have done such a thing for y o u, who care no more—except to laugh at me—oh! Are you sure nobody has touched it?

BLUNTSCHLI. Well, I can't be quite sure. You see I couldn't

---

[5]*Hand aufs Herz!* Cross my heart!

carry it about with me all the time: one can't take much luggage on active service.

RAINA. What did you do with it?

BLUNTSCHLI. When I got through to Peerot I had to put it in safekeeping somehow. I thought of the railway cloak room; but that's the surest place to get looted in modern warfare. So I pawned it.

RAINA. P a w n e d it!!!

BLUNTSCHLI. I know it doesn't sound nice; but it was much the safest plan. I redeemed it the day before yesterday. Heaven only knows whether the pawnbroker cleared out the pockets or not.

RAINA (*furious — throwing the words right into his face*). You have a low, shopkeeping mind. You think of things that would never come into a gentleman's head.

BLUNTSCHLI (*phlegmatically*).[6] That's the Swiss national character, dear lady.

RAINA. Oh, I wish I had never met you. (*She flounces away and sits at the window fuming.*)

(LOUKA *comes in with a heap of letters and telegrams on her salver, and crosses, with her bold, free gait, to the table. Her left sleeve is looped up to the shoulder with a brooch, showing her naked arm, with a broad gilt bracelet covering the bruise.*)

LOUKA (*to* BLUNTSCHLI). For you. (*She empties the salver recklessly on the table.*) The messenger is waiting. (*She is determined not to be civil to a Servian, even if she must bring him his letters.*)

BLUNTSCHLI (*to* RAINA). Will you excuse me: the last postal delivery that reached me was three weeks ago. These are the subsequent accumulations. Four telegrams — a week old. (*He opens one.*) Oho! Bad news!

RAINA (*rising and advancing a little remorsefully*). Bad news?

BLUNTSCHLI. My father's dead. (*He looks at the telegram with his lips pursed, musing on the unexpected change in his arrangements.*)

[6]*phlegmatically:* calmly

RAINA.　Oh, how very sad!

BLUNTSCHLI.　Yes: I shall have to start for home in an hour. He has left a lot of big hotels behind him to be looked after. (*Takes up a heavy letter in a long blue envelope.*) Here's a whacking letter from the family solicitor. (*He pulls out the enclosures and glances over them.*) Great Heavens! Seventy! Two hundred! (*In a crescendo of dismay.*) Four hundred! Four t h o u s a n d ! ! Nine thousand six hundred!!! What on earth shall I do with them all?

RAINA (*timidly*).　Nine thousand hotels?

BLUNTSCHLI.　Hotels! Nonsense. If you only knew!—oh, it's too ridiculous! Excuse me: I must give my fellow orders about starting. (*He leaves the room hastily, with the document in his hand.*)

LOUKA (*tauntingly*).　He has not much heart, that Swiss, though he is so fond of the Servians. He has not a word of grief for his poor father.

RAINA (*bitterly*).　Grief!—a man who has been doing nothing but killing people for years! What does he care? What does any soldier care? (*She goes to the door, evidently restraining her tears with difficulty.*)

LOUKA.　Major Saranoff has been fighting, too; and he has plenty of heart left. (RAINA, *at the door, looks haughtily at her and goes out.*) Aha! I thought you wouldn't get much feeling out of y o u r soldier. (*She is following* RAINA *when* NICOLA *enters with an armful of logs for the fire.*)

NICOLA (*grinning amorously at her*).　I've been trying all the afternoon to get a minute alone with you, my girl. (*His countenance changes as he notices her arm.*) Why, what fashion is that of wearing your sleeve, child?

LOUKA (*proudly*).　My own fashion.

NICOLA.　Indeed! If the mistress catches you, she'll talk to you.

(*He throws the logs down on the ottoman, and sits comfortably beside them.*)

LOUKA.　Is that any reason why y o u should take it on yourself to talk to me?

NICOLA.　Come: don't be so contrary with me. I've some good

news for you. *(He takes out some paper money.* LOUKA, *with an eager gleam in her eyes, comes close to look at it.)* See, a twenty leva bill![7] Sergius gave me that out of pure swagger. A fool and his money are soon parted. There's ten levas more. The Swiss gave me that for backing up the mistress's and Raina's lies about him. He's no fool, he isn't. You should have heard old Catherine downstairs as polite as you please to me, telling me not to mind the Major being a little impatient; for they knew what a good servant I was—after making a fool and a liar of me before them all! The twenty will go to our savings; and you shall have the ten to spend if you'll only talk to me so as to remind me I'm a human being. I get tired of being a servant occasionally.

LOUKA *(scornfully).* Yes: sell your manhood for thirty levas, and buy me for ten! Keep your money. You were born to be a servant. I was not. When you set up your shop you will only be everybody's servant instead of somebody's servant.

NICOLA *(picking up his logs, and going to the stove).* Ah, wait till you see. We shall have our evenings to ourselves; and I shall be master in my own house, I promise you. *(He throws the logs down and kneels at the stove.)*

LOUKA. You shall never be master in mine. *(She sits down on* SERGIUS'S *chair.)*

NICOLA *(turning, still on his knees, and squatting down rather forlornly, on his calves, daunted by her impacable disdain).* You have a great ambition in you, Louka. Remember: if any luck comes to you, it was I that made a woman of you.

LOUKA. You!

NICOLA *(with dogged self-assertion).* Yes, me. Who was it made you give up wearing a couple of pounds of false black hair on your head and reddening your lips and cheeks like any other Bulgarian girl? I did. Who taught you to trim your nails, and keep your hands clean, and be dainty about yourself, like a fine Russian lady? Me! do

[7]*twenty leva bill:* about six cents

you hear that? me! (*She tosses her head defiantly; and he rises, ill-humoredly, adding more coolly:*) I've often thought that if Raina were out of the way, and you just a little less of a fool and Sergius just a little more of one, you might come to be one of my grandest customers, instead of only being my wife and costing me money.

LOUKA. I believe you would rather be my servant than my husband. You would make more out of me. Oh, I know that soul of yours.

NICOLA (*going up close to her for greater emphasis*). Never you mind my soul; but just listen to my advice. If you want to be a lady, your present behaviour to me won't do at all, unless when we're alone. It's too sharp and impudent; and impudence is a sort of familiarity: it shows affection for me. And don't you try being high and mighty with me either. You're like all country girls: you think it's genteel to treat a servant the way I treat a stable-boy. That's only your ignorance; and don't you forget it. And don't be so ready to defy everybody. Act as if you expected to have your own way, not as if you expected to be ordered about. The way to get on as a lady is the same as the way to get on as a servant: you've got to know your place; that's the secret of it. And you may depend on me to know my place if you get promoted. Think over it, my girl. I'll stand by you: one servant should always stand by another.

LOUKA (*rising impatiently*). Oh, I must behave in my own way. You take all the courage out of me with your cold-blooded wisdom. Go and put those logs on the fire: that's the sort of thing y o u understand.

(*Before* NICOLA *can retort*, SERGIUS *comes in. He checks himself a moment on seeing* LOUKA; *then goes to the stove.*)

SERGIUS (*to* NICOLA). I am not in the way of your work, I hope.

NICOLA (*in a smooth, elderly manner*). Oh, no, sir, thank you kindly. I was only speaking to this foolish girl about her habit of running up here to the library whenever she gets a chance, to look at the books. That's the worst of her education, sir: it gives her habits above her station. (*To* LOUKA.) Make that table tidy, Louka, for the Major. (*He goes out sedately.*)

(LOUKA, *without looking at* SERGIUS, *begins to arrange the papers on the table. He crosses slowly to her, and studies the arrangement of her sleeve reflectively.*)

SERGIUS.   Let me see: is there a mark there? (*He turns up the bracket and sees the bruise made by his grasp. She stands motionless, not looking at him: fascinated, but on her guard.*) Ffff! Does it hurt!

LOUKA.   Yes.

SERGIUS.   Shall I cure it?

LOUKA (*instantly withdrawing herself proudly, but still not looking at him*).   No. You cannot cure it now.

SERGIUS (*masterfully*).   Quite sure? (*He makes a movement as if to take her in his arms.*)

LOUKA.   Don't trifle with me, please. An officer should not trifle with a servant.

SERGIUS (*touching the arm with a merciless stroke of his forefinger*).   That was no trifle, Louka.

LOUKA.   No. (*Looking at him for the first time.*) Are you sorry?

SERGIUS (*with measured emphasis, folding his arms*).   I am n e v e r sorry.

LOUKA (*wistfully*).   I wish I could believe a man could be so unlike a woman as that. I wonder are you really a brave man?

SERGIUS (*unaffectedly, relaxing his attitude*).   Yes: I am a brave man. My heart jumped like a woman's at the first shot; but in the charge I found that I was brave. Yes: that at least is real about me.

LOUKA.   Did you find in the charge that the men whose fathers are poor like mine were any less brave than the men who are rich like you?

SERGIUS (*with bitter levity*).   Not a bit. They all slashed and cursed and yelled like heroes. Psha! the courage to rage and kill is cheap. I have an English bull terrier who has as much of that sort of courage as the whole Bulgarian nation, and the whole Russian nation at its back. But he lets my groom thrash him, all the same. That's your soldier all over! No, Louka, your poor men can cut throats; but they are afraid of their officers; they put up with insults and blows; they stand by and see one another punished like children—aye, and help to do it when they are ordered. And the officers!—well *(with a short, bitter laugh)* I am an officer. Oh, *(fervently)* give me the man who will defv to the death any power on earth or in heaven that sets itself up against his own will and conscience: he alone is the brave man.

LOUKA.   How easy it is to talk! Men never seem to me to grow up: they all have schoolboy's ideas. You don't know what true courage is.

SERGIUS *(ironically).*   Indeed! I am willing to be instructed.

LOUKA.   Look at me! how much am I allowed to have my own will? I have to get your room ready for you—to sweep and dust, to fetch and carry. How could that degrade me if it did not degrade you to have it done for you? But *(with subdued passion)* if I were Empress of Russia, above everyone in the world, then—ah, then, though according to you I could show no courage at all—you should see, you should see.

SERGIUS.   What would you do, most noble Empress?

LOUKA.   I would marry the man I loved, which no other queen in Europe has the courage to do. If I loved you, though you would be as far beneath me as I am beneath you, I would dare to be the equal of my inferior. Would you dare as much if you loved me? No: if you felt the beginnings of love for me you would not let it grow. You dare not: you would marry a rich man's daughter because you would be afraid of what other people would say of you.

SERGIUS *(carried away).*   You lie: it is not so, by all the stars! If I loved you, and I were the Czar himself, I would set you on the throne by my side. You know that I love another woman, a woman as high above you as heaven is above earth. And you are jealous of her.

LOUKA. I have no reason to be. She will never marry you now. The man I told you of has come back. She will marry the Swiss.

SERGIUS *(recoiling)*. The Swiss!

LOUKA. A man worth ten of you. Then you can come to me; and I will refuse you. You are not good enough for me. *(She turns to the door)*.

SERGIUS *(springing after her and catching her fiercely in his arms)*. I will kill the Swiss, and afterwards I will do as I please with you.

LOUKA *(in his arms, passive and steadfast)*. The Swiss will kill you, perhaps. He has beaten you in love. He may beat you in war.

SERGIUS *(tormentedly)*. Do you think I believe that she — s h e ! whose worst thoughts are higher than your best ones, is capable of trifling with another man behind my back?

LOUKA. Do you think s h e would believe the Swiss if he told her now that I am in your arms?

SERGIUS *(releasing her in despair)*. Damnation! Oh, damnation! Mockery, mockery everywhere: everything I think is mocked by everything I do. *(He strikes himself frantically on the breast.)* Coward, liar, fool! Shall I kill myself like a man, or live and pretend to laugh at myself? *(She again turns to go.)* Louka! *(She stops near the door.)* Remember: you belong to me.

LOUKA *(quietly)*. What does that mean — an insult?

SERGIUS *(commandingly)*. It means that you love me, and that I have had you here in my arms, and will perhaps have you there again. Whether that is an insult I neither know nor care: take it as you please. But *(vehemently)* I w i l l not be a coward and a trifler. If I choose to love you, I dare marry you, in spite of all Bulgaria. If these hands ever touch you again, they shall touch my affianced bride.

LOUKA. We shall see whether you dare keep your word. But take care. I will not wait long.

SERGIUS *(again folding his arms and standing motionless in the middle of the room)*. Yes, we shall see. And you shall wait my pleasure.

(BLUNTSCHLI, *much preoccupied, with his papers still in his hand, enters, leaving the door open for* LOUKA *to go out. He goes across to the table, glancing at her as he passes.* SERGIUS, *without altering his resolute attitude, watches him steadily.* LOUKA *goes out, leaving the door open.*)

BLUNTSCHLI (*absently, sitting at the table as before, and putting down his papers*).   That's a remarkable looking young woman.

SERGIUS (*gravely, without moving*).   Captain Bluntschli.

BLUNTSCHLI.   Eh?

SERGIUS.   You have deceived me. You are my rival. I brook no rivals. At six o'clock I shall be in the drilling-ground on the Klissoura road, alone, on horseback, with my sabre. Do you understand?

BLUNTSCHLI (*staring, but sitting quite at his ease*).   Oh, thank you: that's a cavalry man's proposal. I'm in the artillery; and I have the choice of weapon. If I go, I shall take a machine gun. And there shall be no mistake about the cartridges this time.

SERGIUS (*flushing, but with deadly coldness*).   Take care, sir. It is not our custom in Bulgaria to allow invitations of that kind to be trifled with.

BLUNTSCHLI (*warmly*).   Pooh! don't talk to me about Bulgaria. You don't know what fighting is. But have it your own way. Bring your sabre along. I'll meet you.

SERGIUS (*fiercely delighted to find his opponent a man of spirit*).   Well said, Switzer. Shall I lend you my best horse?

BLUNTSCHLI.   No: damn your horse!—thank you all the same, my dear fellow. (RAINA *comes in, and hears the next sentence.*) I shall fight you on foot. Horseback's too dangerous: I don't want to kill you if I can help it.

RAINA (*hurrying forward anxiously*).   I have heard what Captain Bluntschli said, Sergius. You are going to fight. Why? (SERGIUS *turns away in silence, and goes to the stove, where he stands watching her as she continues, to* BLUNTSCHLI:) What about?

BLUNTSCHLI.   I don't know: he hasn't told me. Better not

interfere, dear young lady. No harm will be done: I've often acted as sword instructor. He won't be able to touch me; and I'll not hurt him. It will save explanations. In the morning I shall be off home; and you'll never see me or hear of me again. You and he will then make it up and live happily ever after.

RAINA *(turning away deeply hurt, almost with a sob in her voice).* I never said I wanted to see you again.

SERGIUS *(striding forward).* Ha! That is a confession.

RAINA *(haughtily).* What do you mean?

SERGIUS. You love that man!

RAINA *(scandalized).* Sergius!

SERGIUS. You allow him to make love to you behind my back, just as you accept me as your affianced husband behind his. Bluntschli: you knew our relations; and you deceived me. It is for that I call you to account, not for having received favours that I never enjoyed.

BLUNTSCHLI *(jumping up indignantly).* Stuff! Rubbish! I have received no favours. Why, the young lady doesn't even know whether I'm married or not.

RAINA *(forgetting herself).* Oh! *(Collapsing on the ottoman.)* A r e you?

SERGIUS. You see the young lady's concern, Captain Bluntschli. Denial is useless. You have enjoyed the privilege of being received in her own room, late at night—

BLUNTSCHLI *(interrupting him pepperily).* Yes; you blockhead! She received me with a pistol at her head. Your cavalry were at my heels. I'd have blown out her brains if she'd uttered a cry.

SERGIUS *(taken aback).* Bluntschli! Raina: is this true?

RAINA *(rising in wrathful majesty).* Oh, how dare you, how dare you?

BLUNTSCHLI. Apologize, man, apologize! *(He resumes his seat at the table).*

SERGIUS *(with the old measured emphasis, folding his arms).* I n e v e r apologize.

RAINA *(passionately).* This is the doing of that friend of yours, Captain Bluntschli. It is he who is spreading this horrible story about me. *(She walks about excitedly.)*

BLUNTSCHLI.   No: he's dead—burnt alive.

RAINA *(stopping, shocked)*.   Burnt alive!

BLUNTSCHLI.   Shot in the hip in a wood-yard. Couldn't drag himself out. Your fellows' shells set the timber on fire and burnt him, with half a dozen other poor devils in the same predicament.

RAINA.   How horrible!

SERGIUS.   And how ridiculous! Oh, war! war! the dream of patriots and heroes! A fraud, Bluntschli, a hollow sham, like love.

RAINA *(outraged)*.   Like love! You say that before me.

BLUNTSCHLI.   Come, Saranoff: that matter is explained.

SERGIUS.   A hollow sham, I say. Would you have come back here if nothing had passed between you, except at the muzzle of your pistol? Raina is mistaken about our friend who was burnt. He was not my informant.

RAINA.   Who then? *(Suddenly guessing the truth.)* Ah, Louka! my maid, my servant! You were with her this morning all that time after—after— Oh, what sort of god is this I have been worshipping! *(He meets her gaze with sardonic enjoyment of her disenchantment. Angered all the more, she goes closer to him, and says, in a lower, intenser tone:)* Do you know that I looked out of the window as I went upstairs, to have another sight of my hero; and I saw something that I did not understand then. I know now that you were making love to her.

SERGIUS *(with grim humor)*.   You saw that?

RAINA.   Only too well. *(She turns away, and throws herself on the divan under the center window, quite overcome.)*

SERGIUS *(cynically)*.   Raina: our romance is shattered. Life's a farce.

BLUNTSCHLI *(to RAINA, goodhumoredly)*.   You see: h e ' s found himself out now.

SERGIUS.   Bluntschli: I have allowed you to call me a blockhead. You may now call me a coward as well. I refuse to fight you. Do you know why?

BLUNTSCHLI.   No; but it doesn't matter. I didn't ask the reason when you cried on; and I don't ask the reason now that you cry off. I'm a professional soldier. I fight when I have to, and am very glad to get out of it when I haven't to. You're only an amateur: you think fighting's an amusement.

SERGIUS.   You shall hear the reason all the same, my professional. The reason is that it takes two men—real men— men of heart, blood and honor—to make a genuine combat. I could no more fight with you than I could make love to an ugly woman. You've no magnetism: you're not a man, you're a machine.

BLUNTSCHLI *(apologetically)*.   Quite true, quite true. I always w a s that sort of chap. I'm very sorry. But now that you've found that life i s n ' t a farce, but something quite sensible and serious, what further obstacle is there to your happiness?

RAINA *(rising)*.   You are very solicitous about my happiness and his. Do you forget his new love—Louka? It is not you that he must fight now, but his rival, Nicola.

SERGIUS.   Rival!! *(striking his forehead.)*

RAINA.   Did you not know that they are engaged?

SERGIUS.   Nicola! Are fresh abysses opening? Nicola!!

RAINA *(sarcastically)*.   A shocking sacrifice, isn't it? Such beauty, such intellect, such modesty, wasted on a middle-aged servant man! Really, Sergius, you cannot stand by and allow such a thing It would be unworthy of your chivalry.

SERGIUS *(losing all self-control)*.   Viper! Viper! *(He rushes to and fro, raging.)*

BLUNTSCHLI.   Look here, Saranoff; you're getting the worst of this.

RAINA *(getting angrier)*.   Do you realize what he has done, Captain Bluntschli? He has set this girl as a spy on us; and her reward is that he makes love to her.

SERGIUS.   False! Monstrous!

RAINA.   Monstrous! *(Confronting him.)* Do you deny that she told you about Captain Bluntschli being in my room?

SERGIUS.   No; but—

RAINA *(interrupting)*.   Do you deny that you were making love to her when she told you?

SERGIUS.   No; but I tell you—

RAINA *(cutting him short contemptuously).*   It is unnecessary
to tell us anything more. That is quite enough for us. *(She
turns her back on him and sweeps majestically back to
the window.)*
BLUNTSCHLI *(quietly, as* SERGIUS, *in an agony of mortifica-
tion, sinks on the ottoman, clutching his averted head between his fists).*   I told you you were getting the worst of
it, Saranoff.
SERGIUS.   Tiger cat!
RAINA *(running excitedly to* BLUNTSCHLI*).*   You hear this man
calling me names, Captain Bluntschli?
BLUNTSCHLI.   What else can he do, dear lady? He must defend himself somehow. Come *(very persuasively),* don't
quarrel. What good does it do?

(RAINA, *with a gasp, sits down on the ottoman, and after
a vain effort to look vexedly at* BLUNTSCHLI, *she falls a
victim to her sense of humor, and is attacked with a disposition to laugh.)*

SERGIUS.   Engaged to Nicola! *(He rises.)* Ha! ha! *(Going to the
stove and standing with his back to it.)* Ah, well, Bluntschli, you are right to take this huge imposture of a world
coolly.
RAINA *(to* BLUNTSCHLI, *with an intuitive guess at his state of
mind).*   I daresay you think us a couple of grown up
babies, don't you?
SERGIUS *(grinning a little).*   He does, he does. Swiss civilization nursetending Bulgarian barbarism, eh?
BLUNTSCHLI *(blushing).*   Not at all, I assure you. I'm only
very glad to get you two quieted. There now, let's be
pleasant and talk it over in a friendly way. Where is this
other young lady?
RAINA.   Listening at the door, probably.
SERGIUS *(shivering as if a bullet had struck him, and speaking with quiet but deep indignation).*   I will prove that
that, at least, is a calumny. *(He goes with dignity to the
door and opens it. A yell of fury bursts from him as he
looks out. He darts into the passage, and returns dragging*

in LOUKA, *whom he flings against the table, right, as he cries:*) Judge her, Bluntschli—you, the moderate, cautious man: judge the eavesdropper.

(LOUKA *stands her ground, proud and silent.*)

BLUNTSCHLI (*shaking his head*). I mustn't judge her. I once listened myself outside a tent when there was a mutiny brewing. It's all a question of the degree of provocation. My life was at stake.

LOUKA. My love was at stake. (SERGIUS *flinches, ashamed of her in spite of himself.*) I am not ashamed.

RAINA (*contemptuously*). Your love! Your curiosity, you mean.

LOUKA (*facing her and restoring her contempt with interest*). My love, stronger than anything y o u can feel, even for your chocolate cream soldier.

SERGIUS (*with quick suspicion—to* LOUKA). What does that mean?

LOUKA (*fiercely*). It means—

SERGIUS (*interrupting her slightingly*). Oh, I remember, the ice pudding. A paltry taunt, girl.

(MAJOR PETKOFF *enters, in his shirtsleeves.*)

PETKOFF. Excuse my shirtsleeves, gentlemen. Raina: somebody has been wearing that coat of mine: I'll swear it—somebody with bigger shoulders than mine. It's all burst open at the back. Your mother is mending it. I wish she'd make haste. I shall catch cold. (*He looks more attentively at them.*) Is anything the matter?

RAINA. No. (*She sits down at the stove with a tranquil air.*)

SERGIUS. Oh, no! (*He sits down at the end of the table, as at first.*)

BLUNTSCHLI (*who is already seated*). Nothing, nothing.

PETKOFF (*sitting down on the ottoman in his old place*). That's all right. (*He notices* LOUKA.) Anything the matter, Louka?

LOUKA. No, sir.
PETKOFF *(genially)*. T h a t' s all right. *(He sneezes.)* Go and
ask your mistress for my coat, like a good girl, will you?

(She turns to obey; but NICOLA *enters with the coat; and
she makes a pretence of having business in the room by
taking the little table with the hookah away to the wall
near the windows.)*
RAINA *(rising quickly, as she sees the coat on* NICOLA'S *arm).*
Here it is, papa. Give it to me, Nicola; and do you put
some more wood on the fire. *(She takes the coat, and
brings it to the* MAJOR, *who stands up to put it on.* NICOLA
attends to the fire.)
PETKOFF *(to* RAINA, *teasing her affectionately).* Aha! Going
to be very good to poor old papa just for one day after his
return from the wars, eh?
RAINA *(with solemn reproach).* Ah, how can you say that to
me, father?
PETKOFF. Well, well, only a joke, little one. Come, give me
a kiss. *(She kisses him.)* Now give me the coat.
RAINA. Now, I am going to put it on for you. Turn your back.
*(He turns his back and feels behind him with his arms for
the sleeves. She dexterously takes the photograph from
the pocket and throws it on the table before* BLUNTSCHLI,
*who covers it with a sheet of paper under the very nose
of* SERGIUS, *who looks on amazed, with his suspicions
roused in the highest degree. She then helps* PETKOFF *on
with his coat.)* There dear! Now are you comfortable?
PETKOFF. Quite, little love. Thanks. *(He sits down; and
RAINA returns to her seat near the stove.)* Oh, by the bye,
I've found something funny. What's the meaning of this?
(He puts his hand into the picked pocket.) Eh? Hollo!
(He tries the other pocket.) Well, I could have sworn—
(Much puzzled, he tries the breast pocket.) I wonder—
(Tries the original pocket.) Where can it—*(A light flashes
on him; he rises, exclaiming:)* Your mother's taken it.
RAINA *(very red).* Taken what?
PETKOFF. Your photograph, with the inscription: "Raina, to

her Chocolate Cream Soldier—a souvenir." Now you
know there's something more in this than meets the eye;
and I'm going to find it out. *(Shouting:)* Nicola?

NICOLA *(dropping a log, and turning).*   Sir!

PETKOFF.   Did you spoil any pastry of Miss Raina's this
morning?

NICOLA.   You heard Miss Raina say that I did, sir.

PETKOFF.   I know that, you idiot. Was it true?

NICOLA.   I am sure Miss Raina is incapable of saying anything that is not true, sir.

PETKOFF.   Are you? Then I'm not. *(Turning to the others.)*
Come: do you think I don't see it all? *(Goes to* SERGIUS,
and slaps him on the shoulder.) Sergius: you're the
chocolate cream soldier, aren't you.

SERGIUS *(starting up).*   I! a chocolate cream soldier! Certainly not.

PETKOFF.   Not! *(He looks at them. They are all very serious
and very conscious.)* Do you mean to tell me that Raina
sends photographic souvenirs to other men?

SERGIUS *(enigmatically).*   The world is not such an innocent
place as we used to think, Petkoff.

BLUNTSCHLI *(rising).*   It's all right, Major. I'm the chocolate
cream soldier. *(PETKOFF and SERGIUS are equally astonished.)* The gracious young lady saved my life by giving
me chocolate creams when I was starving—shall I ever
forget their flavour! My late friend Stolz told you the story
at Peerot. I was the fugitive.

PETKOFF.   You! *(He gasps.)* Sergius: do you remember how
those two women went on this morning when we mentioned it? *(SERGIUS smiles cynically. PETKOFF confronts
RAINA severely.)* you're a nice young woman, aren't
you?

RAINA *(bitterly).*   Major Saranoff has changed his mind. And
when I wrote that on the photograph, I did not know that
Captain Bluntschli was married.

BLUNTSCHLI *(much startled—protesting vehemently).*   I'm
not married.

RAINA *(with deep reproach).*   You said you were.

BLUNTSCHLI.   I did not. I positively did not. I never was
married in my life.

PETKOFF *(exasperated)*. Raina: will you kindly inform me, if I am not asking too much, which gentleman you a r e engaged to?

RAINA. To neither of them. T h i s young lady *(introducing* LOUKA, *who faces them all proudly)* is the object of Major Saranoff's affections at present.

PETKOFF. Louka! Are you mad, Sergius? Why, this girl's engaged to Nicola.

NICOLA *(coming forward)*. I beg your pardon, sir. There is a mistake. Louka is not engaged to me.

PETKOFF. Not engaged to you, you scoundrel! Why, you had twenty-five levas from me on the day of your betrothal; and she had that gilt bracelet from Miss Raina.

NICOLA *(with cool unction)*. We gave it out so, sir. But it was only to give Louka protection. She had a soul above her station; and I have been no more than her confidential servant. I intend, as you know, sir, to set up a shop later on in Sofia; and I look forward to her custom and recommendation should she marry into the nobility. *(He goes out with impressive discretion, leaving them all staring after him.)*

PETKOFF *(breaking the silence)*. Well, I a m—hm!

SERGIUS. This is either the finest heroism or the most crawling baseness. Which is it, Bluntschli?

BLUNTSCHLI. Never mind whether it's heroism or baseness. Nicola's the ablest man I've met in Bulgaria. I'll make him manager of a hotel if he can speak French and German.

LOUKA *(suddenly breaking out at* SERGIUS*)*. I have been insulted by everyone here. Y o u set them the example. You owe me an apology. (SERGIUS *immediately, like a repeating clock of which the spring has been touched, begins to fold his arms.)*

BLUNTSCHLI *(before he can speak)*. It's no use. He never apologizes.

LOUKA. Not to you, his equal and his enemy. To me, his poor servant, he will not refuse to apologize.

SERGIUS *(approvingly)*. You are right. *(He bends his knee in his grandest manner.)* Forgive me!

LOUKA. I forgive you. *(She timidly gives him her hand,*

which he kisses.) That touch makes me your affianced
wife.

SERGIUS *(springing up).* Ah, I forgot that!

LOUKA *(coldly).* You can withdraw if you like.

SERGIUS. Withdraw! Never! You belong to me! *(He puts his
arm about her and draws her to him.)*

*(CATHERINE comes in and finds LOUKA in SERGIUS'S
arms, and all the rest gazing at them in bewildered astonishment.)*

CATHERINE. What does this mean?

(SERGIUS releases LOUKA.)

PETKOFF. Well, my dear, it appears that Sergius is going to
marry Louka instead of Raina. *(She is about to break out
indignantly at him: he stops her by exclaiming testily.)*
Don't blame m e; I ' v e nothing to do with it. *(He retreats
to the stove.)*

CATHERINE. Marry Louka! Sergius: you are bound by your
word to us!

SERGIUS *(folding his arms).* Nothing binds me.

BLUNTSCHLI *(much pleased by this piece of common sense).*
Saranoff: your hand. My congratulations. These heroics
of yours have their practical side after all. *(To LOUKA.)*
Gracious young lady: the best wishes of a good Repub-
lican! *(He kisses her hand, to RAINA'S great disgust.)*

CATHERINE *(threateningly).* Louka: you have been telling
stories.

LOUKA. I have done Raina no harm.

CATHERINE *(haughtily).* Raina! *(RAINA is equally indignant
at the liberty.)*

LOUKA. I have a right to call her Raina: she calls me Louka.
I told Major Saranoff she would never marry him if the
Swiss gentleman came back.

BLUNTSCHLI *(surprised).* Hollo!

LOUKA *(turning to RAINA).* I thought you were fonder of
him than of Sergius. You know best whether I was right.

BLUNTSCHLI. What nonsense! I assure you, my dear Major,

my dear Madame, the gracious young lady simply saved my life, nothing else. She never cared two straws for me. Why, bless my heart and soul, look at the young lady and look at me. She, rich, young, beautiful, with her imagination full of fairy princes and noble natures and cavalry charges and goodness knows what! And I, a commonplace Swiss soldier who hardly knows what a decent life is after fifteen years of barracks and battles—a vagabond—a man who has spoiled all his chances in life through an incurably romantic disposition—a man—

SERGIUS (*starting as if a needle had pricked him and interrupting* BLUNTSCHLI *in incredulous amazement*). Excuse me, Bluntschli: w h a t did you say had spoiled your chances in life?

BLUNTSCHLI (*promptly*). An incurably romantic disposition. I ran away from home twice when I was a boy. I went into the army instead of into my father's business. I climbed the balcony of this house when a man of sense would have dived into the nearest cellar. I came sneaking back here to have another look at the young lady when any other man of my age would have sent the coat back—

PETKOFF. My coat!

BLUNTSCHLI. —Yes: that's the coat I mean—would have sent it back and gone quietly home. Do you suppose I am the sort of fellow a young girl falls in love with? Why, look at our ages! I'm thirty-four: I don't suppose the young lady is much over seventeen. (*This estimate produces a marked sensation, all the rest turning and staring at one another. He proceeds innocently.*) All that adventure which was life or death to me, was only a schoolgirl's game to her—chocolate creams and hide and seek. Here's the proof! (*He takes the photograph from the table.*) Now, I ask you, would a woman who took the affair seriously have sent me this and written on it: "Raina, to her chocolate cream soldier—a souvenir"? (*He exhibits the photograph triumphantly, as if it settled the matter beyond all possibility of refutation.*)

PETKOFF. That's what I was looking for. How the deuce did it get there?

BLUNTSCHLI *(to* RAINA *complacently).* I have put everything right, I hope, gracious young lady!

RAINA *(in uncontrollable vexation).* I quite agree with your account of yourself. You are a romantic idiot. (BLUNTSCHLI *is unspeakably taken aback.)* Next time I hope you will know the difference between a schoolgirl of seventeen and a woman of twenty-three.

BLUNTSCHLI *(stupefied).* Twenty-three! *(She snaps the photograph contemptuously from his hands; tears it across and throws the pieces at his feet.)*

SERGIUS *(with grim enjoyment of* BLUNTSCHLI'S *discomfiture).* Bluntschli: my one last belief is gone. Your sagacity is a fraud, like all the other things. You have less sense than even I have.

BLUNTSCHLI *(overwhelmed).* Twenty-three! Twenty-three!! *(He considers.)* Hm! *(Swiftly making up his mind.)* In that case, Major Petkoff, I beg to propose formally to become a suitor for your daughter's hand, in place of Major Saranoff retired.

RAINA. You dare!

BLUNTSCHLI. If you were twenty-three when you said those things to me this afternoon, I shall take them seriously.

CATHERINE *(loftily polite).* I doubt, sir, whether you quite realize either my daughter's position or that of Major Sergius Saranoff, whose place you propose to take. The Petkoffs and the Saranoffs are known as the richest and most important families in the country. Our position is almost historical: we can go back for nearly twenty years.

PETKOFF. Oh, never mind that, Catherine *(To* BLUNTSCHLI.) We should be most happy, Bluntschli, if it were only a question of your position; but hang it, you know, Raina is accustomed to a very comfortable establishment. Sergius keeps twenty horses.

BLUNTSCHLI. But what on earth is the use of twenty horses? Why, it's a circus.

CATHERINE *(severely).* My daughter, sir, is accustomed to a first-rate stable.

RAINA. Hush, mother, you're making me ridiculous.

BLUNTSCHLI. Oh, well, if it comes to a question of an establishment, here goes! *(He goes impetuously to the table and seizes the papers in the blue envelope.)* How many horses did you say?

SERGIUS.   Twenty, noble Switzer!

BLUNTSCHLI.   I have two hundred horses. *(They are amazed.)* How many carriages?

SERGIUS.   Three.

BLUNTSCHLI.   I have seventy. Twenty-four of them will hold twelve inside, besides two on the box, without counting the driver and conductor. How many tablecloths have you?

SERGIUS.   How the deuce do I know?

BLUNTSCHLI.   Have you four thousand?

SERGIUS. No.

BLUNTSCHLI.   I have. I have nine thousand six hundred pairs of sheets and blankets, with two thousand four hundred eiderdown quilts. I have ten thousand knives and forks, and the same quantity of dessert spoons. I have six hundred servants. I have six palatial establishments, besides two livery stables, a tea garden and a private house. I have four medals for distinguished services; I have the rank of an officer and the standing of a gentleman; and I have three native languages. Show me any man in Bulgaria that can offer as much.

PETKOFF *(with childish awe)*.   Are you Emperor of Switzerland?

BLUNTSCHLI.   My rank is the highest known in Switzerland: I'm a free citizen.

CATHERINE.   Then Captain Bluntschli, since you are my daughter's choice, I shall not stand in the way of her happiness. (PETKOFF *is about to speak.)* That is Major Petkoff's feeling also.

PETKOFF.   Oh, I shall be only too glad. Two hundred horses! Whew!

SERGIUS.   What says the lady!

RAINA *(pretending to sulk)*.   The lady says that he can keep his tablecloths and his omnibuses. I am not here to be sold to the highest bidder.

BLUNTSCHLI.   I won't take that answer. I appealed to you as a fugitive, a beggar, and a starving man. You accepted me. You gave me your hand to kiss, your bed to sleep in, and your roof to shelter me —

RAINA *(interrupting him).* I did not give them to the Emperor of Switzerland!

BLUNTSCHLI. That's just what I say. *(He catches her hand quickly and looks her straight in the face as he adds, with confident mastery:)* Now tell us who you did give them to.

RAINA *(succumbing with a shy smile).* To my chocolate cream soldier!

BLUNTSCHLI *(with a boyish laugh of delight).* That'll do. Thank you. *(Looks at his watch and suddenly becomes businesslike.)* Time's up, Major. You've managed those regiments so well that you are sure to be asked to get rid of some of the Infantry of the Teemok division. Send them home by way of Lom Palanka. Saranoff: don't get married until I come back: I shall be here punctually at five in the evening on Tuesday fortnight. Gracious ladies — good evening. *(He makes them a military bow, and goes.)*

SERGIUS. What a man! What a man!

Curtain

FOR DISCUSSION

Act I

1. Why are Catherine and Raina so pleased over the battle? What does Raina find "all true" that leads her to exclaim "What happiness! What unspeakable fulfillment!" From her words and actions, what impression do you gain of her age, social position, character, and attitude toward life and love?

2. How does the conversation between Louka and Raina set the stage for the entrance of the Man and for Raina's treatment of him? By what means does he try to intimidate her, and how does she react? Why is she able to deceive the Officer but not Louka? At this point in the play, what impression have you gained of the Man? What is Raina's attitude toward him?

3. As the Man waits for a quiet interval, what does he do and say

that makes Raina scornful of him? What does she learn about the "great cavalry charge"? Why does the Man agree that the first man in the charge was a hero? How well does he succeed in soothing her injured feelings? What incident leads her to call him a "chocolate cream soldier"?

4. What plan does Raina propose for saving the Man, and on what "notion" is it based? How do you explain his reactions to her account of her family, home, countrymen? How does the playwright prepare you for the Man's falling asleep? Are the reactions of Raina and Catherine to this complication consistent with the opinion you have formed of them? Explain.

5. How would you describe Raina's feelings toward the Man? Do you think he is, or is not, attracted to her? Have her feelings toward Sergius changed? What determines her attitudes and feelings? In what ways are they similar to, or very different from, the attitudes and feelings of the Man?

Act II

1. Why does Nicola disapprove of Louka's attitude toward her employers? What opinions does he express that lead her to accuse him of having "the soul of a servant"? What impression do you gain of the relationship between master and servant in the Petkoff household, and probably in others like it?

2. How does Catherine react to her husband's unexpected arrival? Do you think he takes her remarks seriously? What is of major importance to both of them? What has each learned about "civilized people"?

3. Petkoff is not as enthusiastic as Catherine about the heroic Sergius. Why? To what is Sergius referring when he says, "Madam: it was the cradle and the grave of my military reputation"? What explanation does he give for resigning from the army? How do he and Petkoff feel about the Swiss officer, and for what reasons?

4. When Sergius tells the "queer story" about the Swiss soldier's escape, how do you think Catherine and Raina feel? How does each react? What kind of relationship exists between Raina and Sergius that she describes as "the higher love"?

5. How do you explain Sergius' behavior with Louka? What is she trying to do: (1) win him away from Raina, (2) use him to get even with her employers, (3) make a fool of him because he considers himself above her? Does this scene turn out as either

of them hoped or expected? What kind of people do they reveal
themselves to be? Give reasons to support your answers to
these questions.

6. From the conversation between Catherine and Raina—after
Sergius goes to help Petkoff—what do you learn of Raina's
feelings toward Sergius and toward the Swiss officer? Why
is Catherine justifiably upset over the arrival of Captain Bluntschli? What reasons does she give for insisting that he leave
at once? How are her plans upset? Do the reactions of Sergius
and Petkoff support or contradict her earlier statements? Explain.

7. What amusing complications add interest and humor to the last
minutes of Act II? How does Nicola prove himself the perfect
servant? Why do you think Raina wants Bluntschli to stay?
Is she in love with him? Does she want to make him pay for
telling the story of his escape? Is it that she is intrigued by
the situation that has developed and wants to see how it will
come out? Support your opinions with evidence drawn from
the play.

Act III

1. The opening scene in the library provides the audience with a
chance to observe the various relationships among the Petkoffs and their guests. With what "unfinished business" are
Petkoff and Catherine concerned, and how do the others react to
it? What is ironic about the part Bluntschli plays in this scene?
What "business" takes the Petkoffs and Sergius offstage so that
Bluntschli and Raina can be alone? Why does Bluntschli remark, "What a country"?

2. In what *mood* (see Glossary) does the conversation between
Raina and Bluntschli begin? What causes her to accuse him of
insulting her? Why can't he believe a single word she says?
How does she react to being "found out"? At the end of this
scene, is your opinion of her the same or different? Are Bluntschli's words and actions consistent with your previous impression of him? Discuss.

3. Why is Raina upset by the missing portrait? What has Bluntschli
done that she finds inexcusable? Earlier Sergius compared
Bluntschli to "a commercial traveler." Does Raina's accusation
reflect a similar or different attitude? What effect does it have
on Bluntschli?

4. When Louka brings Bluntschli his letters, he doesn't seem surprised, but he has come to the Petkoff home only to return the coat. Was he so certain of an invitation to remain? Has he written the supposed letters and telegrams to himself so that he can impress Raina and the family with his wealth and position? Did he want an excuse to leave hurriedly if Raina's attitude had changed? Or are both the letters and telegrams and their delivery believable and not prearranged? Discuss. What use does Louka make of this incident to hurt Raina?

5. By what "good news" does Nicola hope to gain a little consideration from Louka? How does she receive it? What does he claim he has done for her? In his opinion, how will she have to change her ways if she is to achieve her "great ambition"? Why do you think his advice upsets her?

6. Part of Louka's "great ambition" involves marriage, a subject she maneuvers Sergius into discussing by questioning (1) whether or not he is a brave man, and (2) whether poor men are less brave than rich men. What does he say that provokes her into remarking, "You don't know what true courage is"? What would she dare to do that he would never dare, and why? How does she torment him into swearing, "If these hands ever touch you again, they shall touch my affianced bride"? Tell why you think that Sergius does, or does not, deserve the treatment he receives.

7. What reason does Sergius give for challenging Bluntschli to a duel? What other reasons might there be? How does Bluntschli react to the challenge and to Raina's involvement in it? What seems to be his main interest throughout the entire discussion? How do you interpret his comment about Sergius: "He's found himself out now"? Why does Sergius decide not to fight Bluntschli? What is Bluntschli's reaction?

8. When Sergius makes the mistake of revealing that Louka is his "informant," Raina is quick to put "two and two together." Of what does she accuse him? Why does she propose that he fight Nicola? What happens when Bluntschli suggests that Louka be called and they "talk it over in a friendly way"? How different is Raina's behavior during this scene from Louka's behavior in the preceding scene?

9. How does Petkoff become involved in the mystery of the photograph? Why does Bluntschli think it necessary to confess? When Raina names Louka as the object of Sergius' affections, what "mistake" does Nicola clear up? How do Petkoff and the others react? Do you think that Louka has deliberately tricked Sergius

into keeping his word? Do you think he is pleased or displeased at the turn of events? Discuss.

10. Why does Louka's explanation to Catherine bring a surprised protest from Bluntschli? What does he say that, he hopes, will "put everything right"? Why is Raina furious and Sergius amused? How consistent is Bluntschli's account of himself with the kind of person his words and actions have revealed him to be? Explain.

11. In true storybook fashion, Bluntschli first asks permission from Raina's father. What reservations do Catherine and Petkoff have and how does he satisfy them? How does he win Raina's consent? Why, in your opinion, did Shaw not end the play with Bluntschli's remark, "That'll do. Thank you"? What *dramatic purpose* (see Glossary) is served by the lines that follow?

ON THE PLAY AS A WHOLE

1. One critic has written about *Arms and the Man:* "A prosaic professional soldier is introduced in a situation between a typical romantic hero and a typical romantic heroine with disastrous consequences to both." Obviously the hero and heroine are Sergius and Raina. What is the "situation" between them? What are the "consequences" of Bluntschli's entrance into this situation? In what ways, if any, do you think they are "disastrous"? In choosing the word *disastrous,* do you think the critic was being satirical? Support your answers to these questions.

2. At the end of the play, how do you think each of the characters feels about the way things have turned out? Who has benefited the most by the romantic upset? Are either Sergius or Raina worse off financially or socially? Have any of their romantic illusions been destroyed? In what ways, if at all, will their future lives be much different? Give examples to support your answers.

3. One target of Shaw's comic satire is the Petkoffs' belief that they are "civilized people." How is this belief revealed in the kind of life they live, in what they value, and in the way they treat people whom they consider inferior? How do they know what "civilized people" do or do not do? Tell why you think Shaw is satirizing (1) civilized people in general, (2) the idea of being civilized, or (3) the pretensions which some people con-

fuse with being civilized. What pretensions does he succeed in making seem especially ridiculous?

4. Characters in a play can be significant in and for themselves. You like or dislike them, as you do people in real life, because of what they are. Characters can also be significant principally for the values, ideas, attitudes, or customs they represent. In which of these ways do you think Shaw intended the characters in this play to be principally significant? If some characters seem significant to you in one way and some in the other, explain why. As you were reading the play, what interested you especially about the characters: (1) what they were like, (2) what would happen to them, or (3) what they did and said in response to each other and to new situations? Discuss.

5. Louka says to Sergius, "I know the difference between the sort of manner you and she [Raina] put on before one another and the real manner." What do Sergius and Raina say and do that represents that "sort of manner"? In what ways, if any, is this related to Raina's idea of "the higher love"? What do you think Louka means by "the real manner"? Between what characters, if any, does the "real manner" exist? What romantic illusions is Shaw satirizing? Explain.

6. During the course of the play, Bluntschli is called a "commercial traveler in uniform," a "romantic idiot," a "machine," and, somewhat sarcastically, a "moderate, cautious man." What evidence can you find in the play that he is all of these? In spite of his "incurably romantic disposition," what reason do you have for believing that he does—as Sergius claims—"take this huge imposture of a world coolly"? In what situations does he appear to be very much the realist? When, if ever, is he a "romantic" in the way Sergius is? What false pretensions does he help to tear down? What illusions does he expose? Give reasons to support your answers.

7. Louka says of Raina, "She's a liar; and her fine airs are a cheat; and I'm worth six of her." How different are these young ladies in what they want and in the tactics they use to get it? How similar or different are their values? In what ways do you think Louka considers herself worth six of Raina? Does her behavior support or refute her claims? Of what "fine airs" is Raina guilty? Does Louka call them "a cheat" because she is envious or because she is more honest? Explain. Which of the two ladies catches your fancy and why?

8. In true Byronesque fashion, Sergius declares, "Which of the six

is the real man—that's the question that torments me." To what six is he referring? Before Raina becomes disillusioned, what kind of man does she think him to be? Is he also, as Louka claims, made out of the same "common clay" as she? Judging from their remarks, what opinion do Petkoff and Bluntschli have of Sergius? State your own opinion of Sergius and support it by referring to specific incidents and to conversations between him and other characters.

9. To Nicola, having the soul of a servant is an advantage; it is "the secret of success in service." What does he have to endure in order to be a success in the Petkoff household? Why is he willing to do it? In what ways could Louka be of help to him? Why does he claim that she is indebted to him? At the end of the play, what does he say that leads Bluntschli to remark, "Nicola's the ablest man I've met in Bulgaria"? Why would Bluntschli be impressed by him? What impressed you most about him? Through Nicola's relationship with the Petkoffs and his remarks to Louka, what attitudes, values, and ideas was Shaw exposing or making seem ridiculous?

10. Would you say that Petkoff and Catherine are happy in spite of their romantic ideas or because of them? What is the relationship between them? In what ways are they alike and different? Point out scenes involving one or both of them which you found especially amusing.

11. In *Arms and the Man*, Shaw's aim was to tear down false pretensions and to destroy illusions—always, of course, with the "utmost levity." He wrote this play in the 1890's, both to entertain his fellow Englishmen and to compel them, for an hour or two, to face realities. Why, then, did he choose an earlier time and a foreign country as the setting? Why did he create a plot and characters that had little relation to English life and people? Why do you think he wanted to make it seem that he was satirizing Bulgarian pretensions and illusions? What advantage can you see in his using a non-English storybook plot and non-English characters to poke fun at English ideas? How did it help him to achieve his dual aim in writing the play? Discuss.

12. Even in a romantic comedy, the playwright must create some kind of *conflict* (see Glossary) or there will be no action. In this comedy, what is the conflict of the main plot? Who are the opposing forces in it: the *protagonist* (see Glossary) and *antagonist* (see Glossary)? Before this conflict is resolved, a second conflict develops, which is the basis of the *subplot*. What is this second conflict, and who are the opposing forces in it? How,

and in what order, is each of these conflicts resolved? In what way, if any, is the outcome of one plot dependent on the outcome of the other? Is either outcome a surprise, or are both what you have been led to expect? Explain.

13. If the action of the main plot reaches a climax, where does it occur? Is this the point of highest interest in the play? Does it mark the end of the suspense? Why or why not? Does the action of the subplot also reach a climax? If so, where does it occur? Why is it important to the play? Be specific in your answers.

14. If you were viewing this play, you would have to depend upon the stage set, the costumes, and the actors' facial expressions, gestures, and manner of speaking for the details and interpretations which Shaw has provided in the stage directions. In most plays, such directions are as brief as possible, serving merely as guides for stage designer, director, and actors to follow. In what ways are the stage directions in this play different, both in the way they are written and in what they contribute to the play? Explain why you do, or do not, think they are an important part of the pleasure of reading *Arms and the Man.*

15. In both the popular and the literary sense, this play could be called a typical romantic comedy. It has a strong love interest and it presents life as people would like it to be, not as it actually is. What reasons can you see for Shaw's creating such a typical romantic comedy to satirize typical romantic ideas? What are these ideas? Could he have satirized them as effectively in any other kind of play? How do you explain his calling this play an anti-romantic comedy? Discuss.

16. *Arms and the Man* is a catchy title, but what does it mean? Does the word *Arms* stand for guns and swords, soldiers, heroism, war, romantic ideas about war? Does the word *Man* stand for one of the characters, for a particular kind of man, for man in general? What idea or observation on life do you think Shaw intended to convey through the combination of these words in the title? Give reasons to support your answer.

FOR COMPOSITION

1. Shaw could not write any play—even a comedy—without presenting ideas through incidents and situations, and particularly through the dialogue spoken by the characters. In three short paragraphs state three of the ideas you think he presented in

Arms and the Man. In each paragraph refer to one or more incidents or conversations through which he brought out the idea.

2. When Nicola is warning Louka, he says, "Child, you don't know the power such high people have over the likes of you and me when we try to rise out of our poverty against them." In a paragraph present evidence gathered from the play that what he believes to be true is, or is not, an illusion.

3. According to Raina, Bluntschli's account—"all that about me and my room"—must have made a "lovely story." Write this story as you think Bluntschli might have told it to his soldier friend, using the first person point-of-view. Begin with his scramble up the water pipe and end with his departure wearing Major Petkoff's coat. Use whatever details you were given in the play and invent others where they are needed.

4. When Bluntschli mentions "the great cavalry charge," Raina says, "Describe it to me." From the different versions given by Bluntschli and Sergius, try to picture in your mind what the charge might have been like. Then write your own graphic account of it. Follow Shaw's example and make it, and the participants in it, amusing.

5. Both Bluntschli and Sergius express some unromantic opinions about soldiers, amateur and professional, young and old, brave and cowardly. Find these opinions in the play and list them under the three headings. Then state in your own words what "realities" about war and soldiers you think Shaw hoped to make his readers and audiences face.

6. Suppose you were a talent scout looking for a leading lady and a leading man for *Arms and the Man.* In separate paragraphs describe the kind of person you think each one should be. Give a general picture of the physical appearance of each, but focus major attention on those qualities of personality and character which you feel each actor should be able to portray through his actions and through the way he speaks his lines.

7. Choose a character in the play whom you found especially amusing. Write a sketch of him or her that will convey the kind of person you picture this character to be. Include in your sketch several examples of what he or she said and did that are especially revealing.

Sean O'Casey

The birth of Sean O'Casey in 1880 coincided with a growing nationalist movement in Ireland for a revival of Irish culture and the establishment of an independent Irish nation. The resulting literary renaissance centered around the founding of an Irish National Theater in 1904, the famous Abbey Theatre of Dublin. The Abbey Theatre group, led by William Butler Yeats, adopted as its purpose the writing and production of plays about the Irish people and the encouragement of promising young playwrights toward this end. Among the members of this illustrious group were, besides Yeats, Lady Augusta Gregory, John Millington Synge, and, later, Sean O'Casey.

At the time the Abbey was established, young O'Casey was devoting most of his time and energy to the cause of labor. Having worked as a common laborer from the age of thirteen, he was active at this time in the Irish Transport and General Workers Union. When the Union formed the Irish Citizen Army in 1913, he became its first secretary, pledging allegiance with his fellow workers to "The Plough and the Stars," its flag. This army of laborers and its middle-class rival, the Irish Volunteers, had one goal in common: total independence from Britain. When Irish bitterness toward Britain erupted in the abortive Dublin rebellion of Easter Week, 1916, O'Casey's sympathies lay with these nationalist soldiers, though he had previously resigned his post with the Citizen Army. Unlike the ranks of idealistic patriots, however, he refused to take a romantic view of the war. He saw the Dublin rebellion realistically, in terms of its sacrifice and bloodshed. When, ten years later, he used the events of Easter Week as the background for his drama, *The Plough and the Stars*, his blunt realism was still capable of bringing angry demonstrations from some of the more sensitive nationalists.

O'Casey did not write his first full-length drama until he was over forty. His writing up to that time had consisted largely of articles and occasional pieces for labor periodicals, though he had written several one-act plays. Nevertheless, his first three full-length plays, *The Shadow of a Gunman* (1923), *Juno and the Paycock* (1924), and *The Plough and the Stars* (1926), were produced by the Abbey Theatre, largely through the efforts of W. B. Yeats. The two latter plays are acknowledged to be the best of his twelve full-length plays and are considered to be two of the best dramas written during this century. Both of them capture the sparkle and poetry of Irish speech; and both give a realistic, indeed naturalistic, portrayal of Dublin tenement life with its humor and high spirits, its tragedy and sorrow. O'Casey was well acquainted with the existence he dramatized, for he, too, was a product of the Dublin slums. His meager sustenance and malnutrition as a child had left him a ready victim to the chronic eye disease that seriously impaired his vision. The success of his first two plays, however, enabled him to leave those all-too-familiar surroundings.

The production of his third play, *The Plough and the Stars*, brought him instant notoriety when a riot broke out in the theater at its fourth performance. During the third act, as Nora is describing the fighting of the soldiers at the barricades, more than a dozen Dubliners—mostly women—swarmed onto the stage, instigating a battle with the Abbey Players that halted the performance of the play. A similar disturbance had occurred in 1907 over an obscene word in Synge's comedy, *The Playboy of the Western World*. This time, the disturbance arose over O'Casey's implicit criticism of Irish nationalist romanticism in his portrayal of the Easter Rebellion. The police soon arrived to throw the rioters out of the theater, and Yeats appeared onstage to shout his disapproval at the minority who had threatened to disgrace the city:

> "Is this going to be a recurring celebration of Irish genius? Synge first, and then O'Casey! The news of the happenings of the last few minutes here will flash from country to country. Dublin has once more rocked the cradle of a reputation. From such a scene in this theater went forth the fame of Synge. Equally, the fame of O'Casey is born here tonight."[1]

Yeats's words proved to be prophetic; for today O'Casey, along with George Bernard Shaw, is regarded as one of the greatest dramatists of the twentieth century.

The Abbey Theatre incident, however, had serious consequences. It was partly responsible for O'Casey's decision to leave Ireland. Convinced that he could not write freely in Ireland and disillusioned by the political failure of the labor cause, O'Casey left Dublin in 1926 to take up permanent residence in London. In his later plays, O'Casey broke away from the realism of his first three plays, branching into a freer, more experimental, more expressionistic kind of drama. Most notable, perhaps, among these later works were *Purple Dust* (1944); *Cock-a-Doodle Dandy* (1949), his favorite play; *The Bishop's Bonfire* (1955); and *The Drums of Father Ned* (1958). Though his later dramas may eventually be accorded a place beside *Juno and the Paycock* and *The Plough and the Stars*, it is upon the brilliant blending of comedy and tragedy in these two early plays that his reputation rests today.

[1]*The Irish Times*, February 12, 1926.

The Plough and the Stars

CHARACTERS

JACK CLITHEROE, a bricklayer; Commandant in
the Irish Citizen Army
NORA CLITHEROE, his wife
PETER FLYNN, a labourer; Nora's uncle
THE YOUNG COVEY, a fitter; Clitheroe's cousin
BESSIE BURGESS, a street fruit-vendor
MRS. GOGAN, a charwoman
MOLLSER, her consumptive child
FLUTHER GOOD, a carpenter

} Residents in
the Tenement

LIEUT. LANGON, a Civil Servant; member of the Irish
Volunteers
CAPT. BRENNAN, a chicken butcher; member of the Irish
Citizen Army
CORPORAL STODDART, of the Wiltshires
SERGEANT TINLEY, of the Wiltshires
ROSIE REDMOND
A BAR-TENDER
A WOMAN
THE FIGURE IN THE WINDOW

SCENE: A slum in Dublin, Ireland.
TIME: Acts I and II, November 1915; Acts III and IV, Easter
Week, 1916. A few days elapse between Acts III and IV.

274

Act I

The home of the CLITHEROES *in a Dublin tenement. It consists of the front and back drawing-rooms in a fine old Georgian house, struggling for its life against the assaults of time, and the more savage assaults of the tenants. The room shown is the back drawing-room, wide, spacious, and lofty. At back is the entrance to the front drawing-room. The space, originally occupied by folding doors, is now draped with casement cloth of a dark purple, decorated with a design in reddish-purple and cream. One of the curtains is pulled aside, giving a glimpse of the front drawing-room, at the end of which can be seen the wide, lofty windows looking out into the street. The room directly in front of the audience is furnished in a way that suggests an attempt towards a finer expression of domestic life. The large fireplace on the right is of wood, painted to look like marble (the original has been taken away by the landlord). On the mantelshelf are two candlesticks of dark carved wood. Between them is a small clock. Over the clock is hanging a calendar which displays a picture of "The Sleeping Venus."[1] In the centre of the breast of the chimney hangs a picture of Robert Emmet.[2] On the right of the entrance to the front drawing-room is a copy of "The Gleaners," on the opposite side a copy of "The Angelus."[3] Underneath "The Gleaners" is a chest of drawers on which stands a green bowl filled with scarlet dahlias and white chrysanthemums. Near to*

[1]*The Sleeping Venus:* painting of a sleeping nude by Il Giorgione (1478?-1511), a Venetian painter

[2]*Robert Emmet:* Irish nationalist (1778-1803), hanged after leading an unsuccessful revolt against the British

[3]*The Gleaners. . . The Angelus:* two paintings of peasants in the fields by Jean François Millet (1814-1875), a French painter

the fireplace is a settee which at night forms a double bed for CLITHEROE *and* NORA. *Underneath "The Angelus" are a number of shelves containing saucepans and a frying-pan. Under these is a table on which are various articles of delf ware. Near the end of the room, opposite to the fireplace is a gate-legged table, covered with a cloth. On top of the table a huge cavalry sword is lying. To the right is a door which leads to a lobby from which the staircase leads to the hall. The floor is covered with a dark green linoleum. The room is dim except where it is illuminated from the glow of the fire. Through the window of the room at back can be seen the flaring of the flame of a gasoline lamp giving light to workmen repairing the street. Occasionally can be heard the clang of crowbars.* FLUTHER GOOD *is repairing the lock of door, Right. A claw-hammer is on a chair beside him, and he has a screw-driver in his hand. He is a man of forty years of age, rarely surrendering to thoughts of anxiety, fond of his "oil"[4] but determined to conquer the habit before he dies. He is square-jawed and harshly featured; under the left eye is a scar, and his nose is bent from a smashing blow received in a fistic battle long ago. He is bald, save for a few peeping tufts of reddish hair around his ears; and his upper lip is hidden by a scrubby red moustache, embroidered here and there with a grey hair. He is dressed in a seedy black suit, cotton shirt with a soft collar, and wears a very respectable little black bow. On his head is a faded jerry[5] hat, which, when he is excited, he has a habit of knocking farther back on his head, in a series of taps. In an argument he usually fills with sound and fury generally signifying a row. He is in his shirtsleeves at present, and wears a soiled white apron, from a pocket in which sticks a carpenter's two-foot rule. He has just finished the job of putting on a new lock, and, filled with satisfaction, he is opening and shutting the*

---

[4]*oil:* any alcoholic beverage (slang)
[5]*jerry:* German soldier (slang)

door, *enjoying the completion of a work well done. Sitting
at the fire, airing a white shirt, is* PETER FLYNN. *He is a
little, thin bit of a man, with a face shaped like a loz-
enge; on his cheeks and under his chin is a straggling wiry
beard of a dirty-white and lemon hue. His face invariably
wears a look of animated anguish, mixed with irritated
defiance, as if everybody was at war with him, and he at
war with everybody. He is cocking his head in a way that
suggests resentment at the presence of* FLUTHER, *who
pays no attention to him, apparently, but is really
furtively watching him. Peter is clad in a singlet,[6] white
whipcord knee-breeches, and is in his stocking-feet.*

*A voice is heard speaking outside of door, Left (it is
that of* MRS. GOGAN*).*

MRS. GOGAN (*outside*).   Who are you lookin' for, sir? Who?
Mrs. Clitheroe? . . . Oh, excuse me. Oh ay, up this way.
She's out, I think: I seen her goin'. Oh, you've somethin'
for her; oh, excuse me. You're from Arnott's. . . . I see. . . .
You've a parcel for her. . . . Righto. . . . I'll take it. . . .
I'll give it to her the minute she comes in. . . . It'll be
quite safe. . . . Oh, sign that. . . . Excuse me. . . . Where?
. . . Here? . . . No, there; righto. Am I to put Maggie or
Mrs.? What is it? You dunno? Oh, excuse me.

MRS. GOGAN *opens the door and comes in. She is a
doleful-looking little woman of forty, insinuating manner and sallow complexion. She is fidgety and nervous,
terribly talkative, has a habit of taking up things that
may be near her and fiddling with them while she is
speaking. Her heart is aflame with curiosity, and a fly
could not come into nor go out of the house without her
knowing. She has a draper's parcel in her hand, the knot
of the twine tying it is untied.* PETER, *more resentful of
this intrusion than of* FLUTHER'S *presence, gets up from
the chair, and without looking around, his head carried
at an angry cock, marches into the room at back.*)

[6]*singlet:* undershirt

MRS. GOGAN (*removing the paper and opening the cardboard box it contains*). I wondher what's that now? A hat! (*She takes out a hat, black, with decorations in red and gold.*) God, she's going' to th' divil lately for style! That hat, now, cost more than a penny. Such notions of upperosity she's gettin'. (*Putting the hat on her head.*) Oh, swank, what! (*She replaces it in parcel.*)

FLUTHER. She's a pretty little Judy,[7] all the same.

MRS. GOGAN. Ah, she is, an' she isn't. There's prettiness an' prettiness in it. I'm always sayin' that her skirts are a little too short for a married woman. An' to see her, sometimes of an evenin', in her glad-neck gown would make a body's blood run cold. I do be ashamed of me life before her husband. An' th' way she thries to be polite, with her "Good mornin', Mrs. Gogan," when she's goin' down, an' her "Good evenin', Mrs. Gogan," when she's comin' up. But there's politeness an' politeness in it.

FLUTHER. They seem to get on well together, all th' same.

MRS. GOGAN. Ah, they do, an' they don't. The pair o' them used to be like two turtle doves always billin' an' cooin'. You couldn't come into th' room but you'd feel, instinctive like, that they'd just been afther kissin' an' cuddlin' each other. . . . It often made me shiver, for, afther all, there's kissin' an' cuddlin' in it. But I'm thinkin' he's beginnin' to take things more quietly; the mystery of havin' a woman's a mystery no longer. . . . She dhresses herself to keep him with her, but it's no use—afther a month or two, th' wondher of a woman wears off.

FLUTHER. I dunno, I dunno. Not wishin' to say anything derogatory,[8] I think it's all a question of location: when a man finds th' wondher of one woman beginnin' to die, it's usually beginnin' to live in another.

MRS. GOGAN. She's always grumblin' about havin' to live in a tenement house. "I wouldn't like to spend me last hour in one, let alone live me life in a tenement," says

[7]*Judy:* girl (slang)
[8]*derogatory:* Fluther uses the word frequently without concern for its meaning.

she. "Vaults," says she, "that are hidin' th' dead, instead of homes that are sheltherin' th' livin'." "Many a good one," says I, "was reared in a tenement house." Oh, you know, she's a well-up little lassie, too; able to make a shillin' go where another would have to spend a pound. She's wipin' th' eyes of th' Covey an' poor oul' Pether—everybody knows that—screwin' every penny she can out o' them, in ordher to turn th' place into a babby-house.[9] An' she has th' life frightened out o' them; washin' their face, combin' their hair, wipin' their feet, brushin' their clothes, thrimmin' their nails, cleanin' their teeth—God Almighty, you'd think th' poor men were undher-goin' penal servitude.

FLUTHER *(with an exclamation of disgust).* A-a-ah, that's goin' beyond th' beyonds in a tenement house. That's a little bit too derogatory.

(PETER *enters from room, Back, head elevated and resentful fire in his eyes; he is still in his singlet and trousers, but is now wearing a pair of unlaced boots—possibly to be decent in the presence of* MRS. GOGAN. *He places the white shirt, which he has carried in on his arm, on the back of a chair near the fire, and, going over to the chest of drawers, he opens drawer after drawer, looking for something; as he fails to find it he closes each drawer with a snap; he pulls out pieces of linen neatly folded, and bundles them back again any way.)*

PETER *(in accents of anguish).* Well, God Almighty, give me patience! *(He returns to room, Back, giving the shirt a vicious turn as he passes.)*

MRS. GOGAN. I wondher what he is foostherin'[10] for now?

FLUTHER. He's adornin' himself for th' meeting to-night. *(Pulling a handbill from his pocket and reading)* "Great Demonstration an' torchlight procession around places in th' city sacred to th' memory of Irish Patriots, to be

[9]*babby-house:* dollhouse
[10]*foostherin':* (foostering) bustling around

concluded be a meetin', at which will be taken an oath of fealty to th' Irish Republic.[11] Formation in Parnell Square at eight o'clock." Well, they can hold it for Fluther. I'm up th' pole; no more dhrink for Fluther. It's three days now since I touched a dhrop, an' I feel a new man already.

MRS. GOGAN. Isn't oul' Peter a funny-lookin' little man? . . . Like somethin' you'd pick off a Christmas Tree. . . . When he's dhressed up in his canonicals, you'd wondher where he'd been got. God forgive me, when I see him in them, I always think he must ha' had a Mormon for a father! He an' th' Covey can't abide each other; th' pair o' them is always at it, thryin' to best each other. There'll be blood dhrawn one o' these days.

FLUTHER. How is it that Clitheroe himself, now, doesn't have anythin' to do with th' Citizen Army?[12] A couple o' months ago, an' you'd hardly ever see him without his gun, an' th' Red Hand o' Liberty Hall in his hat.

MRS. GOGAN. Just because he wasn't made a Captain of. He wasn't goin' to be in anything where he couldn't be con-spishuous. He was so cocksure o' being made one that he bought a Sam Browne belt,[13] an' was always puttin' it on an' standin' at th' door showing it off, till th' man came an' put out th' street lamps on him. God, I think he used to bring it to bed with him! But I'm tellin' you herself was delighted that that cock didn't crow, for she's like a clockin' hen if he leaves her sight for a minute.

(While she is talking, she takes up book after book from the table, looks into each of them in a near-sighted way, and then leaves them back. She now lifts up the sword, and proceeds to examine it.)

[11]The goal of these Irish nationalists was the establishment of an Irish Republic, thus making the government of Ireland completely independent of the British Parliament.
[12]*Citizen Army:* The Irish Citizen Army, formed in 1913 by the Irish Transport and General Workers Union
[13]*Sam Browne belt:* leather army officer's belt held by a strap over the right shoulder

MRS. GOGAN. Be th' look of it, this must ha' been a general's
    sword . . . All th' gold lace an' th' fine figaries on it. . . .
    Sure it's twiced too big for him.

FLUTHER. A-ah; it's a baby's rattle he ought to have, an' he
    as he is with thoughts tossin' in his head of what may
    happen to him on th' day o' judgment.

(PETER *has entered, and seeing* MRS. GOGAN *with the
sword, goes over to her, pulls it resentfully out of her
hands, and marches into the room, Back, without speaking.*)

MRS. GOGAN (*as* PETER *whips the sword*). Oh, excuse me!
    . . . (*To* FLUTHER) Isn't he th' surly oul' rascal!

FLUTHER. Take no notice of him. . . . You'd think he was
    dumb, but when you get his goat, or he has a few jars[14]
    up, he's vice versa. (*He coughs.*)

MRS. GOGAN (*she has now sidled over as far as the shirt hang-
    ing on the chair*). Oh, you've got a cold on you, Fluther.

FLUTHER (*carelessly*). Ah, it's only a little one.

MRS. GOGAN. You'd want to be careful, all th' same. I knew
    a woman, a big lump of a woman, red-faced an' round-
    bodied, a little awkward on her feet; you'd think to look
    at her, she could put out her two arms an' lift a two-storied
    house on th' top of her head; got a ticklin' in her throat,
    an' a little cough, an' the' next mornin' she had a little
    catchin' in her chest, an' they had just time to wet her lips
    with a little rum, an' off she went. *She begins to look at
    and handle the shirt.*)

FLUTHER (*a little nervously*). It's only a little cold I have;
    there's nothing derogatory wrong with me.

MRS. GOGAN. I dunno; there's many a man this minute
    lowerin' a pint, thinkin' of a woman, or pickin' out a win-
    ner, or doin' work as you're doin', while th' hearse dhrawn
    be th' horses with the black plumes is dhrivin' up to his
    own hall door, an' a voice that he doesn't hear is mutther-
    in' in his ear, "Earth to earth, an' ashes t' ashes, an' dust
    to dust."

----

[14]*jars:* tankards of beer or stout

FLUTHER (*faintly*).   A man in th' pink o' health should have a holy horror of allowin' thoughts o' death to be festherin' in his mind, for—(*with a frightened cough*) be God, I think I'm afther gettin' a little catch in me chest that time —it's a creepy thing to be thinkin' about.

MRS. GOGAN.   It is, an' it isn't; it's both bad an' good. . . . It always gives meself a kind o' thresspassin' joy to feel meself movin' along in a mournin' coach, an' me thinkin' that, maybe, th' next funeral 'll be me own, an' glad, in a quiet way, that this is somebody else's.

FLUTHER.   An' a curious kind of a gaspin' for breath—I hope there's nothin' derogatory wrong with me.

MRS. GOGAN (*examining the shirt*).   Frills on it, like a woman's petticoat.

FLUTHER.   Suddenly gettin' hot, an' then, just as suddenly, gettin' cold.

MRS. GOGAN (*holding out the shirt toward* FLUTHER).   How would you like to be wearin' this Lord Mayor's nightdhress, Fluther?

FLUTHER (*vehemently*).   Blast you an' your nightshirt! Is a man fermentin' with fear to stick th' showin' off to him of a thing that looks like a shinin' shroud?

MRS. GOGAN.   Oh, excuse me!

(PETER *has again entered, and he pulls the shirt from the hands of* MRS. GOGAN, *replacing it on the chair. He returns to room.*)

PETER (*as he goes out*).   Well, God Almighty, give me patience!

MRS GOGAN. (*to Peter*).   Oh, excuse me!

(*There is heard a cheer from the men working outside on the street, followed by the clang of tools being thrown down, then silence. The glare of the gasoline light diminishes and finally goes out.*)

MRS. GOGAN (*running into the back room to look out of the*

window).   What's the men repairin' th' streets cheerin'
for?

FLUTHER *(sitting down weakly on a chair).*   You can't sneeze
but that oul' one wants to know th' why an' th' wherefore.
. . . I feel as dizzy as bedamned! I hope I didn't give up
th' beer too suddenly.

(The COVEY[15] *comes in by door, Right. He is about
twenty-five, tall, thin, with lines on his face that form a
perpetual protest against life as he conceives it to be.
Heavy seams fall from each side of his nose, down around
his lips, as if they were suspenders keeping his mouth
from falling. He speaks in a slow, wailing drawl; more
rapidly when he is excited. He is dressed in dungarees,
and is wearing a vividly red tie. He flings his cap with a
gesture of disgust on the table, and begins to take off his
overalls.)*

MRS. GOGAN *(to the* COVEY, *as she runs back into the room).*
What's after happenin', Covey?

THE COVEY *(with contempt).*   Th' job's stopped. They've
been mobilized to march in th' demonstration to-night
undher th' Plough an' th' Stars.[16] Didn't you hear them
cheerin', th' mugs! They have to renew their political
baptismal vows to be faithful in seculo seculorum.[17]

FLUTHER *(forgetting his fear in his indignation).*   There's no
reason to bring religion into it. I think we ought to have
as great a regard for religion as we can, so as to keep it
out of as many things as possible.

THE COVEY *(pausing in the taking off of his dungarees).*   Oh,
you're one o' the boys that climb into religion as high as
a short Mass on Sunday mornin's? I suppose you'll be
singin' songs o' Sion an' songs o' Tara at th' meetin', too.

FLUTHER.   We're all Irishmen, anyhow; aren't we?

---

[15]*covey:* young fellow (slang)
[16]*Plough . . . Stars:* the flag of the Irish Citizen Army, so-called because
of the symbols that appear upon it
[17]*in seculo seculorum:* into the hereafter, forever

THE COVEY (*with hand outstretched, and in a professional tone*).   Look here, comrade, there's no such thing as an Irishman, or an Englishman, or a German or a Turk; we're all only human bein's. Scientifically speakin', it's all a question of the accidental gatherin' together of mollycewels an' atoms.

(PETER *comes in with a collar in his hand. He goes over to mirror, Left, and proceeds to try to put it on.*)

FLUTHER.   Mollycewels an' atoms! D'ye think I'm goin' to listen to you thryin' to juggle Fluther's mind with complicated cunundhrums[18] of mollycewels an' atoms?

THE COVEY (*rather loudly*).   There's nothin' complicated in it. There's no fear o' th' Church tellin' you that mollycewels is a stickin' together of millions of atoms o' sodium, carbon, potassium o' iodide, etcetera, that, accordin' to th' way they're mixed, make a flower, a fish, a star that you see shinin' in th' sky, or a man with a big brain like me, or a man with a little brain like you!

FLUTHER (*more loudly still*).   There's no necessity to be raisin' your voice; shoutin's no manifestin' forth of a growin' mind.

PETER (*struggling with his collar*).   God, give me patience with this thing. . . . She makes these collars as stiff with starch as a shinin' band o' solid steel! She does it purposely to thry an' twart me.[19] If I can't get it on th' singlet, how, in th' Name o' God, am I goin' to get it on th' shirt?

THE COVEY (*loudly*).   There's no use o' arguin' with you; it's education you want, comrade.

FLUTHER.   The Covey an' God made th' world, I suppose, wha'?

THE COVEY.   When I hear some men talkin' I'm inclined to disbelieve that th' world's eight-hundred million years old, for it's not long since th' fathers o' some o' them crawled out o' th' sheltherin' slime o' the sea.

MRS. GOGAN (*from room at back*).   There, they're afther formin' fours, an' now they're goin' to march away.

[18]*cunundhrums:* (conundrums) riddles
[19]*twart:* (thwart) frustrate. Peter uses the word continually.

FLUTHER (*scornfully*).   Mollycewels! *He begins to untie his apron.)* What about Adam an' Eve?

THE COVEY.   Well, what about them?

FLUTHER (*fiercely*).   What about them, you?

THE COVEY.   Adam an' Eve! Is that as far as you've got? Are you still thinkin' there was nobody in th' world before Adam an' Eve? (*Loudly*) Did you ever hear, man, of th' skeleton of th' man o' Java?[20]

PETER (*casting the collar from him*).   Blast it, blast it, blast it!

FLUTHER (*viciously folding his apron*).   Ah, you're not goin' to be let tap your rubbidge o' thoughts into th' mind o' Fluther.

THE COVEY.   You're afraid to listen to th' thruth!

FLUTHER.   Who's afraid?

THE COVEY.   You are!

FLUTHER.   G'way, you wurum!

THE COVEY.   Who's a worum?

FLUTHER.   You are, or you wouldn't talk th' way you're talkin'.

THE COVEY.   Th' oul', ignorant savage leppin' up in you, when science shows you that th' head of your god is an empty one. Well, I hope you're enjoyin' th' blessin' o' havin' to live be th' sweat of your brow.

FLUTHER.   You'll be kickin' an' yellin' for th' priest yet, me boyo. I'm not goin' to stand silent an' simple listenin' to a thick[21] like you makin' a maddenin' mockery o' God Almighty. It 'ud be a nice derogatory thing on me conscience, an' me dyin', to look back in rememberin' shame of talkin' to a word-weavin' little ignorant yahoo of a red flag Socialist!

MRS. GOGAN (*she has returned to the front room, and has wandered around looking at things in general, and is now in front of the fireplace looking at the picture hanging over it*).   For God's sake, Fluther, dhrop it; there's always th' makin's of a row in th' mention of religion . . .

[20]*man o' Java:* (Java man) a type of primitive man known from fossil remains found in Java in 1891
[21]*thick:* stupid person (colloquial)

(Looking at picture) God bless us, it's a naked woman!

FLUTHER *(coming over to look at it)*. What's undher it? *(Reading)* "Georgina: The Sleepin' Vennis".[22] Oh, that's a terrible picture; oh, that's a shockin' picture! Oh, th' one that got that taken, she must have been a prime lassie!

PETER *(who also has come over to look, laughing, with his body bent at the waist, and his head slightly tilted back).* Hee, hee, hee, hee, hee!

FLUTHER *(indignantly, to* PETER*).* What are you hee, hee-in' for? That's a nice thing to be hee, hee-in' at. Where's your morality, man?

MRS. GOGAN. God forgive us, it's not right to be lookin' at it.

FLUTHER. It's nearly a derogatory thing to be in th' room where it is.

MRS. GOGAN *(giggling hysterically).* I couldn't stop any longer in th' same room with three men, afther lookin' at it! *(She goes out.)*

(The COVEY, *who has divested himself of his dungarees, throws them with a contemptuous motion on top of* PETER'S *white shirt.)*

PETER *(plaintively).* Where are you throwin' them? Are you thryin' to twart an' torment me again?

THE COVEY. Who's thryin' to twart you?

PETER *(flinging the dungarees violently on the floor).* You're not goin' to make me lose me temper, me young Covey.

THE COVEY *(flinging the white shirt on the floor).* If you're Nora's pet, aself, you're not goin' to get your way in everything.

PETER *(plaintively, with his eyes looking up at the ceiling).* I'll say nothin'. . . . I'll leave you to th' day when th' all-pitiful, all-merciful, all-lovin' God 'll be handin' you to th' angels to be rievin' an' roastin' you, tearin' an' tormentin' you, burnin' an' blastin' you!

THE COVEY. Aren't you th' little malignant oul' lemon-whiskered oul' swine!

[22]*The Sleeping Venus:* See page 275.

(PETER *runs to the sword, draws it, and makes for the* COVEY, *who dodges him around the table;* PETER *has no intention of striking, but the* COVEY *wants to take no chances.*)

THE COVEY (*dodging*).　Fluther, hold him, there. It's a nice thing to have a lunatic like this lashin' around with a lethal weapon! (*He darts out of the room, Right, slamming the door in the face of* PETER.)

PETER (*battering and pulling at the door*).　Lemme out, lemme out; isn't it a poor thing for a man who wouldn't say a word against his greatest enemy to have to listen to that Covey's twartin' animosities, shovin' poor, patient people into a lashin' out of curses that darken his soul with th' shadow of th' wrath of th' last day!

FLUTHER.　Why d'ye take notice of him? If he seen you didn't, he'd say nothin' derogatory.

PETER.　I'll make him stop his laughin' an' lerrin', jibin' an' jeerin' an' scarifyin' people with his corner-boy insinuations! . . . He's always thryin' to rouse me: if it's not a song, it's a whistle; if it isn't a whistle, it's a cough. But you can taunt an' taunt—I'm laughin' at you; he, hee, hee, hee, hee, heee!

THE COVEY (*singing through the keyhole*):

Dear harp o' me counthry, in darkness I found thee,
The dark chain of silence had hung o'er thee long—

PETER (*frantically*).　Jasus, d'ye hear that? D'ye hear him soundin' forth his divil-souled song o' provocation?

THE COVEY (*singing as before*):

When proudly, me own island harp, I unbound thee,
An' gave all thy chords to light, freedom an' song!

PETER (*battering at door*).　When I get out I'll do for you, I'll do for you, I'll do for you!

THE COVEY (*through the keyhole*).　Cuckoo-oo!

(NORA *enters by door, Right. She is a young woman of twenty-two, alert, swift, full of nervous energy, and a little anxious to get on in the world. The firm lines of her face are considerably opposed by a soft, amorous mouth and gentle eyes. When her firmness fails her, she persuades with her feminine charm. She is dressed in a tailor-made costume, and wears around her neck a silver fox fur.*)

NORA (*running in and pushing* PETER *away from the door*). Oh, can I not turn me back but th' two o' yous are at it like a pair o' fightin' cocks! Uncle Peter . . . Uncle Peter . . . UNCLE PETER!

PETER (*vociferously*). Oh, Uncle Peter, Uncle Peter be damned! D'ye think I'm goin' to give a free pass to th' young Covey to turn me whole life into a Holy Manual o' penances an' martyrdoms?

THE COVEY (*angrily rushing into the room*). If you won't exercise some sort o' conthrol over that Uncle Peter o' yours, there'll be a funeral, an' it won't be me that'll be in th' hearse!

NORA (*between* PETER *and the* COVEY, *to the* COVEY). Are yous always goin' to be tearin' down th' little bit of respectability that a body's thryin' to build up? Am I always goin' to be havin' to nurse yous into th' hardy habit o' thryin' to keep up a little bit of appearance?

THE COVEY. Why weren't you here to see th' way he run at me with th' sword?

PETER. What did you call me a lemon-whiskered oul' swine for?

NORA. If th' two o' yous don't thry to make a generous altheration in your goin's on, an' keep on thryin' t' inaugurate th' customs o' th' rest o' th' house into this place, yous can flit into other lodgin's where your bowsey[23] battlin' 'ill meet, maybe, with an encore.

PETER (*to* NORA). Would you like to be called a lemon-whiskered oul' swine?

[23]*bowsey*: rowdy

NORA. If you attempt to wag that sword of yours at anybody again, it'll have to be taken off you an' put in a safe place away from babies that don't know th' danger o' them things.

PETER *(at entrance to room, Back).* Well, I'm not goin' to let anybody call me a lemon-whiskered oul' swine. *(He goes in.)*

FLUTHER *(trying the door).* Openin' an' shuttin' now with a well-mannered motion, like a door of a select bar in a high-class pub.

NORA *(to the* COVEY, *as she lays table for tea).* An', once for all, Willie, you'll have to thry to deliver yourself from th' desire of provokin' oul' Pether into a wild forgetfulness of what's proper an' allowable in a respectable home.

THE COVEY. Well, let him mind his own business, then. Yestherday, I caught him hee-hee-in' out of him an' he readin' bits out of Jenersky's *Thesis on th' Origin, Development, an' Consolidation of th' Evolutionary Idea of th' Proletariat.*

NORA. Now, let it end at that, for God's sake; Jack'll be in any minute, an' I'm not goin' to have th' quiet of his evenin' tossed about in an everlastin' uproar between you an' Uncle Pether. *(To* FLUTHER*)* Well, did you manage to settle th' lock, yet, Mr. Good?

FLUTHER *(opening and shutting door).* It's betther than a new one, now, Mrs. Clitheroe; it's almost ready to open and shut of its own accord.

NORA *(giving him a coin).* You're a whole man. How many pints will that get you?

FLUTHER *(seriously).* Ne'er a one at all, Mrs. Clitheroe, for Fluther's on th' wather waggon now. You could stan' where you're stannin' chantin', "Have a glass o' malt, Fluther; Fluther, have a glass o' malt," till th' bells would be ringin' th' ould year out an' th' New Year in, an' you'd have as much chance o' movin' Fluther as a tune on a tin whistle would move a deaf man an' he dead.

(As NORA *is opening and shutting door,* MRS. BESSIE BURGESS *appears at it. She is a woman of forty, vigorously*

built. Her face is a dogged one, hardened by toil, and a little coarsened by drink. She looks scornfully and viciously at NORA *for a few moments before she speaks.)*

BESSIE. Puttin' a new lock on her door . . . afraid her poor neighbours ud break through an' steal. . . . *(In a loud tone)* Maybe, now, they're a damn sight more honest than your ladyship . . . checkin' th' children playin' on th' stairs . . . gettin' on th' nerves of your ladyship . . . Complainin' about Bessie Burgess singin' her hymns at night, when she has a few up. . . . *(She comes in half-way on the threshold, and screams)* Bessie Burgess 'll sing whenever she damn well likes!

*(*NORA *tries to shut door, but* BESSIE *violently shoves it in, and, gripping* NORA *by the shoulders, shakes her.)*

BESSIE. You little over-dressed throllope, you, for one pin I'd paste th′ white face o' you!
NORA *(frightened)*. Fluther, Fluther!
FLUTHER *(running over and breaking the hold of* BESSIE *from* NORA*)*. Now, now, Bessie, Bessie, leave poor Mrs. Clitheroe alone; she'd do no one any harm, an' minds no one's business but her own.
BESSIE. Why is she always thryin' to speak proud things, an' lookin' like a mighty one in th' congregation o' th' people!

*(*NORA *sinks frightened on to the couch as* JACK CLITHEROE *enters. He is a tall, well-made fellow of twenty-five. His face has none of the strength of* NORA'S. *It is a face in which is the desire for authority, without the power to attain it.*

CLITHEROE *(excitedly)*. What's up? what's afther happenin'?
FLUTHER. Nothin', Jack. Nothin'. It's all over now. Come on, Bessie, come on.
CLITHEROE *(to* NORA*)*. What's wrong, Nora? Did she say anything to you?
NORA. She was bargin' out of her, an' I only told her to g'up

ower o' that[24] to her own place; an' before I knew where I
was, she flew at me like a tiger, an' thried to guzzle me!
CLITHEROE *(going to door and speaking to* BESSIE*).*   Get up
to your own place, Mrs. Burgess, and don't you be interferin' with my wife, or it'll be th' worse for you. . . . Go
on, go on!
BESSIE *(as* CLITHEROE *is pushing her out).*   Mind who you're
pushin', now. . . . I attend me place o' worship, anyhow
. . . not like some o' them that go to neither church, chapel
nor meetin'-house. . . . If me son was home from th'
threnches[25] he'd see me righted.

(BESSIE *and* FLUTHER *depart, and* CLITHEROE *closes the
door.)*

CLITHEROE *(going over to* NORA*, and putting his arm round
her).*   There, don't mind that old witch, Nora, darling;
I'll soon put a stop to her interferin'.
NORA.   Some day or another, when I'm here be meself, she'll
come in an' do somethin' desperate.
CLITHEROE *(kissing her).*   Oh, sorra[26] fear of her doin' anythin' desperate. I'll talk to her tomorrow when she's sober.
A taste o' me mind that'll shock her into the sensibility
of behavin' herself!

(NORA *gets up and settles the table. She sees the dungarees on the floor and stands looking at them, then she
turns to the* COVEY*, who is reading Jenersky's "Thesis"
at the fire.)*

NORA.   Willie, is that th' place for your dungarees?
THE COVEY *(getting up and lifting them from the floor).*   Ah,
they won't do th' floor any harm, will they? *(He carries
them into room, Back.)*
NORA *(calling).*   Uncle Peter, now, Uncle Peter; tea's ready.

---

[24]*ower o' that:* enough of that
[25]*threnches:* (trenches) meaning the combat zone of the Allies in World
War I (1914-1918)
[26]*sorra:* (an Irish expression of negation) no

(PETER and the COVEY come in from room, Back; they all sit down to tea. PETER is in full dress of the Foresters:[27] green coat, gold braided; white breeches, top boots, frilled shirt. He carries the slouch hat, with the white ostrich plume, and the sword in his hands. They eat for a few moments in silence, the COVEY furtively looking at PETER with scorn in his eyes. PETER knows it and is fidgety.)

THE COVEY *(provokingly).* Another cut o' bread, Uncle Peter? *(PETER maintains a dignified silence.)*

CLITHEROE.   It's sure to be a great meetin' to-night. We ought to go, Nora.

NORA *(decisively).*   I won't go, Jack; you can go if you wish.

(A pause.)

THE COVEY.   D'ye want th' sugar, Uncle Peter?

PETER *(explosively).*   Now, are you goin' to start your thryin' an' your twartin' again?

NORA.   Now, Uncle Peter, you musn't be so touchy; Willie has only asked you if you wanted th' sugar.

PETER.   He doesn't care a damn whether I want th' sugar or no. He's only thryin' to twart me!

NORA *(angrily, to the COVEY).*   Can't you let him alone, Willie? If he wants the sugar, let him stretch his hand out an' get it himself!

THE COVEY *(to PETER).*   Now, if you want the sugar, you can stretch out your hand and get it yourself!

CLITHEROE.   Tonight is th' first chance that Brennan has got of showing himself off since they made a Captain of him —why, God only knows. It'll be a treat to see him swankin' it at th' head of the Citizen Army carryin' th' flag of the Plough an' th' Stars. . . . *(Looking roguishly at NORA)* He was sweet on you, once, Nora?

NORA.   He may have been. . . . I never liked him. I always thought he was a bit of a thick.

---

[27]*Foresters:* The Ancient Order of Foresters, a benevolent society

THE COVEY.   They're bringin' nice disgrace on that banner now.

CLITHEROE (*remonstratively*).   How are they bringin' disgrace on it?

THE COVEY (*snappily*).   Because it's a Labour[28] flag, an' was never meant for politics. . . . What does th' design of th' field plough, bearin' on it th' stars of th' heavenly plough, mean, if it's not Communism? It's a flag that should only be used when we're buildin' th' barricades to fight for a Workers' Republic!

PETER (*with a puff of derision*).   P-phuh.

THE COVEY (*angrily*).   What are you phuhin' out o' you for? Your mind is th' mind of a mummy. (*Rising*) I betther go an' get a good place to have a look at Ireland's warriors passin' by. (*He goes into room, Left, and returns with his cap.*

NORA (*to the* COVEY).   Oh, Willie, brush your clothes before you go.

THE COVEY.   Oh, they'll do well enough.

NORA.   Go an' brush them; th' brush is in th' drawer there.

(*The* COVEY *goes to the drawer, muttering, gets the brush, and starts to brush his clothes.*)

THE COVEY (*singing at* PETER, *as he does so*):

> Oh, where's th' slave so lowly,
> Condemn'd to chains unholy,
> Who, could he burst his bonds at first,
> Would pine beneath them slowly?

> We tread th' land that . . . bore us,
> Th' green flag glitters . . . o'er us,
> Th' friends we've tried are by our side,
> An' th' foe we hate . . . before us!

PETER (*leaping to his feet in a whirl of rage*).   Now, I'm

---

[28]*Labour:* the political party of Great Britain organized to protect and further the rights of workers

tellin' you, me young Covey, once for all, that I'll not
stick any longer these tittherin' taunts of yours, rovin'
around to sing your slights an' slandhers, reddenin' th'
mind of a man to th' thinkin' an' sayin' of things that
sicken his soul with sin! *(Hysterically; lifting up a cup
to fling at the* COVEY*)* Be God, I'll—

CLITHEROE *(catching his arm).*   Now then, none o' that, none
o' that!

NORA.   Uncle Pether, Uncle Pether, UNCLE PETHER!

THE COVEY *(at the door, about to go out).*   Isn't that th'
malignant oul' varmint! Lookin' like th' illegitimate son
of an illegitimate child of a corporal in th' Mexican army!
(He goes out.)

PETER *(plaintively).*   He's afther leavin' me now in such a
state of agitation that I won't be able to do meself justice
when I'm marchin' to th' meetin'.

NORA *(jumping up).*   Oh, for God's sake, here, buckle your
sword on, and go to your meetin', so that we'll have at
least one hour of peace! *(She proceeds to belt on the
sword.)*

CLITHEROE *(irritably).*   For God's sake hurry him up ou' o'
this, Nora.

PETER.   Are yous all goin' to thry to start to twart me now?

NORA *(putting on his plumed hat).*   S-s-sh. Now, your hat's
on, your house is thatched; off you pop! *(She gently pushes
him from her.)*

PETER *(going, and turning as he reaches the door).*   Now, if
that young Covey—

NORA.   Go on, go on.

(PETER goes. CLITHEROE *sits down in the lounge, lights a
cigarette, and looks thoughtfully into the fire.* NORA *takes
the things from the table, placing them on the chest of
drawers. There is a pause, then she swiftly comes over to
him and sits beside him.)*

NORA *(softly).*   A penny for them, Jack!

CLITHEROE.   Me? Oh, I was thinkin' of nothing.

NORA. You were thinkin' of th' . . . meetin' . . . Jack. When
we were courtin' an' I wanted you to go, you'd say, "Oh,
to hell with meetin's," an' that you felt lonely in cheerin'
crowds when I was absent. An' we weren't a month married when you began that you couldn't keep away from
them.

CLITHEROE. Oh, that's enough about th' meetin'. It looks as
if you wanted me to go, th' way you're talkin'. You were
always at me to give up th' Citizen Army, an' I gave it
up; surely that ought to satisfy you

NORA. Ay, you gave it up—because you got th' sulks when
they didn't make a Captain of you. It wasn't for my sake,
Jack.

CLITHEROE. For your sake or no, you're benefitin' by it,
aren't you? I didn't forget this was your birthday, did I?
(He puts his arms around her) And you liked your new
hat; didn't you, didn't you? *(He kisses her rapidly several
times.)*

NORA. Jack, Jack; please, Jack! I thought you were tired of
that sort of thing long ago.

CLITHEROE. Well, you're finding out now that I amn't tired
of it yet, anyhow. Mrs. Clitheroe doesn't want to be
kissed, sure she doesn't? *(He kisses her again.)* Little,
little red-lipped Nora!

NORA *(coquettishly removing his arm from around her).* Oh,
yes, your little, little red-lipped Nora's a sweet little girl
when th' fit seizes you; but your little, little red-lipped
Nora has to clean your boots every mornin', all the same.

CLITHEROE *(with a movement of irritation).* Oh, well, if
we're goin' to be snotty!

(A pause.)

NORA. It's lookin' like as if it was you that was goin' to be . . .
snotty! Bridlin' up with bittherness, th' minute a body
attempts t'open her mouth.

CLITHEROE. Is it any wondher, turnin' a tendher sayin' into
a meanin' o' malice an' spite!

NORA.   It's hard for a body to be always keepin' her mind bent on makin' thoughts that'll be no longer than th' length of your own satisfaction.   *(A pause.)*

NORA *(standing up).*   If we're goin' to dhribble th' time away sittin' here like a pair o' cranky mummies, I'd be as well sewin' or doin' something about th' place.

(She looks appealingly at him for a few moments; he doesn't speak. She swiftly sits down beside him, and puts her arm around his neck.)

NORA *(imploringly).*   Ah, Jack, don't be so cross!

CLITHEROE *(doggedly).*   Cross? I'm not cross; I'm not a bit cross. It was yourself started it.

NORA *(coaxingly).*   I didn't mean to say anything out o' the way. You take a body up too quickly, Jack. *(In an ordinary tone as if nothing of an angry nature had been said.)* You didn't offer me me evenin' allowance yet.

(CLITHEROE silently takes out a cigarette for her and himself and lights both.)

NORA *(trying to make conversation).*   How quiet th' house is now; they must be all out.

CLITHEROE *(rather shortly).*   I suppose so.

NORA *(rising from the seat).*   I'm longin' to show you me new hat, to see what you think of it. Would you like to see it?

CLITHEROE.   Ah, I don't mind.

(NORA suppresses a sharp reply, hesitates for a moment, then gets the hat, puts it on, and stands before CLITHEROE.)

NORA.   Well, how does Mr. Clitheroe like me new hat?

CLITHEROE.   It suits you, Nora, it does right enough.

(He stands up, puts his hand beneath her chin, and tilts her head up. She looks at him roguishly. He bends down and kisses her.)

NORA. Here, sit down, an' don't let me hear another cross
  word out of you for th' rest o' the night. *(They sit down.)*
CLITHEROE *(with his arms around her)*. Little, little, red-
  lipped Nora!
NORA. Jack!
CLITHEROE *(tightening his arms around her)*. Well?
NORA. You haven't sung me a song since our honeymoon.
  Sing me one now, do . . . please, Jack!
CLITHEROE. What song? "Since Maggie Went Away"?
NORA. Ah, no, Jack, not that; it's too sad. "When You Said
  You Loved Me."

(Clearing his throat, CLITHEROE *thinks for a moment, and
then begins to sing.* NORA, *putting an arm around him,
nestles her head on his breast and listens delightedly.)*

CLITHEROE *(singing verses following to the air of "When You
and I Were Young, Maggie")*:

  Th' violets were scenting th' woods, Nora,
    Displaying their charm to th' bee,
  When I first said I lov'd only you, Nora,
    An' you said you lov'd only me!

  Th' chestnut blooms gleam'd through th' glade,
      Nora,
    A robin sang loud from a tree,
  When I first said I lov'd only you, Nora,
    An' you said you lov'd only me!

  Th' golden-rob'd daffodils shone, Nora,
    An' danc'd in th' breeze on th' lea,
  When I first said I lov'd only you, Nora,
    An' you said you lov'd only me!

  Th' trees, birds, an' bees sang a song, Nora,
    Of happier transports to be,
  When I first said I lov'd only you, Nora,
    An' you said you lov'd only me!

298 ε Sean O'Casey

*(NORA kisses him. A knock is heard at the door, Right; a
pause as they listen. NORA clings closely to CLITHEROE.
Another knock, more imperative than the first.)*

CLITHEROE.   I wonder who can that be, now?

NORA *(a little nervous)*.   Take no notice of it, Jack; they'll go
away in a minute. *(Another knock, followed by a voice.)*

VOICE.   Commandant Clitheroe, Commandant Clitheroe, are
you there? A message from General Jim Connolly.

CLITHEROE.   Damn it, it's Captain Brennan.

NORA *(anxiously)*.   Don't mind him, don't mind, Jack. Don't
break our happiness . . . Pretend we're not in. Let us forget everything tonight but our two selves!

CLITHEROE *(reassuringly)*.   Don't be alarmed, darling; I'll
just see what he wants, an' send him about his business.

NORA *(tremulously)*.   No, no. Please, Jack; don't open it.
Please, for your own little Nora's sake!

CLITHEROE *(rising to open the door)*.   Now don't be silly,
Nora.

*(CLITHEROE opens door, and admits a young man in the
full uniform of the Irish Citizen Army — green suit; slouch
green hat caught up at one side by a small Red Hand
badge; Sam Browne belt, with a revolver in the holster.
He carries a letter in his hand. When he comes in he
smartly salutes CLITHEROE. The young man is CAPTAIN
BRENNAN.)*

CAPT. BRENNAN *(giving the letter to CLITHEROE)*.   A dispatch
from General Connolly.

CLITHEROE *(reading. While he is doing so, BRENNAN'S eyes
are fixed on NORA, who droops as she sits on the lounge)*.
"Commandant Clitheroe is to take command of the eighth
battalion of the I.C.A. which will assemble to proceed to
the meeting at nine o'clock. He is to see that all units are
provided with full equipment; two days' rations and fifty
rounds of ammunition. At two o'clock A.M. the army will
leave Liberty Hall for a reconnaissance attack on Dublin
Castle.[29] — Com.-Gen. Connolly."

[29]*Dublin Castle:* headquarters of the British authorities in Ireland

CLITHEROE. I don't understand this. Why does General Connolly call me Commandant?

CAPT. BRENNAN. Th' Staff appointed you Commandant, and th' General agreed with their selection.

CLITHEROE. When did this happen?

CAPT. BRENNAN. A fortnight ago.

CLITHEROE. How is it word was never sent to me?

CAPT. BRENNAN. Word was sent to you. . . . I meself brought it.

CLITHEROE. Who did you give it to, then?

CAPT. BRENNAN *(after a pause)*. I think I gave it to Mrs. Clitheroe, there.

CLITHEROE. Nora, d'ye hear that? (NORA *makes no answer.*)

CLITHEROE *(there is a note of hardness in his voice)*. Nora . . . Captain Brennan says he brought a letter to me from General Connolly, and that he gave it to you. . . . Where is it? What did you do with it?

NORA *(running over to him, and pleadingly putting her arms around him)*. Jack, please, Jack, don't go out tonight an' I'll tell you; I'll explain everything. . . . Send him away, an' stay with your own little red-lipp'd Nora.

CLITHEROE *(removing her arms from around him)*. None o' this nonsense, now; I want to know what you did with th' letter?

(NORA *goes slowly to the lounge and sits down.*)

CLITHEROE *(angrily)*. Why didn't you give me th' letter? What did you do with it? . . . *(He shakes her by the shoulder)* What did you do with th' letter?

NORA *(flaming up)*. I burned it, I burned it! That's what I did with it! Is General Connolly an' th' Citizen Army goin' to be your only care? Is your home goin' to be only a place to rest in? Am I goin' to be only somethin' to provide merry-makin' for you? Your vanity'll be th' ruin of you an' me yet. . . . That's what's movin' you: because they've made an officer of you, you'll make a glorious cause of what you're doin', while your little red-lipp'd Nora can go on sittin' here, makin' a companion of th' loneliness of th' night!

CLITHEROE *(fiercely).* You burned it, did you? *(He grips her arm.)* Well, me good lady—
NORA. Let go—you're hurtin' me!
CLITHEROE. You deserve to be hurt. . . . Any letter that comes to me for th' future, take care that I get it. . . . D'ye hear—take care that I get it!

(He goes to the chest of drawers and takes out a Sam Browne belt, which he puts on, and then puts a revolver in the holster. He puts on his hat, and looks towards Nora. While this dialogue is proceeding, and while CLITHEROE *prepares himself,* BRENNAN *softly whistles "The Soldiers' Song.")*

CLITHEROE *(at door, about to go out).* You needn't wait up for me; if I'm in at all, it won't be before six in th' morning.
NORA *(bitterly).* I don't care if you never come back!
CLITHEROE *(to* CAPT. BRENNAN*).* Come along, Ned.

(They go out; there is a pause. NORA *pulls the new hat from her head and with a bitter movement flings it to the other end of the room. There is a gentle knock at door, Right, which opens, and* MOLLSER *comes into the room. She is about fifteen, but looks to be only about ten, for the ravages of consumption have shrivelled her up. She is pitifully worn, walks feebly, and frequently coughs. She goes over to* NORA.*)*

MOLLSER *(to* NORA*).* Mother's gone to th' meetin', an' I was feelin' terrible lonely, so I come down to see if you'd let me sit with you, thinkin' you mightn't be goin' yourself. . . . I do be terrible afraid I'll die sometime when I'm be meself. . . . I often envy you, Mrs. Clitheroe, seein' th' health you have, an' th' lovely place you have here, an' wondherin' if I'll ever be sthrong enough to be keepin' a home together for a man. Oh, this must be some more o' the Dublin Fusiliers[30] flyin' off to the front.

[30]*Dublin Fusiliers:* Irish regiment fighting along with the British in World War I

(Just before MOLLSER *ceases to speak, there is heard in the distance the music of a brass band playing a regiment to the boat on the way to the front. The tune that is being played is "It's a Long Way to Tipperary"; as the band comes to the chorus, the regiment is swinging into the street by* NORA'S *house, and the voices of the soldiers can be heard lustily singing the chorus of the song.)*

It's a long way to Tipperary, it's a long way to go;
It's a long way to Tipperary, to th' sweetest girl I know!
Goodbye Piccadilly, farewell Leicester Square.
It's a long, long way to Tipperary, but my heart's right
   there!

*(*NORA *and* MOLLSER *remain silently listening. As the chorus ends and the music is faint in the distance again,* BESSIE BURGESS *appears at door, Right, which* MOLLSER *has left open.)*

BESSIE *(speaking in towards the room).* There's th' men marchin' out into th' dhread dimness o' danger, while th' lice is crawlin' about feedin' on th' fatness o' the land! But yous'll not escape from th' arrow that flieth be night, or th' sickness that wasteth be day. . . . An' ladyship an' all, as some o' them may be, they'll be scattered abroad, like th' dust in th' darkness!

*(*BESSIE *goes away;* NORA *steals over and quietly shuts the door. She comes back to the lounge and wearily throws herself on it beside* MOLLSER.)*

MOLLSER *(after a pause and a cough).* Is there anybody goin', Mrs Clitheroe, with a titther o' sense?

Curtain

Act II

A commodious public-house at the corner of the street in which the meeting is being addressed from Platform No. 1. It is the south corner of the public-house that is visible to the audience. The counter, beginning at Back about one-fourth of the width of the space shown, comes across two-thirds of the length of the stage, and, taking a circular sweep, passes out of sight to Left. On the counter are beer-pulls, glasses, and a carafe. The other three-fourths of the Back is occupied by a tall, wide, two-paned window. Beside this window at the Right is a small, box-like, panelled snug.[1] Next to the snug is a double swing door, the entrance to that particular end of the house. Farther on is a shelf on which customers may rest their drinks. Underneath the windows is a cushioned seat. Behind the counter at Back can be seen the shelves running the whole length of the counter. On these shelves can be seen the end (or the beginning) of rows of bottles. The BARMAN *is seen wiping the part of the counter which is in view.* ROSIE *is standing at the counter toying with what remains of a half of whisky in a wine-glass. She is a sturdy, well-shaped girl of twenty; pretty, and pert in manner. She is wearing a cream blouse, with an obviously suggestive glad neck; a grey tweed dress, brown stockings and shoes. The blouse and most of the dress are hidden by a black shawl. She has no hat, and in her hair is jauntily set a cheap, glittering, jewelled ornament. It is an hour later.*

BARMAN *(wiping counter).*   Nothin' much doin' in your line tonight, Rosie?

ROSIE.   Curse o' God on th' haporth,[2] hardly, Tom. There isn't much notice taken of a pretty petticoat of a night like this. . . . They're all in a holy mood. Th' solemn-lookin' dials[3] on th' whole o' them an' they marchin' to

[1]*snug:* booth
[2]*haporth:* halfpenny's worth
[3]*dials:* faces (slang)

th' meetin.' You'd think they were th' glorious company
of th' saints, an' th' noble army of martyrs thrampin'
through th' sthreets of paradise. They're all thinkin' of
higher things than a girl's garthers. . . . It's a tremendous
meetin'; four platforms they have—there's one o' them
just outside opposite th' window.

BARMAN.   Oh, ay; sure when th' speaker comes (*motioning
with his hand*) to th' near end, here, you can see him
plain, an' hear nearly everythin' he's spoutin' out of him.

ROSIE.   It's no joke thrying' to make up fifty-five shillin's a
week for your keep an' laundhry, an' then taxin' you a
quid[4] for your own room if you bring home a friend. . . .
If I could only put by a couple of quid for a swankier outfit, everythin' in th' garden ud look lovely—

BARMAN.   Whisht,[5] till we hear what he's sayin'.

(*Through the window is silhouetted the figure of a tall
man who is speaking to the crowd. The* BARMAN *and*
ROSIE *look out of the window and listen.*)

THE VOICE OF THE MAN.   It is a glorious thing to see arms in
the hands of Irishmen. We must accustom ourselves to the
thought of arms, we must accustom ourselves to the sight
of arms, we must accustom ourselves to the use of arms.
. . . Bloodshed is a cleansing and sanctifying thing, and
the nation that regards it as the final horror has lost its
manhood. . . . There are many things more horrible than
bloodshed, and slavery is one of them!

(*The figure moves away towards the Right, and is lost to
sight and hearing.*)

ROSIE.   It's th' sacred thruth, mind you, what that man's afther
sayin'.

BARMAN.   If I was only a little younger, I'd be plungin' mad
into th' middle of it!

ROSIE (*who is still looking out of the window*).   Oh, here's
the two gems runnin' over again for their oil!

---

[4]*quid:* one pound (slang)
[5]*whisht:* hush

(PETER *and* FLUTHER *enter tumultuously. They are hot, and full and hasty with the things they have seen and heard. Emotion is bubbling up in them, so that when they drink, and when they speak, they drink and speak with the fullness of emotional passion.* PETER *leads the way to the counter.*)

PETER (*splutteringly to* BARMAN). Two halves[6] ... (*To* FLUTHER) A meetin' like this always makes me feel as if I could dhrink Loch Erinn dhry!

FLUTHER. You couldn't feel any way else at a time like this when th' spirit of a man is pulsin' to be out fightin' for th' thruth with his feet thremblin' on th' way, maybe to th' gallows, an' his ears tinglin' with th' faint, far-away sound of burstin' rifle-shots that'll maybe whip th' last little shock o' life out of him that's left lingerin' in his body!

PETER. I felt a burnin' lump in me throat when I heard th' band playin' "The Soldiers' Song," rememberin' last hearin' it marchin' in military formation, with th' people starin' on both sides at us, carryin' with us th' pride an' resolution o' Dublin to th' grave of Wolfe Tone.[7]

FLUTHER. Get th' Dublin men goin' an' they'll go on full force for anything that's thryin' to bar them away from what they're wantin', where th' slim thinkin' counthry boyo ud limp away from th' first faintest touch of compromization!

PETER (*hurriedly to the* BARMAN). Two more, Tom! ... (*To* FLUTHER) Th' memory of all th' things that was done, an' all th' things that was suffered be th' people, was boomin' in me brain. ... Every nerve in me body was quiverin' to do somethin' desperate!

FLUTHER. Jammed as I was in th' crowd, I listened to th' speeches patherin' on th' people's head, like rain fallin' on th' corn; every derogatory thought went out o' me mind, an' I said to meself, "You can die now, Fluther, for you've seen th' shadow-dhreams of th' past leppin' to life

---

[6]*halves:* half-pints (beer or stout)
[7]*Wolfe Tone:* leader of an unsuccessful nationalist uprising for independence from England in 1798.

in th' bodies of livin' men that show, if we were without a titther o' courage for centuries, we're vice versa now!" Looka here. [*He stretches out his arm under Peter's face and rolls up his sleeve.*] The blood was BOILIN' in me veins!

(*The silhouette of the tall figure again moves into the frame of the window speaking to the people.*)

PETER (*unaware, in his enthusiasm, of the speaker's appearance, to* FLUTHER). I was burnin' to dhraw me sword, an' wave an' wave it over me——

FLUTHER (*overwhelming* PETER). Well you stop your blatherin' for a minute, man, an' let us hear what he's sayin'!

VOICE OF THE MAN. Comrade soldiers of the Irish Volunteers[8] and of the Citizen Army, we rejoice in this terrible war. The old heart of the earth needed to be warmed with the red wine of the battlefields. . . . Such august homage was never offered to God as this: the homage of millions of lives given gladly for love of country. And we must be ready to pour out the same red wine in the same glorious sacrifice, for without shedding of blood there is no redemption! (*The figure moves out of sight and hearing.*)

FLUTHER (*gulping down the drink that remains in his glass, and rushing out*). Come on, man; this is too good to be missed!

(PETER *finishes his drink less rapidly, and as he is going out wiping his mouth with the back of his hand he runs into the* COVEY *coming in. He immediately erects his body like a young cock, and with his chin thrust forward, and a look of venomous dignity on his face, he marches out.*)

THE COVEY (*at counter*). Give us a glass o' malt, for God's sake, till I stimulate meself from th' shock o' seein' th' sight that's afther goin' out!

---

[8]*Irish Volunteers:* rivals of the Irish Citizen Army. Though both groups were nationalistic, the Volunteers—being a middle-class group—were largely unconcerned with the cause of labor. The goal of the Volunteers was an Irish Free State rather than a Workers' Republic.

ROSIE *(all business, coming over to the counter, and standing near the* COVEY*).* Another one for me, Tommy; *(to the* BARMAN*)* th' young gentleman's ordherin' it in th' corner of his eye.

(The BARMAN *brings the drink for the* COVEY, *and leaves it on the counter.* ROSIE *whips it up.)*

BARMAN. Ay, houl' on there, houl' on there, Rosie!

ROSIE *(to the* BARMAN*).* What are you houldin' on out o' you for? Didn't you hear th' young gentleman say that he couldn't refuse anything to a nice little bird?[9] *(To the* COVEY*)* Isn't that right, Jiggs? *(The* COVEY *says nothing.)* Didn't I know, Tommy, it would be all right? It takes Rosie to size a young man up, an' tell th' thoughts that are thremblin' in his mind. Isn't that right, Jiggs?

(The COVEY *stirs uneasily, moves a little farther away, and pulls his cap over his eyes.)*

ROSIE *(moving after him).* Great meetin' that's gettin' held outside. Well, it's up to us all, anyway, to fight for our freedom.

THE COVEY *(to* BARMAN*).* Two more, please. *(To* ROSIE*)* Freedom! What's th' use o' freedom, if it's not economic freedom?

ROSIE *(emphasizing with extended arm and moving finger).* I used them very words just before you come in. "A lot o' thricksters," says I, "that wouldn't know what freedom was if they got it from their mother." . . . *(To* BARMAN*)* Didn't I, Tommy?

BARMAN. I disremember.

ROSIE. No, you don't disremember. Remember you said, yourself, it was all "only a flash in th' pan." Well, "flash in th' pan, or no flash in th' pan," says I, "they're not goin' to get Rosie Redmond," says I, "to fight for freedom that wouldn't be worth winnin' in a raffle!"

---

[9]*bird:* girl (slang)

THE COVEY. There's only one freedom for th' workin' man: conthrol o' th' means o' production, rates of exchange, an' th' means of disthribution. *(Tapping Rosie on the shoulder)* Look here, comrade, I'll leave here tomorrow night for you a copy of Jenersky's *Thesis on the Origin, Development, an' Consolidation of the Evolutionary Idea of the Proletariat.*

ROSIE *(throwing off her shawl on to the counter, and showing an exemplified glad neck, which reveals a good deal of a white bosom).* If y'ask Rosie, it's heartbreakin' to see a young fella thinkin' of anything, or admirin' anything, but silk thransparent stockin's showin' off the shape of a little lassie's legs!

(The COVEY, *frightened, moves a little away)*

ROSIE *(following on).* Out in th' park in th' shade of a warm summery evenin', with your little darlin' bridie to be, kissin' an' cuddlin' *(she tries to put her arm around his neck),* kissin' an' cuddlin', ay?

THE COVEY *(frightened).* Ay, what are you doin'? None o' that, now; none o' that. I've something else to do besides shinannickin' afther Judies! *(He turns away, but* ROSIE *follows, keeping face to face with him.)*

ROSIE. Oh, little duckey, oh, shy little duckery! Never held a mot's hand, an' wouldn't know how to tittle a little Judy! *(She clips him under the chin.)* Tittle him undher th' chin, tittle him undher th' chin!

THE COVEY *(breaking away and running out).* Ay, go on, now; I don't want to have any meddlin' with a lassie like you!

ROSIE *(enraged).* Jasus, it's in a monasthery some of us ought to be, spendin' our holidays kneelin' on our adorers, tellin' our beads,[10] an' knockin' hell out of our buzzums!

THE COVEY *(outside).* Cuckoo-oo!

(PETER and FLUTHER come in again, followed by MRS.

---

[10]*tellin' our beads:* saying our rosaries

GOGAN, *carrying a baby in her arms. They go over to the counter.)*

PETER *(with plaintive anger).* It's terrible that young Covey can't let me pass without proddin' at me! Did you hear him murmurin' "cuckoo" when we were passin'?

FLUTHER *(irritably).* I wouldn't be everlastin' cockin' me ear to hear every little whisper that was floatin' around about me! It's my rule never to lose me temper till it would be dethrimental to keep it. There's nothin' derogatory in th' use o' th' word "cuckoo," is there?

PETER *(tearfully).* It's not th' word; it's th' way he says it: he never says it straight out, but murmurs it with curious quiverin' ripples, like variations on a flute!

FLUTHER. Ah, what odds if he gave it with variations on a thrombone! *(To MRS. GOGAN)* What's yours goin' to be, ma'am?

MRS. GOGAN. Ah, a half o' malt, Fluther.

FLUTHER *(to BARMAN).* Three halves, Tommy.

(The BARMAN brings the drinks.)

MRS. GOGAN *(drinking).* The Foresthers' is a gorgeous dhress! I don't think I've seen nicer, mind you, in a pantomime. . . . Th' loveliest part of th' dhress, I think, is th' osthrichess plume. . . . When yous are goin' along, an' I see them wavin' an' noddin' an' waggin', I seem to be lookin' at each of yous hangin' at th' end of a rope, your eyes bulgin' an' your legs twistin' an' jerkin', gaspin' an' gaspin' for breath while yous are thryin' to die for Ireland!

FLUTHER. If any o' them is hangin' at the end of a rope, it won't be for Ireland!

PETER. Are you goin' to start th' young Covey's game o' proddin' an' twartin' a man? There's not many that's talkin' can say that for twenty-five years he never missed a pilgrimage to Bodenstown!

FLUTHER. You're always blowin' about goin' to Bodenstown. D'ye think no one but yourself ever went to Bodenstown?

PETER *(plaintively).* I'm not blowin' about it; but there's not a year that I go there but I pluck a leaf off Tone's[11] grave, an' this very day me prayer-book is nearly full of them.

FLUTHER *(scornfully).* Then Fluther has a vice versa opinion of them that put ivy leaves into their prayer-books, scabbin' it on th' clergy, an' thryin' to out-do th' haloes o' th' saints be lookin' as if he was wearin' around his head a glittherin' aroree boree allis![12] *(Fiercely)* Sure, I don't care a damn if you slep' in Bodenstown! You can take your breakfast, dinner, an' tea on th' grave in Bodenstown, if you like, for Fluther!

MRS. GOGAN. Oh, don't start a fight, boys, for God's sake; I was only sayin' what a nice costume it is — nicer than th' kilts, for, God forgive me, I always think th' kilts is hardly decent.

FLUTHER. Ah, sure, when you'd look at him, you'd wondher whether th' man was makin' fun o' th' costume, or th' costume was makin' fun o' th' man!

BARMAN. Now, then, thry to speak asy, will yous! We don't want no shoutin' here.

(The COVEY *followed by* BESSIE BURGESS *comes in. They go over to the opposite end of the counter, and direct their gaze on the other group.)*

THE COVEY *(to* BARMAN*).* Two glasses o' malt.

PETER. There he is, now; I knew he wouldn't be long till he folleyed me in.

BESSIE *(speaking to the* COVEY, *but really at the other party).* I can't for th' life o' me undherstand how they can call themselves Catholics, when they won't lift a finger to help poor little Catholic Belgium.

MRS. GOGAN *(rising her voice).* What about poor little Catholic Ireland?

BESSIE *(over to* MRS. GOGAN*).* You mind your own business, ma'am, an' stupefy your foolishness be gettin' dhrunk.

PETER *(anxiously).* Take no notice of her; pay no attention

to her. She's just tormentin' herself towards havin' a row
with somebody.

BESSIE.   There's a storm of anger tossin' in me heart, thinkin'
of all th' poor Tommies,[13] an' with them me own son,
dhrenched in water an' soaked in blood, gropin' their way
to a shattherin' death, in a shower o' shells! Young men
with th' sunny lust o' life beamin' in them, layin' down
their white bodies, shredded into torn an' bloody pieces,
on th' althar that God Himself has built for th' sacrifice
of heroes!

MRS. GOGAN.   Isn't it a nice thing to have to be listenin' to a
lassie an' hangin' our heads in a dead silence, knowin'
that some persons think more of a ball of malt than they
do of th' blessed saints.

FLUTHER.   Whisht; she's always dangerous an' derogatory
when she's well oiled. Th' safest way to hindher her from
havin' any enjoyment out of her spite, is to dip our
thoughts into the fact of her bein' a female person that
has moved out of th' sight of ordinary sensible people.

BESSIE.   To look at some o' th' women that's knockin' about,
now, is a thing to make a body sigh. . . . A woman on her
own, dhrinkin' with a bevy o' men, is hardly an example
to her sex. . . . A woman dhrinkin' with a woman is one
thing, an' a woman dhrinkin' with herself is still a woman
—flappers[14] may be put in another category altogether—
but a middle-aged married woman makin' herself th'
centre of a circle of men is as a woman that is loud an'
stubborn, whose feet abideth not in her own house.

THE COVEY *(to* BESSIE*).*   When I think of all th' problems in
front o' th' workers, it makes me sick to be lookin' at oul'
codgers goin' about dhressed up like green-accoutred
figures gone asthray out of a toyshop!

PETER.   Gracious God, give me patience to be listenin' to
that blasted young Covey proddin' at me from over at th'
other end of th' shop!

MRS. GOGAN *(dipping her finger in the whisky, and moistening
with it the lips of her baby).*   Cissie Gogan's a woman

[13]*Tommies:* British soldiers
[14]*flappers:* girls in the late teens

livin' for nigh on twenty-five years in her own room, an'
beyond biddin' th' time o' day to her neighbours, never
yet as much as nodded her head in th' direction of other
people's business, while she knows some as are never
content unless they're standin' senthry over other people's doin's!

(BESSIE *is about to reply, when the tall, dark figure is
again silhouetted against the window, and the voice of
the speaker is heard speaking passionately.)*

VOICE OF SPEAKER.   The last sixteen months have been the
most glorious in the history of Europe.[15] Heroism has
come back to the earth. War is a terrible thing, but war is
not an evil thing People in Ireland dread war because
they do not know it. Ireland has not known the exhilara-
tion of war for over a hundred years. When war comes to
Ireland she must welcome it as she would welcome the
Angel of God! *(The figure passes out of sight and hearing.)*

THE COVEY *(towards all present).*   Dope, dope. There's only
one war worth havin': th' war for th' economic emancipation of th' proletariat.

BESSIE.   They may crow away out o' them; but it ud be fitther
for some o' them to mend their ways, an' cease from havin'
scouts out watchin' for th' comin' of th' Saint Vincent de
Paul man, for fear they'd be nailed lowerin'[16] a pint of
beer, mockin' th' man with an angel face, shinin' with th'
glamour of deceit an' lies!

MRS. GOGAN.   An' a certain lassie standin' stiff behind her
own door with her ears cocked listenin' to what's being
said, stuffed till she's sthrained with envy of a neighbour
thryin' for a few little things that may be got be hard
sthrivin' to keep up to th' letther an' th' law, an' th' prac-
tices of th' Church!

PETER *(to MRS. GOGAN).*   If I was you, Mrs. Gogan, I'd parry
her jabbin' remarks be a powerful silence that'll keep her
tantalizin' words from penethratin' into your feelin's. It's

[15]He is referring to World War I, which began in 1914.
[16]*lowerin':* drinking down

always betther to leave these people to th' vengeance o' God!

BESSIE.   Bessie Burgess doesn't put up to know much, never havin' a swaggerin' mind, thanks be to God, but goin' on packin' up knowledge accordin' to her conscience: precept upon precept, line upon line; here a little, an there a little. But *(with a passionate swing of her shawl)*, thanks be to Christ, she knows when she was got, where she was got, an' how she was got; while there's some she knows, decoratin' their finger with a well-polished weddin' ring, would be hard put to it if they were asked to show their weddin' lines!

MRS. GOGAN *(plunging out into the centre of the floor in a wild tempest of hysterical rage).*   Y' oul' rip of a blasted liar, me weddin' ring's been well earned be twenty years be th' side o' me husband, now takin' his rest in heaven, married to me be Father Dempsey, in th' Chapel o' Saint Jude's, in th' Christmas Week of eighteen hundhred an' ninety-five; an' any kid, livin' or dead, that Jinnie Gogan's had since, was got between th' bordhers of th' Ten Commandments! . . . An' that's more than some o' you can say that are kep' from th' dhread o' desthruction be a few drowsy virtues, that th' first whisper of temptation lulls into a sleep, that'll know one sin from another only on th' day of their last anointin'! . . .

BESSIE *(jumping out to face* MRS. GOGAN, *and bringing the palms of her hands together in sharp claps to emphasize her remarks).*   Liar to you, too, ma'am, y' oul' hardened thresspasser on other people's good nature, wizenin' up your soul in th' arts o' dodgeries, till every dhrop of respectability in a female is dhried up in her, lookin' at your readymade manœuverin' with th' menkind!

BARMAN.   Here, there; here, there; speak asy there. No rowin' here, no rowin' here, now.

FLUTHER *(trying to calm* MRS. GOGAN).   Now Jinnie, Jinnie, it's a derogatory thing to be smirchin' a night like this with a row; it's rompin' with th' feelin's of hope we ought to be, instead o' bein' vice versa!

PETER (*trying to quiet* BESSIE). I'm terrible dawny,[17] Mrs.
   Burgess, an' a fight leaves me weak for a long time afther-
   wards. . . . Please, Mrs. Burgess, before there's damage
   done, thry to have a little respect for yourself.

BESSIE (*with a push of her hand that sends* PETER *tottering
   to the end of the shop*). G'way, you little sermonizing,
   little yella-faced, little consequential,[18] little pudgy, little
   bum, you!

MRS. GOGAN (*screaming*). Fluther, leggo! I'm not goin' to
   keep an unresistin' silence, an' her scattherin' her festherin' words in me face, stirrin' up every dhrop of decency
   in a respectable female, with her restless rally o' lies that
   would make a saint say his prayer backwards!

BESSIE (*shouting*). Ah, everybody knows well that th' best
   charity that can be shown to you is to hide th' thruth as
   much as our thrue worship of God Almighty will allow us!

MRS. GOGAN (*frantically*). Here, houl' th' kid, one o' yous;
   houl' th' kid for a minute! There's nothin' for it but to
   show this lassie a lesson or two. . . . (*To* PETER) Here,
   houl' th' kid, you. (*Before* PETER *is aware of it, she places
   the infant in his arms.*)

MRS. GOGAN (*to* BESSIE, *standing before her in a fighting attitude*). Come on, now, me loyal lassie, dyin' with grief
   for little Catholic Belgium! When Jinnie Gogan's done
   with you, you'll have a little leisure lyin' down to think
   an' pray for your king an' counthry!

BARMAN (*coming from behind the counter, getting between
   the women, and proceeding to push them towards the
   door*). Here, now, since yous can't have a little friendly
   argument quietly, you'll get out o' this place in quick
   time. Go on, an' settle your differences somewhere else—
   I don't want to have another endorsement[19] on me licence.

PETER (*anxiously, over to* MRS. GOGAN). Here, take your kid
   back, ower this.[20] How nicely I was picked, now, for it to
   be plumped into me arms!

---

[17]*dawny:* puny
[18]*consequential:* pompous, self-important
[19]*endorsement:* record of an offense written on the back of one's licence
[20]*ower this:* enough of this, stop this

THE COVEY. She knew who she was givin' it to, maybe.

PETER *(hotly to the* COVEY*)*. Now, I'm givin' you fair warnin', me young Covey, to quit firin' your jibes an' jeers at me. . . . For one o' these days, I'll run out in front o' God Almighty an' take your sacred life!

BARMAN *(pushing Bessie out after* MRS. GOGAN*)*. Go on, now; out you go.

BESSIE *(as she goes out)*. If you think, me lassie, that Bessie Burgess has an untidy conscience, she'll soon show you to th' differ!

PETER *(leaving the baby down on the floor)*. Ay, be Jasus, wait there, till I give her back her youngster! *(He runs to the door.)* Ay, there, ay! *(He comes back.)* There, she's afther goin' without her kid. What are we goin' to do with it, now?

THE COVEY. What are we goin' to do with it? Bring it outside an' show everybody what you're afther findin'!

PETER *(in a panic to* FLUTHER*)*. Pick it up, you, Fluther, an' run afther her with it, will you?

FLUTHER. What d'ye take Fluther for? You must think Fluther's a right gom.[21] D'ye think Fluther's like yourself, destitute of a titther of undherstandin'?

BARMAN *(imperatively to* PETER*)*. Take it up, man, an' run out afther her with it, before she's gone too far. You're not goin' to leave th' bloody thing here, are you?

PETER *(plaintively, as he lifts up the baby)*. Well, God Almighty, give me patience with all th' scorners, tormentors, an' twarters that are always an' ever thryin' to goad me into prayin' for their blindin' an' blastin' an' burnin' in th' world to come! *(He goes out.)*

FLUTHER. God, it's a relief to get rid o' that crowd. Women is terrible when they start to fight. There's no holdin' them back. *(To the* COVEY*)* Are you goin' to have anything?

THE COVEY. Ah, I don't mind if I have another half.

FLUTHER *(to* BARMAN*)*. Two more, Tommy, me son.

(The BARMAN *gets the drinks.)*

[21]*gom:* a clumsy, stupid fellow

FLUTHER. You know, there's no conthrollin' a woman when she loses her head.

(ROSIE *enters and goes over to the counter on the side nearest to* FLUTHER.)

ROSIE (*to* BARMAN). Divil a use o' havin' a thrim little leg on a night like this; things was never worse. . . . Give us a half till tomorrow, Tom, duckey.

BARMAN (*coldly*). No more to-night, Rosie; you owe me for three already.

ROSIE (*combatively*). You'll be paid, won't you?

BARMAN. I hope so.

ROSIE. You hope so! Is that th' way with you, now?

FLUTHER (*to* BARMAN). Give her one; it'll be all right.

ROSIE (*clapping* FLUTHER *on the back*). Oul' sport!

FLUTHER. Th' meetin' should be soon over, now.

THE COVEY. Th' sooner th' bether. It's all a lot o' blasted nonsense, comrade.

FLUTHER. Oh, I wouldn't say it was all nonsense. Afther all, Fluther can remember th' time, an' him only a dawny chiselur,[22] bein' taught at his mother's knee to be faithful to th' Shan Van Vok![23]

THE COVEY. That's all dope, comrade; th' sort o' thing that workers are fed on be th' Boorzwawzee.

FLUTHER (*a little sharply*). What's all dope? Though I'm sayin' it that shouldn't: (*catching his cheek with his hand, and pulling down the flesh from the eye*) d'ye see that mark there, undher me eye? . . . A sabre slice from a dragoon[24] in O'Connell Street! (*Thrusting his head forward towards* ROSIE) Feel that dint in th' middle o' me nut!

ROSIE (*rubbing* FLUTHER'S *head, and winking at the* COVEY). My God, there's a holla!

FLUTHER (*putting on his hat with quiet pride*). A skelp[25]

[22]*dawny chiselur:* small child
[23]*Shan Van Vok* [Sean Bhean Bhocht]: "the poor old woman," a poetical reference to Ireland (Gaelic)
[24]*dragoon:* cavalryman
[25]*skelp:* smack, slap

from a bobby's[26] baton at a Labour meetin' in th' Phœnix
Park!

THE COVEY.   He must ha' hitten you in mistake. I don't know
what you ever done for th' Labour movement.

FLUTHER *(loudly)*.   D'ye not? Maybe, then, I done as much,
an' know as much about th' Labour movement as th'
chancers that are blowin' about it!

BARMAN.   Speak easy, Fluther, thry to speak easy.

THE COVEY.   There's no necessity to get excited about it,
comrade.

FLUTHER *(more loudly)*.   Excited? Who's gettin' excited?
There's no one gettin' excited! It would take something
more than a thing like you to flutther a feather o' Fluther.
Blatherin', an', when all is said, you know as much as th'
rest in th' wind up!

THE COVEY.   Well, let us put it to th' test, then, an' see what
you know about th' Labour movement: what's the mecha-
nism of exchange?

FLUTHER *(roaring, because he feels he is beaten)*.   How th'
hell do I know what it is? There's nothin' about that in
th' rules of our Thrades Union!

BARMAN.   For God's sake, thry to speak easy, Fluther.

THE COVEY.   What does Karl Marx say about th' Relation of
Value to th' Cost o' Production?

FLUTHER *(angrily)*.   What th' hell do I care what he says?
I'm Irishman enough not to lose me head be follyin'
foreigners!

BARMAN.   Speak easy, Fluther.

THE COVEY.   It's only waste o' time talkin' to you, comrade.

FLUTHER.   Don't be comradin' me, mate. I'd be on me last
legs if I wanted you for a comrade.

ROSIE *(to the COVEY)*.   It seems a highly rediculous thing to
hear a thing that's only an inch or two away from a kid,
swingin' heavy words about he doesn't know th' meanin'
of, an' uppishly thryin' to down a man like Misther
Fluther here, that's well flavoured in th' knowledge of
th' world he's livin' in.

---

[26]*bobby:* policeman

THE COVEY (*savagely to* ROSIE). Nobody's askin' you to be buttin' in with your prate. . . . I have you well taped, me lassie. . . . Just you keep your opinions for your own place. . . . It'll be a long time before th' Covey takes any insthructions or reprimandin' from a prostitute!

ROSIE (*wild with humiliation*). You louse, you louse, you! . . . You're no man. . . . You're no man . . . I'm a woman, anyhow, an' if I'm a prostitute aself, I have me feelin's. . . . Thryin' to put his arm around me a minute ago, an' givin' me th' glad eye, th' little wrigglin' lump o' desolation turns on me now, because he saw there was nothin' doin'. . . . You louse, you! If I was a man, or you were a woman, I'd bate th' puss o' you![27]

BARMAN. Ay, Rosie, ay! You'll have to shut your mouth altogether , if you can't learn to speak easy!

FLUTHER (*to* ROSIE). Houl' on there, Rosie; houl' on there. There's no necessity to flutther yourself when you're with Fluther. . . . Any lady that's in th' company of Fluther is goin' to get a fair hunt. . . . This is outside your province. . . . I'm not goin' to let you demean yourself be talkin' to a tittherin' chancer. . . . Leave this to Fluther— this is a man's job. (*To the* COVEY) Now, if you've anything to say, say it to Fluther, an', let me tell you, you're not goin' to be pass-remarkable to any lady in my company.

THE COVEY. Sure I don't care if you were runnin' all night afther your Mary o' th' Curlin' Hair, but, when you start tellin' luscious lies about what you done for th' Labour movement, it's nearly time to show y'up!

FLUTHER (*fiercely*). Is it you show Fluther up? G'way, man, I'd beat two o' you before me breakfast!

THE COVEY (*contemptuously*). Tell us where you bury your dead, will you?

FLUTHER (*with his face stuck into the face of the* COVEY). Sing a little less on th' high note, or, when I'm done with you, you'll put a Christianable consthruction on things, I'm tellin' you!

[27] *I'd . . . you:* "I'd smash your face in!"

THE COVEY. You're a big fella, you are.

FLUTHER (*tapping the* COVEY *threateningly on the shoulder*). Now, you're temptin' Providence when you're temptin' Fluther!

THE COVEY (*losing his temper, and bawling*). Easy with them hands, there, easy with them hands! You're startin' to take a little risk when you commence to paw the Covey!

(FLUTHER *suddenly springs into the middle of the shop, flings his hat into the corner, whips off his coat, and begins to paw the air.*)

FLUTHER (*roaring at the top of his voice*). Come on, come on, you lowser; put your mits up now, if there's a man's blood in you! Be God, in a few minutes you'll see some snots flyin' around, I'm tellin' you. . . . When Fluther's done with you, you'll have a vice versa opinion of him! Come on, now, come on!

BARMAN (*running from behind the counter and catching hold of the* COVEY). Here, out you go, me little bowsey.[28] Because you got a couple o' halves you think you can act as you like. (*He pushes the* COVEY *to the door.*) Fluther's a friend o' mine, an' I'll not have him insulted.

THE COVEY (*struggling with the* BARMAN). Ay, leggo, leggo there; fair hunt, give a man a fair hunt! One minute with him is all I ask; one minute alone with him, while you're runnin' for th' priest an' th' doctor.

FLUTHER (*to the* BARMAN). Let him go, let him go, Tom: let him open th' door to sudden death if he wants to!

BARMAN (*to the* COVEY). Go on, out you go an' do th' bowsey somewhere else. (*He pushes the* COVEY *out and comes back.*)

ROSIE (*getting Fluther's hat as he is putting on his coat*). Be God, you put th' fear o' God in his heart that time! I thought you'd have to be dug out of him. . . . Th' way you lepped out without any of your fancy side-steppin'! "Men like Fluther," say I to meself, "is gettin' scarce nowadays."

---

[28]*bowsey:* rowdy, drunkard

FLUTHER (*with proud complacency*). I wasn't goin' to let meself be malignified by a chancer. . . . He got a little bit too derogatory for Fluther. . . . Be God, to think of a cur like that comin' to talk to a man like me!

ROSIE (*fixing on his hat*). Did j'ever!

FLUTHER. He's lucky he got off safe. I hit a man last week, Rosie, an' he's fallin' yet!

ROSIE. Sure, you'd ha' broken him in two if you'd ha' hitten him one clatther!

FLUTHER (*amorously, putting his arm around* ROSIE). Come on into th' snug, me little darlin', an' we'll have a few dhrinks before I see you home.

ROSIE. Oh, Fluther, I'm afraid you're a terrible man for th' women.

(*They go into the snug as* CLITHEROE, CAPTAIN BRENNAN, *and* LIEUT. LANGON *of the Irish Volunteers enter hurriedly.* CAPTAIN BRENNAN *carries the banner of The Plough and the Stars, and* LIEUT. LANGON *a green, white, and orange Tri-color.*[29] *They are in a state of emotional excitement. Their faces are flushed and their eyes sparkle; they speak rapidly, as if unaware of the meaning of what they said. They have been mesmerized by the fervency of the speeches.*)

CLITHEROE (*almost pantingly*). Three glasses o' port!

(*The* BARMAN *brings the drinks.*)

CAPT. BRENNAN. We won't have long to wait now.

LIEUT. LANGON. Th' time is rotten ripe for revolution.

CLITHEROE. You have a mother, Langon.

LIEUT. LANGON. Ireland is greater than a mother.

CAPT. BRENNAN. You have a wife, Clitheroe.

CLITHEROE. Ireland is greater than a wife.

LIEUT. LANGON. Th' time for Ireland's battle is now—th' place for Ireland's battle is here.

[29]*green . . . Tri-color:* flag of the Irish Volunteers

320 🐾 *Sean O'Casey*

(The tall, dark figure again is silhouetted against the window. The three men pause and listen.)

VOICE OF THE MAN.   Our foes are strong, but strong as they are, they cannot undo the miracles of God, who ripens in the heart of young men the seeds sown by the young men of a former generation. They think they have pacified Ireland; think they have foreseen everything; think they have provided against everything; but the fools, the fools, the fools!—they have left us our Fenian[30] dead, and, while Ireland holds these graves, Ireland, unfree, shall never be at peace!

CAPT. BRENNAN *(catching up The Plough and the Stars).*   Imprisonment for th' Independence of Ireland!

LIEUT. LANGON *(catching up the Tri-colour).*   Wounds for th' Independence of Ireland!

CLITHEROE.   Death for th' Independence of Ireland!

THE THREE *(together).*   So help us God!

(They drink. A bugle blows the Assembly. They hurry out. A pause. FLUTHER *and* ROSIE *come out of the snug;* ROSIE *is linking* FLUTHER, *who is a little drunk. Both are in a merry mood.)*

ROSIE.   Come on home, ower o' that, man. Are you afraid or what? Are you goin' to come home, or are you not?

FLUTHER.   Of course I'm goin' home. What ud ail me that I wouldn't go?

ROSIE *(lovingly).*   Come on then, oul' sport. *(They go out with their arms round each other.)*

OFFICER'S VOICE *(giving command outside).*   Irish Volunteers, by th' right, quick march!

CLITHEROE'S VOICE *(in command outside).*   Dublin Battalion of the Irish Citizen Army, by th' right, quick march!

Curtain

[30]*Fenian:* The Fenian Brotherhood was a secret organization, founded in 1856, whose objective was to secure home rule for Ireland.

Act III

The corner house in a street of tenements: it is the home of the CLITHEROES. *The house is a long, gaunt, five-story tenement; its brick front is chipped and scarred with age and neglect. The wide and heavy hall door, flanked by two pillars, has a look of having been charred by a fire in the distant past. The door lurches a little to one side, disjointed by the continual and reckless banging when it is being closed by most of the residents. The diamond-paned fanlight is destitute of a single pane, the frame-work alone remaining. The windows, except the two look-ing into the front parlour (*CLITHEROE'S *room), are grimy, and are draped with fluttering and soiled fragments of lace curtains. The front parlour windows are hung with rich, comparatively, casement cloth. Five stone steps lead from the door to the path on the street. Branching on each side are railings to prevent people from falling into the area. At the left corner of the house runs a narrow lane, bisecting the street, and connecting with another of the same kind. At the corner of the lane is a street lamp.*

As the house is revealed, MRS. GOGAN *is seen helping* MOLLSER *to a chair, which stands on the path beside the railings, at the left side of the steps. She then wraps a shawl around* MOLLSER'S *shoulders. It is some months later.*[1]

MRS. GOGAN (*arranging shawl around* MOLLSER). Th' sun'll do you all th' good in th' world. A few more weeks o' this weather, an' there's no knowin' how well you'll be. . . . Are you comfy, now?

MOLLSER (*weakly and wearily*). Yis, ma; I'm all right.

MRS. GOGAN. How are you feelin'?

---

[1]Acts III and IV take place during Easter Week, 1916, the time of the bloody rebellion of the Irish nationalist armies against the British. Though the Irish were able to seize important public buildings in Dublin, they were forced to surrender after holding out against the British for a week.

MOLLSER.   Betther, ma, betther. If th' horrible sinkin' feelin' ud go, I'd be all right.

MRS. GOGAN.   Ah, I wouldn't put much pass on that. Your stomach maybe's out of ordher. . . . Is th' poor breathin' any betther, d'ye think?

MOLLSER.   Yis, yis, ma; a lot betther.

MRS. GOGAN.   Well, that's somethin' anyhow. . . . With th' help o' God, you'll be on th' mend from this out. . . . D'your legs feel any sthronger undher you, d'ye think?

MOLLSER *(irritably).*   I can't tell, ma. I think so. . . . A little.

MRS. GOGAN.   Well, a little aself is somethin'. . . . I thought I heard you coughin' a little more than usual last night. . . . D'ye think you were?

MOLLSER.   I wasn't, ma, I wasn't.

MRS. GOGAN.   I thought I heard you, for I was kep' awake all night with th' shootin'. An' thinkin' o' that madman, Fluther, runnin' about through th' night lookin' for Nora Clitheroe to bring her back when he heard she'd gone to folly her husband, an' in dhread any minute he might come staggerin' in covered with bandages, splashed all over with th' red of his own blood, an' givin' us barely time to bring th' priest to hear th' last whisper of his final confession, as his soul was passin' through th' dark doorway o' death into th' way o' th' wondherin' dead. . . . You don't feel cold, do you?

MOLLSER.   No, ma; I'm all right.

MRS. GOGAN.   Keep your chest well covered, for that's th' delicate spot in you . . . if there's any danger, I'll whip you in again. . . . *(Looking up the street)* Oh, here's th' Covey an' oul' Pether hurryin' along. God Almighty, sthrange things is happenin' when them two is pullin' together.

(The COVEY *and* PETER *come in, breathless and excited.)*

MRS. GOGAN *(to the two men).*   Were yous far up th' town? Did yous see any sign o' Fluther or Nora? How is things lookin'? I hear they're blazin' away out o' th' G.P.O.[2] That

²*G.P.O.*: General Post Office

th' Tommies is sthretched in heaps around Nelson's Pillar an' th' Parnell Statue, an' that th' pavin' sets in O'Connell Street is nearly covered be pools o' blood.

PETER.   We seen no sign o' Nora or Fluther anywhere.

MRS. GOGAN.   We should ha' held her back be main force from goin' to look for her husband. . . . God knows what's happened to her—I'm always seein' her sthretched on her back in some hospital, moanin' with th' pain of a bullet in her vitals, an' nuns thryin' to get her to take a last look at th' crucifix!

THE COVEY.   We can do nothin'. You can't stick your nose into O'Connell Street, an' Tyler's is on fire.

PETER.   An' we seen th' Lancers—[3]

THE COVEY *(interrupting).*   Throttin' along, heads in th' air; spurs an' sabres jinglin', an' lances quiverin', an' lookin' as if they were askin' themselves, "Where's these blighters, till we get a prod at them?" when there was a volley from th' Post Office that stretched half o' them, an' sent th' rest gallopin' away wondherin' how far they'd have to go before they'd feel safe.

PETER *(rubbing his hands).*   "Damn it," says I to meself, "this looks like business!"

THE COVEY.   An' then out comes General Pearse[4] an' his staff, an', standin' in th' middle o' th' street, he reads th' Proclamation.

MRS. GOGAN.   What proclamation?

PETER.   Declarin' an Irish Republic.

MRS. GOGAN.   Go to God!

PETER.   The gunboat *Helga's* shellin' Liberty Hall, an' I hear the people livin' on th' quays had to crawl on their bellies to Mass with th' bullets that were flyin' around from Boland's Mills.

MRS. GOGAN.   God bless us, what's goin' to be th' end of it all!

BESSIE *(looking out of the top window).*   Maybe yous are satisfied now; maybe yous are satisfied now. Go on an' get guns if yous are men—Johnny get your gun, get your

[3]*Lancers:* British light cavalry soldiers armed with lances

[4]*General Pearse:* Patrick Pearse—poet, teacher, and a leader of the Easter Rebellion—read a proclamation declaring Ireland a Republic on Easter Monday, 1916.

gun, get your gun! Yous are all nicely shanghaied now; th' boyo hasn't a sword on his thigh now! Oh, yous are all nicely shanghaied now!

MRS. GOGAN (*warningly to* PETER *and the* COVEY). S-s-sh, don't answer her. She's th' right oul' Orange[5] witch! She's been chantin' "Rule, Britannia" all th' mornin'.

PETER. I hope Fluther hasn't met with any accident, he's such a wild card.

MRS. GOGAN. God grant it; but last night I dreamt I seen gettin' carried into th' house a sthretcher with a figure lyin' on it, stiff an' still, dhressed in th' habit of Saint Francis. An, then, I heard th' murmurs of a crowd no one could see sayin' th' litany for th' dead; an' then it got so dark that nothin' was seen but th' white face of th' corpse, gleamin' like a white wather-lily floatin' on th' top of a dark lake. Then a tiny whisper thrickled into me ear, sayin', "Isn't the face very like th' face o' Fluther?" an' then, with a thremblin flutther, th' dead lips opened, an', although I couldn't hear, I knew they were sayin', "Poor oul' Fluther, afther havin' handed in his gun at last, his shakin' soul moored in th' place where th' wicked are at rest an' th' weary cease from throublin'."

PETER (*who has put on a pair of spectacles, and has been looking down the street*). Here they are, be God, here they are; just afther turnin' th' corner—Nora an' Fluther!

THE COVEY. She must be wounded or something—he seems to be carryin' her.

(FLUTHER *and* NORA *enter.* FLUTHER *has his arm around her and is half leading, half carrying her in. Her eyes are dim and hollow, her face pale and strained-looking; her hair is tossed, and her clothes are dusty.*)

MRS. GOGAN (*running over to them*). God bless us, is it wounded y'are, Mrs. Clitheroe, or what?

FLUTHER. Ah, she's all right, Mrs. Gogan; only worn out from thravellin' an' want o' sleep. A night's rest, now, an'

[5]*Orange:* The Orangemen were members of a secret society organized in northern Ireland in 1795 to uphold Protestantism and British rule in Ireland.

she'll be as fit as a fiddle. Bring her in, an' make her lie down.

MRS. GOGAN *(to* NORA*).*   Did you hear e'er a whisper o' Mr. Clitheroe?

NORA *(wearily).*   I could find him nowhere, Mrs. Gogan. None o' them would tell me where he was. They told me I shamed my husband an' th' women of Ireland be carryin' on as I was. . . . They said th' women must learn to be brave an' cease to be cowardly. . . . Me who risked more for love than they would risk for hate. . . . *(Raising her voice hysterical in protest)* My Jack will be killed, my Jack will be killed! . . . He is to be butchered as a sacrifice to th' dead!

BESSIE *(from upper window).*   Yous are all nicely shanghaied now! Sorra mend th' lasses that have been kissin' an' cuddlin' their boys into th' sheddin' of blood! . . . Fillin' their minds with fairy tales that had no beginnin', but, please God, 'll have a bloody quick endin'! . . . Turnin' bitther into sweet, an' sweet into bitther. . . . Stabbin' in th' back th' men that are dyin' in th' threnches for them! It's a bad thing for any one that thries to jilt th' Ten Commandments, for judgements are prepared for scorners an' sthripes for th' back o' fools! *(Going away from window as she sings:)*

> Rule, Britannia, Britannia rules th' waves,
> Britons never, never, never shall be slaves!

FLUTHER *(with a roar up at the window).*   Y'ignorant oul' throllope, you!

MRS. GOGAN *(to* NORA*).*   He'll come home safe enough to you, you'll find, Mrs. Clitheroe; afther all, there's a power[6] o' women that's handed over sons an' husbands to take a runnin' risk in th' fight they're wagin'.

NORA.   I can't help thinkin' every shot fired 'll be fired at Jack, an' every shot fired at Jack 'll be fired at me. What do I care for th' others? I can think only of me own self.

---

[6]*a power:* a large number

. . . An' there's no woman gives a son or a husband to be killed—if they say it, they're lyin', lyin', against God, Nature, an' against themselves! . . . One blasted hussy at a barricade told me to go home an' not be thryin' to dishearten th' men. . . That I wasn't worthy to bear a son to a man that was out fightin' for freedom. . . . I clawed at her, an' smashed her in th' face till we were separated. . . . I was pushed down th' street, an' I cursed them—cursed the rebel ruffians an' Volunteers that had dhragged me ravin' mad into th' sthreets to seek me husband!

PETER. You'll have to have patience, Nora. We all have to put up with twarthers an' tormentors in this world.

THE COVEY. If they were fightin' for anything worth while, I wouldn't mind.

FLUTHER (to NORA). Nothin' derogatory 'll happen to Mr. Clitheroe. You'll find, now, in th' finish up it'll be vice versa.

NORA. Oh, I know that wherever he is, he's thinkin' of wantin' to be with me. I know he's longin' to be passin' his hand through me hair, to be caressin' me neck, to fondle me hand an' to feel me kisses clingin' to his mouth. . . . An' he stands wherever he is because he's brave? (Vehmently) No, but because he's a coward, a coward, a coward!

MRS. GOGAN. Oh, they're not cowards anyway.

NORA (with denunciatory anger). I tell you they're afraid to say they're afraid! . . . Oh, I saw it, I saw it, Mrs. Gogan. . . . At th' barricade in North King Street I saw fear glowin' in all their eyes. . . . An' in th' middle o' th' sthreet was somethin' huddled up in a horrible tangled heap. . . . His face was jammed again th' stones, an' his arm was twisted round his back. . . . An' every twist of his body was a cry against th' terrible thing that had happened to him. . . . An' I saw they were afraid to look at it. . . . An' some o' them laughed at me, but th' laugh was a frightened one. . . . An' some o' them shouted at me, but th' shout had in it th' shiver o' fear. . . . I tell you they were afraid, afraid, afraid!

MRS. GOGAN (leading her towards the house). Come on in,

dear. If you'd been a little longer together, th' wrench
asundher wouldn't have been so sharp.

NORA.   Th' agony I'm in since he left me has thrust away
every rough thing he done, an' every unkind word he
spoke; only th' blossoms that grew out of our lives are
before me now; shakin' their colours before me face, an'
breathin' their sweet scent on every thought springin' up
in me mind, till, sometimes, Mrs. Gogan, sometimes I
think I'm goin' mad!

MRS. GOGAN.   You'll be a lot betther when you have a little
lie down.

NORA *(turning towards* FLUTHER *as she is going in).*   I don't
know what I'd have done, only for Fluther. I'd have been
lyin' in th' streets, only for him. . . . *(As she goes in)* They
have dhriven away th' little happiness life had to spare
for me.   He has gone from me for ever, for ever. . . . Oh,
Jack, Jack, Jack!

(She is led in by MRS. GOGAN *as* BESSIE *comes out with a
shawl around her shoulders. She passes by them with her
head in the air. When they have gone in, she gives a mug
of milk to* MOLLSER *silently.)*

FLUTHER.   Which of yous has th' tossers?[7]

THE COVEY.   I have.

BESSIE *(as she is passing them to go down the street).*   You
an' your Leadhers an' their sham-battle soldiers has
landed a body in a nice way, havin' to go an' ferret out a
bit o' bread God knows where. . . . Why aren't yous in th'
G.P.O. if yous are men? It's paler an' paler yous are
gettin'. . . . A lot o' vipers, that's what th' Irish people is!
(She goes out.)

FLUTHER.   Never mind her. . . . *(To the* COVEY*)* Make a start
an' keep us from th' sin o' idleness. *(To* MOLLSER*)* Well,
how are you to-day, Mollser, oul' son? What are you
dhrinkin', milk?

MOLLSER.   Grand, Fluther, grand, thanks. Yis, milk.

---

[7]*tossers:* coins to use in a toss-up

FLUTHER. You couldn't get a bethter thing down you. . . . This turn-up has done one good thing, anyhow; you can't get dhrink anywhere, an' if it lasts a week, I'll be so used to it that I won't think of a pint.

THE COVEY (*who has taken from his pocket two worn coins and a thin strip of wood about four inches long*). What's th' bettin'?

PETER. Heads, a juice.

FLUTHER. Harps, a tanner.

(*The* COVEY *places the coins on the strip of wood, and flips them up into the air. As they jingle on the ground the distant boom of a big gun is heard. They stand for a moment listening.*)

FLUTHER. What th' hell's that?

THE COVEY. It's like th' boom of a big gun!

FLUTHER. Surely to God they're not goin' to use artillery on us?

THE COVEY (*scornfully*). Not goin'! (*Vehemently*) Wouldn't they use anything on us, man?

FLUTHER. Aw, holy Christ, that's not playin' th' game!

PETER (*plaintively*). What would happen if a shell landed here now?

THE COVEY (*ironically*). You'd be off to heaven in a fiery chariot.

PETER. In spite of all th' warnin's that's ringin' around us, are you goin' to start your pickin' at me again?

FLUTHER. Go on, toss them again, toss them again. . . . Harps, a tanner.

PETER. Heads, a juice.

(*The* COVEY *tosses the coins.*)

FLUTHER (*as the coins fall*). Let them roll, let them roll. Heads, be God!

(BESSIE *runs in excitedly. She has a new hat on her head, a fox fur round her neck over her shawl, three umbrellas*

*under her right arm, and a box of biscuits under her left.
She speaks rapidly and breathlessly.)*

BESSIE. They're breakin' into th' shops, they're breakin'
into th' shops! Smashin' th' windows, battherin' in th'
doors, an' whippin' away everything! An' th' Volunteers
is firin' on them. I seen two men an' a lassie pushin' a
piano down th' sthreet, an' th' sweat rollin' off them thryin' to get it up on th' pavement; an' an oul' wan that must
ha' been seventy lookin' as if she'd dhrop every minute
with th' dint o' heart beatin', thryin' to pull a big double
bed out of a broken shop-window! I was goin' to wait till
I dhressed meself from th' skin out.

MOLLSER *(to BESSIE, as she is going in).*   Help me in, Bessie;
I'm feelin' curious.

*(BESSIE leaves the looted things in the house, and, rapidly
returning, helps MOLLSER in.)*

THE COVEY. Th' selfishness of that one—she waited till she
got all she could carry before she'd come to tell anyone!

FLUTHER *(running over to the door of the house and shouting
in to BESSIE).* Ay, Bessie, did you hear of e'er a pub
gettin' a shake up?[8]

BESSIE *(inside).*   I didn't hear o' none.

FLUTHER *(in a burst of enthusiasm).*   Well, you're goin' to
hear of one soon!

THE COVEY.   Come on, man, an' don't be wastin' time.

PETER *(to them as they are about to run off).*   Ay, ay, are you
goin' to leave me here?

FLUTHER.   Are you goin' to leave yourself here?

PETER *(anxiously).*   Didn't yous hear her sayin' they were
firin' on them?

THE COVEY *and* FLUTHER *(together).*   Well?

PETER.   Supposin' I happened to be potted?

FLUTHER.   We'd give you a Christian burial, anyhow.

THE COVEY *(ironically).*   Dhressed up in your regimentals.

[8]*shake up:* (humor intended) a drastic rearrangement or reorganization

PETER (*to the* COVEY, *passionately*).   May th' all-lovin' God give you a hot knock one o' these days, me young Covey, tuthorin' Fluther up now to be tiltin' at me, an' crossin' me with his mockeries an' jibin'!

(*A fashionably dressed, middle-aged, stout woman comes hurriedly in, and makes for the group. She is almost fainting with fear.*)

THE WOMAN.   For Gawd's sake, will one of you kind men show any safe way for me to get to Wrathmines? . . . . I was foolish enough to visit a friend, thinking the howl thing was a joke, and now I cawn't get a car or a tram to take me home—isn't it awful?

FLUTHER.   I'm afraid, ma'am, one way is as safe as another.

WOMAN.   And what am I gowing to do? Oh, isn't this awful? . . . I'm so different from others . . . The mowment I hear a shot, my legs give way under me—I cawn't stir, I'm paralysed—isn't it awful?

FLUTHER (*moving away*).   It's a derogatory way to be, right enough, ma'am.

WOMAN (*catching* FLUTHER'S *coat*).   Creeping along the street there, with my head down and my eyes half shut, a bullet whizzed past within an inch of my nowse. . . . I had to lean against the wall for a long time, gasping for breath —I nearly passed away—it was awful! . . . I wonder, would you kind men come some of the way and see me safe?

FLUTHER.   I have to go away, ma'am, to thry an' save a few things from th' burnin' buildin's.

THE COVEY.   Come on, then, or there won't be anything left to save. (*The* COVEY *and* FLUTHER *hurry away.*)

WOMEN (*to* PETER).   Wasn't it an awful thing for me to leave my friend's house? Wasn't it an idiotic thing to do? . . . I haven't the slightest idea where I am. . . . You have a kind face, sir. Could you possibly come and pilot me in the direction of Wrathmines?

PETER (*indignantly*).   D'ye think I'm goin' to risk me life throttin' in front of you? An' maybe get a bullet that would

gimmie a game leg or something that would leave me a
jibe an' a jeer to Fluther an' th' young Covey for th' rest
o' me days! (*With an indignant toss of his head he walks
into the house.*)

THE WOMAN (*going out*). I know I'll fall down in a dead faint
if I hear another shot go off anyway near me — isn't it
awful!

(MRS. GOGAN *comes out of the house pushing a pram*[9] *before her. As she enters the street,* BESSIE *rushes out, follows* MRS. GOGAN, *and catches hold of the pram, stopping*
MRS. GOGAN'S *progress.*)

BESSIE. Here, where are you goin' with that? How quick
you were, me lady, to clap your eyes on th' pram. . . .
Maybe you don't know that Mrs. Sullivan, before she
went to spend Easther with her people in Dunboyne,
gave me sthrict injunctions to give an accasional look to
see if it was still standin' where it was left in th' corner
of th' lobby.

MRS. GOGAN. That remark of yours, Mrs. Bessie Burgess,
requires a little considheration, seein' that th' pram was
left on our lobby, an' not on yours; a foot or two a little to
th' left of th' jamb of me own room door; nor is it needful
to mention th' name of th' person that gave a squint to see
if it was there th' first thing in th' mornin', an' th' last
thing in th' stillness o' th' night; never failin' to realize
that her eyes couldn't be goin' wrong, be sthretchin' out
her arm an' runnin' her hand over th' pram, to make sure
that th' sight was no deception! Moreover, somethin's
tellin' me that th' runnin' hurry of an inthrest you're takin'
in it now is a sudden ambition to use th' pram for a purpose that a loyal woman of law an' ordher would stagger
away from! (*She gives the pram a sudden push that pulls*
BESSIE *forward.*)

BESSIE (*still holding the pram*). There's not as much as one
body in th' house that doesn't know that it wasn't Bessie

[9]*pram:* (perambulator) baby carriage

Burgess that was always shakin' her voice complainin'
about people leavin' bassinettes[10] in th' way of them that,
week in an' week out, had to pay their rent, an' always
had to find a regular accommodation for her own furniture
in her own room. . . . An' as for law an' ordher, puttin'
aside th' harp an' shamrock,[11] Bessie Burgess 'll have as
much respect as she wants for th' lion an' unicorn![12]

PETER (*appearing at the door*). I think I'll go with th' pair
of yous an' see th' fun. A fella might as well chance it,
anyhow.

MRS. GOGAN (*taking no notice of* PETER, *and pushing the
pram on another step*). Take your rovin' lumps o' hands
from pattin' th' bassinette, if you please, ma'am; an',
steppin' from th' threshold of good manners, let me tell
you, Mrs. Burgess, that's it's a fat wondher to Jennie
Gogan that a lady-like singer o' hymns like yourself would
lower her thoughts from sky-thinkin' to sthretch out her
arm in a sly-seekin' way to pinch anything dhriven asthray
in th' confusion of th' battle our boys is makin' for th'
freedom of their counthry!

PETER (*laughing and rubbing his hands together*). Hee,
hee, hee, hee, hee! I'll go with th' pair o' yous an' give
yous a hand.

MRS. GOGAN (*with a rapid turn of her head as she shoves the
pram forward*). Get up in th' prambulator an' we'll
wheel you down.

BESSIE (*to* MRS. GOGAN). Poverty an' hardship has sent
Bessie Burgess to abide with sthrange company, but she
always knew them she had to live with from backside to
breakfast time; an' she can tell them, always havin' had
a Christian kinch on her conscience, that a passion for
thievin' an' pinchin' would find her soul a foreign place
to live in, an' that her present intention is quite th' lofty-
hearted one of pickin' up anything shaken up an' scat-
thered about in th' loose confusion of a general plundher!

[10]*bassinette:* in this case, she is referring to the baby carriage
[11]*harp ... shamrock:* symbols of Ireland
[12]*lion ... unicorn:* symbols of Great Britain

(By this time they have disappeared from view. PETER *is following, when the boom of a big gun in the distance brings him to a quick halt.)*

PETER.   God Almighty, that's th' big gun again! God forbid any harm would happen to them, but sorra mind I'd mind if they met with a dhrop in their mad endeyvours to plundher an' desthroy.

(He looks down the street for a moment, then runs to the hall door of the house, which is open, and shuts it with a vicious pull; he then goes to the chair in which MOLLSER *had sat, sits down, takes out his pipe, lights it and begins to smoke with his head carried at a haughty angle. The* COVEY *comes staggering in with a ten-stone sack of flour on his back. On the top of the sack is a ham. He goes over to the door, pushes it with his head, and finds he can't open it; he turns slightly in the direction of* PETER.*)*

THE COVEY *(to* PETER*).*   Who shut th' door? . . . *(He kicks at it)* Here, come on an' open it, will you? This isn't a mot's hand-bag I've got on me back.

PETER.   Now, me young Covey, d'ye think I'm goin to be your lackey?

THE COVEY *(angrily).*   Will you open th' door, y'oul'—

PETER *(shouting).*   Don't be assin' me to open any door, don't be assin' me to open any door for you. . . . Makin' a shame an' a sin o' th' cause that good men are fightin' for. . . . Oh, God forgive th' people that, instead o' burnishin' th' work th' boys is doin' to-day with quiet honesty an' patience, is revilin' their sacrifices with a riot of lootin' an' roguery!

THE COVEY.   Isn't your own eyes leppin' out o' your head with envy that you haven't th' guts to ketch a few o' th' things that God is givin' to His chosen people? . . . Y'oul' hypocrite, if everyone was blind you'd steal a cross off an ass's back!

PETER *(very calmly).*   You're not going to make me lose me temper; you can go on with your proddin' as long as you like; goad an' goad an' goad away; hee, hee, heee! I'll not lose me temper.

(*Somebody opens door and the* COVEY *goes in.*)

THE COVEY (*inside, mockingly*).   Cuckoo-oo!
PETER (*running to the door and shouting in a blaze of passion as he follows the* COVEY *in*).   You lean, long, lanky lath of a lowsey . . . (*Following him in*).

(BESSIE *and* MRS. GOGAN *enter, the pride of a great joy illuminating their faces.* BESSIE *is pushing the pram, which is filled with clothes and boots; on the top of the boots and clothes is a fancy table, which* MRS. GOGAN *is holding on with her left hand, while with her right hand she holds a chair on the top of her head. The are heard talking to each other before they enter.*)

MRS. GOGAN (*outside*).   I don't remember ever havin' seen such lovely pairs as them, (*they appear*) with th' pointed toes an' th' cuban heels.
BESSIE.   They'll go grand with th' dhresses we're afther liftin', when we've stitched a sthray bit o' silk to lift th' bodices up a little bit higher, so as to shake th' shame out o' them, an' make them fit for women that hasn't lost themselves in th' nakedness o' th' times.

(*They fussily carry in the chair, the table, and some of the other goods. They return to bring in the rest.*)

PETER (*at door, sourly to* MRS. GOGAN).   Ay, you. Mollser looks as if she was goin' to faint, an' your youngster is roarin' in convulsions in her lap.
MRS. GOGAN (*snappily*).   She's never any other way but faintin'!

(*She goes to go in with some things in her arms, when a shot from a rifle rings out. She and* BESSIE *make a bolt for the door, which* PETER, *in a panic, tries to shut before they have got inside.)*

MRS. GOGAN.   Ay, ay, ay, you cowardly oul' fool, what are you thryin' to shut th' door on us for?

(They retreat tumultuously inside. A pause; then CAPTAIN BRENNAN *comes in supporting* LIEUTENANT LANGON, *whose arm is around* BRENNAN'S *neck.* LANGON'S *face, which is ghastly white, is momentarily convulsed with spasms of agony. He is in a state of collapse, and* BREN-NAN *is almost carrying him. After a few moments* CLIT-HEROE, *pale, and in a state of calm nervousness, follows, looking back in the direction from which he came, a rifle, held at the ready, in his hands.)*

CAPT. BRENNAN *(savagely to* CLITHEROE*).*   Why did you fire over their heads? Why didn't you fire to kill?

CLITHEROE.   No, no, Bill; bad as they are they're Irish men an' women.

CAPT. BRENNAN *(savagely).*   Irish be damned! Attackin' an' mobbin' th' men that are riskin' their lives for them. If these slum lice gather at our heels again, plug one o' them, or I'll soon shock them with a shot or two meself!

LIEUT. LANGON *(moaningly).*   My God, is there ne'er an ambulance knockin' around anywhere? . . . Th' stomach is ripped out o' me; I feel it — o-o-oh, Christ!

CAPT. BRENNAN.   Keep th' heart up, Jim; we'll soon get help, now.

*(*NORA *rushes wildly out of the house and flings her arms round the neck of* CLITHEROE *with a fierce and joyous insistence. Her hair is down, her face is haggard, but her eyes are agleam with the light of happy relief.)*

NORA.   Jack, Jack, Jack; God be thanked . . . be thanked. . . . He has been kind and merciful to His poor handmaiden. . . . My Jack, my own Jack, that I thought was lost is found, that I thought was dead is alive again! . . . Oh, God be

praised for ever, evermore! . . . My poor Jack. . . . Kiss
me, kiss me, Jack, kiss your own Nora!

CLITHEROE (*kissing her, and speaking brokenly*). My Nora;
my little, beautiful Nora, I wish to God I'd never left you.

NORA. It doesn't matter—not now, not now, Jack. It will
make us dearer than ever to each other. . . . Kiss me, kiss
me again.

CLITHEROE. Now, for God's sake, Nora, don't make a scene.

NORA. I won't, I won't; I promise, I promise, Jack; honest to
God. I'll be silent an' brave to bear th' joy of feelin' you
safe in my arms again. . . . It's hard to force away th' tears
of happiness at th' end of an awful agony.

BESSIE (*from the upper window*). Th' Minsthrel Boys aren't
feelin' very comfortable now. Th' big guns has knocked
all th' harps out of their hands. General Clitheroe 'd rather
be unlacin' his wife's bodice than standin' at a barricade
. . . An' th' professor of chicken-butcherin' there, finds
he's up against somethin' a little tougher even than his
own chickens, an' that's sayin' a lot!

CAPT. BRENNAN (*up to* BESSIE). Shut up, y'oul' hag!

BESSIE (*down to* BRENNAN). Choke th' chicken, choke th'
chicken, choke th' chicken!

LIEUT. LANGON. For God's sake, Bill, bring me some place
where me wound 'll be looked afther. . . . Am I to die before anything is done to save me?

CAPT. BRENNAN (*to* CLITHEROE). Come on Jack. We've got
to get help for Jim, here—have you no thought for his
pain an' danger?

BESSIE. Choke th' chicken, choke th' chicken, choke th'
chicken!

CLITHEROE (*to* NORA). Loosen me, darling, let me go.

NORA (*clinging to him*). No, no, no, I'll not let you go! Come
on, come up to our home, Jack, my sweetheart, my lover,
my husband, an' we'll forget th' last few terrible days! . . .
I look tired now, but a few hours of happy rest in your
arms will bring back th' bloom of freshness again, an' you
will be glad, you will be glad, glad . . . glad!

LIEUT. LANGON. Oh, if I'd kep' down only a little longer,
I mightn't ha' been hit! Everyone else escapin', an' me

gettin' me belly ripped asundher! . . . I couldn't scream, couldn't even scream. . . . D'ye think I'm really badly wounded, Bill? Me clothes seem to be all soakin' wet. . . . It's blood . . . My God, it must be me own blood!

CAPT. BRENNAN (*to* CLITHEROE). Go on, Jack, bid her good-bye with another kiss, an' be done with it! D'ye want Langon to die in me arms while you're dallyin' with your Nora?

CLITHEROE (*to* NORA). I must go, I must go, Nora. I'm sorry we met at all. . . . It couldn't be helped—all other ways were blocked be th' British. . . . Let me go, can't you, Nora? D'ye want me to be unthrue to me comrades?

NORA. No, I won't let you go. . . . I want you to be thrue to me, Jack. . . . I'm your dearest comrade; I'm your thruest comrade. . . . They only want th' comfort of havin' you in th' same danger as themselves. . . . Oh, Jack, I can't let you go!

CLITHEROE. You must, Nora, you must.

NORA. All last night at th' barricades I sought you, Jack. . . . I didn't think of th' danger—I could only think of you. . . . I asked for you everywhere. . . . Some o' them laughed. . . . I was pushed away, but I shoved back. . . . Some o' them even sthruck me. . . . an' I screamed an' screamed your name!

CLITHEROE (*in fear her action would give him future shame*). What possessed you to make a show of yourself, like that? . . What way d'ye think I'll feel when I'm told my wife was bawlin' for me at th' barricades? What are you more than any other woman?

NORA. No more, maybe; but you are more to me than any other man, Jack. . . . I didn't mean any harm, honestly, Jack. . . . I couldn't help it. . . . I shouldn't have told you. . . . My love for you made me mad with terror.

CLITHEROE (*angrily*). They'll say now that I sent you out th' way I'd have an excuse to bring you home. . . . Are you goin' to turn all th' risks I'm takin' into a laugh?

LIEUT. LANGON. Let me lie down, let me lie down, Bill; th' pain would be easier, maybe, lyin' down. . . . Oh, God, have mercy on me!

CAPT. BRENNAN (*to* LANGON). A few steps more, Jim, a few steps more; thry to stick it for a few steps more.

LIEUT. LANGON. Oh, I can't, I can't, I can't!

CAPT. BRENNAN (*to* CLITHEROE). Are you comin', man, or are you goin' to make an arrangement for another honeymoon? . . . If you want to act th' renegade, say so, an' we'll be off!

BESSIE (*from above*). Runnin' from th' Tommies—choke th' chicken. Runnin' from th' Tommies—choke th' chicken!

CLITHEROE (*savagely to* BRENNAN). Damn you, man, who wants to act th' renegade? (*To* NORA) Here, let go your hold; let go, I say!

NORA (*clinging to* CLITHEROE, *and indicating* BRENNAN). Look, Jack, look at th' anger in his face; look at th' fear glintin' in his eyes. . . . He himself's afraid, afraid, afraid! . . . He wants you to go th' way he'll have th' chance of death sthrikin you an' missin' him! . . . Turn round an' look at him, Jack, look at him, look at him! . . . His very soul is cold . . . shiverin' with th' thought of what may happen to him. . . . It is his fear that is thryin' to frighten you from recognizin' th' same fear that is in your own heart!

CLITHEROE (*struggling to release himself from* NORA). Damn you, woman, will you let me go!

CAPT. BRENNAN (*fiercely, to* CLITHEROE). Why are you beggin' her to let you go? Are you afraid of her, or what? Break her hold on you, man, or go up, an' sit on her lap! (CLITHEROE *trying roughly to break her hold.*)

NORA (*imploringly*). Oh, Jack. . . . Jack. . . . Jack!

LIEUT. LANGON (*agonisingly*). Brennan, a priest; I'm dyin', I think, I'm dyin'!

CLITHEROE (*to* NORA). If you won't do it quietly, I'll have to make you! (*To* BRENNAN) Here, hold this gun, you, for a minute. (*He hands the gun to Brennan.*)

NORA (*pitifully*). Please, Jack. . . . You're hurting me, Jack. . . . Honestly. . . . Oh, you're hurting . . . me! . . . I won't, I won't, I won't! . . . Oh, Jack, I gave you everything you asked of me. . . . Don't fling me from you, now!

(He roughly loosens her grip, and pushes her away from him. NORA *sinks to the ground and lies there.)*

NORA *(weakly).*   Ah, Jack. . . . Jack. . . . Jack!

CLITHEROE *(taking the gun back from* BRENNAN*).*   Come on, come on.

(They go out. BESSIE *looks at* NORA *lying on the street, for a few moments, then, leaving the window, she comes out, runs over to* NORA *lifts her up in her arms, and carries her swiftly into the house. A short pause, then down the street is heard a wild, drunken yell; it comes nearer, and* FLUTHER *enters, frenzied, wild-eyed, mad, roaring drunk. In his arms is an earthen half-gallon jar of whisky; streaming from one of the pockets of his coat is the arm of a new tunic shirt; on his head is a woman's vivid blue hat with gold lacing, all of which he has looted.)*

FLUTHER *(singing in a frenzy):*
Fluther's a jolly good fella! . . . Fluther's a jolly good fella!
Up the rebels! . . . That nobody can deny!
(He beats on the door.) Get us a mug or a jug, or somethin', some o' yous, one o' yous, will yous, before I lay one o' yous out! . . . *(Looking down the street)* Bang an' fire away for all Fluther cares. . . . *(Banging at door)* Come down an' open th' door, some of yous, one o' yous, will yous, before I lay some o' yous out! . . . Th' whole city can topple home to hell, for Fluther!

(Inside the house is heard a scream from NORA, *followed by a moan.)*

FLUTHER *(singing furiously):*
That nobody can deny, that nobody can deny,
For Fluther's a jolly good fella, Fluther's a jolly good fella,
Fluther's a jolly good fella . . . Up th' rebels! That nobody
can deny!

(His frantic movements cause him to spill some of the whisky out of the jar.) Blast you, Fluther, don't be spillin' th' precious liquor! *(He kicks at the door.)* Ay, give us a mug or a jug, or somethin', one o' yous, some o' yous, will yous, before I lay one o' yous out!

(The door suddenly opens, and BESSIE, *coming out, grips him by the collar.)*

BESSIE *(indignantly)*.   You bowsey, come in ower o' that. . . . I'll thrim your thricks o' dhrunken dancin' for you, an' none of us knowin' how soon we'll bump into a world we were never in before!

FLUTHER *(as she is pulling him in)*.   Ay, th' jar, th' jar, th' jar!

(A short pause, then again is heard a scream of pain from NORA. *The door opens and* MRS. GOGAN *and* BESSIE *are seen standing at it.)*

BESSIE.   Fluther would go, only he's too dhrunk. . . . Oh, God, isn't it a pity he's so dhrunk! We'll have to thry to get a docthor somewhere.

MRS. GOGAN.   I'd be afraid to go. . . . Besides, Mollser's terrible bad. I don't think you'll get a docthor to come. It's hardly any use goin'.

BESSIE *(determinedly)*.   I'll risk it. . . . Give her a little of Fluther's whisky. . . . It's th' fright that's brought it on her so soon. . . . Go on back to her, you.

*(*MRS. GOGAN *goes in, and* BESSIE *softly closes the door. She is moving forward, when the sound of some rifle shots, and the tok, tok, tok of a distant machine-gun bring her to a sudden halt. She hesitates for a moment, then she tightens her shawl round her, as if it were a shield, then she firmly and swiftly goes out.)*

BESSIE *(as she goes out)*.   Oh, God, be Thou my help in time o' throuble. An' shelter me safely in th' shadow of Thy wings!

Curtain

Act IV

The living-room of BESSIE BURGESS. *It is one of two small attic rooms (the other, used as a bedroom, is to the Left), the ceiling slopes up towards the back, giving to the apartment a look of compressed confinement. In the centre of the ceiling is a small skylight. There is an unmistakable air of poverty bordering on destitution. The paper on the walls is torn and soiled, particularly near the fire where the cooking is done, and near the washstand where the washing is done. The fireplace is to the Left. A small armchair near fire. One small window at Back. A pane of this window is starred by the entrance of a bullet. Under the window to the Right is an oak coffin standing on two kitchen chairs. Near the coffin is a home-manufactured stool, on which are two lighted candles. Beside the window is a worn-out dresser on which is a small quantity of delf. Tattered remains of cheap lace curtains drape the window. Standing near the window on Left is a brass standard-lamp with a fancy shade; hanging on the wall near the same window is a vividly crimson silk dress, both of which have been looted. A door on Left leading to the bedroom. Another opposite giving a way to the rest of the house. To the Left of this door a common washstand. A tin kettle, very black, and an old saucepan inside the fender. There is no light in the room but that given from the two candles and the fire. The dusk has well fallen, and the glare of the burning buildings in the town can be seen through the window, in the distant sky. The* COVEY *and* FLUTHER *have been playing cards, sitting on the floor by the light of the candles on the stool near the coffin. When the curtain rises the* COVEY *is shuffling the cards,* PETER *is sitting in a stiff, dignified way beside him, and* FLUTHER *is kneeling beside the window, cautiously looking out. It is a few days later.)*

FLUTHER *(furtively peeping out of the window).*   Give them a good shuffling. . . . Th' sky's gettin' reddher an' reddher.

. . . You'd think it was afire. . . . Half o' th' city must be burnin'.

THE COVEY.   If I was you, Fluther, I'd keep away from that window. . . . It's dangerous, an', besides, if they see you, you'll only bring a nose on th' house.

PETER.   Yes; an' he knows we had to leave our own place th' way they were riddlin' it with machine-gun fire. . . . He'll keep on pimpin'[1] an' pimpin' there, till we have to fly out o' this place too.

FLUTHER *(ironically).*   If they make any attack here, we'll send you out in your green an' glory uniform, shakin' your sword over your head, an' they'll fly before you as th' Danes flew before Brian Boru.[2]

THE COVEY *(placing the cards on the floor, after shuffling them).*   Come on, an' cut.

(FLUTHER *comes over, sits on floor, and cuts the cards.*)

THE COVEY *(having dealt the cards).*   Spuds[3] up again.

(NORA *moans feebly in room on Left.*)

FLUTHER.   There, she's at it again. She's been quiet for a long time, all th' same.

THE COVEY.   She was quiet before, sure, an' she broke out again worse than ever. . . . What was led that time?

PETER.   Thray o' Hearts, Thray o' Hearts, Thray o' Hearts.

FLUTHER.   It's damned hard lines to think of her dead-born kiddie lyin' there in th' arms o' poor little Mollser. Mollser snuffed it[4] sudden too, afther all.

THE COVEY.   Sure she never got any care. How could she get it, an' th' mother out day an' night lookin' for work, an' her consumptive husband leavin' her with a baby to be born before he died!

---

[1]*pimpin':* acting as informer

[2]*Brian Boru:* (926-1014) king of Ireland who routed the Danes (Vikings) at the Battle of Clontarf (1014), thus ending an era of plundering Viking raids on the Irish coast

[3]*spuds:* spades

[4]*snuffed it:* died (slang)

VOICES *(in a lilting chant to the Left in a distant street).*   Red Cr . . . oss, Red Cr . . . oss! . . . Ambu . . . lance, Ambu . . . lance!

THE COVEY *(to FLUTHER).*   Your deal, Fluther.

FLUTHER *(shuffling and dealing the cards).*   It'll take a lot out of Nora—if she'll ever be th' same.

THE COVEY.   Th' docthor thinks she'll never be th' same; thinks she'll be a little touched here. *(He touches his forehead.)* She's ramblin' a lot; thinkin' she's out in th' counthry with Jack; or gettin' his dinner ready for him before he comes home; or yellin' for her kiddie. All that, though, might be th' chloroform she got. . . . I don't know what we'd have done only for oul' Bessie: up with her for th' past three nights, hand runnin'.

FLUTHER.   I always knew there was never anything really derogatory wrong with poor oul' Bessie. *(To PETER, who is taking a trick)* Ay, houl' on, there, don't be so damn quick—that's my thrick.

PETER.   What's your thrick? It's my thrick, man.

FLUTHER *(loudly).*   How is it your thrick?

PETER *(answering as loudly).*   Didn't I lead th' deuce!

FLUTHER.   You must be gettin' blind, man; don't you see th' ace?

BESSIE *(appearing at door of room, Left; in a tense whisper).*   D'ye want to waken her again on me, when she's just gone asleep? If she wakes will yous come an' mind her? If I hear a whisper out o' one o' yous again, I'll . . . gut yous!

THE COVEY *(in a whisper).*   S-s-s-h. She can hear anything above a whisper.

PETER *(looking up at the ceiling).*   Th' gentle an' merciful God 'll give th' pair o' yous a scawldin' an' a scarifyin' one o' these days!

(FLUTHER takes a bottle of whisky from his pocket, and takes a drink.)

THE COVEY *(to FLUTHER).*   Why don't you spread that out, man, an' thry to keep a sup[5] for to-morrow?

----

[5]*sup:* sip

FLUTHER. Spread it out? Keep a sup for to-morrow? How th' hell does a fella know there'll be any to-morrow? If I'm goin' to be whipped away, let me be whipped away when it's empty, an' not when it's half full! *(To Bessie, who has seated herself in an armchair at the fire)* How is she, now, Bessie?

BESSIE. I left her sleeping quietly. When I'm listenin' to her babblin', I think she'll never be much betther than she is. Her eyes have a hauntin' way of lookin' in instead of lookin' out, as if her mind had been lost alive in madly minglin' memories of th' past. . . . *(Sleepily)* Crushin' her thoughts . . . together . . . in a fierce . . . an' fanciful . . . *(she nods her head and starts wakefully)* idea that dead things are livin', an' livin' things are dead. . . . *(With a start)* Was that a scream I heard her give? *(Reassured)* Blessed God, I think I hear her screamin' every minute! An' it's only there with me that I'm able to keep awake.

THE COVEY. She'll sleep, maybe, for a long time, now. Ten there.

FLUTHER. Ten here. If she gets a long sleep, she might be all right. Peter's th' lone five.

THE COVEY. Whisht! I think I hear somebody movin' below. Whoever it is, he's comin' up.

(A pause. Then the door opens and CAPTAIN BRENNAN *comes into the room. He has changed his uniform for a suit of civvies. His eyes droop with the heaviness of exhaustion; his face is pallid and drawn. His clothes are dusty and stained here and there with mud. He leans heavily on the back of a chair as he stands.)*

CAPT. BRENNAN. Mrs. Clitheroe; where's Mrs. Clitheroe? I was told I'd find her here.

BESSIE. What d'ye want with Mrs. Clitheroe?

CAPT. BRENNAN. I've a message, a last message for her from her husband.

BESSIE. Killed! He's not killed, is he!

CAPT. BRENNAN *(sinking stiffly and painfully on to a chair)*. In th' Imperial Hotel; we fought till th' place was in flames. He was shot through th' arm, an' then through th' lung. . . . I could do nothin' for him—only watch his breath comin' an' goin' in quick, jerky gasps, an' a tiny sthream o' blood thricklin' out of his mouth, down over his lower lip. . . . I said a prayer for th' dyin', an' twined his Rosary beads around his fingers. . . . Then I had to leave him to save meself. . . . *(He shows some holes in his coat)* Look at th' way a machine-gun tore at me coat, as I belted out o' th' buildin' an' darted across th' sthreet for shelter. . . . An' then, I seen The Plough an' th' Stars fallin' like a shot as th' roof crashed in, an' where I'd left poor Jack was nothin but a leppin' spout o' flame!

BESSIE *(with partly repressed vehemence).* Ay, you left him! You twined his Rosary beads round his fingers, an' then you run like a hare to get out o' danger!

CAPT. BRENNAN. I took me chance as well as him. . . . He took it like a man. His last whisper was to "Tell Nora to be brave; that I'm ready to meet my God, an' that I'm proud to die for Ireland." An' when our General heard it he said that "Commandant Clitheroe's end was gleam of glory." Mrs. Clitheroe's grief will be a joy when she realizes that she has had a hero for a husband.

BESSIE. If you only seen her, you'd know to th' differ.

(NORA appears at door, Left. She is clad only in her night-dress; her hair, uncared for some days, is hanging in disorder over her shoulders. Her pale face looks paler still because of a vivid red spot on the tip of each cheek. Her eyes are glimmering with the light of incipient insanity; her hands are nervously fiddling with her nightgown. She halts at the door for a moment, looks vacantly around the room, and then comes slowly in. The rest do not notice her till she speaks.)

NORA *(in a quiet and monotonous tone).* No . . . Not there, Jack. . . . I can feel comfortable only in our own familiar place beneath th' bramble tree. . . . We must be walking for a long time; I feel very, very tired. . . . Have we to go farther, or have we passed it by? *(Passing her hand across her eyes)* Curious mist on my eyes. . . . Why don't you hold my hand, Jack. . . . *(Excitedly)* No, no, Jack, it's not. Can't you see it's a goldfinch. Look at th' black-satiny wings with th' gold bars, an' th' splash of crimson on its head. . . . *(Wearily)* Something ails me, something ails me. . . . Don't kiss me like that; you take my breath away, Jack. . . . Why do you frown at me? . . . You're going away, and *(frightened)* I can't follow you. Something's keeping me from moving. . . . *(Crying out)* Jack, Jack, Jack!

BESSIE *(who has gone over and caught* NORA'S *arm).* Now, Mrs. Clitheroe, you're a terrible woman to get up out of bed. . . . You'll get cold if you stay here in them clothes.

NORA. Cold? I'm feelin' very cold; it's chilly out here in th' counthry. . . . *(Looking around frightened)* What place is this? Where am I?

BESSIE *(coaxingly).* You're all right, Nora; you're with friends, an' in a safe place. Don't you know your uncle an' your cousin, an' poor oul' Fluther?

PETER *(about to go over to* NORA*).* Nora, darlin', now —

FLUTHER *(pulling him back).* Now, leave her to Bessie, man. A crowd 'll only make her worse.

NORA *(thoughtfully).* There is something I want to remember, an' I can't. *(With agony)* I can't, I can't, I can't! My head, my head! *(Suddenly breaking from* BESSIE *and running over to the men, and gripping* FLUTHER *by the shoulders)* Where is it? Where's my baby! Tell me where you've put it, where've you hidden it? My baby, my baby; I want my baby! My head, my poor head. . . . Oh, I can't tell what is wrong with me. *(Screaming)* Give him to me, give me my husband!

BESSIE. Blessin' o' God on us, isn't this pitiful!

NORA *(struggling with* BESSIE*).* I won't go away for you; I won't. Not till you give me back my husband. *(Screaming)* Murderers, that's what yous are; murderers, murderers!

BESSIE. S-s-sh. We'll bring Mr. Clitheroe back to you, if you'll only lie down an' stop quiet. . . . *(Trying to lead her in)* Come on, now, Nora, an' I'll sing something to you.

NORA. I feel as if my life was thryin' to force its way out of

my body. . . . I can hardly breathe . . . I'm frightened,
I'm frightened, I'm frightened! For God's sake, don't
leave me, Bessie. Hold my hand, put your arms around
me!

FLUTHER *(to* BRENNAN*)*. Now you can see th' way she is,
man.

PETER. An' what way would she be if she heard Jack had
gone west?

THE COVEY *(to* PETER*)*. Shut up, you, man!

BESSIE *(to* NORA*)*. We'll have to be brave, an' let patience
clip away th' heaviness of th' slow-movin' hours, rememberin' that sorrow may endure for th' night, but joy
cometh in th' mornin'. . . . Come on in, an' I'll sing to you,
an' you'll rest quietly.

NORA *(stopping suddenly on her way to the room)*. Jack an'
me are goin' out somewhere this evenin'. Where I can't
tell. Isn't it curious I can't remember. . . . Maura, Maura,
Jack, if th' baby's a girl; any name you like, if th' baby's
a boy! . . . He's there. *(Screaming)* He's there, an' they
won't give him back to me!

BESSIE. S-ss-s-h, darlin', s-ssh. I won't sing to you, if you're
not quiet.

NORA *(nervously holding* BESSIE*)*. Hold my hand, hold my
hand, an' sing to me, sing to me!

BESSIE. Come in an' lie down, an' I'll sing to you.

NORA *(vehemently)*. Sing to me, sing to me; sing, sing!

BESSIE *(singing as she leads* NORA *into room)*:

   Lead, kindly light, amid th' encircling gloom,
      Lead Thou me on.
   Th' night is dark an' I am far from home,
      Lead Thou me on.
   Keep Thou my feet, I do not ask to see
   Th' distant scene—one step enough for me.

   So long that Thou hast blessed me, sure Thou still
      Wilt lead me on;

(They go in.)

BESSIE *(singing in room):*

> O'er moor an' fen, o'er crag an' torrent, till
> > Th' night is gone.
> An' in th' morn those angel faces smile
> That I have lov'd long since, an' lost awhile!

THE COVEY *(to* BRENNAN*).* Now that you've seen how bad she is, an' that we daren't tell her what has happened till she's betther, you'd best be slippin' back to where you come from.

CAPT. BRENNAN. There's no chance o' slippin' back now, for th' military are everywhere: a fly couldn't get through. I'd never have got here, only I managed to change me uniform for what I'm wearin'. . . . I'll have to take me chance, an' thry to lie low here for a while.

THE COVEY *(frightened).* There's no place here to lie low. Th' Tommies 'll be hoppin' in here, any minute!

PETER *(aghast).* An' then we'd all be shanghaied!

THE COVEY. Be God, there's enough afther happenin' to us!

FLUTHER *(warningly, as he listens).* Whisht, whisht, th' whole o' yous. I think I heard th' clang of a rifle butt on th floor of th' hall below. *(All alertness.)* Here, come on with th' cards again. I'll deal. *(He shuffles and deals the cards to all.)*

FLUTHER. Clubs up. *(To* BRENNAN*)* Thry to keep your hands from shakin', man. You lead, Peter. *(As Peter throws out a card)* Four o' Hearts led.

(The door opens and CORPORAL STODDART *of the Wilt-shires[6] enters in full war kit; steel helmet, rifle and bayonet, and trench tool. He looks round the room. A pause and a palpable silence.)*

FLUTHER *(breaking the silence).* Two tens an' a five.

CORPORAL STODDART. 'Ello. *(Indicating the coffin)* This the stiff?

THE COVEY. Yis.

CORPORAL STODDART. Who's gowing with it? Ownly one allowed to gow with it, you know.

[6]*Wiltshires:* a British regiment

THE COVEY. I dunno.

CORPORAL STODDART. You dunnow?

THE COVEY. I dunno.

BESSIE *(coming into the room).* She's afther slippin' off to sleep again, thanks be to God. I'm hardly able to keep me own eyes open. *(To the soldier)* Oh, are yous goin' to take away poor little Mollser?

CORPORAL STODDART. Ay; 'oo's agowing with 'er?

BESSIE. Oh, th' poor mother, o' course. God help her, it's a terrible blow to her!

FLUTHER. A terrible blow? Sure, she's in her element now, woman, mixin' earth to earth, an' ashes t'ashes an' dust to dust, an' revellin' in plumes an' hearses, last days an' judgements!

BESSIE *(falling into chair by the fire).* God bless us! I'm jaded!

CORPORAL STODDART. Was she plugged?

THE COVEY. Ah, no; died o' consumption.

CORPORAL STODDART. Ow, is that all? Thought she moight 'ave been plugged.

THE COVEY. Is that all? Isn't it enough? D'ye know, comrade, that more die o' consumption than are killed in th' wars? An' it's all because of th' system we're livin' undher?

CORPORAL STODDART. Ow, I know. I'm a Sowcialist moiself, but I 'as to do my dooty.

THE COVEY *(ironically).* Dooty! Th' only dooty of a Socialist is th' emancipation of th' workers.

CORPORAL STODDART. Ow, a man's a man, an 'e 'as to foight for 'is country, 'asn't 'e?

FLUTHER *(aggressively).* You're not fightin' for your counthry here, are you?

PETER *(anxiously, to* FLUTHER*).* Ay, ay, Fluther, none o' that, none o' that!

THE COVEY. Fight for your counthry! Did y'ever read, comrade, Jenersky's *Thesis on the Origin, Development, an' Consolidation of th' Evolutionary Idea of the Proletariat?*

CORPORAL STODDART. Ow, cheese it, Paddy,[7] cheese it!

⎯⎯⎯⎯⎯⎯

[7]*Paddy:* nickname for any Irishman

BESSIE *(sleepily).* How is things in th' town, Tommy?

CORPORAL STODDART. Ow, I fink it's nearly hover. We've got 'em surrounded, and we're clowsing in on the bloighters. Ow, it was only a little bit of a dawg-foight.

(The sharp ping of the sniper's rifle is heard, followed by a squeal of pain.)

VOICES *(to the Left in a chant).* Red Cr . . . oss, Red Cr . . . ss! Ambu . . . lance, Ambu . . . lance!

CORPORAL STODDART *(excitedly).* Christ, that's another of our men 'it by that blawsted sniper! 'E's knocking abaht 'ere, somewheres. Gawd, when we gets th' bloighter, we'll give 'im the cold steel, we will. We'll jab the belly aht of 'im, we will!

(MRS. GOGAN comes in tearfully, and a little proud of the importance of being directly connected with death.)

MRS. GOGAN *(to FLUTHER).* I'll never forget what you done for me, Fluther, goin' around at th' risk of your life settlin' everything with th' undhertaker an' th' cemetery people. When all me own were afraid to put their noses out, you plunged like a good one through hummin' bullets, an' they knockin' fire out o' th' road, tinklin' through th' frightened windows, an' splashin' themselves to pieces on th' walls! An' you'll find, that Mollser, in th' happy place she's gone to, won't forget to whisper, now an' again, th' name o' Fluther.

CORPORAL STODDART. Git it aht, mother, git it aht.

BESSIE *(from the chair).* It's excusin' me you'll be, Mrs. Gogan, for not stannin' up, seein' I'm shaky on me feet for want of a little sleep, an' not desirin' to show any disrespect to poor little Mollser.

FLUTHER. Sure, we all know, Bessie, that it's vice versa with you.

MRS. GOGAN *(to BESSIE).* Indeed, it's meself that has well chronicled, Mrs. Burgess, all your gentle hurryin's to me

little Mollser, when she was alive, bringin her somethin'
to dhrink, or somethin' t'eat, an' never passin' her without liftin' up her heart with a delicate word o' kindness.

CORPORAL STODDART (*impatiently, but kindly*). Git it aht,
git it aht, mother.

(*The* COVEY, FLUTHER, BRENNAN, *and* PETER *carry out
the coffin, followed by* MRS. GOGAN.)

CORPORAL STODDART (*to* BESSIE, *who is almost asleep*). 'Ow
many men is in this 'ere 'ouse? (*No answer. Loudly*) 'Ow
many men is in this 'ere 'ouse?

BESSIE (*waking with a start*). God, I was nearly asleep! . . .
How many men? Didn't you see them?

CORPORAL STODDART. Are they all that are in the 'ouse?

BESSIE. Oh, there's none higher up, but there may be more
lower down. Why?

CORPORAL STODDART. All men in the district 'as to be
rounded up. Somebody's giving 'elp to the snipers, and
we 'as to take precautions. If I 'ad my woy, I'd make 'em
all join hup, and do their bit! But I suppowse they and you
are all Shinners.⁸

BESSIE (*who has been sinking into sleep, waking up to a
sleepy vehemence*). Bessie Burgess is no Shinner, an'
never had no thruck with anything spotted be th' fingers
o' th' Fenians; but always made it her business to harness
herself for Church whenever she knew that "God Save
the King"⁹ was goin' to be sung at t'end of th' service;
whose only son went to th' front in th' first contingent of
the Dublin Fusiliers,¹⁰ an' that's on his way home carryin'
a shatthered arm that he got fightin' for his King an'
counthry!

---

⁸*Shinners:* members of the Sinn Fein, a political party and movement
founded in Ireland, about 1905, with the goals of reviving Irish culture and
securing Ireland's independence from Britain
⁹*God Save the King:* British national anthem, sung at the end of Protestant
services
¹⁰*Dublin Fusiliers:* See page 300.

(Her head sinks slowly forward again. PETER *comes into the room; his body is stiffened and his face is wearing a comically indignant look. He walks to and fro at the back of the room, evidently repressing a violent desire to speak angrily. He is followed in by* FLUTHER, *the* COVEY, *and* BRENNAN, *who slinks into an obscure corner of the room, nervous of notice.)*

FLUTHER *(after an embarrassing pause).* Th' air in th' sthreet outside's shakin' with the firin' o' rifles an' machine-guns. It must be a hot shop in th' middle o' th' scrap.

CORPORAL STODDART. We're pumping lead in on 'em from every side, now; they'll soon be shoving up th' white flag.

PETER *(with a shout).* I'm tellin' you either o' yous two

lowsers 'ud make a betther hearse-man than Peter; proddin' an' pokin' at me an' I helpin' to carry out a corpse!

FLUTHER. It wasn't a very derogatory thing for th' Covey to say that you'd make a fancy hearse-man, was it?

PETER *(furiously).* A pair o' redjesthered bowserys pondherin' from mornin' till night on how they'll get a chance to break a gap through th' quiet nature of a man that's alway endeavourin' to chase out of him any sthray thought of venom against his fella-man!

THE COVEY. Oh, shut it, shut it, shut it!

PETER. As long as I'm a livin' man, responsible for me thoughts, words, an' deeds to th' Man above, I'll feel meself instituted to fight again' th' sliddherin' ways of a pair o' picaroons, whisperin', concurrin', concoctin', an' conspirin' together to rendher me unconscious of th' life I'm thryin' to live!

CORPORAL STODDART *(dumbfounded).* What's wrong, Daddy; wot 'ave they done to you?

PETER *(savagely to the Corporal).* You mind your own business! What's it got to do with you, what's wrong with me?

BESSIE *(in a sleepy murmur).* Will yous thry to conthrol yourselves into quietness? Yous'll waken her . . . up . . . on . . . me . . . again. *(She sleeps.)*

FLUTHER. Come on, boys, to th' cards again, an' never mind him.

CORPORAL STODDART.   No use of you gowing to start cawds;
   you'll be gowing out of 'ere, soon as Sergeant comes.
FLUTHER.   Goin' out o' here? An' why're we goin' out o'
   here?
CORPORAL STODDART.   All men in district to be rounded up,
   and 'eld in till the scrap is hover.
FLUTHER.   An' where're we goin' to be held in?
CORPORAL STODDART.   They're puttin 'em in a church.
THE COVEY.   A church?
FLUTHER.   What sort of a church? Is it a Protestan' Church?
CORPORAL STODDART.   I dunnow; I suppowse so.
FLUTHER *(dismayed)*.   Be God, it'll be a nice thing to be
   stuck all night in a Protestan' Church!
CORPORAL STODDART.   Bring the cawds; you moight get a
   chance of a goime.
FLUTHER.   Ah, no, that wouldn't do. . . . I wondher? *(After
   a moment's thought)* Ah, I don't think we'd be doin' any-
   thing derogatory be playin' cards in a Protestan' Church.
CORPORAL STODDART.   If I was you I'd bring a little snack
   with me; you moight be glad of it before the mawning.
   (Sings):

> I do loike a snoice mince poy,
> I do loike a snoice mince poy!

*(The snap of the sniper's rifle rings out again, followed
simultaneously by a scream of pain.* CORPORAL STODDART
goes pale, and brings his rifle to the ready, listening.)

VOICES *(chanting to the Right.*   Red Cro . . . ss, Red Cro . . .
   ss! Ambu . . . lance, Ambu . . . lance!

(SERGEANT TINLEY *comes rapidly in, pale, agitated, and
fiercely angry.)*

CORPORAL STODDART *(to Sergeant).*   One of hour men 'it,
   Sergeant?
SERGEANT TINLEY.   Private Taylor; got 'it roight through the
   chest, 'e did; an 'ole in front of 'im as 'ow you could put
   your fist through, and 'arf 'is back blown awoy! Dum-

dum bullets they're using. Gang of Hassassins potting at us from behind roofs. That's not playing the goime: why down't they come into the owpen and foight fair!

FLUTHER *(unable to stand the slight).* Fight fair! A few hundhred scrawls o' chaps with a couple o' guns an' Rosary beads, again' a hundhred thousand thrained men with horse, fut, an' artillery . . . an' he wants us to fight fair! *(To* SERGEANT*)* D'ye want us to come out in our skins an' throw stones?

SERGEANT TINLEY *(to* CORPORAL*).* Are these four all that are 'ere?

CORPORAL STODDART. Four; that's all, Sergeant.

SERGEANT TINLEY *(vindictively).* Come on, then; get the blighters aht. *(To the men)* 'Ere 'op it aht! Aht into the streets with you, and if a snoiper sends another of our men west, you gow with 'im! *(He catches Fluther by the shoulder)* Gow on, git aht!

FLUTHER. Eh, who are you chuckin', eh?

SERGEANT TINLEY *(roughly).* Gow on, git aht, you blighter.

FLUTHER. Who are you callin' a blighter to, eh? I'm a Dublin man, born an' bred in th' city, see?

SERGEANT TINLEY. I down't care if you were Broin Buroo;[11] git aht, git aht.

FLUTHER *(halting as he is going out).* Jasus, you an' your guns! Leave them down, an' I'd beat th' two o' yous without sweatin'!

(PETER, BRENNAN, the COVEY, and FLUTHER, followed by the soldiers, go out. BESSIE is sleeping on the chair by the fire. After a pause, NORA appears at door, Left, in her nightdress. Remaining at door for a few moments she looks vaguely around the room. She then comes in quietly, goes over to the fire, pokes it, and puts the kettle on. She thinks for a few moments, pressing her hand to her forehead. She looks questioningly at the fire, and then at the press at back. She goes to the press, opens it, takes out a soiled cloth and spreads it on the table. She then places things for tea on the table.)

[11]*Broin Buroo:* Brian Boru (see page 342)

NORA. I imagine th' room looks very odd somehow. . . . I was nearly forgetting Jack's tea. . . . Ah, I think I'll have everything done before he gets in. . . . (*She lilts gently, as she arranges the table.*)

> Th' violets were scenting th' woods, Nora,
>   Displaying their charms to th' bee,
> When I first said I lov'd only you, Nora,
>   An' you said you lov'd only me.
>
> Th' chesnut blooms gleam'd through th' glade,
>   Nora,
> A robin sang loud from a tree,
> When I first said I lov'd only you, Nora,
>   An' you said you lov'd only me.

(*She pauses suddenly, and glances round the room.*)

NORA (*doubtfully*). I can't help feelin' this room very strange. . . . What is it? . . . What is it? . . . I must think. . . . I must thry to remember. . . .

VOICES (*chanting in a distant street*). Ambu . . . lance, Ambu . . . lance! Red Cro . . . ss, Red Cro . . . ss!

NORA (*startled and listening for a moment, then resuming the arrangement of the table*):

> Trees, birds, an' bees sang a song, Nora,
>   Of happier transports to be,
> When I first said I lov'd only you, Nora,
>   An' you said you lov'd only me.

(*A burst of rifle fire is heard in a street near by, followed by the rapid rok, tok, tok of a machine-gun.*

NORA (*staring in front of her and screaming*). Jack, Jack, Jack! My baby, my baby, my baby!

BESSIE (*waking with a start*). You divil, are you afther gettin' out o' bed again! (*She rises and runs towards* NORA, *who rushes to the window, which she frantically opens.*)

NORA (*at window, screaming*). Jack, Jack, for God's sake, come to me!

356 ?~ *Sean O'Casey*

SOLDIER (*outside, shouting*). Git away, git away from that
window there!

BESSIE (*seizing hold of* NORA). Come away, come away,
woman, from that window!

NORA (*struggling with* BESSIE). Where is it; where have you
hidden it? Oh, Jack, Jack, where are you?

BESSIE (*imploringly*). Mrs. Clitheroe, for God's sake, come
away!

NORA (*fiercely*). I won't; he's below. Let . . . me . . . go!
You're thryin' to keep me from me husband. I'll follow
him. Jack, Jack, come to your Nora!

BESSIE. Hus-s-sh, Nora, Nora! He'll be here in a minute. I'll
bring him to you, if you'll only be quiet—honest to God,
I will.

(*With a great effort* BESSIE *pushes* NORA *away from the
window, the force used causing her to stagger against it
herself. Two rifle shots ring out in quick succession.*
BESSIE *jerks her body convulsively; stands stiffly for a
moment, a look of agonized astonishment on her face,
then she staggers forward, leaning heavily on the table
with her hands.*)

BESSIE (*with an arrested scream of fear and pain*). Merciful
God, I'm shot, I'm shot, I'm shot! . . . Th' life's pourin'
out o' me! (*To Nora*) I've got this through . . . through you
. . . through you, you witch, you! . . . O God, have mercy
on me! . . . (*To Nora*) You wouldn't stop quiet, no, you
wouldn't, you wouldn't, blast you! Look at what I'm
afther gettin', look at what I'm afther gettin' . . . I'm
bleedin' to death, an' no one's here to stop th' flowin'
blood! (*Calling*) Mrs. Gogan, Mrs. Gogan! Fluther,
Fluther, for God's sake, somebody, a doctor, a doctor!

(*She staggers frightened towards the door, to seek for aid,
but, weakening half-way across the room, she sinks to her
knees, and bending forward, supports herself with her
hands resting on the floor.* NORA *is standing rigidly with
her back to the wall opposite, her trembling hands held*

*out a little from the sides of her body, her lips quivering,
her breast heaving, staring wildly at the figure of* BESSIE.)

NORA *(in a breathless whisper)*.   Jack, I'm frightened. . . .
I'm frightened, Jack. . . . Oh, Jack, where are you?

BESSIE *(moaningly)*.   This is what afther comin' on me for
nursin' you day an' night. . . . I was a fool, a fool, a fool!
Get me a dhrink o' wather, you jade, will you? There's a
fire burnin' in me blood! *(Pleadingly)* Nora, Nora, dear,
for God's sake, run out an' get Mrs. Gogan, or Fluther, or
somebody to bring a doctor, quick, quick, quick! *(As* NORA
does not stir) Blast you, stir yourself, before I'm gone!

NORA.   Oh, Jack, Jack, where are you?

BESSIE *(in a whispered moan)*.   Jesus Christ, me sight's goin'!
It's all dark, dark! Nora, hold me hand!

*(*BESSIE'S *body lists over and she sinks into a prostrate
position on the floor.)*

BESSIE.   I'm dyin', I'm dyin' . . . I feel it. . . . Oh God, oh
God! *(She feebly sings:)*

> I do believe, I will believe
>   That Jesus died for me;
> That on th' cross He shed His blood,
>   From sin to set me free. . . .
>
> I do believe . . . I will believe
>   . . . Jesus died . . . me;
> . . . th' cross He shed . . . blood,
>   From sin . . . free.

*(She ceases singing, and lies stretched out, still and very
rigid. A pause. Then* MRS. GOGAN *runs hastily in.)*

MRS. GOGAN *(quivering with fright)*.   Blessed be God, what's
afther happenin'? *(To* NORA) What's wrong, child, what's
wrong? *(She sees* BESSIE, *runs to her and bends over the
body)* Bessie, Bessie! *(She shakes the body)* Mrs. Burgess,

Mrs. Burgess! *(She feels* BESSIE's *forehead)* My God, she's as cold as death. They're afther murdherin' th' poor inoffensive woman!

*(*SERGEANT TINLEY *and* CORPORAL STODDART *enter agitatedly, their rifles at the ready.)*

SERGEANT TINLEY *(excitedly).* This is the 'ouse. That's the window!

NORA *(pressing back against the wall).* Hide it, hide it; cover it up, cover it up!

SERGEANT TINLEY *(going over to the body).* 'Ere, what's this? Who's this? *(Looking at* BESSIE*)* Oh, Gawd, we've plugged one of the women of the 'ouse.

CORPORAL STODDART. Whoy the 'ell did she gow to the window? Is she dead?

SERGEANT TINLEY. Oh, dead as bedamned. Well, we couldn't affort to toike any chawnces.

NORA *(screaming).* Hide it, hide it; don't let me see it! Take me away, take me away, Mrs. Gogan!

*(*MRS. GOGAN *runs into room, Left, and runs out again with a sheet which she spreads over the body of* BESSIE*.)*

MRS. GOGAN *(as she spreads the sheet).* Oh, God help her, th' poor woman, she's stiffenin' out as hard as she can! Her face has written on it th' shock o' sudden agony, an' her hands is whitenin' into th' smooth shininess of wax.

NORA *(whimperingly).* Take me away, take me away; don't leave me here to be lookin' an' lookin' at it!

MRS. GOGAN *(going over to Nora and putting her arm around her).* Come on with me, dear, an' you can doss[12] in poor Mollser's bed, till we gather some neighbors to come an' give th' last friendly touches to Bessie in th' lonely layin' of her out.

*(*MRS. GOGAN *and* NORA *go slowly out.)*

[12]*doss:* sleep

CORPORAL STODDART (*who has been looking around, to* SER-
GEANT TINLEY). Tea here, Sergeant. Wot abaht a cup of
scald?

SERGEANT TINLEY. Pour it aht, Stoddart, pour it aht. I could
scoff hanything just now.

(CORPORAL STODDART *pours out two cups of tea, and the
two soldiers begin to drink. In the distance is heard a
bitter burst of rifle and machine-gun fire, interspersed
with the boom, boom of artillery. The glare in the sky
seen through the window flares into a fuller and a deeper
red.*)

SERGEANT TINLEY. There gows the general attack on the
Powst Office.

VOICES (*in a distant street*). Ambu . . . lance, Ambu . . .
lance! Red Cro . . . ss, Red Cro . . . ss!

(*The voices of soldiers at a barricade outside the house
are heard singing:*)

> They were summoned from the 'illside,
> They were called in from the glen,
> And the country found 'em ready
> At the stirring call for men.
> Let not tears add to their 'ardship,
> As the soldiers pass along,
> And although our 'eart is breaking,
> Make it sing this cheery song.

SERGEANT TINLEY *and* CORPORAL STODDART (*joining in the
chorus, as they sip the tea*):

> Keep the 'owme fires burning,
> While your 'earts are yearning;
> Though your lads are far away
> They dream of 'owme;
> There's a silver loining

Through the dark cloud shoining,
Turn the dark cloud inside out,
Till the boys come 'owme!

Curtain

FOR DISCUSSION

Act I

1. The long opening conversation between Mrs. Gogan and Fluther Good provides some of the *exposition* (see Glossary) for the play. How does Mrs. Gogan characterize Nora Clitheroe? What conflict is suggested between Nora and Jack? Judging from the stage directions and from her own comments, tell what sort of person Mrs. Gogan is.

2. Peter says very little during his numerous entrances and exits, and yet he performs a definite dramatic function. What is his effect on the rather lengthy dialogue between Fluther and Mrs. Gogan? Why do you think this effect is desirable?

3. What is the main function of the "mollycewel" argument between Fluther and the Covey? What sort of person is Fluther? What is your impression of the Covey? What do you learn about his political beliefs?

4. What resolution does Fluther announce to Nora concerning his drinking?

5. At what points does the playwright introduce background information about the political situation in Ireland? How does he provide this information in a natural manner?

6. How does the playwright link Peter and the Covey together during Act I? Do you see any similarities in their attitudes or behavior? What is your impression of Peter?

7. Mrs. Gogan characterizes Nora and Jack before either of them appears onstage. In what ways are they consistent with her characterization? What situation arises late in the act to confirm her intimations of a conflict between them?

8. What is your impression of the playwright's presentation of the love scene between Nora and Jack? Do you consider it realistic, romantic, naive, overly sentimental? Explain.

9. What is your impression of Bessie Burgess from her two brief appearances during Act I? How do she and Nora feel toward

each other? What is the dramatic effect of her speech at the end of the act?

10. Who is Mollser? In what sense is her final question a commentary upon the entire act?

Act II

1. Rosie Redmond characterizes the mood of the soldiers as "a holy mood." How do the words of the soldier Voice reinforce this idea? What is the attitude of the patriots toward war?

2. The playwright has structured Act II as an alternation between the words of the soldier Voice outside the public-house and the actions of the main characters inside. What ironic effect does he achieve by this arrangement? What specific contrasts between the soldiers and the non-combatants do you find particularly ironic? (See Glossary, *irony*.)

3. On the basis of what you have learned about them so far, compare the characters and attitudes of Mrs. Gogan and Bessie Burgess. In what ways are they similar? How do their political views differ? In what sense is Bessie an "outsider"?

4. In view of Fluther's remarks about his drinking in Act I, why are his actions in Act II ironic? What other examples do you find throughout the act in which a character's actions belie his words or his words are cast into doubt by another character? In bringing the words of the non-combatants under suspicion, how is the playwright able to control your reaction to the words of Clitheroe, Brennan, and Langon near the end of the act?

Act III

1. This act takes place several months later, during the Easter Week Rebellion, and Mrs. Gogan and Mollser provide the exposition in their conversation. What do you learn about the present state of affairs? What ironic change has occurred in Mrs. Gogan's behavior since Act II?

2. How does Nora's view of the war contrast with that of the Irish patriots? In what respect is Bessie's view similar to hers?

3. How is Bessie's isolation from the others emphasized by her physical position during most of the act? What is the dramatic effect of her gesture to Mollser in respect to her isolation? In view of her behavior during the preceding acts, is her gesture unexpected? Explain. What new aspect of her character does it reveal? How is this aspect of her character reconfirmed by her behavior at the end of the act?

4. What does Fluther's search for Nora reveal about him? Why is his behavior a direct contrast to that of the other men in the tenement? In what sense does his behavior transcend the limits of the political situation?

5. The woman from Wrathmines thinks she is "so different from others" because the shooting terrifies her. What irony do you find in her remarks?

6. How does the appearance of Clitheroe, Brennan, and Langon in this act contrast with their appearance in Act II? How does their present behavior contrast with the high-sounding sentiments they expressed in Act II? Have you been prepared in any way for their present behavior? Explain.

7. At what point in the act does the Clitheroe strand of the plot reach its *climax* (see Glossary)? What do you suspect will be the outcome in Act IV? Give evidence for your view.

8. In this act, the playwright again presents two contrasting aspects of the war. Which scenes are particularly ironic in contrast to the fighting and to the idealistic sentiments of those at the barricades?

9. The relationship between Mrs. Gogan and Bessie Burgess at the end of Act III presents a marked contrast to their relationship in Act II. What has caused the change? What is Bessie Burgess' position now in relation to the other tenants? In what sense has her behavior transcended the confines of the political situation?

Act IV

1. During the opening moments of the act, how does the playwright provide the necessary exposition in a natural manner? How were Mollser's death and Nora's miscarriage *foreshadowed* (see Glossary) in Act III? Were you prepared in any way for Nora's insanity?

2. In considering the fate of each tenant, do you feel that he has shaped his own destiny, or do you feel that his destiny has been controlled by his environment? Explain. Why is Bessie's fate particularly ironic?

3. What elements make the war more obtrusive and more immediate in this act than in the previous acts? What is the dramatic effect of this obtrusion? In what respect is the final scene of the play a culmination of this dramatic effect?

4. O'Casey's irony has been constantly evident in the interplay between the exterior action of the war and the interior actions

of the main characters. In what sense is the final chorus of the British soldiers the culminating irony of both the exterior and the interior actions?

ON THE PLAY AS A WHOLE

1. Bessie's speech at the end of Act I has the overtones of a prophecy of doom. How do the subsequent events of the play fulfill her prophecy?

2. The complex plot of this play results from an interplay between two structures of action: an *interior action*, showing the lives of various members of a tenement; and an *exterior action*, showing the rise and decline of the Easter Week Rebellion. The exterior action provides a framework for the progressive episodes of the interior action. The plot of the exterior action more or less follows the traditional plot development in terms of exposition, complication, climax, and denouement. Trace this development act by act. Where does the *climax* (see Glossary) of the exterior action occur? Which of the individual plot strands of the interior action show traditional plot development? At what point in each of these strands does the climax occur? Does the plot development of the exterior action coincide with that of the interior action at any point? If so, where?

3. Though the play is generally considered to be a tragicomedy, combining elements of both comedy and tragedy, O'Casey labeled it as "A Tragedy in Four Acts." Do you see the play as a tragedy of individual characters, a tragedy of the characters as a group, a tragedy of the Dublin rebellion, or as a tragedy of war itself? Give evidence to support your view. In what sense does the tragedy of this play combine all of these elements?

4. The juxtaposition of comedy and tragedy within the confines of a single play is a practice that very few dramatists since Shakespeare have been able to accomplish successfully. A delicate balance must be maintained between the two elements if the comedy is to be truly comic and the tragedy truly tragic. What happens to the comedy in this play as its tragic aspects become more apparent? Do you feel that the comedy softens the effect of the tragedy, emphasizes the effect of the tragedy, or spoils the effect of the tragedy? Give reasons for your view. Do you feel that O'Casey has succeeded or failed in maintaining the necessary balance between the two elements? Why?

5. Ironically, the characters who emerge as the "heroes" in this play are not the soldiers, but the non-combatants. Which of the non-combatants do you feel exhibit heroic qualities? What are these qualities? In what specific situations are these qualities exhibited?

6. O'Casey describes his characters in a wealth of detail, displaying them from several points of view. Which of his characters are *dynamic characters* (see Glossary, *character*)? In what ways do their personalities change and develop during the play? Which incidents or experiences are responsible for their change and development? Which of the characters are *static characters* (see Glossary, *character*)? What are their distinguishing traits? In general, who are the stronger characters, the women or the men? Explain.

7. O'Casey achieves his comic effects in several different ways. Some of the humor rises directly from the dialogue, as in the argument of Fluther and the Covey over "mollycewels" and atoms. What other lines of dialogue do you find particularly amusing? Part of the humor arises not only from what the characters say but from their manner of saying it. Of which characters is this especially true? Explain. The most obvious comic effects are achieved by O'Casey's skillful integration of farcical elements (see Glossary, *farce*) into the action of the play. What broadly humorous or ridiculous incidents occur in connection with Peter's Foresters outfit in Act I? What other examples of farce do you find?

8. O'Casey sought to render the speech patterns of his characters as realistically as possible. How does he distinguish the speech differences of the lady from Wrathmines, the British soldiers, and the tenement dwellers in his dialogue? What speech characteristics are immediately apparent in the spelling of the words? What does the spelling indicate about the differences between British and Irish speech in respect to rhythm and tempo? What further differences are evident in grammar, usage, and choice of words?

9. The theory of *naturalism* (see Glossary) holds that man's character and behavior are determined by the forces of heredity and environment. The naturalist's conviction is that literature should depict life with scientific objectivity without avoiding anything regarded as repulsive. What elements of naturalism do you find in the play?

FOR COMPOSITION

1. Imagine that you are one of the idealistic Irish patriots and that you are part of the opening night audience for this play. In view of the fact that O'Casey sees the war realistically rather than romantically, which characters and scenes might you find particularly objectionable? In essay form, describe your imagined reactions to the play, citing specific characters, scenes, or lines of dialogue.

2. From among O'Casey's major or minor characters, choose the one you find most interesting. Write a character sketch showing his outstanding traits, his values and motives, his attitudes and ideas, and his significance in the play as a whole. Organize your sketch in such a way as to show why you find this character interesting.

3. The flag of the Citizen Army showed a field plough, symbol of the laborers, on which were superimposed the stars of the "plough constellation" (the Big Dipper). In a brief essay, explain why this combination of the real and the ideal on the flag makes the name of the play, "The Plough and the Stars," an appropriate title for the play. Refer to specific situations in the play to illuminate your explanation.

4. Write an essay in which you compare the romantic attitude of the patriots toward war with the attitudes of members of your community toward war or with your own attitudes toward war. To what extent do you think people's attitudes toward a war are determined by the causes and objectives of the war? Do you feel that a person's economic or educational background affects his attitudes? If so, in what ways?

5. The Bessie Burgess who goes for the doctor at the end of Act III is quite a different person from the belligerent woman of Acts I and II. In an essay, discuss the transformation that occurs in her behavior. What qualities of her personality are evident throughout the play? What new qualities appear in Act III? In view of her political beliefs, what decision or change of attitude do you think is responsible for her transformation? In what respects is her transformation responsible for her death?

Terence Rattigan

Terence Rattigan has devoted his life to the theater ever since he was a stage-struck boy of ten—when he read plays unceasingly and attended performances at every opportunity. Even the plays he wrote as a schoolboy showed an unerring sense of theater; and when he was only twenty-five, this "sixth sense" guided him to immediate success on the London stage with the production of his farce-comedy, *French Without Tears*. It played over a thousand consecutive performances for one of the longest runs in British theater history. Since that first successful production in 1936, hardly a theater season has passed that has not included a play by Rattigan. Among his most memorable productions have been *The Winslow Boy* (1946), which won the New York Drama Critics' Circle Award as the best foreign play of 1947; *The Browning Version* (1948); and *Separate Tables* (1955). All three plays were later made into popular motion pictures.

The young Rattigan entered the theater at a time when it was still dominated by the presence of George Bernard Shaw and his "play of ideas." Rattigan objected to Shaw's use of comedy as a vehicle for social propaganda and moral instruction, and he sharply challenged Shaw's view that the quality of a play is no better than the quality of its ideas. Rattigan was quick to explain that he had no objection to ideas but that he felt the theater was not the proper place to express them. After all, he countered, the audience was in no position to "talk back."

Rattigan insists that the human element of the drama is its most important aspect. He firmly believes that it is the quality of a playwright's treatment of character, feeling, and narrative that ultimately determines the quality of a play.

The quality of Rattigan's characterization in *The Browning Version* was largely responsible for the critical acclaim it received when it opened in London in 1948. His firm, sure grasp of character makes this one-act play a bitter, yet sympathetic, study of failure. The play won an Ellen Terry Award as the best play of the 1948 season in London, and it was produced that same year in New York with similar critical success.

Since the days of his open disagreement with Shaw, Rattigan's views on playwriting have been challenged again and again by dramatists and critics who feel that the theater *is* the proper place for the expression of ideas. At a time when the trend in drama has been toward a looser, more flexible dramatic construction, he has also been chided for his "old-fashioned" preference for the "well-made" play—of which he is an acknowledged master. This type of play is characterized by a tightly constructed plot, a unity of time and space, and a discernable beginning, middle, and end. In spite of attacks by critics, the long and profitable runs that nearly all of his plays have enjoyed are evidence that Rattigan is one of England's most popular and most successful playwrights today.

The Browning Version

CHARACTERS

ANDREW CROCKER-HARRIS, retiring schoolmaster of Latin
MILLIE CROCKER-HARRIS, his wife
JOHN TAPLOW, a student
FRANK HUNTER, young schoolmaster of science
DR. FROBISHER, headmaster of the school
PETER GILBERT, Crocker-Harris's younger replacement
MRS. GILBERT, his wife

SCENE: *The sitting-room of the Crocker-Harrises' rooms in a public school in the South of England. It is between six and seven o'clock on a July evening. The building in which the rooms are situated is large and Victorian, and at some fairly recent date has been converted into flats of varying size for masters, married and unmarried. The Crocker-Harrises have the ground floor and their sitting-room is probably the biggest—and gloomiest—room in the house. It boasts, however, access (through a stained-glass door, L.) to a small garden, and is furnished with*

*chintzy and genteel cheerfulness. Another door, back
R., leads into the hall and the rest of the flat. This door
is concealed by a screen.*

*The room is empty at the rise of the curtain, but we
hear the front-door opening and closing and, immediately
after, a timorous knock on the door, repeated after a
pause.*

Finally the door opens and JOHN TAPLOW *makes his
appearance. He is a plain, moon-faced boy of about sixteen, with glasses. He stands in doubt at the door for a
moment, then goes back into the hall, where we hear
him calling.*

TAPLOW *(calling off).*   Sir! Sir!

> *(After a pause, he re-enters. He is dressed in gray flannels,
> a dark blue coat, and white scarf. He goes to the garden
> door and opens it.)*

> *(Calling.)*   Sir!

> *(There is no reply.* TAPLOW, *standing in the bright sun-
> shine at the door, emits a plaintive sigh, then closes it
> firmly and goes to a table on which he places a book, a
> notebook, and a pen.*
> *On the table is a small box of chocolates, probably the
> Crocker-Harrises' ration for the month.* TAPLOW *opens
> the box, counts the number inside, and removes two. One
> of these he eats and the other, after a second's struggle,
> either with his conscience or his judgment of what he
> might be able to get away with, he virtuously replaces
> in the box. Finally he picks up a walking-stick with a
> crooked handle and makes a couple of golf swings, with
> an air of great concentration.*
> FRANK HUNTER *appears from behind the screen covering
> the door. He is a rugged young man—not perhaps quite
> as rugged as his deliberately-cultivated manner of ruth-
> less honesty makes him appear, but wrapped in all the*

self-confidence of the popular master. He watches TAPLOW, *whose back is to the door, making his swing.)*

FRANK. Roll the wrists away from the ball. Don't break them like that.

(He walks over quickly and puts his large hands over the abashed TAPLOW'S.)

Now swing.

*(*TAPLOW, *guided by* FRANK'S *evidently expert hands, succeeds in hitting the carpet with more effect than before.)*

Too quick. Slow back and stiff left arm. It's no good just whacking the ball as if you were the headmaster and the ball was you. It'll never go more than fifty yards if you do. Get a rhythm. A good golf swing is a matter of aesthetics, not of brute strength.

*(*TAPLOW *is only half-listening, gazing at the carpet.)*

What's the matter?

TAPLOW. I think we've made a tear in the carpet, sir. *(*FRANK *examines the carpet perfunctorily.)*

FRANK. Nonsense. That was there already. *(He puts the stick in a corner of the room.)* Do I know you?

TAPLOW. No, sir.

FRANK. What's your name?

TAPLOW. Taplow.

FRANK. Taplow! No, I don't. You're not a scientist I gather?

TAPLOW. No, sir. I'm still in the lower fifth. I can't specialize until next term—that's to say if I've got my remove[1] all right.

FRANK. Don't you know yet if you've got your remove?

TAPLOW. No, sir. Mr. Crocker-Harris doesn't tell us the results like the other masters.

FRANK. Why not?

[1]*remove:* promotion of a pupil to the next form

TAPLOW.   Well, you know what he's like, sir.

FRANK.   I believe there *is* a rule that form[2] results should only be announced by the headmaster on the last day of term.

TAPLOW.   Yes—but who else pays any attention to it—except Mr. Crocker-Harris?

FRANK.   I don't, I admit—but that's no criterion. So you've got to wait until tomorrow to know your fate, have you?

TAPLOW.   Yes, sir.

FRANK.   Supposing the answer is favourable—what then?

TAPLOW.   Oh—science, sir, of course.

FRANK *(sadly)*.   Yes. We get all the slackers.

TAPLOW *(protestingly)*.   I'm extremely interested in science, sir.

FRANK.   Are you? I'm not. Not at least in the science I have to teach.

TAPLOW.   Well, anyway, sir, it's a good deal more exciting than this muck. *(Indicating his book.)*

FRANK.   What is this muck?

TAPLOW.   Aeschylus, sir. The *Agamemnon.*

FRANK.   And your considered view is that the *Agamemnon* of Aeschylus is muck, is it?

TAPLOW.   Well, no, sir. I don't think the play is muck—exactly. I suppose, in a way, it's rather a good plot, really, a wife murdering her husband and having a lover and all that. I only meant the way it's taught to us—just a lot of Greek words strung together and fifty lines if you get them wrong.

FRANK.   You sound a little bitter, Taplow.

TAPLOW.   I am rather, sir.

FRANK.   Kept in, eh?

TAPLOW.   No, sir. Extra work.

FRANK.   Extra work—on the last day of school?

TAPLOW.   Yes, sir—and I might be playing golf. You'd think *he'd* have enough to do anyway himself, considering he's leaving tomorrow for good—but oh no. I missed a day last week when I had 'flu—so here I am—and look at the weather, sir.

FRANK.   Bad luck. Still, there's one consolation. You're pretty

[2]*form:* a class or grade in a British secondary school

well bound to get your remove tomorrow for being a good
boy in taking extra work.

TAPLOW.   Well, I'm not so sure, sir. That would be true of the
ordinary masters, all right. They just wouldn't dare not
give a chap a remove after his taking extra work — it would
be such a bad advertisement for them. But those sort of
rules don't apply to the Crock — Mr. Crocker-Harris. I
asked him yesterday outright if he'd given me a remove
and do you know what he said, sir?

FRANK.   No. What?

TAPLOW *(mimicking a very gentle, rather throaty voice).*   My
dear Taplow, I have given you exactly what you deserve.
No less; and certainly no more.' Do you know, sir, I
think he may have marked me down, rather than up, for
taking extra work. I mean, the man's barely human. *(He
breaks off quickly.)* Sorry, sir. Have I gone too far?

FRANK.   Yes. Much too far.

TAPLOW.   Sorry, sir. I got sort of carried away.

FRANK.   Evidently. *(He picks up* The Times *and opens it.)*
Er — Taplow.

TAPLOW.   Yes, sir?

FRANK.   What was that Mr. Crocker-Harris said to you? Just
— er — repeat it, would you?

TAPLOW *(mimicking again).*   'My dear Taplow, I have given
you exactly what you deserve. No less; and certainly no
more.'

FRANK *snorts, then looks stern.*

FRANK.   Not in the least like him. Read your nice Aeschylus
and be quiet.

TAPLOW *(with weary disgust).*   Aeschylus.

FRANK.   Look, what time did Mr. Crocker-Harris tell you to
be here?

TAPLOW.   Six-thirty, sir.

FRANK.   Well, he's ten minutes late. Why don't you cut?
You could still get nine holes in before lock-up.

TAPLOW *(genuinely shocked).*   Oh, no, I couldn't cut. Cut the
Crock — Mr. Crocker-Harris? I shouldn't think it's ever
been done in the whole time he's been here. God knows

what would happen if I did. He'd probably follow me home, or something—

FRANK. I must admit I envy him the effect he seems to have on you boys in his form. You all seem scared to death of him. What does he do—beat you all, or something?

TAPLOW. Good lord, no. He's not a sadist, like one or two of the others.

FRANK. I beg your pardon?

TAPLOW. A sadist, sir, is someone who gets pleasure out of giving pain.

FRANK. Indeed? But I think you went on to say that some other masters—

TAPLOW. Well, of course they are, sir. I won't mention names, but you know them as well as I do. Of course I know most masters think we boys don't understand a thing—but dash it, sir, you're different. You're young— well comparatively anyway—and you're science and you canvassed for Labour in the last election. You must know what sadism is.

FRANK (*after a pause*). Good lord! What are the public schools coming to?

TAPLOW. Anyway the Crock isn't a sadist. That's what I'm saying. He wouldn't be so frightening if he were— because at least it would show he had some feelings. But he hasn't. He's all shrivelled up inside like a nut and he seems to hate people to like him. It's funny, that. I don't know any other master who doesn't like being liked—

FRANK. And I don't know any boy who doesn't trade on that very foible.

TAPLOW. Well, it's natural, sir. But not with the Crock—

FRANK (*making a feeble attempt at re-establishing the correct relationship*). Mr. Crocker-Harris.

TAPLOW. Mr. Crocker-Harris. The funny thing is that in spite of everything, I do rather like him. I can't help it. And sometimes I think he sees it and that seems to shrivel him up even more—

FRANK. I'm sure you're exaggerating.

TAPLOW. No, sir. I'm not. In form the other day he made one

of his little classical jokes. Of course nobody laughed because nobody understood it, myself included. Still, I knew he'd meant it as funny, so I laughed. Not out of sucking-up[3], sir, I swear, but ordinary common politeness, and feeling a bit sorry for him having made a dud joke. *(He goes to the table and sits down.)* Now I can't remember what the joke was—but let's say it was *(adopting his imitative voice again.)* benedictus, benedicatur, benedictine . . . Now, you laugh, sir—

(FRANK laughs. TAPLOW looks at him over an imaginary pair of spectacles, and then, very gently, crooks his forefinger to him in indication to approach the table. FRANK does so—simply, not clowning. He is genuinely interested in the incident.)

(In a gentle, throaty voice). 'Taplow—you laughed at my little pun, I noticed. I must confess I am flattered at the evident advance your Latinity has made that you should so readily have understood what the rest of the form did not. Perhaps, now, you would be good enough to explain it to them, so that they too can share your pleasure.'

(The door behind the screen is pushed open and MILLIE CROCKER-HARRIS appears. She is a thin woman in the late thirties, rather more smartly dressed than the general run of schoolmasters' wives. She stands by the screen pulling off her gloves and watching TAPLOW and FRANK. It is a few seconds before they notice her.)

'Come along, Taplow. Do not be so selfish as to keep a good joke to yourself. Tell the others—' *(He breaks off suddenly, seeing MILLIE.)* Oh lord!

(FRANK turns quickly, and seems infinitely relieved at seeing MILLIE.)

FRANK. Oh, hullo.

[3]*sucking-up:* apple-polishing

MILLIE (*without expression*).   Hullo. (*She puts down a couple
of parcels she has been carrying, and goes back into the
hall to take off her hat.*)
TAPLOW (*frantically whispering to* FRANK).   Do you think
she heard?

(FRANK *shakes his head comfortably.*)

I think she did. She was standing there quite a time. If
she did and she tells him, there goes my remove—
FRANK.   Nonsense—

(MILLIE *comes back into the room.*)

MILLIE (*to* TAPLOW).   Waiting for my husband?
TAPLOW.   Er—yes.
MILLIE.   He's at the Bursar's and might be there quite a time.
If I were you I'd go.
TAPLOW (*doubtfully*).   He said most particularly I was to
come—
MILLIE.   Well, why don't you run away for a quarter of an
hour and come back?
TAPLOW.   Supposing he gets here before me?
MILLIE (*smiling*).   I'll take the blame. I tell you what—you
can do a job for him. Take this prescription to the chemist[4]
and get it made up.
TAPLOW.   All right, Mrs. Crocker-Harris.
MILLIE.   And while you're there you might as well slip into
Stewarts and have an ice. Here. Catch. (*She takes a shill-
ing from her bag and throws it to him.*)
TAPLOW.   Thanks awfully. (*He passes* FRANK *on his way to
the door. In a whisper.*) See she doesn't tell him.
FRANK.   O.K.
MILLIE (*turning as* TAPLOW *is going*).   Oh, Taplow—
TAPLOW.   Yes, Mrs. Crocker-Harris.
MILLIE.   I had a letter from my father today in which he says
he once had the pleasure of meeting your mother—
TAPLOW (*uninterested, but polite*).   Oh, really?

[4]*chemist:* druggist

MILLIE. Yes. It was at some fête or other in Bradford. My uncle—that's Sir William Bartop, you know—made a speech and so did your mother. My father met her afterwards at tea—

TAPLOW. Oh, really?

MILLIE. He said he found her quite charming.

TAPLOW. Yes, she's jolly good at those sort of functions. *(Aware of his lack of tact.)* I mean—I'm sure she found him charming, too. Well, I'd better get going. So long. *(He goes out.)*

MILLIE. Thank you for coming round.

FRANK. That's all right.

MILLIE. You're staying for dinner?

FRANK. If I may.

MILLIE. If you may! Give me a cigarette.

(He extends his case. She takes a cigarette.)

(Indicating case.) You haven't given it away yet, I see.

FRANK. Do you think I would?

MILLIE. Frankly, yes. Luckily it's a man's case. I don't suppose any of your girl friends would want it—

FRANK. Don't be silly.

MILLIE. Where have you been all this week?

FRANK. Correcting exam papers—making reports. You know what end of term is like—

MILLIE. I do know what end of term is like. But even Andrew has managed this last week to take a few hours off to say goodbye to people—

FRANK. I really have been appallingly busy. Besides I'm coming to stay with you in Bradford—

MILLIE. Not for over a month. Andrew doesn't start his new job until September first. That's one of the things I had to tell you.

FRANK. Oh, I had meant to be in Devonshire in September.

MILLIE *(quickly).* Who with?

FRANK. My family.

MILLIE. Surely you can go earlier, can't you? Go in August.

FRANK. It'll be difficult.

MILLIE.   Then you'd better come to me in August.
FRANK.   But Andrew will still be there.
MILLIE.   Yes.

(Pause.)

FRANK.   I think I can manage September.
MILLIE.   That'd be better—from every point of view. Except that it means I shan't see you for six weeks.
FRANK *(lightly)*.   You'll survive that, all right.
MILLIE.   Yes, I'll survive it—but not as easily as you will. (FRANK *says nothing.*) I haven't much pride, have I? *(She approaches him.)* Frank, darling, I love you so much—

(He kisses her, on the mouth, but a trifle perfunctorily, and then breaks quickly away, as if afraid someone had come into the room.)

(Laughing.) You're very nervous.
FRANK.   I'm afraid of that screen arrangement. You can't see people coming in—
MILLIE.   Oh, yes. That reminds me. What were you and Taplow up to when I came in just now? Making fun of my husband?
FRANK.   Afraid so. Yes.
MILLIE.   It sounded rather a good imitation. I must get him to do it for me some time. It was very naughty of you to encourage him.
FRANK.   I know. It was.
MILLIE *(ironically)*.   Bad for discipline.
FRANK.   Exactly. Currying favour with the boys, too. My God, how easy it is to be popular. I've only been a master three years but I've already slipped into an act and a vernacular that I just can't get out of. Why can't anyone ever be natural with the little blighters?
MILLIE.   They probably wouldn't like it if you were.
FRANK.   I don't see why not. No one seems to have tried it yet, anyway. I suppose the trouble is—we're all too scared of them. Either one gets forced into an attitude of false

and hearty and jocular bonhomie[5] like myself, or into the
sort of petty, soulless tyranny which your husband uses
to protect himself against the lower fifth.

MILLIE *(rather bored with this).*   He'd never be popular whatever he did—

FRANK.   Possibly not. He ought never to have become a
schoolmaster, really. Why did he?

MILLIE.   It was his vocation, he said. He was sure he'd make
a big success of it, especially when he got his job here
first go off. *(Bitterly.)* Fine success he's made, hasn't he?

FRANK.   You should have stopped him.

MILLIE.   How was I to know? He talked about getting a
house, then a headmastership.

FRANK.   The Crock a headmaster! That's a pretty thought.

MILLIE.   Yes, it's funny to think of it now, all right. Still he
wasn't always the Crock, you know. He had a bit more
gumption once. At least I thought he had. Don't let's talk
any more about him—it's too depressing.

FRANK.   I'm sorry for him.

MILLIE *(indifferently).*   He's not sorry for himself, so why
should you be? It's me you should be sorry for.

FRANK.   I am.

MILLIE *(smiling).*   Then show me.

*(She stretches out her arms to him. He kisses her again
quickly and lightly, but she holds him hungrily. He has
to free himself almost roughly.)*

FRANK.   What have you been doing all day?

MILLIE.   Calling on the other masters' wives—saying fond
farewells. I've worked off twelve. I've another seven to
do tomorrow.

FRANK.   You poor thing! I don't envy you.

MILLIE.   It's the housemasters' wives that are the worst.
They're all so damn patronizing. You should have heard
Betty Carstairs. 'My dear—it's such terrible bad luck on

[5]*bonhomie:* good nature

you both — that your husband should get this heart trouble
just when, if only he'd stayed on, he'd have been bound
to get a house. I mean, he's considerably senior to my
Arthur as it is, and they simply couldn't have gone on
passing him over, could they?'

FRANK. There's a word for Betty Carstairs, my dear, that I
would hesitate to employ before a lady.

MILLIE. She's got her eye on you, anyway.

FRANK. Betty Carstairs? What utter rot!

MILLIE. Oh, yes, she has. I saw you at that concert. Don't
think I didn't notice.

FRANK. Millie, darling! Really! I detest the woman.

MILLIE. Then what were you doing in her box at Lord's?

FRANK. Carstairs invited me. I went there because it was a
good place to see the match from.

MILLIE. Yes, I'm sure it was. Much better than the grand-
stand, anyway.

FRANK (*as if remembering something suddenly*). Oh, my
God!

MILLIE. It's all right, my dear. Don't bother to apologize.
We gave the seat away, as it happens —

FRANK. I'm most terribly sorry.

MILLIE. It's all right. We couldn't afford a box, you see —

FRANK. It wasn't that. You know it wasn't that. It's just that
I — well, I clean forgot.

MILLIE. Funny you didn't forget the Carstairs's invitation —

FRANK. Millie — don't be a fool.

MILLIE. It's you who are the fool. (*Appealingly.*) Frank —
have you never been in love? I know you're not in love
with me — but haven't you ever been in love with anyone?
Don't you realize what torture you inflict on someone who
loves you when you do a thing like that?

FRANK. I've told you I'm sorry — I don't know what more I
can say.

MILLIE. Why not the truth?

FRANK. The truth is — I clean forgot.

MILLIE. The truth is — you had something better to do — and
why not say it?

FRANK. All right. Believe that if you like. It happens to be a
lie, but believe it all the same. Only for God's sake stop
this—

MILLIE. Then for God's sake show me some pity. Do you
think it's any pleasanter for me to believe that you cut me
because you forgot? Do you think that doesn't hurt either?
(FRANK *turns away.*) Oh, damn! I was so determined to be
brave and not mention Lord's. Why did I? Frank, just tell
me one thing. Just tell me you're not running away from
me—that's all I want to hear.

FRANK. I'm coming to Bradford.

MILLIE. I think, if you don't, I'll kill myself.

FRANK. I'm coming to Bradford.

(*The door is pushed open.* FRANK *has made a move towards* MILLIE, *but stops at the sound.* MILLIE *has recovered herself as* ANDREW CROCKER-HARRIS *appears by
the screen. Despite the summer sun he wears a serge suit
and a stiff collar. He carries a portfolio and looks, as ever,
neat, complacent, and unruffled. He speaks in a very
gentle voice which he rarely raises.*)

ANDREW. Is Taplow here?

MILLIE. I sent him to the chemist to get your prescription
made up—

ANDREW. What prescription?

MILLIE. Your heart medicine. Don't you remember? You
told me this morning it had run out—

ANDREW. Of course I remember, my dear, but there was no
need to send Taplow for it. If you had telephoned the
chemist he would have sent it round in plenty of time. He
knows the prescription. Now Taplow will be late and I
am so pressed for time I hardly know how to fit him in.

(*This colloquy*[6] *has taken place near the door, the screen
and* MILLIE *blocking* ANDREW'S *view of the room. As he
now comes in he sees* FRANK.)

Ah, Hunter! How are you?

[6]*colloquy:* a somewhat formal conversation

FRANK. Very well, thanks.

(They shake hands.)

ANDREW. Most kind of you to drop in, but, as Millie should have warned you, I am expecting a pupil for extra work and—
MILLIE. He's staying to dinner, Andrew.
ANDREW. Good. Then I shall see something of you. However, when Taplow returns I'm sure you won't mind—
FRANK *(making a move)*. No, of course not. I'll make myself scarce now, if you'd rather—I mean, if you're busy—
ANDREW. Oh, no. There is no need for that. Sit down, do. Will you smoke? I don't, as you know, but Millie does. Millie, give our guest a cigarette—
MILLIE. I haven't any, I'm afraid. I've had to cadge[7] from him.

(FRANK takes out his cigarette case and offers it to MILLIE who exchanges a glance with him as she takes one.)

ANDREW. We expected you at Lord's, Hunter.
FRANK. What? Oh, yes. I'm most terribly sorry. I—
MILLIE. He clean forgot, Andrew. Imagine.
ANDREW. Forgot?
MILLIE. Not everyone is blessed with your superhuman memory, you see.
FRANK. I really can't apologize enough—
ANDREW. Please don't bother to mention it. On the second day we managed to sell the seat to a certain Dr. Lambert, who wore, I regret to say, the colours of the opposing faction, but who otherwise seemed a passably agreeable person. You liked him, didn't you, Millie?
MILLIE *(looking at FRANK)*. Very much, indeed. I thought him quite charming.
ANDREW. A charming old gentleman. *(To FRANK.)* You have had tea?

[7]*cadge:* beg

FRANK. Yes — thank you —

ANDREW. Is there any other refreshment I can offer you?

FRANK. No, thank you.

ANDREW. Would it interest you to see the new timetable I have drafted for next term?

FRANK. Yes, very much.

(ANDREW *has taken out a long roll of paper, made by pasting pieces of foolscap together and which is entirely covered by his meticulous writing.*)

I never knew you drafted our timetables —

ANDREW. Didn't you? I have done so for the last fifteen years. Of course they are always issued in mimeograph under the headmaster's signature — Now what form do you take? upper fifth Science — there you are — that's the general picture, but on the back you will see each form specified under separate headings — there — that's a new idea of mine — Millie, this might interest you —

MILLIE *(suddenly harsh).* You know it bores me to death —

(FRANK *looks up, surprised and uncomfortable.* ANDREW *does not remove his eyes from the timetable.*)

ANDREW. Millie has no head for this sort of work. There you see. Now here you can follow the upper fifth Science throughout every day of the week.

FRANK *(indicating timetable).* I must say, I think this is a really wonderful job.

ANDREW. Thank you. It has the merit of clarity, I think.

FRANK. I don't know what they'll do without you.

ANDREW *(without expression).* They'll find somebody else, I expect.

(Pause.)

FRANK. What sort of job is this you're going to?

ANDREW *(looking at his wife for the first time).* Hasn't Millie told you?

FRANK.   She said it was a cr—a private school.

ANDREW.   A crammer's[8]—for backward boys. It is run by an old Oxford contemporary of mine who lives in Dorset. The work will not be so arduous as here and my doctor seems to think I will be able to undertake it without—er—danger—

FRANK *(with genuine sympathy)*.   It's the most rotten bad luck for you. I'm awfully sorry.

ANDREW *(raising his voice a little)*.   My dear Hunter, there is nothing whatever to be sorry for. I am looking forward to the change—

(There is a knock at the door.)

ANDREW.   Come in. (TAPLOW *appears a trifle breathless and guilty-looking. He carries a medicine bottle wrapped and sealed.)* Ah, Taplow. Good. You have been running, I see.

TAPLOW.   Yes, sir. *(He hands the bottle to* MILLIE.*)*

ANDREW.   There was a queue at the chemist's, I suppose?

TAPLOW.   Yes, sir.

ANDREW.   And doubtless an even longer one at Stewarts?

TAPLOW.   Yes, sir—I mean—no, sir—I mean—*(He looks at* MILLIE.*)*—yes, sir.

MILLIE.   You were late, yourself, Andrew.

ANDREW.   Exactly. And for that I apologize, Taplow.

TAPLOW.   That's all right, sir.

ANDREW.   Luckily we have still a good hour before lock-up, so nothing has been lost—

FRANK *(to* MILLIE*)*.   May I use the short cut? I'm going back to my digs.

MILLIE.   Yes. Go ahead. Come back soon. If Andrew hasn't finished we can sit in the garden. *(Moving to door.)* I'd better go and see about dinner. *(She goes out at back.)*

ANDREW *(to* FRANK*)*.   Taplow is desirous of obtaining a remove from my form, Hunter, so that he can spend the rest of his career here playing happily with the crucibles, retorts, and bunsen burners of your Science fifth.

---

[8]*crammer:* a British school that crams students for college

FRANK (*at door*).   Oh. Has he?
ANDREW.   Has he what?
FRANK.   Obtained his remove?
ANDREW (*after a pause*).   He has obtained exactly what he deserves. No less; and certainly no more.

(TAPLOW *utters an explosion of mirth.* FRANK *nods, thoughtfully, and goes out through the garden door.* ANDREW *has caught sight of* TAPLOW'S *contorted face, but passes no remark on it. He sits at the table and makes a sign for* TAPLOW *to sit beside him. He picks up a text of the* Agamemnon *and* TAPLOW *does the same.*)

Line thirteen hundred and ninety-nine. Begin.
TAPLOW.   Chorus. We—are surprised at—
ANDREW (*automatically*).   We marvel at.
TAPLOW.   We marvel at—thy tongue—how bold thou art—that you—
ANDREW.   Thou. (ANDREW'S *interruptions are automatic. His thoughts are evidently far distant.*)
TAPLOW.   Thou—can—
ANDREW.   Canst—
TAPLOW.   Canst—boastfully speak—
ANDREW.   Utter such a boastful speech—
TAPLOW.   Utter such a boastful speech—over—(*In a sudden rush of inspiration.*)—the bloody corpse of the husband you have slain—

(ANDREW *looks down at his text for the first time.* TAPLOW *looks apprehensive.*)

ANDREW.   Taplow—I presume you are using a different text from mine—
TAPLOW.   No, sir.
ANDREW.   That is strange for the line as I have it reads: ἥτις τοιόνδ'ἐπ' ἀν δρὶ κομπάζεις λόγον.   However diligently I search I can discover no 'bloody'—no 'corpse'—no 'you have slain'. Simply husband'—
TAPLOW.   Yes, sir. That's right.

ANDREW.　Then why do you invent words that simply are not there?

TAPLOW.　I thought they sounded better, sir. More exciting. After all she did kill her husband, sir. *(With relish.)* She's just been revealed with his dead body and Cassandra's weltering in gore—

ANDREW.　I am delighted at this evidence, Taplow, of your interest in the rather more lurid aspects of dramaturgy, but I feel I must remind you that you are supposed to be construing Greek, not collaborating with Aeschylus.

TAPLOW *(greatly daring).*　Yes, but still, sir, translator's licence, sir—I didn't get anything wrong—and after all it *is* a play and not just a bit of Greek construe.

ANDREW *(momentarily at a loss).*　I seem to detect a note of end of term in your remarks. I am not denying that the *Agamemnon* is a play. It is perhaps the greatest play ever written—

TAPLOW *(quickly).*　I wonder how many people in the form think that? *(Pause.* TAPLOW *is instantly frightened of what he has said.)* Sorry, sir. Shall I go on? *(*ANDREW *does not answer. He sits motionless staring at his book.)* Shall I go on, sir?

(There is another pause. ANDREW *raises his head slowly from his book.)*

ANDREW *(murmuring gently, not looking at* TAPLOW*).*　When I was a very young man, only two years older than you are now, Taplow, I wrote, for my own pleasure, a translation of the *Agamemnon*—a very free translation—I remember—in rhyming couplets.

TAPLOW.　The whole *Agamemnon*—in verse? That must have been hard work, sir.

ANDREW.　It was hard work; but I derived great joy from it. The play had so excited and moved me that I wished to communicate, however imperfectly, some of that emotion to others. When I had finished it, I remember, I thought it very beautiful—almost more beautiful than the original.

TAPLOW.　Was it ever published, sir?

ANDREW.   No. Yesterday I looked for the manuscript while I was packing my papers. I was unable to find it. I fear it is lost—like so many other things. Lost for good.

TAPLOW.   Hard luck, sir. (ANDREW *is silent again.* TAPLOW *steals a timid glance at him.*) Shall I go on, sir?

(ANDREW, *with a slight effort, lowers his eyes again to his text.*)

ANDREW *(raising his voice slightly).*   No. Go back and get that last line right.

(TAPLOW, *out of* ANDREW'S *vision, as he thinks, makes a disgusted grimace in his direction.*)

TAPLOW.   That—thou canst utter such a boastful speech over thy husband—

ANDREW.   Yes. And, now, if you would be so kind, you will do the line again, without the facial contortion which you just found necessary to accompany it—

(TAPLOW *is just beginning the line again, when* MILLIE *appears hurriedly. She has on an apron.*)

MILLIE.   The headmaster's just coming up the drive. Don't tell him I'm in. The fish pie isn't in the oven yet. (*She disappears.*)

(TAPLOW, *who has jumped up on* MILLIE'S *entrance, turns hopefully to* ANDREW.)

TAPLOW.   I'd better go, hadn't I, sir? I mean—I don't want to be in the way—

ANDREW.   We do not yet know that it is I the headmaster wishes to see. Other people live in this building.

(*There is a knock at the door.*)

ANDREW. Come in.

(DR. FROBISHER *comes in. He looks more like a distinguished diplomat than a doctor of literature and classical scholar. He is in the middle fifties and goes to a very good tailor.*)

FROBISHER. Ah, Crocker-Harris, I've caught you in. I'm so glad. I hope I'm not disturbing you?

ANDREW. I have been taking a pupil in extra work—

FROBISHER. On the penultimate[9] day of term? That argues either great conscientiousness on your part or considerable backwardness on his.

ANDREW. Perhaps a combination of both—

FROBISHER. Quite so, but as this is my only chance of speaking to you before tomorrow, I think that perhaps your pupil will be good enough to excuse us—(*He turns politely to* TAPLOW.)

TAPLOW. Oh, yes, sir. That's really quite all right. (*He collects his books and dashes to the door.*)

ANDREW. I'm extremely sorry, Taplow. You will please explain to your father exactly what occurred over this lost hour and tell him that I shall in due course be writing to him to return the money involved—

TAPLOW (*hurridly*). Yes, sir. But please don't bother, sir. I know it's all right, sir. Thank you, sir. (*He darts out.*)

FROBISHER. Have the Gilberts called on you, yet?

ANDREW. The Gilberts, sir? Who are they?

FROBISHER. Gilbert is your successor with the lower fifth. He is down here today with his wife, and as they will be taking over this flat I thought perhaps you wouldn't mind if they came in to look it over.

ANDREW. Of course not.

FROBISHER. I've told you about him, I think. He is a very brilliant young man and won exceptionally high honours at Oxford.

[9]*penultimate:* next to the last

388 🐚 *Terence Rattigan*

ANDREW.   So I understand, sir.

FROBISHER.   Not, of course, as high as the honours you yourself won there. He didn't, for instance, win the Chancel-
lor's prize for Latin verse or the Gaisford.

ANDREW.   He won the Hertford Latin, then?

FROBISHER.   No. *(Mildly surprised.)* Did you win that, too?
(ANDREW nods.) It's sometimes rather hard to remember
that you are perhaps the most brilliant classical scholar
we have ever had at the school—

ANDREW.   You are very kind.

FROBISHER *(urbanely[10] correcting his gaffe[11]).*   Hard to remember, I mean—because of your other activities—your
brilliant work on the school timetable, for instance, and
also for your heroic battle for so long and against such
odds with the soul-destroying lower fifth.

ANDREW.   I have not found that my soul has been destroyed
by the lower fifth, headmaster.

FROBISHER.   I was joking, of course.

ANDREW.   Oh. I see.

FROBISHER.   Is your wife in?

ANDREW.   Er—no. Not at the moment.

FROBISHER.   I shall have a chance of saying goodbye to her
tomorrow. I am rather glad I have got you to myself. I
have a delicate matter—two rather delicate matters—to
broach.

ANDREW.   Please sit down.

FROBISHER.   Thank you. *(He sits.)* Now you have been with
us, in all, eighteen years, haven't you? *(ANDREW nods.)*
It is extremely unlucky that you should have had to retire
at so comparatively early an age and so short a time before
you would have been eligible for a pension.

(The HEADMASTER *is regarding his nails, as he speaks,
studiously avoiding* ANDREW'S *gaze.)*

ANDREW.   Pension? *(After a pause.)* You have decided then,
not to award me a pension?

[10]*urbanely:* smoothly, suavely
[11]*gaffe:* blunder

FROBISHER.   Not I, my dear fellow. It has nothing at all to do with me. It's the governors who, I'm afraid, have been forced to turn down your application. I put your case to them as well as I could, but they decided, with great regret, that they couldn't make an exception to the rule.

ANDREW.   But I thought—my wife thought, that an exception was made some five years ago—

FROBISHER.   Ah. In the case of Buller, you mean? True. But the circumstances with Buller were quite remarkable. It was, after all, in playing rugger against the school that he received that injury—

ANDREW.   Yes. I remember.

FROBISHER.   And then the governors received a petition from boys, old boys, and parents with over five hundred signatures.

ANDREW.   I would have signed that petition myself, but through some oversight I was not asked—

FROBISHER.   He was a splendid fellow, Buller. Splendid. Doing very well, too, now, I gather.

ANDREW.   I'm delighted to hear it.

FROBISHER.   Your own case, of course, is equally deserving. If not more so—for Buller was a younger man. Unfortunately—rules are rules—and are not made to be broken every few years; at any rate that is the governors' view.

ANDREW.   I quite understand.

FROBISHER.   I knew you would. Now might I ask you a rather impertinent question?

ANDREW.   Certainly.

FROBISHER.   You have, I take it, private means?

ANDREW.   My wife has some.

FROBISHER.   Ah, yes. Your wife has often told me of her family connections. I understand her father has a business in—Bradford—isn't it?

ANDREW.   Yes. He runs a men's clothing shop in the Arcade.

FROBISHER.   Indeed? Your wife's remarks had led me to imagine something a little more—extensive.

ANDREW.   My father-in-law made a settlement on my wife at the time of our marriage. She has about three hundred a year of her own. I have nothing. Is that the answer to your question, headmaster?

FROBISHER. Yes. Thank you for your frankness. Now, this private school you are going to —

ANDREW. My salary at the crammer's is to be two hundred pounds a year.

FROBISHER. Quite so. With board and lodging, of course?

ANDREW. For eight months of the year.

FROBISHER. Yes, I see. *(He ponders a second.)* Of course, you know, there is the School Benevolent Fund that deals with cases of actual hardship —

ANDREW. There will be no actual hardship, headmaster.

FROBISHER. No. I am glad you take that view. I must admit, though, I had hoped that your own means had proved a little more ample. Your wife had certainly led me to suppose —

ANDREW. I am not denying that a pension would have been very welcome, headmaster, but I see no reason to quarrel with the governors' decision. What is the other delicate matter you have to discuss?

FROBISHER. Well, it concerns the arrangements at prize-giving tomorrow. You are, of course, prepared to say a few words.

ANDREW. I had assumed you would call on me to do so.

FROBISHER. Of course. It is always done, and I know the boys appreciate the custom.

ANDREW. I have already made a few notes of what I am going to say. Perhaps you would care —

FROBISHER. No, no. That isn't necessary at all. I know I can trust your discretion — not to say your wit. It will be, I know, a very moving moment for you — indeed for us all — but, as I'm sure you realize, it is far better to keep these occasions from becoming too heavy and distressing. You know how little the boys appreciate sentiment —

ANDREW. I do.

FROBISHER. That is why I've planned my own reference to you at the end of my speech to be rather more light and jocular than I would otherwise have made it.

ANDREW. I quite understand. I too have prepared a few little jokes and puns for my speech. One — a play of words on *vale,* farewell, and Wally, the Christian name of a backward boy in my class, is, I think, rather happy.

FROBISHER. Yes. *(He laughs belatedly.)* Very neat. That should go down extremely well.

ANDREW. I'm glad you like it.

FROBISHER. Well, now—there is a particular favour I have to ask of you in connection with the ceremony, and I know I shall not have to ask in vain. Fletcher, as you know, is leaving, too.

ANDREW. Yes. He is going into the City, they tell me.

FROBISHER. Yes. Now he is, of course, considerably junior to you. He has only been here—let me see—five years. But, as you know, he has done great things for our cricket —positive wonders, when you remember what doldrums we were in before he came—

ANDREW. Our win at Lord's this year was certainly most inspiriting—

FROBISHER. Exactly. Now I'm sure that tomorrow the boys will make the occasion of his farewell speech a tremendous demonstration of gratitude. The applause might go on for minutes—you know what the boys feel about Lord's —and I seriously doubt my ability to cut it short or even, I admit, the propriety of trying to do so. Now, you see the quandary in which I am placed?

ANDREW. Perfectly. You wish to refer to me and for me to make my speech before you come to Fletcher?

FROBISHER. It's extremely awkward, and I feel wretched about asking it of you—but it's more for your own sake than for mine or Fletcher's that I do. After all, a climax is what one must try to work up to on these occasions.

ANDREW. Naturally, headmaster, I wouldn't wish to provide an anti-climax.

FROBISHER. You really mustn't take it amiss, my dear fellow. The boys, in applauding Fletcher for several minutes and yourself say—for—well, for not quite so long—won't be making any personal demonstration between you. It will be quite impersonal—I assure you—quite impersonal.

ANDREW. I understand.

FROBISHER. *(warmly).* I knew you would, and I can hardly tell you how wisely I think you have chosen. Well now— as that is all my business, I think perhaps I had better be getting along. This has been a terribly busy day for me— for you too, I imagine.

ANDREW. Yes.

(MILLIE comes in. She has taken off her apron, and tidied herself up.)

MILLIE *(in her social manner).* Ah, headmaster. How good of you to drop in.

FROBISHER *(more at home with her than with Andrew).* Mrs. Crocker-Harris. How are you? *(They shake hands.)* You're looking extremely well, I must say. Has anyone ever told you, Crocker-Harris, that you have a very attractive wife?

ANDREW. Many people, sir. But then I hardly need to be told.

MILLIE. Can I persuade you to stay a few moments and have a drink, headmaster. It's so rarely we have the pleasure of seeing you—

FROBISHER. Unfortunately, dear lady, I was just on the point of leaving. I have two frantic parents waiting for me at home. You are dining with us tomorrow—both of you, aren't you?

MILLIE. Yes, indeed—and so looking forward to it.

FROBISHER. I'm so glad. We can say our sad farewells then. *(To ANDREW.)* *Au revoir,*[12] Crocker-Harris, and thank you very much.

(ANDREW bows. MILLIE holds the door open for FROBISHER and follows him out into the hall.)

MILLIE *(to ANDREW as she goes out with FROBISHER).* Don't forget to take your medicine, dear, will you?

ANDREW. No.

FROBISHER *(in the hall).* Lucky invalid! To have such a very charming nurse—

[12]*Au revoir:* goodbye (French)

MILLIE *(also in the hall).* I really don't know what to say to all these compliments, headmaster. I don't believe you mean a word of them.

FROBISHER. Every word. Till tomorrow, then? Goodbye.

(We hear the door slam. ANDREW *is staring out of the window.* MILLIE *reappears.)*

MILLIE. Well? Do we get it?

ANDREW *(absently).* Get what?

MILLIE. The pension, of course. Do we get it?

ANDREW. No.

MILLIE. My God! Why not?

ANDREW. It's against the rules.

MILLIE. Buller got it, didn't he? Buller got it? What's the idea of giving it to him and not to us?

ANDREW. The governors are afraid of establishing a precedent.

MILLIE. The mean old brutes! My God, what I wouldn't like to say to them! *(Rounding on* ANDREW.*)* And what did you say? Just sat there and made a joke in Latin, I suppose?

ANDREW. There wasn't very much I could say, in Latin or any other language.

MILLIE. Oh, wasn't there? I'd have said it all right. I wouldn't just have sat there twiddling my thumbs and taking it from that old phoney of a headmaster. But then, of course, I'm not a man. *(*ANDREW *is turning the pages of the* Agamemnon, *not looking at her.)* What do they expect you to do? Live on my money, I suppose.

ANDREW. There has never been any question of that. I shall be perfectly able to support myself.

MILLIE. Yourself? Doesn't the marriage service say something about the husband supporting his wife? Doesn't it? you ought to know?

ANDREW. Yes, it does.

MILLIE. And how do you think you're going to do that on two hundred a year?

ANDREW. I shall do my utmost to save some of it. You're welcome to it, if I can.

MILLIE. Thank you for precisely nothing. (ANDREW *under-lines a word in the text he is reading.*) What else did the old fool have to say?

ANDREW. The headmaster? He wants me to make my speech tomorrow before instead of after Fletcher.

MILLIE. Yes. I knew he was going to ask that.

ANDREW (*without surprise*). You knew?

MILLIE. Yes. He asked my advice about it a week ago. I told him to go ahead. I knew you wouldn't mind, and as there isn't a Mrs. Fletcher to make *me* look a fool, I didn't give two hoots.

(*There is a knock on the door.*)

Come in.

(MR. *and* MRS. GILBERT *come in. He is about twenty-two, and his wife a year or so younger.*)

GILBERT. Mr. Crocker-Harris?

ANDREW (*rising*). Yes. Is it Mr. and Mrs. Gilbert? The head-master told me you might look in.

MRS. GILBERT. I do hope we're not disturbing you.

ANDREW. Not at all. This is my wife.

MRS. GILBERT. How do you do.

ANDREW. Mr. and Mrs. Gilbert are our successors to this flat my dear.

MILLIE. Oh, yes. How nice to meet you both.

GILBERT. How do you do? We really won't keep you more than a second—my wife thought as we were here you wouldn't mind us taking a squint at our future home.

MRS. GILBERT (*unnecessarily*). This is the drawing-room, I suppose?

MILLIE. That's right. Well, it's really a living-room. Andrew uses it as a study.

MRS. GILBERT. How charmingly you've done it!

MILLIE. Oh, do you think so? I'm afraid it isn't nearly as nice as I'd like to make it—but a schoolmaster's wife has to think of so many other things besides curtains and covers. Boys with dirty boots and a husband with leaky fountain pens, for instance.

MRS. GILBERT. Yes, I suppose so. Of course I haven't been a schoolmaster's wife for very long, you know.

GILBERT. Don't swank,[13] darling. You haven't been a schoolmaster's wife at all yet.

MRS. GILBERT. Oh yes, I have—for two months. You were a schoolmaster when I married you.

GILBERT. Prep school doesn't count.

MILLIE. Have you only been married two months?

MRS. GILBERT. Two months and sixteen days.

GILBERT. Seventeen.

MILLIE *(sentimentally)*. Andrew, did you hear? They've only been married two months.

ANDREW. Indeed? Is that all?

MRS. GILBERT *(at the garden door)*. Oh, look, darling. They've got a garden. It is yours, isn't it?

MILLIE. Oh, yes. It's only a pocket handkerchief, I'm afraid but it's very useful to Andrew. He often works out there, don't you, dear?

ANDREW. Yes, indeed. I find it very agreeable.

MILLIE. Shall I show you the rest of the flat? It's a bit untidy, I'm afraid, but you must forgive that.

MRS. GILBERT. Oh, of course.

MILLIE *(as they move to the door)*. And the kitchen is in a terrible mess. I'm in the middle of cooking dinner—

MRS. GILBERT *(breathlessly)*. Oh. Do you cook?

MILLIE. Oh, yes. I have to. We haven't had a maid for five years.

MRS. GILBERT. Oh, I do think that's wonderful of you. I'm scared stiff of having to do it for Peter—I know the first dinner I have to cook for him will wreck our married life—

GILBERT. Highly probable.

---

[13]*swank:* show off, swagger

MILLIE *(following* MRS. GILBERT *out).* Well, these days we've all got to try and do things we weren't really brought up to do. *(They disappear.)*

ANDREW *(to* GILBERT*).* Don't you want to see the rest of the flat?

GILBERT. No. I leave all that sort of thing to my wife. She's the boss. I thought perhaps you could tell me something about the lower fifth.

ANDREW. What would you like to know?

GILBERT. Well, sir, quite frankly, I'm petrified.

ANDREW. I don't think you need to be. May I give you some sherry?

GILBERT. Thank you.

ANDREW. They are mostly boys of about fifteen or sixteen. They are not very difficult to handle.

GILBERT. The headmaster said you ruled them with a rod of iron. He called you the Himmler of the lower fifth.

ANDREW. Did he? The Himmler of the lower fifth? I think he exaggerated. I hope he exaggerated. The Himmler of the lower fifth?

GILBERT *(puzzled).* He only meant that you kept the most wonderful discipline. I must say I do admire you for that. I couldn't even manage that with eleven-year-olds, so what I'll be like with fifteens and sixteens I shudder to think.

ANDREW. It is not so difficult. They aren't bad boys. Some-times—a little wild and unfeeling, perhaps—but not bad. The Himmler of the lower fifth? Dear me!

GILBERT. Perhaps I shouldn't have said that. I've been tact-less, I'm afraid.

ANDREW. Oh, no, please sit down.

GILBERT. Thank you, sir.

ANDREW. From the very beginning I realized that I didn't possess the knack of making myself liked—a knack that you will find you do possess.

GILBERT. Do you think so?

ANDREW. Oh, yes. I am quite sure of it. It is not a quality of great importance to a schoolmaster, though, for too much of it, as you may also find, is as great a danger as the total lack of it. Forgive me lecturing, won't you?

GILBERT. I want to learn.

ANDREW. I can only teach you from my own experience. For two or three years I tried very hard to communicate to the boys some of my own joy in the great literature of the past. Of course, I failed, as you will fail, nine hundred and ninety-nine times out of a thousand. But a single success can atone and more than atone for all the failures in the world. And sometimes—very rarely, it is true—but sometimes I had that success. That was in the early years.

GILBERT *(eagerly listening).* Please go on, sir.

ANDREW. In early years, too, I discovered an easy substitute for popularity. I had, of course, acquired—we all do—many little mannerisms and tricks of speech, and I found that the boys were beginning to laugh at me. I was very happy at that, and encouraged the boys' laughter by playing up to it. It made our relationship so very much easier. They didn't like me as a man, but they found me funny as a character, and you can teach more things by laughter than by earnestness—for I never did have much sense of humour. So, for a time, you see, I was quite a success as a schoolmaster—*(He stops.)*—I fear this is all very personal and embarrassing to you. Forgive me. You need have no fears about the lower fifth.

GILBERT *(after a pause).* I'm afraid I said something that hurt you very much. It's myself you must forgive, sir. Believe me, I'm desperately sorry.

ANDREW. There's no need. You were merely telling me what I should have known for myself. Perhaps I did in my heart, and hadn't the courage to acknowledge it. I knew, of course, that I was not only not liked, but now positively disliked. I had realized, too, that the boys—for many long years now—had ceased to laugh at me. I don't know why they no longer found me a joke. Perhaps it was my illness. No, I don't think it was that. Something deeper than that. Not a sickness of the body, but a sickness of the soul. At all events it didn't take much discernment on my part to realize I had become an utter failure as a schoolmaster. Still, stupidly enough, I hadn't realized that I was also feared. The Himmler of the lower fifth! I suppose that will become my epitaph.

(GILBERT *is now deeply embarrassed and rather upset, but he remains silent.*)

(*With a mild laugh.*) I cannot for the life of me imagine why I should choose to unburden myself to you—a total stranger—when I have been silent to others for so long. Perhaps it is because my very unworthy mantle is about to fall on your shoulders. If that is so I shall take a prophet's privilege and foretell that you will have a very great success with the lower fifth.

GILBERT. Thank you, sir. I shall do my best.

ANDREW. I can't offer you a cigarette, I'm afraid. I don't smoke.

GILBERT. That's all right, sir. Nor do I.

(MILLIE *and* MRS. GILBERT *can be heard in the hall outside.*)

MRS. GILBERT (*off*). Thank you so much for showing me round.

(MILLIE *and* MRS. GILBERT *come in.*)

ANDREW. I trust your wife has found no major snags in your new flat.

MRS. GILBERT. No. None at all. Just imagine, Peter. Mr. and Mrs. Crocker-Harris first met each other on a holiday in the Lake District. Isn't that a coincidence!

GILBERT (*a little distrait[14]*). Yes. Yes, it certainly is. On a walking tour, too?

MILLIE. Andrew was on a walking tour. No walking for me. I can't abide it. I was staying with my uncle—that's Sir William Bartop, you know—you may have heard of him?

(GILBERT *and* MRS. GILBERT *try to look as though they had heard of him constantly.*)

He'd taken a house near Windermere—quite a mansion

[14]*distrait:* absent-minded

it was really—rather silly for an old gentleman living
alone—and Andrew knocked on our front-door one day
and asked the footman for a glass of water. So my uncle
invited him in to tea.

MRS. GILBERT.　Our meeting wasn't quite as romantic as that.

GILBERT.　I knocked her flat on her face.

MRS. GILBERT.　Not with love at first sight. With the swing
doors of our hotel bar. So, of course, then he apologized
and—

GILBERT (*brusquely*).　Darling. The Crocker-Harrises, I'm
sure, have far more important things to do than to listen
to your detailed but inaccurate account of our very sordid
little encounter. Why not just say I married you for your
money and leave it at that? Come on, we must go.

MRS. GILBERT (*to* MILLIE).　Isn't he awful to me?

MILLIE.　Men have no souls, my dear. My husband is just as
bad.

MRS. GILBERT.　Goodbye, Mr. Crocker-Harris.

ANDREW (*bowing*).　Goodbye.

MRS. GILBERT (*as she goes out with* MILLIE).　I think your
idea about the dining-room is awfully good—if only I can
get the permit—

(MILLIE *and* MRS. GILBERT *go out.* GILBERT *has dallied
to say goodbye alone to* ANDREW.)

GILBERT.　Goodbye, sir.

ANDREW.　Er—you will, I know, respect the confidences I
have just made to you—

GILBERT.　I should hate you to think I wouldn't.

ANDREW.　I am sorry to have embarrassed you. I don't know
what come over me. I have not been very well, you know.
Goodbye, my dear fellow, and my best wishes.

GILBERT.　Thank you. The very best of good luck to you too,
sir, in your future career.

ANDREW.　My future career? Yes. Thank you.

GILBERT.　Well, goodbye, sir. (*He goes out.*)

(*We hear voices in the hall, cut short as the front-door
closes.* MILLIE *comes back.*)

MILLIE.   Good-looking couple.

ANDREW.   Very.

MILLIE.   He looks as if he'd got what it takes. I should think he'll be a success all right.

ANDREW.   That's what I thought.

MILLIE.   I don't think it's much of a career, though—a schoolmaster—for a likely young chap like that.

ANDREW.   I know you don't.

MILLIE.   Still I bet when he leaves this place it won't be without a pension. It'll be roses, roses all the way, and tears and cheers and goodbye, Mr. Chips.[15]

ANDREW.   I expect so.

MILLIE.   What's the matter with you?

ANDREW.   Nothing.

MILLIE.   You're not going to have another of your attacks, are you? You look dreadful.

ANDREW.   I'm perfectly all right.

MILLIE *(indifferently).* You know best. Your medicine's there, anyway, if you want it. *(She goes out.)*

(ANDREW, left alone, continues for a time staring at the text he has been pretending to read. Then he puts one hand over his eyes. There is a knock on the door.)

ANDREW.   Come in.

(TAPLOW appears timidly from behind the screen.)

(Sharply.) Yes, Taplow? What is it?

TAPLOW.   Nothing, sir.

ANDREW.   What do you mean, nothing?

TAPLOW *(timidly).*   I just came back to say goodbye, sir.

ANDREW.   Oh. *(He gets up.)*

TAPLOW.   I didn't have a chance with the head here. I rather dashed out, I'm afraid. I thought I'd just come back and — and wish you luck, sir.

ANDREW.   Thank you, Taplow. That's good of you.

[15]*Mr. Chips:* the beloved and respected schoolmaster of the short novel, *Goodbye, Mr. Chips,* by James Hilton

TAPLOW.　I—er—thought this might interest you, sir. *(He quickly thrusts a small book into* ANDREW'S *hand.)*
ANDREW.　What is it?
TAPLOW.　Verse translation of the *Agamemnon,* sir. The Browning version. It's not much good. I've been reading it in the Chapel gardens.

(ANDREW very deliberately turns over the pages of the book.)

ANDREW.　Very interesting, Taplow. *(He seems to have a little difficulty in speaking. He clears his throat and then goes on in his level, gentle voice.)* I know the translation, of course. It has its faults, I agree, but I think you will enjoy it more when you get used to the meter he employs. *(He hands it to* TAPLOW *who brusquely thrusts it back to him.)*
TAPLOW.　It's for you, sir.
ANDREW.　For me?
TAPLOW.　Yes, sir. I've written in it.

(ANDREW opens the fly-leaf and reads whatever is written there.)

ANDREW.　Did you buy this?
TAPLOW.　Yes, sir. It was only second-hand.
ANDREW.　You shouldn't have spent your pocket-money this way.
TAPLOW.　That's all right, sir. It wasn't very much. The price isn't still inside, is it?

(ANDREW carefully wipes his glasses and puts them on again.)

ANDREW *(at length).*　No. Just what you've written. Nothing else.
TAPLOW.　Good. I'm sorry you've got it already. I thought you probably would have—
ANDREW.　I haven't got it already. I may have had it once. I can't remember. But I haven't got it now.

TAPLOW.   That's all right, then.

(ANDREW *continues to stare at* TAPLOW'S *inscription on the fly-leaf.*)

(*Suspiciously.*) What's the matter, sir? Have I got the accent wrong on εὐμενῶς?
ANDREW.   No. The perispomenon is perfectly correct.

(*He lowers the book and we notice his hands are shaking from some intense inner effort as he takes off his spectacles.*)

Taplow, would you be good enough to take that bottle of medicine, which you so kindly brought in, and pour me out one dose in a glass which you will find in the bathroom?
TAPLOW (*seeing something is wrong*).   Yes, sir.

(ANDREW *sits at his seat by the table.*)

ANDREW.   The doses are clearly marked on the bottle. I usually put a little water with it.
TAPLOW.   Yes, sir. (*He takes the bottle and darts out.*)

(ANDREW, *the moment he is gone, breaks down and begins to sob uncontrollably. He makes a desperate attempt, after a moment, to control himself, but when* TAPLOW *comes back his emotion is still very apparent.*)

ANDREW (*taking the glass*).   Thank you. (*He drinks it, turning his back on* TAPLOW *as he does so. At length.*) You must forgive this exhibition of weakness, Taplow. The truth is I have been going through rather a strain lately.
TAPLOW.   Of course, sir. I quite understand.

(*There is a knock on the garden door.*)

ANDREW.   Come in.

(FRANK *comes in*)

FRANK.   Oh, sorry. I thought you'd be finished by now —

ANDREW.   Come in, Hunter, do. It's perfectly all right. Our lesson was over some time ago, but Taplow most kindly came back to say goodbye.

(FRANK, *taking in* TAPLOW'S *rather startled face and* ANDREW'S *obvious emotion, looks a little puzzled.*)

FRANK.   Are you sure I'm not intruding?

ANDREW.   No, no. I want you to see this book that Γaplow has given me, Hunter. Look. (*He hands it to* HUNTER.) A translation of the *Agamemnon* by Robert Browning. Do you see the inscription he has put into it?

FRANK.   Yes, but it's no use to me, I'm afraid. I never learnt Greek.

ANDREW.   Then we'll have to translate it for him, won't we, Taplow? (*Reciting by heart.*) τὸν κρατοῦντα μαλθακῶς θεὸς πρόσωθεν εὐμενῶς προσδέρκεται. That means — in a rough translation: 'God from afar looks graciously upon a gentle master.' It comes from a speech of Agamemnon's to Clytaemnestra.

FRANK.   I see. Very pleasant and very apt. (*He hands the book back to* ANDREW.)

ANDREW.   Very pleasant. But perhaps not, after all, so very apt.

(*He turns quickly away from both of them as emotion once more seems about to overcome him.* FRANK *brusquely jerks his head to the bewildered* TAPLOW *to get out.* TAPLOW *nods.*)

TAPLOW.   Goodbye, sir, and the best of luck.

ANDREW.   Goodbye, Taplow, and thank you very much.

(TAPLOW *flees quickly.* FRANK *watches* ANDREW'S *back with a mixture of embarrassment and sympathy.*)

(*Turning at length, slightly recovered.*) Dear me, what a fool I made of myself in front of that boy. And in front of you, Hunter. I can't imagine what you must think of me.

FRANK.   Nonsense.

ANDREW.   I am not a very emotional person, as you know, but
there was something so very touching and kindly about
his action, and coming as it did just after—*(He stops, then
glances at the book in his hand.)* This is a very delightful
thing to have, don't you think?

FRANK.   Delightful.

ANDREW.   The quotation, of course, he didn't find entirely
by himself. I happened to make some little joke about the
line in form the other day. But he must have remembered
it all the same to have found it so readily—and perhaps
he means it.

FRANK.   I'm sure he does, or he wouldn't have written it.

(MILLIE comes in.)

MILLIE.   Hullo, Frank. I'm glad you're in time. *(She picks up
the medicine bottle and the glass from the table and puts
them aside. To FRANK.)* Lend me a cigarette. I've been
gasping for one for an hour.

*(FRANK once more extends his case and MILLIE takes a
cigarette which he lights.)*

FRANK.   Your husband has just had a very nice present.

MILLIE.   Oh? Who from?

FRANK.   Taplow.

MILLIE *(smiling).*   Oh, Taplow. Let's see. *(She takes the book
from ANDREW.)*

ANDREW.   He bought it with his own pocket-money, Millie,
and wrote a very charming inscription inside.

FRANK.   God looks kindly upon a gracious master.

ANDREW.   No—not gracious—gentle, I think—τὸω κρατοῦντα
μαλθακῶς —yes I think gentle is the better translation.
I would rather have had this present than almost anything
I can think of.

Pause. MILLIE *laughs suddenly.*

MILLIE.   The artful little beast—

FRANK.   *(urgently).*   Millie—

ANDREW. Artful? Why artful? (MILLIE *looks at* FRANK *who is staring meaningly at her.*) Why artful, Millie? (MILLIE *laughs again, quite lightly, and turns from* FRANK *to* ANDREW.)

MILLIE. My dear, because I came into this room this afternoon to find him giving an imitation of you to Frank here. Obviously he was scared stiff I was going to tell you, and you'd ditch his remove or something. I don't blame him for trying a few bobs' worth of appeasement. (*She hands the book back to* ANDREW *who stands quite still looking down at it.*)

ANDREW (*nodding, at length*). I see. (*He puts the book gently on the table and walks to the door.*)

MILLIE. Where are you going, dear? Dinner's nearly ready.

ANDREW. Only to my room for a moment. I won't be long. (*He takes the medicine bottle and a glass.*)

MILLIE. You've just had a dose of that, dear. I shouldn't have another, if I were you.

ANDREW. I am allowed two at a time.

MILLIE. Well, see it is two and no more, won't you?
ANDREW *meets her eye for a moment, at the door, then goes out quietly. She turns to* FRANK *with an expression half defiant and half ashamed.*

FRANK (*with a note of real repulsion in his voice*). Millie! My God! How could you?

MILLIE. Well, why not? Why should he be allowed his comforting little illusions? I'm not.

FRANK (*advancing on her*). Listen. You're to go to his room now and tell him that was a lie.

MILLIE. Certainly not. It wasn't a lie.

FRANK. If you don't, I will.

MILLIE. I shouldn't, if I were you. It'll only make things worse. He won't believe you.

FRANK (*moving*). We'll see about that.

MILLIE. Go ahead. See what happens. He knows I don't lie to him. He knows what I told him was the truth, and he won't like your sympathy. He'll think you're making fun of him, like Taplow.

(FRANK *hesitates at the door then comes slowly back into the room.* MILLIE *watches him, a little frightened.*)

FRANK (*at length*).   We're finished, Millie—you and I.

MILLIE (*laughing*).   Frank, really! Don't be hysterical.

FRANK.   I'm not. I mean it.

MILLIE (*lightly*).   Oh, yes, you mean it. Of course you mean it. Now just sit down, dear, and relax and forget all about artful little boys and their five-bob presents, and talk to me. (*She touches his arm. He moves away from her brusquely.*)

FRANK.   Forget? If I live to be a hundred I shall never forget that little glimpse you've just given me of yourself.

MILLIE.   Frank—you're making a frightening mountain out of an absurd little molehill.

FRANK.   Of course, but the mountain. I'm making in my imagination is so frightening that I'd rather try to forget both it and the repulsive little molehill that gave it birth. But as I know I never can, I tell you, Millie—from this moment you and I are finished.

MILLIE (*quietly*).   You can't scare me, Frank. I know that's what you're trying to do, but you can't do it.

FRANK (*quietly*).   I'm not trying to scare you, Millie. I'm telling you the simple truth. I'm not coming to Bradford.

MILLIE (*after a pause, with an attempt at bravado*).   All right, my dear, if that's the way you feel about it. Don't come to Bradford.

FRANK.   Right. Now I think you ought to go to your room and look after Andrew. I'm leaving. (MILLIE *runs quickly to stop him.*)

MILLIE.   What is this? Frank, I don't understand, really I don't. What have I done?

FRANK.   I think you know what you've done, Millie. Go and look after Andrew.

MILLIE.   Andrew? Why this sudden concern for Andrew?

FRANK.   Because I think he's just been about as badly hurt as a human being can be; and as he's a sick man and in a rather hysterical state it might be a good plan to go and see how he is.

MILLIE *(scornfully).* Hurt? Andrew hurt? You can't hurt Andrew. He's dead.

FRANK. Why do you hate him so much, Millie?

MILLIE. Because he keeps me from you.

FRANK. That isn't true.

MILLIE. Because he's not a man at all.

FRANK. He's a human being.

MILLIE. You've got a fine right to be so noble about him, after deceiving him for six months.

FRANK. Twice in six months—at your urgent invitation.

(MILLIE *slaps his face, in a violent paroxysm[16] of rage.*)

Thank you for that. I deserved it. I deserve a lot worse than that, too—

MILLIE *(running to him).* Frank, forgive me—I didn't mean it—

FRANK *(quietly).* You'd better have the truth, Millie. It had to come some time. I've never loved you. I've never told you I loved you.

MILLIE. I know, Frank, I know—I've always accepted that.

FRANK. You asked me just now if I was running away from you. Well, I was.

MILLIE. I knew that too.

FRANK. But I was coming to Bradford. It was going to be the very last time I was ever going to see you and at Bradford I would have told you that.

MILLIE. You wouldn't. You wouldn't. You've tried to tell me that so often before—and I've always stopped you some-how—somehow. I would have stopped you again.

FRANK. *(quietly).* I don't think so, Millie. Not this time.

MILLIE. Frank, I don't care what humiliations you heap on me. I know you don't give two hoots for me as a person. I've always known that. I've never minded so long as you cared for me as a woman. And you do, Frank. You do. You do, don't you? (FRANK *is silent.*)

---

[16]*paroxysm:* fit, spasm

It'll be all right at Bradford, you see. It'll be all right, there—

FRANK.   I'm not coming to Bradford, Millie.

(The door opens slowly and ANDREW *comes in, carrying the bottle of medicine. He hands it to* MILLIE *and passes on.* MILLIE *quickly holds the bottle up to the light.* ANDREW *turns and sees her.)*

ANDREW *(gently).*   You should know me well enough by now, my dear, to realize how unlikely it is that I should ever take an overdose.

*(*MILLIE, *without a word, puts the bottle down and goes out.* ANDREW *goes to a cupboard at back and produces a decanter of sherry and a glass.)*

FRANK.   I'm not staying to dinner, I'm afraid.

ANDREW.   Indeed? I'm sorry to hear that. You'll have a glass of sherry?

FRANK.   No, thank you.

ANDREW.   You will forgive me if I do.

FRANK.   Of course. (ANDREW *pours himself a glass.)* Perhaps I'll change my mind. (ANDREW *pours* FRANK *a glass.)* About Taplow—

ANDREW.   Oh, yes?

FRANK.   It *is* perfectly true that he was imitating you. I, of course, was mostly to blame in that, and I'm very sorry.

ANDREW.   That is perfectly all right. Was it a good imitation?

FRANK.   No.

ANDREW.   I expect it was. Boys are often very clever mimics.

FRANK.   We talked about you, of course, before that. He said —you probably won't believe this, but I thought I ought to tell you—he said he liked you very much. (ANDREW *smiles slightly.)*

ANDREW.   Indeed?

FRANK.   I can remember very clearly his exact words. He said: 'He doesn't seem to like people to like him—but in spite of that, I do—very much.' *(Lightly.)* So you see it looks after all as if the book might not have been a mere question of—appeasement.

ANDREW. The book? *(He picks it up.)* Dear me! What a lot of fuss about a little book—and a not very good little book at that. *(He drops it on the table.)*

FRANK. I would like you to believe me.

ANDREW. Possibly you would, my dear Hunter; but I can assure you I am not particularly concerned about Taplow's views of my character: or about yours either, if it comes to that.

FRANK *(hopelessly).* I think you should keep that book all the same. You may find it'll mean something to you after all.

ANDREW. Exactly. It will mean a perpetual reminder to myself of the story with which Taplow is at this very moment regaling his friends in the House. 'I gave the Crock a book, to buy him off, and he blubbed. The Crock blubbed. I tell you I was there, I saw it. The Crock blubbed.' My mimicry is not as good as his, I fear. Forgive me. And now let us leave this idiotic subject and talk of more pleasant things. Do you like this sherry? I got it on my last visit to London—

FRANK. If Taplow ever breathes a word of that story to any one at all, I'll murder him. But he won't. And if you think I will you greatly underestimate my character as well as his. *(He drains his glass.)* Goodbye.

ANDREW. Are you leaving so soon? Goodbye, my dear fellow.

(He does not get up nor offer to shake hands. FRANK goes to the window.)

FRANK. As this is the last time I shall probably ever see you I'm going to offer you a word of advice.

ANDREW *(politely).* I shall be glad to listen to it.

FRANK. Leave your wife.

(Pause. ANDREW takes a sip of his sherry.)

ANDREW (*at length*).   So that you may the more easily carry on your intrigue with her?

(FRANK *stares at him, then comes back into the room.*)

FRANK.   How long have you known that?
ANDREW.   Since it first began.
FRANK.   How did you find out?
ANDREW.   By information.
FRANK.   By whose information?
ANDREW.   By someone's whose word I could hardly discredit.

(*Pause.*)

FRANK (*slowly, with repulsion*).   No! That's too horrible to think of.
ANDREW.   Nothing is ever too horrible to think of, Hunter. It is simply a question of facing facts.
FRANK.   She might have told you a lie. Have you faced that fact?
ANDREW.   She never tells me a lie. In twenty years she has never told me a lie. Only the truth.
FRANK.   This was a lie.
ANDREW.   No, my dear Hunter. Do you wish me to quote you dates?
FRANK (*still unable to believe it*).   And she told you six months ago?
ANDREW.   Isn't it seven?
FRANK (*savagely*).   Then why have you allowed me inside your home? Why haven't you done something—reported me to the governors—anything—made a scene, knocked me down?
ANDREW.   Knocked you down?
FRANK.   You didn't have to invite me to dinner.
ANDREW.   My dear Hunter, if, over the last twenty years, I had allowed such petty considerations to influence my choice of dinner guests I would have found it increasingly hard to remember which master to invite and which to refuse. You see, Hunter, you mustn't flatter yourself you

are the first. My information is a good deal better than yours, you understand. It's authentic.

(Pause.)

FRANK.   She's evil.

ANDREW.   That's hardly a kindly epithet to apply to a lady whom, I gather, you have asked to marry.

FRANK.   Did she tell you that?

ANDREW.   She's a dutiful wife. She tells me everything.

FRANK.   That, at least, was a lie.

ANDREW.   She never lies.

FRANK.   That was a lie. Do you want the truth? Can you bear the truth?

ANDREW.   I can bear anything.

FRANK.   What I did, I did cold-bloodedly out of weakness and ignorance and crass stupidity. I'm bitterly, bitterly ashamed of myself, but, in a sense, I'm glad you know, though I'd rather a thousand times that you'd heard it from me than from your wife. I won't ask you to forgive me. I can only tell you, with complete truth, that the only emotion she has ever succeeded in arousing in me she aroused in me for the first time ten minutes ago—an intense and passionate disgust.

ANDREW.   What a delightfully chivalrous statement—

FRANK.   Forget chivalry, Crock, for God's sake. Forget all your fine Mosaic[17] scruples. You must leave her—it's your only chance.

ANDREW.   She's my wife, Hunter. You seem to forget that. As long as she wishes to remain my wife, she may.

FRANK.   She's out to kill you.

ANDREW.   My dear Hunter, if that was indeed her purpose, you should know by now that she fulfilled it long ago.

FRANK.   Why won't you leave her?

ANDREW.   Because I wouldn't wish to add another grave wrong to one I have already done her.

FRANK.   What wrong have you done her?

[17]*Mosaic:* having to do with the laws or commandments attributed to Moses

ANDREW. To marry her. (*Pause.* FRANK *stares at him in silence.*) You see, my dear Hunter, she is really quite as much to be pitied as I. We are both of us interesting subjects for your microscope. Both of us needing from the other something that would make life supportable for us, and neither of us able to give it. Two kinds of love. Hers and mine. Worlds apart, as I know now, though when I married her I didn't think they were incompatible. In those days I hadn't thought that her kind of love—the love she requires and which I was unable to give her—was so important that its absence would drive out the other kind of love—the kind of love that I require and which I thought, in my folly, was by far the greater part of love. I may have been, you see, Hunter, a brilliant classical scholar, but I was woefully ignorant of the facts of life. I know better now, of course. I know that in both of us, the love that we should have borne each other has turned to bitter hatred. That's all the problem is. Not a very unusual one, I venture to think—nor nearly as tragic as you seem to imagine. Merely the problem of an unsatisfied wife and a henpecked husband. You'll find it all over the world. It is usually, I believe, a subject for farce. And now, if you have to leave us, my dear fellow, please don't let me detain you any longer.

(*He turns his back deliberately on* FRANK, *who makes no move to go.*)

FRANK. Don't go to Bradford. Stay here, until you take up your new job.

ANDREW. I think I've already told you I'm not interested in your advice.

FRANK. Leave her. It's the only way.

ANDREW (*violently*). Will you please go!

FRANK. All right. I'd just like you to say goodbye to me, properly, though. Will you? I shan't see you again.

(ANDREW *rises and walks slowly over to* FRANK)

I know you don't want my pity, but I would like to be of some help.

ANDREW. If you think, by this expression of kindness, Hunter, that you can get me to repeat the shameful exhibition of emotion I made to Taplow a moment ago, I must tell you that you have no chance. My hysteria over that book just now was no more than a sort of reflex of action of the spirit. The muscular twitchings of a corpse. It can never happen again.

FRANK. A corpse can be revived.

ANDREW. I don't believe in miracles.

FRANK. Don't you? Funnily enough, as a scientist, I do.

ANDREW. Your faith would be touching, if I were capable of being touched by it.

FRANK. You are, I think. (*After a pause.*) I'd like to come and visit you at this crammer's.

ANDREW. This is an absurd suggestion.

FRANK. I suppose it is rather, but all the same I'd like to do it. May I?

ANDREW. Of course not.

FRANK. Your term begins on the first of September, doesn't it?

ANDREW. I tell you the idea is quite childish—

FRANK. I could come about the second week.

ANDREW. You would be bored to death. So, probably, would I.

FRANK (*glancing at pocket calendar*). Let's say Monday the twelfth, then.

ANDREW (*his hands beginning to tremble again*). Say anything you like, only please go. Please go, Hunter.

FRANK (*writing in his book and not looking at* ANDREW). That's fixed, then. Monday, September the twelfth. Will you remember that?

ANDREW (*after a pause, speaking with difficulty*). I suppose I'm at least as likely to remember it as you are.

FRANK. That's fixed, then. (*He slips the book into his pocket and puts out his hand.*) Goodbye, until then.

(ANDREW, *after hesitation, shakes his hand.*)

ANDREW.   Goodbye.

FRANK.   May I go out through your garden?

ANDREW *(nodding).*   Of course.

FRANK.   I'm off to have a quick word with Taplow. By the way, may I take him a message from you?

ANDREW.   What message?

FRANK.   Has he or has he not got his remove?

ANDREW.   He has.

FRANK.   May I tell him?

ANDREW.   It is highly irregular. Yes, you may.

FRANK.   Good. *(He turns to go then turns back.)* Oh, by the way, I'd better have the address of that crammer's.

(FRANK takes out his notebook and points his pencil, ready to write. MILLIE comes in with tray, dishes, and cutlery. She starts to set the table.)

MILLIE.   Dinner's ready. You're staying, Frank, aren't you?

FRANK *(politely).*   No. I'm afraid not. *(To ANDREW.)* What's that address?

ANDREW *(after great hesitation).*   The Old Deanery, Malcombe, Dorset.

FRANK.   I'll write to you and you can let me know about trains. *(To MILLIE.)* Goodbye. *(To ANDREW.)* Goodbye. *(He goes out.)*

(MILLIE is silent for a moment. Then she laughs.)

MILLIE.   That's a laugh, I must say.

ANDREW.   What's a laugh, my dear?

MILLIE.   You inviting him to stay with you.

ANDREW.   I didn't. He suggested it.

MILLIE.   He's coming to Bradford.

ANDREW.   Yes. I remember your telling me so.

(MILLIE comes close to ANDREW.)

MILLIE.   He's coming to Bradford. He's not going to you.

ANDREW.　The likeliest contingency is, that he s not going to either of us. Shall we have dinner?

MILLIE.　He's coming to Bradford.

ANDREW.　I expect so. Oh, by the way, I'm not. I shall be staying here until I go to Dorest.

MILLIE *(indifferently).*　Suit yourself—what makes you think I'll join you there?

ANDREW.　I don't.

MILLIE.　You needn't expect me.

ANDREW.　I don't think either of us has the right to expect anything further from the other.

(The telephone rings.)

ANDREW.　I don't. Excuse me. *(He picks up the receiver.)* Hullo . . . Yes, headmaster . . . The timetable? . . . It's perfectly simple. The middle fourth B division will take a ten-minute break on Tuesdays and a fifteen-minute break on alternate Wednesdays; while exactly the reverse procedure will apply to the lower Shell, C division. I thought I had sufficiently explained that on my chart . . . Oh, I see . . . Thank you, that is very good of you . . . yes, I think you will find it will work out quite satisfactorily . . . Oh, by the way, headmaster. I have changed my mind about the prize-giving ceremony. I intend to speak after, instead of before, Fletcher, as is my privilege . . . Yes, I quite understand, but I am now seeing the matter in a different light. . . . I know, but I am of the opinion that occasionally an anti-climax can be surprisingly effective. Goodbye. *(He rings off and goes and sits at table.)* Come along, my dear. We mustn't let our dinner get cold.

*(*MILLIE *slowly sits and begins to serve dinner.)*

Curtain

FOR DISCUSSION

1. Rattigan uses stage directions rather fully, as did Shaw. In what ways are the stage directions in the two plays similar? How does the use of these directions affect your reading enjoyment? What do you learn about both John Taplow and Frank Hunter before either of them says anything?

2. Taplow and Frank Hunter provide a good deal of *exposition* (see Glossary) about Andrew Crocker-Harris in their conversation. In what ways is he different from "the others"? How, specifically, does Taplow characterize him? What is his opinion of Crocker-Harris as a teacher?

3. What do you learn about Taplow from what he says and does? What sort of student is he? According to what he tells Frank, how does he personally feel toward Crocker-Harris? Do you feel that he is speaking sincerely? Why?

4. What problem arises for Taplow when Millie Crocker-Harris enters the room? From what you know of him, is his reaction a natural one? Why?

5. During the scene between Millie and Frank, what do they reveal about their relationship? What do Millie's insinuations lead you to suspect about Frank's attitude toward her?

6. What is your initial impression of Millie? How does she seem to feel toward her husband? What significant information about him is she able to provide by quoting Betty Carstair's comments?

7. From what you know about Andrew Crocker-Harris, do you feel that his personal appearance is consistent with his character? Explain. What sort of person does Andrew reveal himself to be?

8. The brief episode about the school timetable provides a telling comment on the Crocker-Harrises' relationship. What does it reveal about each? Why do you suppose Frank reacts as he does to Millie's outburst?

9. How are Crocker-Harris' teaching methods with Taplow consistent with Taplow's earlier complaints to Frank? What unexpected aspect of the schoolmaster emerges for a moment in response to one of Taplow's remarks? Does this incident surprise you? Why? In what way does it alter your feeling toward Crocker-Harris?

10. Dr. Frobisher's visit serves several dramatic functions. How does he prepare you in a natural way for the entrance of the

Gilberts? In discussing Peter Gilbert's qualifications, what information about Andrew's own qualifications is he able to reveal naturally and casually? Why is this information particulary *ironic* (see Glossary) in view of Andrew's status at the school and in view of the "two rather delicate matters" that Frobisher has to discuss?

11. What sort of person is Dr. Frobisher? In what way is his personal appearance (see stage directions) consistent with his manner? How would you describe his attitude toward Crocker-Harris? Do you agree with Millie's characterization of him as a "phoney"? Why?

12. When Dr. Frobisher leaves, Millie and Andrew confront each other directly for the first time in the play. Do you feel that each one behaves consistently in the light of what you know about them? Explain.

13. In Millie Crocker-Harris, Rattigan has created a totally "un-sympathetic" character—that is, one with whom the audience or reader does not sympathize. In addition to her blatant infidelity to her husband, what other unpleasant qualities do you find in her behavior?

14. Peter Gilbert innocently repeats the headmaster's remark about Andrew's being "the Himmler of the lower fifth." (Himmler was a German Nazi leader and the head of the Gestapo.) What is the unexpected effect of this remark upon Andrew? What important truth about himself does it force him to voice? How would you characterize Andrew's attitude toward himself?

15. What very important dramatic function does Peter Gilbert perform? Why was it necessary for Rattigan to use a "total stranger" for this function?

16. During the conversation with Gilbert, Andrew states that "a single success can atone and more than atone for all the failures in the world." What does he mean? What occurrence does this statement foreshadow (see Glossary, *foreshadowing*)?

17. Why might you be inclined to suspect Taplow's motives in returning with the book? On the other hand, why might you be inclined to believe in his sincerity, based on what you have learned of him previously?

18. What ironic contrast is presented by Taplow's inscription, in view of the headmaster's remark quoted previously by Peter Gilbert? How do you know that Taplow's gesture has tremendous significance for Andrew? In what ways have you been prepared for his reaction to the gift?

19. When Millie voices her suspicion of Taplow's motives, what

does Andrew do? Why do his actions cause a building of dramatic tension? How do Frank's words to Millie increase the tension? What does he evidently suspect that Andrew might do? What is the dramatic effect of Andrew's reappearance? Do you consider his remark to Millie consistent or inconsistent with his customary behavior? Why?

20. At what point in the play does the *climax* (see Glossary) occur? Is this also the point of greatest intensity for the audience or reader? Explain.

21. Do you feel that Frank's disgust for Millie is justified? Explain. Why does Andrew not feel the same way toward her? What does he mean in saying, "She is really quite as much to be pitied as I"? Do you agree with him? Why?

22. Taplow has previously characterized Andrew as "barely human"; Millie has called him "dead"; and now Andrew refers to himself as a "corpse." In what sense are these descriptions apt? What is the dramatic effect of Frank's reply? Do you feel that there has been anything in Andrew's behavior to warrant optimism? Explain.

23. At what point do you know definitely that Andrew is not the same man that he was when the play began? How has his attitude toward himself changed? What has caused this change? What further evidence of change do you sense in his behavior toward his wife?

24. Does the phone call from the headmaster seem contrived or do you feel that it is sufficiently justified? In what way has Andrew's behavior toward Dr. Frobisher changed since their earlier visit? In what "different light" is Andrew now seeing the matter?

25. A few critics have suggested that a more justifiable conclusion to the play would have been to allow Crocker-Harris to commit suicide. Explain why you do or do not agree with them.

FOR COMPOSITION

1. Rattigan disparaged Shaw's "play of ideas," insisting that the most important elements of a play should be character, mood, and feeling. On the basis of this disagreement, write a critical comparison of *The Browning Version* and *Arms and the Man*. Is Rattigan's position evident in his play? In what ways do the plays differ? In spite of a basic disagreement between the playwrights, are there similarities in their plays?

2. Rattigan's frequently unconventional characters make interesting subjects for study. Choosing one of the less fully developed characters in the play (Dr. Frobisher, John Taplow, Peter Gilbert), use your powers of inference and your imagination to describe how you think he would react to the change in Andrew Crocker-Harris' manner. Make your composition as detailed as possible. You might want to write it in the form of an interior monologue.

3. In a well-organized essay, tell why you agree or disagree with Andrew Crocker-Harris' statement that a "a single success can atone and more than atone for all the failures in the world." Use specific examples either from the play or from your own experience to illustrate your point.

4. From what you learn in the play and from your own experience, write a description of the qualities you feel a good teacher should have. Be sure to explain your reasons for including each particular quality.

5. In Andrew Crocker-Harris, Rattigan has created an absorbing psychological study of failure. Through the hints, implications, and direct statements of various characters and of Andrew himself, you are given a somewhat detailed history of Andrew's gradual decline after his graduation with honors from Oxford. From the information given in the play, write a detailed analysis of the factors that contributed to Andrew's failure. To what degree do you think he himself was responsible? To what degree do you think his wife was responsible? Were there other factors that increased his difficulties? In conclusion, decide which single factor you think was his greatest obstacle to success.

Peter Shaffer

Peter Shaffer (born in 1926) belongs to the generation of British playwrights who came of age in the years after World War II, established their reputations in the 1950's and 1960's, and may have the most productive years of their careers ahead of them in the 1970's and 1980's. This group includes such writers as Anthony Shaffer (Peter's twin brother), Harold Pinter, Arnold Wesker, John Osborne, Shelagh Delaney, David Storey, and Bernard Kops.

The playwrights indicated, and their contemporaries, represent a wide range of characteristics in their backgrounds, their social attitudes, and their dramatic methods and resources. All of them, however, reflect in their own ways the far-reaching changes that Britain has undergone within the last few generations. Their plays portray, directly or indirectly, a society in which the stable institutions and certitudes of earlier years have been strongly challenged but nonetheless still exert a pervasive influence on the social and psychological ambience within which people function. This tension between the old and the new is the basic source of the dramatic interest in many of the best plays of recent years.

Another characteristic of the generation of playwrights to which Peter Shaffer belongs is that they are strongly oriented toward mass communications media. They do not write just for the stage but for radio, TV, and film. Often, the same vehicle (with necessary adaptations, of course) will be offered to the public in several or all of these forms, as well as on the printed page. Shaffer, among others, has shown great facility and craftsmanship in meeting the special needs of the various media.

Still another characteristic aspect of the careers of the post-World War II dramatists is that they are truly "Anglo-Americans." Although they inevitably write as Englishmen, they find audiences and critical appreciation (to say nothing of financial rewards) on both sides of the Atlantic. It is interesting to note that *White Lies* was written expressly for the New York stage. Only after being presented there was it "exported" to London's West End. On the other hand, Shaffer's *Black Comedy* was originally commissioned and produced by Sir Laurence Olivier for the National Theatre of Great Britain. Afterward it was introduced to American audiences.

Shaffer's work, as exemplified by *White Lies*, is "theatrical" in the best sense of the term. Without seeming to espouse any cause or to deliver any protest message, he uses the resources of the drama to give us a striking insight into the values by which people live—or fail to live. The impact can be immediate and shattering, as you may agree after you read *White Lies*.

White Lies

THINGS TO CONSIDER

① EXTENT TO WHICH PEOPLE
DEPEND ON IMAGES IN REAL
LIFE AND IN THE PLAY.

② GOOD & BAD EFFECTS OF IMAGES

③ WHAT IS THE PLAYWRIGHT SAYING
ABOUT DISHONESTY?

CHARACTERS

SOPHIE: BARONESS LEMBERG
FRANK
TOM

The action takes place in the Fortune Teller's parlour of
Sophie, Baroness Lemberg, on the promenade of a run-down
seaside resort on the south coast of England. The time is the
present, around six o'clock in the evening; mid-September.

SCENE: SOPHIE'S *parlour is in fact a seedy living room facing the sea. One side of it is almost entirely occupied by a window, in which is spelt out in cheap gold letters (and in reverse, so that it can be read from outside):* BARONESS LEMBERG, PALMISTE. CLAIRVOYANTE.[1] *And in smaller letters:* CONSULTANT TO ROYALTY. *Through this window you can glimpse a rusting iron balustrade, painted resort-green, and the bleak six o'clock sky of a disastrous English September.*

The entrance is on the other side, and leads into a sort of waiting room, partially visible when the door is open. A second door takes you from the waiting room into the streets; over it is suspended a loud bell to warn SOPHIE *if she has a client.*

The room is occupied by dusty, broken-down furniture. The most noticeable article of this is the fortune-telling table: an old chilblained[2] Victorian thing, covered with baize and placed centrally on a rotting carpet. On either side of it stand an equally bunioned Victorian chair — and the same swollen decreptitude extends to the side-board at the right and the little dressing table at the back.

There are two photographs in the room. One, on a wall, is of a huge man's hand and is clearly visible. The other — larger, and far more important to the action — stands on the side table with its back to the audience and, save for the frame, is invisible. This is a picture of Vassili, SOPHIE'S *friend. It stands as far as possible from the other important friend in her life:* Pericles[3] *the Parakeet — who is equally invisible inside his wire cage*

[1]*clarivoyante:* a person who can perceive things or events beyond the range of ordinary physical perception

[2]*chilblained:* swollen and reddened as a result of exposure to cold, used here in a humorous sense to emphasize the dilapidated condition of the furnishings

[3]*Pericles:* a great statesman of the 5th century B.C.; a rather grand name for a parakeet

by the window. The BARONESS' *life in this room alternates between these two poles, the photograph and the cage.*

As the curtain rises, the stage is apparently empty. Presently, however, we hear the sound of singing, issuing from one of the high-backed Victorian chairs facing directly upstage: "A Hard Day's Night"[4] sung in a Germanic accent. Presently a hand lifts up and throws a whole fan of playing cards irritatedly onto the table. SOPHIE *has evidently been playing patience.[5] She rises wearily and moves over to the window, through which the light comes drear and thick.*

SOPHIE *is a woman about forty-eight years old. Her appearance is rather neglected; bears the palpable signs of poverty; and is not enhanced by a German fondness for blouses and long woolen skirts. When she speaks her voice is marked by a marked, but never incomprehensible, German accent, and her delivery is mainly swift and vigorous.*

Now she stares through the window in bleak distress.

[4]"*A Hard Day's Night":* a rock song popularized by the Beatles
[5]*patience:* a card game designed for one person to play alone; usually called *solitaire* in the United States

SOPHIE. Look at it. The sea. Like they've poured out ten million cups of tea. No wonder they call it the English Channel. Not one gleam of sunlight in ten days! Not one soul out. Not one miserable holidaymaker walking, jetty to jetty. Nothing but wet sand and rusty iron—and salt on the windows. Grinmouth-on-Sea: Fairyland of the South coast! Grinmouth-on-Tea! (*To the photo.*) You hear that, Vassi, I made a joke. (*Sarcastic.*) Oh no, don't laugh. We Germans have no sense of humour, it's well known. Only the Greeks are witty, ja ja, I'm sure. . . . (*To the cage.*) Perry likes it anyway, don't you? No? . . . Are you sulking too? Well, I don't blame you. Poor little Pericles. Look, I'll tell your fortune—cheer you up? . . . Ja? . . . "You are to fly away on a long, long journey!" (*She laughs.*) . . . Only where would you go, poor little thing? Down the promenade to the chemist?[6] Up to the Fish and Chips Shop? . . . One thing is sure, you'd never find your way home again . . . Never mind—soon, guess what? . . . They'll be putting the lights on. Red and blue lights under a sky like God's used handkerchief . . .

(*Gulls and wind.*)

Beloved God, this silence! You would think someone would consult me, if only to ask should they kill themselves! . . . Do you realize there hasn't been an actual human being in this place for six days? And then it was only Mr. Bowler Hat—if you call him human! Next time he comes he'll close us: that's for certain. I haven't paid him a penny rent since June. (*Irritated.*) Oh, Vassili, what's funny *now?* I'm in real difficulties, don't you understand? I owe two months' rent, and not a client for days. Is that so amusing? . . . Sometimes I think you're going to stay a child all your life. . . . (*She walks away*

[6]*chemist:* drug store

from the photograph, then stops.) What's that? . . . How charming! I suppose you think you're talking to one of your upstart ladies from Athens. Well, let me remind you who I am. (*Sharply.*) You came here to learn history, well, so—here's some homework for you. My family was great under Maria Theresa.[7] All you had then in your so wonderful Greece were goats. Human goats, my dear, living on curd milk! Alright? . . . (*Exasperated.*) Oh, for God's sake now, are you going to sulk? Alright—join Perry. Sulks for the evening: how amusing! . . . I spend my life with a bird and a child, and I don't know which is more boring! (*She sits. Her tone becomes penitent.*) I'm sorry, Vassi: my tongue runs off with me sometimes. I know how dreary it is for you in the house. Go out and see Irina. I tell you what: why don't you invite her here tomorrow for tea? . . . (*Sweetly.*) Ja, of course I mean it! If you spent more time with people of nobility you'd know they always mean what they say. Hypocrisy is for the hoi polloi.[8]

(*The bell clashes.* SOPHIE *is startled.*) Who is it? (*Silence. Then, speaking through the crack.*) One minute, please. Would you mind waiting in the room down the corridor? I'll receive you in a moment! . . . (*Shuts the door.*) Beloved God, there are two of them! Two whole clients. I don't believe it. And on a day like this—it's incredible! . . . That's two whole pounds—think of it. Four if they take the crystal ball. (*Sitting and fixing her hair.*) Well, they're going to take the crystal ball whether they like it or not. . . . I only hope I can remember everything. One gets so rusty! . . . (*To Vassili.*) Oh, shut up, you!—that's not funny. . . . Ja, I have news for you. It takes a fraud to call a fraud: that's what I say! You were a liar in your

[7]*Maria Theresa:* ruler of Austria and Hungary in the 18th century; mother of Queen Marie Antoinette of France

[8]*hoi polloi:* the common people (Greek)

baby carriage, I'm sure of it! . . . (*Addressing herself to the plant.*) Oh, don't droop so—boring middle-class plant! . . . Now—come on everyone!—buck up! A little regality around here, please! . . . Thank you. (*She opens the door.*) I'm ready now. Come in, please, one of you!

(*Enter* FRANK.)

SOPHIE (*very winningly*).   Good afternoon. I am the Baroness Lemberg. Welcome and please sit down.

(FRANK *sits, examining her.*)

SOPHIE.   Let me give you my scale of charges, mister. One pound for cards alone. Thirty shillings for cards and palms. Two pounds for the crystal ball. The ball of course is by far the most profound. It costs just a little more, it's true—but in this world if one wants the best one has to pay for it, doesn't one? (*She gives him a ravishing smile.*)

(*He returns it, thinly, nodding Yes.*)

SOPHIE.   Good: You agree. So—you'll take the ball—ja?

(*He shakes his head: No.*)

SOPHIE.   Oh . . . Which do you want then, please?
FRANK.   None.
SOPHIE.   I don't understand
FRANK.   I like your slogan outside. "Lemberg never lies."
SOPHIE.   Thank you.
FRANK.   Is it true?
SOPHIE.   Of course.
FRANK.   Pity.
SOPHIE.   I beg your pardon.

FRANK. White lies never harm you. (*He examines the cage.*) Who's this? Your familiar?[9]

SOPHIE. Please?

FRANK. All witches have familiars, don't they? Creepy little animals they share confidences with . . . ! I suppose you'd lose all your mystic powers without him, wouldn't you?

SOPHIE (*still sitting*). Stand away from there, mister, if you please. He's a very sensitive bird. . . .

FRANK. That's alright. I'm an expert on sensitive birds.

SOPHIE (*controlling herself*). Stand away, please, I asked you.

FRANK (*lightly*). Alright . . . Alright . . . !

SOPHIE. Now, mister, what do you want from me?

FRANK. A giggle, Baroness. (*He smiles at her, unexpectedly.*)

SOPHIE. A giggle? What is that?

FRANK. A laugh. A little fun. You look like you enjoy fun yourself. I hope you do.

SOPHIE. If the situation is amusing, sir, I imagine I can manage a—what?—a giggle.

FRANK. I'm glad to hear that, Baroness. Because that's what I want to consult you about. That's what I want to create right here in this room—an amusing situation.

SOPHIE. Create?

FRANK. Exactly. For him—the boy who's come here with me. You see, him and me, we have this crazy relationship going, like, well, we kid all the time—have the laugh on each other: you know. What they call practical jokes. Some people think it's adolescent. I hope you don't.

SOPHIE. That depends.

FRANK. He's a clever kid—very impressionable. I got him here to see you by telling him you were one of the most famous fortune-tellers in the Western world. Doing a summer season for her health's sake. (*She lowers her*

[9]*familiar:* attendant spirit of a witch or magician, often taking animal form

eyes and makes modest noises.) His name's Tom, and he's lead singer with our group. We're called The White Lies. I don't suppose you've ever heard of us.

SOPHIE. On the contrary, you are singing tonight . . . at the Holiday Camp.

FRANK (*impressed*). How d'you know that?

SOPHIE (*laughing*). I saw it on the poster! You're on the same bill with the Lettuce Leaves. That's a pity: they're lousy. However, you have the Serial Numbers to top the bill, and they're excellent.

FRANK. Well, well, a fan!

SOPHIE. A vulgar word, but true. Are you any good?

FRANK. He's good. A real talent. The girls go mad for him. . . .

SOPHIE. And you? Do you sing also?

FRANK. Me? No. I'm their manager.

SOPHIE. Well!

FRANK (*staring at her*). That's my scene, really. I manage.

SOPHIE (*nervous*). How interesting.

FRANK. It can be. It's why I'm here now — to manage this little scene. . . . (*He smiles at her again.*) When we drove into Grinmouth this afternoon and I saw your sign, I thought to myself immediately: Baroness Lemberg, you're the lady for me. In your mysterious parlour I could stage the best joke ever played. I could get him so brilliantly he'd never forget it.

SOPHIE. Really?

FRANK. With your help, of course. And with someone of your fame — consultant to royalty and all that — I wouldn't expect you to do it for nothing. I'm prepared to offer quite a large fee. I'll do anything for a giggle. I really will. (*He gives his smile.*)

SOPHIE (*interested despite herself*). What kind of giggle would this be exactly, mister?

FRANK. Well, it's sort of a game, really. I'd want you to tell him his past, present and future.

SOPHIE. Well, that's my profession, after all.

FRANK. I mean precisely. I don't mean to be rude—I'm sure you're fine on your own—but with me you'd be perfect, you see? No, you don't! In this envelope are the main facts of Tom's life—the things he's told me over the past year. No one else knows them but me. Some of it's pretty lurid stuff. Unhappy childhood. Coal-mining background. Drunken father who beat him and threw his guitar on the fire. It's all here.

SOPHIE. And are you suggesting I use it?

FRANK. Well now, listen. Tom's a bit dim but he's not an idiot. You'll have your work cut out for you to convince him you're genuine. That's where the fun comes in. By the time you've finished telling back to him what's in here, he'll be fish-mouthed, I tell you!

SOPHIE. Mister, I see no joke in this. It's not funny at all.

(*Pause.*)

FRANK. To be honest, Baroness, this game isn't entirely for laughs. Mainly, but not entirely. I see it as a sort of warning game. Like I'm using it to say something to him. Do you understand? I mean, if you can get Tom to the point when he really believes you have the power to see his whole life, he'll really believe you when you see something a bit nasty in his future. It'll sort of scare him off a bit. Do you see?

SOPHIE. Scare him off what?

FRANK. A girl. I told you I was interested in sensitive birds. What are they? (*Staring at her necklace, which she is fingering.*)

SOPHIE. Greek worry beads.[10]

FRANK. Are you worried?

SOPHIE. Why should I be?

---

[10]*worry beads:* beads which are manipulated to relieve nervous tension; used particularly in Mediterranean and Middle Eastern countries

FRANK. Her name's Helen, and she's the girl in our group.
She's got a nice voice—nothing special, but it can carry
a tune and won't sour the cream. I've known her for a
couple of years, on and off. Mostly *on*, if you follow me.
In fact, these last eighteen months we've had what I'd
call a perfect working relationship.

SOPHIE. It sounds very romantic.

FRANK (*lightly*). It isn't romantic: it works, or did till he
came along. Tom the Talent, then things began to change.
Mostly with her. She found she couldn't resist all that
shy working-class charm. The downcast look . . . York-
shire murmur, very trendy.[11] . . . And when she looked
. . . he looked. I don't exactly know what's been going on
between them: nothing much I should think at the
moment. She's too timid and he's too hung up on his
loyalty to me, which he damn well should be by the way.
I gave that boy a marvelous bloody chance. And this is
his way of repaying me. He thinks I don't know, you
know. Well, it's time we undeceived him, isn't it?

SOPHIE. You are in love with this girl?

FRANK. That word's rather got rigor mortis[12] round the
edges, hasn't it? (*He laughs.*) Look: the way we are is
the way I like it. Cool . . . easy . . . nothing strenuous . . .
Anyway, if there's any leaving ever done in my life I do
it: do you see? (*Quietly.*) Can't you leave them alone?
(*She stops fiddling with the beads. He smiles.*) I suppose
that's why they're called worry beads. Because they
worry other people . . . (*She returns his smile even more
uncertainly. A pause.*) Well, let's get back to my little
game, shall we? By this time you've done his past and
present, and as far as he's concerned you're the hottest
thing since the Witch of Endor.[13] Right. Now you move

[11]*trendy:* fashionable, "with it"

[12]*rigor mortis:* the stiffness of death (Latin)

[13]*Witch of Endor:* a woman referred to in the Old Testament (Book of
Samuel) whom Saul visited to learn about the future

in for the grand finale. I want you to have a vision, Baroness. A strange, symbolic vision. Let's set it right. . . . (*Slowly.*) You look a little deeper into your crystal ball and you see pink. Shocking pink. Helen's dressing gown. Yeh, that's a good touch—very intimate. You see her wearing it, a pretty blonde girl lying on a bed. Describe the bed. Brass rails top and bottom, and above it, a picture on the wall: some droopy tart holding a lily and flopping her tresses over a stone balcony. It's called *Art Nouveau*,[14] which is French for Sentimental Rubbish. Helen loves it, of course! Anyway—use it. Establish the room. *My* room. You'll have him goggling! Now look deeper. "Good heavens, there's someone else on the bed! Why, it's you, Tom! And what are you doing, my dear? Gracious me, what a passionate creature you are. You're kissing her neck, running your fingers through her blonde hair. . . . (*Mockingly.*) Inside that thin frame of yours is a raging animal, isn't there? . . ." (*He laughs.*) I'd love to be here during that bit. They've never even held hands, I shouldn't think.

SOPHIE. Go on, please.

FRANK (*carefully*). Well now, you'll have to darken it a bit, won't you? . . . Change the mood. I'd thought of something like this. I hope you like it. . . . The door opens. A man stands there. You can't see his face but he's wearing a green corduroy jacket, with black piping round the lapels. That'll get him best, a detail like that. The lovers look up, eyes wide and guilty! Corduroy begins to move towards them. They try to rise, but they're like glued on the bed. Slow motion. Him coming on—them tangled in the sheets—trying to escape. He arrives at the foot of the bed and suddenly—his hand shoots out—like an order!—and what? Why, the girl's whole manner alters

[14]*Art Nouveau:* literally, "new art" (French); refers to a style of decoration and architecture, first popular in the 1890's, characterized by floral forms

at once. She smiles—takes the hand—allows herself to be lifted up, light as a pink feather—high over the brass rails to safety. Our Tom is left alone. . . . And now you see scare in the ball! Tom staring at them both. Them staring back, laughing. Yeh. And what's that now in her hands? Something—it looks like a metal can. Yes, a large metal can. She raises it—upends it—begins to pour from it over the sheets. And then, slowly, Corduroy raises his hands too—a matchbox in the air—strikes it— drops a match onto the bed. (*Very quietly.*) Oh, look, the orange! Soft fire like orange squirrels running over the bed, over his legs, over his arms, up onto his head . . . his head bursts into flowers! (*Gesturing dreamily.*) The whole ball becomes orange—flame whirling, raging inside the crystal, obliterating everything. Then slowly it sinks in. Glass pales from orange to pink to grey, it clears. And then you see him. Tom the Talent. Still sitting upright on my bed—mouth open, one arm raised— like a salute to death. The only difference is—the whole figure is made of ash. (*Pause.*) Interpret that vision, Baroness. Question it. "Who is this corduroy jacket?" "That's Frank," he'll say. "Well, know something, Tom. Frank and that girl are right together. Leave them alone."

SOPHIE (*softly*). Right together?

FRANK. If you come between them, it'll mean disaster for you. Maybe even death.

SOPHIE. "Right together."

FRANK. "Right together." "Belong together." What's it matter? Just so long as you scare him out of his wits.

SOPHIE. For a giggle.

FRANK. Yes, a joke, that's it. We all of us have different senses of humour, Baroness.

SOPHIE. Who am I?

FRANK. What's that?

SOPHIE. Who am I? Some silly gypsy bitch in a caravan you can buy for a couple of pounds?

FRANK.   I was thinking of more than that.
SOPHIE.   Four—five—what's the difference? It's what you
think, I can see it: the mad old fake, she'll take anything
I offer. Well, mister, let me tell you: you're dealing with
a very different kind of lady, I assure you!
FRANK.   Oh, come off it.
SOPHIE (*thrusts her hand at him*).   Look at this! It has held
the hand of a Grand Duchess in intimate spiritual com-
munion! It has held those of Governors—Ministers of
Justice—Princes of the Blood!
FRANK.   Yes, I see them now—thronging the outer salon!
SOPHIE.   Very amusing. Look, mister, I'm not mad, you
know; there are no Duchesses out there, I know that.
Mad spinsters, stinking of mothballs, and old red men
with gin in their eyes, begging me to predict just one
horse race to make them rich for life. Rubbish people,
all of them, boring me to death with their second-rate
dreams. Nevertheless, I make adjustment. Other years—
other tears! I have to spend my life now casting prophetic
pearls before middle-class swine. But one thing always:
I may hate them, but I do not cheat them. *Lemberg never
lies.*
FRANK.   Is that how you think of me, Baroness? One of the
swine?
SOPHIE (*frightened*).   Of course not.
FRANK.   I hope not. I really do hope not.
SOPHIE.   I merely say . . .
FRANK.   What do you merely say?
SOPHIE.   That if you think I betray my art for a few pounds,
you are badly mistaken.
FRANK.   Would I be equally mistaken if it was twenty-five
pounds?
SOPHIE.   Twenty-five?
FRANK.   As you said, if you want the best, you've got to pay
for it.

SOPHIE.   I don't understand. Why don't you just tell him to leave her alone?

FRANK.   If I do anything, Baroness, I do it with style. My own style. You do your job right, this'll work a treat.

SOPHIE.   He may guess.

FRANK.   And even if he does—he'll still get the message. What's your answer? . . . Look—we've kept him waiting long enough. Yes or no?

SOPHIE.   Disgusting. It's disgusting! . . .

FRANK.   Twenty-five quid.[15]

SOPHIE.   Alright!

FRANK.   A sensible lady. I'll go and fetch him.

SOPHIE. (*disturbed*).   No—wait!

FRANK.   What?

SOPHIE.   Give me a minute, please, I must learn this. . . . (*She picks up the envelope.*)

FRANK.   Alright. I'll keep him waiting, tell him how great you were, reading me. But hurry it up.

SOPHIE.   Ja, ja . . . I'll call out when I'm ready.

FRANK.   OK. (*He goes to the door.*) *No* tricks now, Baroness. I would hate you to try keeping that money without earning it. When he comes out of this room I want to see scare in his face, like I've never ever seen it. (*He goes out. She stares after him in horror.*)

SOPHIE.   Beloved God! Beloved God, beloved God, beloved God! . . . (*Shouting at the photo.*) Ja, I know, he's a nut— one more horror, so what? You've seen them before. The world is full of perverts. Business is business, for God's sake. And there's almost half the rent here—just for ten minutes' work! Anyway, what's it matter? He'll be another horror, just you see! A little backstreet nothing who wants to be a singer because he can't do a decent day's work! He'll deserve it. . . . Everyone deserves it! Look, everyone cheats a little, my darling, even

[15]*quid:* British slang for a pound (about $2.35)

your Greek witches. What do you think your famous oracle at Delphi[16] was doing?—one silly cow sitting in a lot of smoke, saying exactly what she was paid to say! Anyway, I tell you once more and that's the end. It is the duty of the aristocracy to maintain itself, no matter what! Now kindly leave me to study these! (*She writes on the fan.*) "Born 1945 . . . Coal mines . . . Mother dead. Father drunkard . . . Guitar." Now! (*She tears open the envelope.*) Look! Do you see? I bet you've never seen so much money in all your life! Think what it means! More Beatle records, more little hats like you were starting the Russian Revolution! And next Sunday, if you are good, a taxi—and not a lousy bus! What do you say? . . . Alright, go to her! Always the same threat—the same threat. If that's the best you can manage—then go to her. See if I care! (*Opening the door.*) Misters! (*Returning.*) Go—go—go—go!

(FRANK *returns with* TOM.)

FRANK.   Mrs. Lemberg, this is my friend Tom. Tom, this is the Baroness Lemberg. The greatest fortune-teller in the world.

SOPHIE (*modestly*).   Please! . . . How do you do?

TOM.   Hallo.

FRANK.   I've been telling him how incredible you are. I hope you don't mind.

SOPHIE.   Such powers as I have, mister, I regard as a gift from the Lord God.

FRANK.   Just what I was telling him. It's almost a religious experience, being read by you.

SOPHIE.   I do my best to convey the truth as I see it.

---

[16]*oracle at Delphi:* shrine of Apollo in the ancient Greek world where a priestess was consulted for prophecies

FRANK. And lady, you certainly saw it! I was wondering
    actually if I could sit over here and listen to you read him.
    I'd be very quiet.
SOPHIE. Oh, no—no. I'm afraid that's quite out of the ques-
    tion. Your emanations would be very disturbing.
FRANK. Couldn't you just ignore my emanations?
SOPHIE. I appreciate your enthusiasm, mister. People of art
    are always nourished by enthusiasm. All the same, I have
    a basic rule. One client: one set of emanations.
TOM. Dead right!
FRANK. Very well.
SOPHIE. May I suggest you go for a promenade? When you
    return in fifteen minutes, you will be refreshed and your
    friend, I hope, satisfied.
FRANK. Fine. (*To* TOM.) Good luck, then. Now that's silly
    to say. She's gonna tell ya if you got any or not.—But I
    hope ya have.
SOPHIE. So. Sit down, please. (*He sits.*) Such a flatterer,
    your friend.
TOM. No, I think he means it. I've never seen him so
    excited. He's not easily impressed, I can tell you.
SOPHIE. Nor you.
TOM. Me?
SOPHIE. You have disbelieving eyes.
TOM. Oh, yeah?
SOPHIE (*quickly*). You will take the crystal ball of course!
TOM. Will I?
SOPHIE. Of course, my dear. It's more profound. And I can
    see you deserve the most profound measures.
TOM. Thank you!
SOPHIE (*getting the ball*). You're a musician. (*He is
    startled.*) Oh, don't worry! Remember, I've just read your
    friend. I presume you are in the group he manages. It's
    an easy guess, after all. (*She sets the ball down on the
    table and uncovers it.*) There. Just a ball of glass. Except,
    of course, that nothing is *just* anything. Give me some-

thing you wear, please. A handkerchief will do. Thank
you. You've very pale. Why?

TOM.   No sun, I suppose.

SOPHIE (*sitting*).   Yes, that can do it . . . Every day I look at
the sea and hate it all over again. Not once this year have
I seen it blue. I think: that's not a sea—it's a gutter
between here and France. Hang your coat up: you're
here for a few minutes, after all.

TOM (*rising*).   Thanks.

SOPHIE.   You like winter best, ja?

TOM.   Could be.

SOPHIE.   You're cautious with me. You have no need.

TOM.   Well, Frank told me not to say anything.

SOPHIE.   I think we can discuss the weather without you
thinking me a fraud.

TOM (*smiling*).   Yeah, I think so, too. You're right. I love
days like this. And seaside towns, too, but only out of
season. When no one's there.

SOPHIE.   Like here *in* season.

TOM.   Oh, much worse! I mean, deserted. Dead, dead of
winter, I tell ya. . . . I went to Herne Bay last March. It
was so cold the rims of your ears felt like they were being
gnawed through. The tide was out and there was snow
on the seaweed.

SOPHIE.   Snow?

TOM.   Yes, it popped when you walked on it. All the sea-
gulls were sitting in those little shelters that are for
people in the summertime. They looked like rows of old
convalescents, huddled down in their coat collars. (*She
stares at him. Wind, outside the window.*)

SOPHIE.   Mister, I do not feel so well this evening. I'm afraid
I won't be able to read you.

TOM.   You won't?

SOPHIE.   I have a headache coming. I feel it. In a minute it
will be very painful.

TOM.   How do you know?

SOPHIE.   Migraine[17] is one of the penalties of divination.[18]

TOM.   Oh, yeah?

SOPHIE.   You'll have to go. You can wait for your friend in the room down the corridor.

TOM.   Yes. Well . . . goodbye.

SOPHIE.   Ja. (*He takes his coat and goes to the door. He hesitates.*) You want something?

TOM.   No.

SOPHIE.   Er . . . Your handkerchief.

TOM.   Oh! Yes! (*He comes back to claim it. She hands it to him.*)

SOPHIE.   Can that be only no sun—your paleness?

TOM.   What else?

SOPHIE.   You think I'm a fake. But somewhere in the back of your head, as you walked here tonight, you were thinking something. Well?

TOM.   Well, I suppose what you always think about fortune-tellers. You read stories of people going in for a laugh, coming out changed for life.

SOPHIE.   You want to be changed for life?

TOM.   Sort of, yeah.

SOPHIE.   Sit down again

TOM.   No, I'll be off now. . . . I think I'm a bit mad sometimes: honest . . .

SOPHIE.   Sit, please.

TOM.   No, really—

SOPHIE (*sharply*).   Look, mister, what kind of a gentleman are you? You come here to ask my advice. I settle myself to give it. Then without a word of respect you turn your back and go!

TOM.   You *told* me to go!

SOPHIE.   Don't argue with a Baroness! Why do people know nothing of breeding?

[17]*migraine:* a severe, recurrent headache
[18]*divination:* foretelling future events

TOM. I'm sorry—

SOPHIE. Then sit! (*Bewildered,* TOM *hangs up his coat again.*) Look, mister. Just for a giggle—you with your paleness—me with my headache—why don't we explore a little the possibility of changing your life? Alright?

TOM (*sitting*). Alright.

SOPHIE. I'll tell you a little your past, a little your present: then your future. (*She stares into the ball.*) Mmm. It's very disturbed. There's much confusion . . . 1945. You were born in 1945?

TOM (*surprised*). Yes!

SOPHIE. It's very ritualistic, the ball. Often first it gives the date of birth, then the place . . . Ja! Exactly! . . . Ah! I see now a place. A dirty street. A little narrow house: working-class. Somewhere in the North, maybe . . . In the background a wheel turning. A coal mine! Ja—a coal village. (TOM *reacts to this, very startled.*) I see I'm not too far from the truth. There's no woman in the house. Your mother is dead, Ja? . . . Your father still alive. At least I see a man in working clothes—bad face—brutal face! . . . He ill-treated you? (TOM *stares at her, rivetted.*) And what's this now? I see a child. A little pale face—pale! Eyes frightened. Oh, mister, no! Such a frightened face! . . . He ill-treated you? (*She stares at him. He looks quickly away.*) Beat you, Ja? . . . I must look closer here. . . . What's this now? A fire. On it I see something, burning.

TOM (*nervously*). What? . . .

SOPHIE. A guitar. Can it be a guitar? . . . What is it? A symbol perhaps of your music talent? (TOM *rises, terrified.*)

TOM. You saw *that?* . . .

SOPHIE. Very plain.

TOM. No—it's impossible. It *is!*

SOPHIE. I'm sorry. It was absolutely clear.

TOM. You can't. Just—not! . . . My head—it's here!

SOPHIE. And for me, it's there. You can lock nothing away, my dear. Time that happened once for you, happens now for me. . . . Why did he do that? To stop you from being a musician? . . . To hurt you? . . . (TOM, *who has been walking up and down the room, suddenly stops, and stands rigid, struck by something.*) What is it? Perhaps I should stop now?

TOM. No . . . Go on. . . .

SOPHIE. You are upset.

TOM. Doesn't matter.

SOPHIE. I stop.

TOM (*urgently*). No! What else do you see?

(SOPHIE *stares at him, then returns to the ball.*)

SOPHIE. Ah: it's better now. Happiness I think is coming. I see a dot of bright pink, moving towards me. It's a girl. On her a pink dressing gown. Very pretty: a blonde girl. You know her?

TOM. Go on.

SOPHIE. Now I see you. She is running to you—you reach out to stop her—but no: she runs right past you. Beloved God!

TOM. What?

SOPHIE. There's someone else. A man. I can't see his face. He wears a green jacket in corduroy. He puts out his hand. She takes it. They walk away together—leaving you alone.

TOM. Alone.

SOPHIE. Ja. The alone of alone. More alone than I've ever seen it.

TOM (*dead*). So that's the message. "Alone."

SOPHIE. Does this make sense to you, mister?

TOM. Oh, yes. It makes sense. It makes sense. . . . (*More to himself.*) What a way to do it!

SOPHIE. To do what, please?

TOM. What a crazy way! To arrange all this—just to let me know—I suppose he set it up as a little joke!

SOPHIE. Who, please?

TOM. Then it was a few quid on the side.

SOPHIE. What d'you mean?

TOM. He's crazy!

SOPHIE. Young mister, are you suggesting I've been bribed?

TOM. No, I'm not suggesting it, I'm *saying* it.

SOPHIE. How dare you? How absolutely bloody dare you?

TOM. Because I absolutely know, that's why. There's only one person I've ever told about my childhood—and that's him.

SOPHIE. My dear, to a professional eye like mine, truth does not have to be told. It is evident.

TOM. I dare say. And what if it isn't the truth?

SOPHIE. What?

TOM (*embarrassed*). What if it's a zonking great lie? *Like every word of that story.*

SOPHIE. I don't believe it. . . .

TOM. Well, it's true.

SOPHIE. Impossible. You say this to discredit me.

TOM. Come on, why should I do that?

SOPHIE. Look, mister, what I see, I see. Lemberg never lies.

TOM (*gently*). No, well, I'm afraid I do. . . . The bit with the guitar I invented as late as last week.

SOPHIE. You mean your father is not a miner?

TOM. No. He's a very nice accountant, living up in Hoylake.

SOPHIE. And your mother isn't dead?

TOM. Not in the biological sense, no. She likes her game of golf and gives bridge parties every Wednesday.

SOPHIE. But your accent . . .

TOM (*letting it drop*). I'm afraid that's as put on as everything else. I mean, there's no point changing your background if you're going to keep your accent, is there?

SOPHIE. Beloved God! You mean to say . . . you live your whole life like this. One enormous lie from morning to night?

TOM.   Yes, I suppose I do.

SOPHIE.   Unimaginable.

TOM.   Does it worry you?

SOPHIE.   Doesn't it worry *you?*

TOM.   Yes, sometimes, I guess. But not all the time. I've gotten used to it now. I regard the whole thing as a sort of . . .

SOPHIE.   White lie?

TOM.   Yes—that's good. A white lie!

SOPHIE.   But why? Why? *Why* in heaven's name?

TOM *(with energy)*.   Because it's an image—and that's what people want! That's all they can cope with—images! And in the pop music world it's got to be working class: I soon found out. No one believes you can sing with the authentic voice of the people if you're the son of an accountant.

SOPHIE.   Are you serious?

TOM.   Believe me, Baroness: I've worked it out. Look—everyone makes images—*everyone.* It's like no one can look at anyone direct. The way I see it, the whole world's made up of images—images talking at images—that's what makes it all impossible!

SOPHIE.   And do your parents know you've worked it out like this? Disowning them completely?

TOM.   No. But they might as well. They've virtually disowned me, after all. Dad calls me "minstrel boy" now every time I go home, and mother has a whole bit with her bridge club that I'm in London "studying" music. Studying is a better image than singing in clubs. She can see herself as the mother of a student. Both of them are talking about themselves of course, not me. And I don't blame them. That's what I'm doing, too. All of us . . .

SOPHIE.   What a complicated young mister you are.

TOM.   Do you think I'm a bit mad?

SOPHIE.   Because you choose to be somebody else? No, that's not mad. That's not mad. Not entirely.

TOM. I've never told anyone this before. You must have very special powers.

SOPHIE. Can you really believe that after the way I told your fortune?

TOM. Well, you were pretending then.

SOPHIE. If I were any good, would I need to pretend? Oh, come: it's me to be embarrassed, not you. It serves me right for playing silly games. Let's have a drink—what do you say? Cheer us both up!

TOM. I think it's more than a game to him.

SOPHIE. Why?

TOM. Well, he's always pulling gags, but he's never gone this far before. He can be really marvelous when he wants to. And then there's another side of him—like this . . . Alright, he's guessed about me and Helen—this is still a pretty weird way of telling me, isn't it? Is that all he asked you to say to me? That I was alone.

SOPHIE. Mister, please have a drink. I always take a glass of *retsina*[19] about this hour in the afternoon. It tastes like gasoline, but it can be very encouraging.

TOM. Thank you. I think I will.

SOPHIE. My husband would never let me drink when he was alive. Mind you, he managed a luxury hotel—so he had to be careful.

TOM. It's so strange his coming here like this. What does he think's going on between Helen and me?

SOPHIE. You feel very strongly about this girl?

TOM. Yes.

SOPHIE. And she about you?

TOM. That's part of it.

SOPHIE. Are you afraid of him?

TOM. I don't know.

SOPHIE. Is she?

TOM. Maybe, I think so, yes.

[19]*retsina:* a Greek wine flavored with resin

SOPHIE.   Well, that makes three of us.

TOM.   You don't know what it can be like sometimes in that house.

SOPHIE.   You all three live together?

TOM.   Yes. Me upstairs, them down. I wake up every morning thinking of her in his bed. When I come downstairs, he's lying there smiling at me.

SOPHIE.   Why don't you leave?

TOM.   I can't.

SOPHIE.   Why not?

TOM.   I can't. Isn't it incredible? And every morning I get up and play that part: the coal miner's son frying up breakfast for three, and avoiding her eyes—her great green eyes.

SOPHIE.   You mean you haven't told her the truth?

TOM.   Why should I? The real me, as they say, isn't a wow with women. Look! Truth's the last thing she wants. She's "in love"—that's what she calls it! She's in love with a working-class boy—even though he doesn't exist. And I'm in love with feelings I see in her eyes—and I know they don't exist. I tell you that's what it's all about— images making noises at images: love—love—love— love—(*Pause.*) But God, you should see those eyes. . . .

SOPHIE.   Ja?

TOM.   They're amazing! Like you said, the alone of alone. Well, these are the green of green.

SOPHIE.   Eyes. It's always the eyes.

TOM.   I don't know why I'm telling you all this.

SOPHIE.   Green or black, it's always the same. (*Rises.*)

TOM.   I can stretch out quite still for hours, and imagine I'm lying at the bottom of her eyes.

SOPHIE.   With me it was black. Immense black, like the olives. He said to me once: "A Greek proverb for you, Sophie. 'Black eyes are the olives at the feast of love.'" He made it up, of course.

TOM.   Who?

SOPHIE. Someone who was lied to. (*She indicates photograph.*)

TOM. He's got a marvelous face.

SOPHIE. Oh yes, white—quite white—with eyes stuck in it so huge. I remember the first time I saw him I thought: "Beloved God, he's dying!" He was paler even than you. He stood on my doorstep with a little suitcase in his hand, full of white shirts and a history of the Tudor kings. He was so polite and thin—like a breathing matchstick— like you—and he bowed so formal. "My name is Vassili. I am a student from Greece. Do you have a room, please? I regret I cannot pay more than three pounds."

TOM. When was this?

SOPHIE. Five years ago. I was a landlady then in Notting Hill.[20] My husband had died penniless: I had to do something besides tell fortunes. Oh, well, other years, other tears. He was twenty-six years old, but still exactly like a child. Everything he felt, he gave you, like a present— shoved at you, a joy now, another joy, all day. He used to come into my room in the evening to watch the television. Always so neat and careful. "Excuse me, is there rock and roll entertainment tonight?" He was such a fan —he taught me everything: what groups were good or lousy, Top Ten, Pick of the Pops! Secretly I liked it, but it was vulgar to admit to. After all, I was the Baroness Lemberg. His own family was middle class. They sent him what they could, but it wasn't much. In a while I stopped asking him for rent . . . and he spent the money instead on pink sweets, yellow beads, tributes to his lady. He lived for dancing and history, he was intoxicated by history! And because I was an aristocrat, I was supposed to know all about it. Every Sunday he went on a bus up to Windsor Castle, down to St. Paul's Cathedral. And what he never knew was every Saturday night I

[20]*Notting Hill:* a district of London

would sit up, secretly memorizing the facts—speaking them next day almost yawning. Tourism, after all, is a little common, my dear . . . typically I never looked at the buildings themselves. Only their reflections in his eyes. So one bright spring day, I saw St. Paul's—two tiny little cathedrals swimming in salt water—and I leaned forward and kissed them, and called him *"Mein liebe"*[21] for the first time. (*Pause.*) Can it be you have powers for me, too—to make me say things? . . . to make me see . . .

TOM. Go on.

SOPHIE. All along there was a fiancée. Maybe that's why I chose him to begin with. Her name was Irina—a slouchy little thing, living with her parents in London. She had been chosen for him by the two fathers, who were best friends. Such arrangements are common with Greeks; he was allowed to take her out for walks in the afternoon, but nothing more for two years, till he had finished studies and could marry. Over the months, just because he was forbidden to touch her, he started to whine. "Oh, Sophie, I need her so bad. Help me, help me, help me." And I—because it was so vulgar, you see, to show jealousy —I said to him—

TOM. Invite her home.

SOPHIE. Ja. "Secretly to your room, in the afternoon. If there are any questions, I shall have been chaperone."

TOM. And she came, of course.

SOPHIE. *Every week!*   ❜

TOM. And you?

SOPHIE. I served them tea. . . . Into their room with my little tray. "Hello, Irina: How are you? How well you look. How's your good father?" And underneath, the hate—I, who had never felt hate in my life before, wasted its first flood on her; a timid little nothing who never harmed me. Oh, that hate. Burning me so I would cry

---

[21]*mein liebe:* my dear (German)

out to the wallpaper on the stairs—and then into them immediately—smiling, holding out chocolate biscuits. "Oh, Vassili, don't grab them like that. It's so rude at a lady's tea table!" I was you—frying your breakfasts!

TOM. Yes!

SOPHIE. Oh, mister, what pain comes when you start protecting white lies! (*The lights spring on. She moves towards the window, talking.*) Dishonest pain. Pain not earned. Pain like an escape from real pain . . . You know the terrible thing? Even now part of me wishes him unhappy, wherever he is, back in Greece. But then part of me wished *me* unhappy, and who can explain *that?* Always it escapes me. Though now and then, staring here across the water, I think I see the pattern. Then no. Like wrinkles on the skin of the sea, a cold wind rushes up and it dissolves. (*She stares out of the window.*)

TOM. What happened?

SOPHIE. One day he brought me a present. Him—in his little cage. He said: "Here, Sophie, this is Pericles. In Greece he is known as the bird of truth. No one must ever lie in his presence!" He made that up too, naturally. "What do you mean," I say to Vassi, "no one must lie?" He sits down, giggling. "Sophie, I was talking to Miss Steinberg, that friend who knew you in Germany before the war. She says you were not a Baroness at all. You were a Jewish girl from a poor family: a refugee who married a horrid Englishman who kept a pub. Not a grand hotel, like you said: a pub. And you were not a manageress in a great office. You were only a barmaid."

TOM. He made that up too?

(*Pause.*)

SOPHIE. No . . . No . . . Now I am ice all over. "Darling," I say, "it is time we talked. The two years are almost over. Our relationship is not fair to Irina. You must think of your marriage." He smiles back—giving me his present, so happy! "I have thought, Sophie, and I tell you I do not wish to marry her. I cannot love someone chosen for me by my father." And now I the Baroness speak for the last time. "That's nonsense, Vassili. You are both young. You are both Greek. You are right together. If you wish to make me happy—marry her."

TOM. No!

SOPHIE. Right together. Very, very right together!

TOM. But why?

SOPHIE. Because it was in his face—don't you see?

TOM. What?

SOPHIE. Love! . . . Not despising! Not anger with me! Just love, smiling in those black eyes. Now he could know me. Now we were equal! . . . (*Pause.*) Intolerable.

TOM (*understanding*). Yes.

SOPHIE. You want advice from the witch by the sea? Dare to love, yourself. Go to your girl. Tell her all your lies! She'll laugh, I promise you.

TOM. And Frank? Will he laugh, too?

SOPHIE. What does it matter? You've never really been afraid of him. Only of yourself.

TOM. Yes, maybe! But still—

SOPHIE. What?

TOM. I owe him everything. When he found me singing in a Chelsea pub,[22] I didn't have a penny to my name. He founded the group . . . he set me up . . . What kind of thanks is it to steal his girl?

SOPHIE. Mister, do you want to know what your friend really wanted me to see for you in that crystal ball? Him and your girl burning you to ashes. His word—ashes. . . . I'm sorry.

TOM. He said that?—You wouldn't lie. Not about this.

---

[22]*Chelsea pub:* a bar or saloon in an area of London known for its Bohemian atmosphere, somewhat like Greenwich Village in New York City

(*The bell sounds.*)

SOPHIE.   No, I wouldn't lie to you. Go to her now, before the concert, take a deep breath—and tell her everything. I'll deal with him. Go now! . . . I said you had disbelieving eyes. It's not true. There is still a little hope in them. Don't let it fade out, mister, like the sky into the sea. All grey.

TOM.   Goodbye, Baroness.

SOPHIE.   Sophie!

TOM.   Sophie.

(FRANK *enters.*)

FRANK.   Tom: It worked, didn't it???
(*Pause.*) What happened, then?

(TOM *silently leaves.*)

SOPHIE.   I read his fortune.

FRANK (*excitedly*).   I bet you did! Come on now—give me every detail, right from the beginning. Don't leave anything out!

SOPHIE.   Mister, I'm afraid things have not gone as planned.

FRANK.   What d'you mean?

SOPHIE.   Your friend is more complicated than you think.

FRANK.   Why? What happened?

SOPHIE.   I don't know.

FRANK.   Meaning?

SOPHIE.   It grew dark; the lights came on.

FRANK.   Look, Baroness, I'm in no mood for games. (*Her gaity deserts her.*) Where was he off to in such a hurry?

SOPHIE.   Mister, would you like a drink? Look, maybe I tell your fortune . . . for free!

FRANK.   Where was he going, Baroness?

SOPHIE.   To his concert, naturally!

FRANK. I don't think so. . . . You're lying, aren't you?

SOPHIE. No.

FRANK. Oh, yes, you're lying. . . . There's cheat in this room. I can smell it. It's hanging in the air like smoke. . . . Lady, you cheated me.

SOPHIE. No! I did exactly what you said. I earned my money!

FRANK (*disbelieving*). Lady, you cheated me! . . . He's gone off to—tell Helen, hasn't he? To tell Helen about all this.

SOPHIE. Of course not.

FRANK. To show me up in front of her—to show me up—to show me up. . . . You cheating old cow!!!

SOPHIE. Cheat? *Me*—cheat! Me! After what you asked me to do! . . . Fantastic! . . . (*Furious.*) Listen, mister—Mr. Cool and Easy—nobody ever leaves you, do they? Well, news for you! Bloody marvelous news for you. They do. And they will! Tonight! (*Pause.*) You've lost her. But then, did you ever really have her?

FRANK (*quietly*). Well, well, well. Who'd have guessed it? Here I was thinking Lemberg may be a bore, but inside that frumpy old bag is a real witch—and all the time she's only a provincial pocketbook psychologist. I think we really have to do something about this cheating, don't we? We have to stop you showing people up like you do. . . . (*He looks at the bird.*) I'm afraid we're going to have to take your license away, dear. No witch—no familiar. That seems fair, doesn't it? (*Moving to the cage, he grabs the bird in the cage.*)

SOPHIE. No!

FRANK (*taking the bird from the cage, walks to the window, which he opens; we hear the wind*). A bird for a bird,[23] (*He throws the bird out the window. Pause. He moves to her.*)

SOPHIE (*icy*). I'm afraid you do not frighten me, sir. I told Pericles one hour ago he would be going on a long journey. Perhaps I am not so much a fake, after all.

[23]*a bird for a bird:* a play on words because *bird* is British slang for girl

FRANK (*ironically*).   Very brave, Baroness. Very brave and gallant. Give me the money.

SOPHIE.   I am not a Baroness. My name is Sophie Harburg. And maybe I am not a witch—but I can still read you, mister! . . . for free! (*Slowly she sits, looking at him.*) You want your money? Very well. (*She deals the cards.*) Five of pounds: card of vanity. Five of pounds: card of cruelty. Five of pounds: card of stupidity. Five of pounds: card of fantasy. Five of pounds: card of a loveless life! It's all there in the cards, mister. . . . Harburg never lies. (*She picks up photograph, looks at it and drops it gently to the floor.*) Never.

Curtain

FOR DISCUSSION

1. Why is the playwright so careful and explicit in describing the scene of the play—the living room of the Baroness Lemberg? What single effect is he trying to convey? Do you feel he has done this effectively?

2. The playwright indicates in his introductory directions that "the Baroness' life in this room alternates between two poles, the photograph and the cage." What does this suggest to us about the circumstances and the frame of mind of the character?

3. Incidentally, the people who see a play presented on the stage do not normally read the stage directions. Why, then, does the playwright bother to specify the highly circum- scribed nature of the Baroness' life? To whom is this informa- tion directed? What are they supposed to do about it?

4. The long introductory speech by Sophie serves as exposition to set up the basic situation. What do we learn from this speech about the past of the character? About her present predicament?

5. The playwright's aim in this long opening monologue is not merely to give necessary information but to establish a psy- chological background for the events to follow. In your opinion has he been successful in each of these aims?

6. We know that in real life people do not usually go about delivering long, involved, and coherent statements addressed to a bird and a photograph in an otherwise unoccupied room. Yet the reader or spectator is probably quite willing to believe that Sophie is behaving in this way. How do you explain this "willing suspension of disbelief"?

7. Frank soon tells Sophie that he wants her to create an "amusing situation" and a "little fun." Yet the spectator or reader suspects strongly that his purpose is not as innocent as these words would suggest. How is the playwright able to convey this without any overt indication (at first) that something sinister is afoot?

8. As Frank continues to speak, he confirms the suspicion that he wants Sophie's help in accomplishing something "a bit nasty." Trace the steps in the dialogue that reveal his

intention. Do you agree that it is more effective dramatically to expose his plan in this gradual, fragmented manner than by a single coherent speech at the outset?

9. What is Sophie's first reaction when she begins to understand Frank's proposal? What causes her to change her mind? Do you think that this is psychologically true to life?

10. When Sophie asks Frank if he is in love with Helen, he answers, "That word's got rigor mortis around the edges, hasn't it?" What does he mean by this? What does this suggest about his personality and values? Conversely, what is suggested about Sophie by the fact that she chooses to frame the question in this way?

11. Sophie speaks of having served "Governors—Ministers of Justice—Princes of the Blood." But she is reduced, she says, to "Rubbish people . . . boring me to death with their second-hand dreams." Thus, at a given moment she combines fantasy with unsparing realism. Which is the fantasy, and which is the realism? Is this inconsistency credible? When she speaks of her glorious past, is she seriously trying to deceive Frank? Or, rather, is she playing a sort of game and in a sense deceiving herself?

12. In the speech on page 435, in which Sophie tries to justify what she is about to do, she addresses the photograph of Vassili. But at this point in the play we really do not know who Vassili is, or what part he has played in Sophie's life. Is this deliberate ambiguity dramatically effective? Does the lack of knowledge annoy you, or does it heighten interest by creating a desire to know more about this figure from the past? Does the playwright finally resolve the tension created in this way by giving more information about Vassili?

13. The initial dealings between Sophie and Tom are emotionally confused. He disconcerts her by telling her something about his frame of mind. She tells him to leave, then calls him back and reproves him for going. He indicates skepticism about her powers, but at the same time admits that he wants to be changed for life, and suggests that she may be able to do it. What is the playwright trying to achieve by this counterpoint of indecision? What is he telling us about the two characters? Is the interchange dramatically effective?

14. How does Tom become aware that the whole incident is a hoax, set up by his friend Frank to further some devious scheme of his own? How does Sophie react to this revelation?

15. Why does Tom say to Sophie, even after she has been revealed as a fraud and a tool of Frank, "You must have very special powers"?

16. Sophie and Tom, brought together in this strange emotional relationship, discover that in spite of all the differences of age, background, and sex, they have been playing essentially the same role toward the people they love. How would you characterize this role? Find the speech or speeches in which Sophie advises Tom to break free of this role and to "dare to love."

17. At first Tom is reluctant to follow this advice. Why? How does Sophie convince him that his scruples are unjustified?

18. How does Frank react when he learns that Sophie has cheated him? Why does he free the bird Pericles? What is Sophie's comment on this action?

19. When Sophie returns the pound notes to Frank, she deals them out like playing cards. Why does she do this? At this time, in what sense does she tell Frank's fortune? Do you think that her prediction is valid?

20. In her final speech, Sophie repeats her slogan, but this time she makes it *"Harburg* never lies." What is the significance of the change of name?

21. A critic has called Sophie a "challenging, almost classically proportioned role for a leading woman." Do you agree? Why? Do you know of any actress (on the screen, television, etc.) who you think could handle this difficult role effectively? Explain.

22. Do you find the ending of the play depressing, or rather on the whole upbeat and satisfying? Has Sophie been defeated, or has she won a sort of victory? Explain your answer.

23. If you don't like the ending, can you suggest some other way in which the playwright might have terminated it more effectively?

24. Tom says to Sophie, "The way I see it, the whole world's made up of images, images talking at images. . . ." Does the final outcome justify this view of life? Or does the playwright have another message for us? If so, what is it?

25. Each of the three characters in the play has been depending on a lie or series of lies to deal with the difficulties of life. Explain the deception in each case. What happens to these lies by the end of the play? What is the significance of this?

FOR COMPOSITION

1. Consider the expression "white lies." It suggests that lying at times may be harmless, or even admirable. Do you agree with this? Or do you feel that lying (including lying to oneself) is essentially destructive and self–defeating? Discuss this question in a composition. Make it as short or as long as you need to express your ideas.

2. Several times Sophie quotes the proverb, "Other years, other tears." The attitude toward life that this expression suggests may be natural for a person in Sophie's circumstances, but this is not to say that it is suitable for everyone. Discuss this question in a short composition. Explain clearly what the proverb means, why Sophie feels this way, and whether you accept or reject this philosophy for yourself.

3. In the modern world, we are much concerned with *images.* The word itself constantly comes up in connection with politics, the communication and entertainment media, business and advertising, and other areas of life. *White Lies* has something to say about image-making, as opposed to a frank assessment and acceptance of reality. Perhaps the play has given you some new ideas about this matter. Write a theme entitled "Images and Reality." Try to consider questions such as the following: Why are we so much concerned with images in the modern world? Why has the very word become so popular in this special sense? Is image-making an out-and-out fraud, or may it be a helpful way of handling or influencing reality? Can the creation and manipulation of images be used for a good purpose as well as a bad one?

4. As of the date of writing, *White Lies* has not been produced for television in either England or the United States. Yet, you will probably agree that with effective casting and direction, this play has the potential to make an unusually compelling TV drama.

Imagine that you are a literary agent, and you control the rights to *White Lies*. You are trying to sell it to a major television producer who has not yet had the chance to see it or read it. Prepare a letter or memorandum in which you give this producer relevant information about *White Lies* and explain why you think it is a natural for TV. Your aim should not be to summarize the play (although you may want to give details about this) but to emphasize the values of the play and its potential appeal for a mass audience.

An Outline
of English Drama

This outline is intended to give a brief overview of English drama from its beginning to the twentieth century. In some instances, as in the case of movements, dates are inclusive and approximate. At other times, there may be an overlapping of dates. There is no connection between the classical drama of Greece and Rome and the beginnings of English drama. As is shown, English drama begins in the Church.

9th Century: A simple play, performed at Easter, called the *Quem Quaeritis (Whom seek ye?)*, involves the angel at the tomb of Jesus and the three Marys. This play, performed in the Church and in Latin, is the beginning of English drama.

11th Century: A group of plays, called pastores, are performed during the Christmas season in imitation of the Easter drama.

458

12th Century: Plays in honor of saints, called *miracle plays*, are performed at various times during the year.

12th Century: Two manuscripts, the *Shrewsbury Fragments* and the Anglo-Norman *Mystere d'Adam*, show two important developments: (a) the vernacular instead of Latin is beginning to be used in drama, and (b) drama is being written to be performed outside of the Church.

14th Century: During the celebration of the Feast of Corpus Christi, established in 1311, many plays, called *craft cycle plays*, are performed—all out-of-doors.

15th Century: Probably deriving from the impact of medieval sermons and the medieval preoccupation with allegory, plays called *morality plays* develop. Written to be performed on an outdoor stage, these plays are best exemplified by the play called *Everyman*.

Late 15th Century: The English *folk play* develops. The figure Robin Hood is the hero of some of these plays. Some folk plays, such as the *St. George Plays*, are designed to be performed indoors in the homes of nobility during the Christmas season. Moving the drama back indoors is an important development, leading eventually to the first public theater.

Late 15th Century: A type of play called an *interlude* develops designed to be performed indoors between the parts of a feast. One such interlude, *Fulgens and Lucres*, was performed at Christmas, 1497. It is the first English play to have a non-religious, romantic theme.

16th Century: With the Renaissance, English drama becomes influenced by classical elements. Comedy is heavily influenced by the Latin comedies of Plautus and Terence, and English tragedy—through the writings of a Roman named Seneca—becomes influenced by the works of the Greek tragedians Aeschylus, Sophocles, and Euripides.

1572: A law is passed in which actors are listed among those persons to be punished as vagabonds. This is instrumental in causing actors to seek the patronage of the nobility; thus, theatrical companies were formed and often named after their patrons. (The company to which Shakespeare belonged was known by the following names: Earl of Leicester's Men, Lord Strange's Men, Earl of Derby's Men, Lord Chamberlain's Men, and, after 1603, King's Men.)

1576: The first public theater, called The Theater, is built on the outskirts of London.

1642: Because of opposition, mainly religious, Parliament, on September 2, passes a law making illegal the performance of drama in public. This act is known as the Suppression of the Drama Act.

1660: Charles II comes to the throne, and once more drama is made legal. However, the right to perform public plays is given in the form of patents to two men only — Sir William D'Avenant as head of the Duke's Company and Thomas Killigrew as head of the King's Company. Thus, this period in drama is known as the Patent-Monopoly Period.

1660-1700: There develops, principally under the authorship of John Dryden, a spectacular type of drama called the *rimed heroic tragedy*, characterized by superhuman heroes, grand actions, and dialogue in heroic couplets. During the same period, a new type of comedy called the *comedy of manners* develops, emphasizing the manners, speech, and weaknesses of the fashionable society of the time. The heroic tragedy died a natural death; the comedy of manners continued to be written well into the eighteenth century. A significant development of this period is the fact that actresses, for the first time, become standard features of the drama.

1700-1800: In opposition to the comedy of manners, which was often criticized for its immorality, there develops a less ribald drama called *sentimental comedy* (also called "weeping comedy" because of its emphasis on pity and sentiment). Sir Richard Steele's *The Conscious Lovers* (1722) belongs to this type.

1737: The Licensing Act is passed, requiring all plays to be submitted to the Lord Chamberlain for his approval before they are performed.

1750-1800: Opposition to the sentimental comedy is best represented by two dramatists who write "laughing comedies"; that is, comedies intended solely to entertain. Oliver Goldsmith is one, and his comedy *She Stoops to Conquer* (1773) remains one of the great "laughing comedies" in our language. The other is Richard Brinsley Sheridan, whose comedy *The School for Scandal* (1777) is also a masterpiece of "laughing comedy."

1800-1900: The nineteenth century brings about drastic changes in the physical makeup of theaters. The old apron-like stage, dating back to Shakespeare, which extended out into the audience, is changed to our conventional present-day stage, with the audience sitting in front and all of the action taking place behind a proscenium arch (now a curtain). Also, theaters become larger, and no attention is paid to acoustics. Consequently, actors have to shout their lines to be heard. Finally, gas lights provide better lighting in theaters, encouraging an emphasis on the dazzling and spectacular on the stage. These developments tended to hinder the drama, not to help it.

In 1843, virtually all legal barriers to the drama and theaters are abolished by Parliament. However, the essential features of the Licensing Act of 1737 are retained (and are still in existence today).

The drama of the nineteenth century is not particularly notable. Sentimental comedy continues to be popular, and there are numerous revivals of Shakespeare's plays. Musical comedy comes into vogue through the works of Sir William S. Gilbert and Sir Arthur Sullivan. Toward the end of the century, through the influence of the Norwegian playwright, Henrik Ibsen, a new type of realistic drama arises, emphasizing contemporary social and moral problems. This new realism is brought to the English stage through the efforts of the great critic-dramatist, George Bernard Shaw. This results in a more serious and mature drama in the twentieth century.

About the Playwrights

Oliver Goldsmith (1730?-1774), the sixth of nine children, was born in Ireland, where his father was a Protestant clergyman. He finally received his degree from Trinity College, Dublin, in 1749, though he was lowest in his class. After a walking tour through Europe, earning his way by playing his flute and debating at various universities, Goldsmith returned to England in 1756. He was at various times a doctor, a teacher, and a hack writer for several periodicals. Though constantly in financial difficulty, this small, homely man was good-natured and friendly. His essays, published in 1762, attracted the attention of Dr. Johnson, who became his friend and benefactor.

Goldsmith's literary versatility was unmatched in his time. His long poem, *The Deserted Village* (1770); his sole novel, *The Vicar of Wakefield* (1766); and his farce-comedy, *She Stoops to Conquer* (1773) are among the most widely read works in English literature. His other works include *The Good-Natured Man*, a less successful comedy than *She Stoops to Conquer; The Traveler,* his first poem; *The Citizen of the World,* a collection of his essays; and *History of England.* It was Dr. Johnson who, in composing Goldsmith's epitaph, wrote of him: "He left scarcely any species of writing untouched and touched none that he did not adorn."

Sean O'Casey (1880-1964) was born in the slums of Dublin, Ireland. A sickly, underfed child, he suffered from a painful eye disease that prevented him from attending school. Nevertheless, he learned to read the textbooks of his twelve older brothers and sisters, and when, at thirteen, he went to work as a laborer, he managed to set aside a few pennies from his wages to buy used books. Much of his time and energy were devoted to the cause of labor, and his earliest writings were for union tracts.

O'Casey did not write his first full-length play until he was nearly forty. This play, *The Shadow of a Gunman*, was produced by the famous Abbey Theatre, Dublin, in 1923. His next two plays, regarded as his best, were also produced by the Abbey, *Juno and the Paycock* (1924) and *The Plough and the Stars* (1926). Both plays are peopled with Dublin's poor and are set against the backdrop of Ireland's struggle for independence. Their bluntly realistic portrayal of the war and its effects was offensive to many Dubliners, and was the cause of a notorious riot during the fourth performance of *The Plough and the Stars*.

Realizing that he could not write freely in Ireland, O'Casey decided to move to London, where he remained for the rest of his life. Among the plays produced during the next twenty years were *The Silver Tassie* (1929), *Within the Gates* (1934), and *Red Roses for Me* (1943). In 1944, O'Casey began a comic cycle of plays with the production of *Purple Dust*, which opened in Boston. His favorite among his twelve full-length plays, *Cock-a-DoodleDandy* (1949), came from this cycle. His last plays include a farce melodrama, *The Bishop's Bonfire* (1955), and a comedy, *The Drums of Father Ned* (1958). This last play was to have been presented at the Dublin International Theatre Festival in 1958, but the authorities in charge forced its withdrawal. As a result, O'Casey prohibited all further performances of his plays in Ireland.

In addition to his many plays, O'Casey wrote a six-volume autobiography: *I Knock at the Door* (1939), *Pictures in the Hallway* (1942), *Drums Under the Window* (1945), *Inishfallen, Fare Thee Well* (1949), *Rose and Crown* (1952), and *Sunset and Evening Star* (1954). *Feathers from the Green Crow* (1962) is a collection of his early writings from 1905 to 1925, and *Under a Colored Cap* (1963) contains twelve essays.

Terence Rattigan (1911-   ) was born in London and educated at Harrow and at Trinity College, Oxford. His father wanted him to enter the diplomatic service, but young Rattigan had set his heart on writing drama. His first play received very little attention either from critics or theatergoers; but he achieved immediate success in 1936 when his farce-comedy, *French Without Tears*, ran for more than a thousand consecutive performances on the London stage. After three years of military service during World War II, Rattigan returned to the London stage with *While the Sun Shines,* breaking all English theater records by writing a *second* play to run over a thousand consecutive performances.

Rattigan has often been highly praised by drama critics and is one of England's most prolific and popular playwrights. As a craftsman he has an unfailing sense of theater which enables him to write deftly and effectively. *The Winslow Boy,* which won critical acclaim in both London and New York, was presented the Ellen Terry Award in 1946 for the best play produced on the London stage that year, and was presented the New York Drama Critics' Circle Award during the following year as the best foreign play produced in New York. Rattigan won the Ellen Terry Award again in 1948 for his one-act play, *The Browning Version.*

Many of Rattigan's plays, in addition to those mentioned, have had long runs on both the London and the New York stages, and a number of them have been filmed. *O Mistress Mine* (1945), starring Alfred Lunt and Lynn Fontanne, was well received by American critics and became one of the Lunts' longest engagements. *The Sleeping Prince* (1953) was filmed in 1957 as *The Prince and the Showgirl* with Sir Laurence Olivier and Marilyn Monroe. His play, *Separate Tables,* proved to be the biggest hit of the London season in 1955. It opened in New York in 1956 and later became a popular motion picture. Among Rattigan's more recent successes have been two motion picture scenarios, *The V.I.P.'s* and *The Yellow Rolls-Royce,* and two plays, *Ross* (1960) and *Man and Boy* (1963).

Peter Shaffer (1926-   ), with his twin brother Anthony, was born in Liverpool and spent his early years there in what he has described as a "nice middle-class neighborhood." His father, a fairly affluent real estate dealer, moved the family to London in 1935. Some years later, the twins were enrolled in St. Paul's, a highly regarded public school in London.

In 1944, when the twins were 18, they were drafted for national service, but instead of being inducted into the armed forces they were assigned jobs as coal miners. They spent a grueling tour of duty at this work, after which they entered Cambridge University.

After graduation, the twins sought a literary career and collaborated on two fairly successful mystery novels, under the pseudonym of "Peter Anthony." Then Peter began to write independently, and in 1958 scored a resounding success with the play *Five Finger*

Exercise. This had a long run in London and was cited as the year's "best play by a new playwright." It was just as successful when produced in New York and won the award of the New York Drama Critics' Circle for the "best foreign play" for the 1959-1960 season.

In the years since then, Peter has emerged as one of the most popular and highly regarded dramatists in England. Most of his plays have also been produced and well received in the United States. His works include *The Private Ear* and *The Public Eye,* offered as a double bill (1962); *The Royal Hunt of the Sun* (1964), an impressive drama about the Incas and the Spanish *conquistadores*; and another double bill, *Black Comedy* and *White Lies* (1965). Most recently he wrote *The Battle of Shruways* (1970). Several of his plays have been made into films, and he has also written for radio and TV.

William Shakespeare (1564-1616) represents one of the great ironies of English literary history — though he is its best-known and greatest playwright, his life is the least known. The biographical facts that are known with certainty can be written in a few lines. The date of his birth is fairly certain because his baptism on April 26, 1564, is recorded in the registry of the Church of the Holy Trinity at Stratford. Since baptism normally took place within three days of birth, his birthdate is traditionally recorded as April 23. Beyond this early mention, nothing definite is known of his life up to the time of his marriage to Anne Hathaway on November 28, 1582, at which time he would have been eighteen. His daughter Susanna was baptized in 1583, and the twins, Hamnet and Judith, in 1585.

No other fact is known until 1592, when Robert Greene wrote his angry attack (see introduction on Shakespeare), proving that Shakespeare had come to London and that he was well enough known in dramatic circles to draw the jealousy of a rival playwright.

The remaining known facts are few and scattered: the publication of certain poems in 1593 and 1594; the death and burial of his only son, Hamnet, in 1596; and the purchase of New Place, the largest house in Stratford, in 1597 — which suggests his success in the London theater. Aside from various legal transactions between 1600 and 1610, nothing else is known of him until his death in 1616 on April 23, the same day as his birth. The fact that he was buried in the chancel of Stratford Church indicates the respect he had won at home. What is known of his will leaves no doubt that he died a prosperous man.

George Bernard Shaw (1856-1950) was born in Dublin, Ireland, "escaped" from school at fourteen, came to London at twenty, and before he was thirty had written five unsuccessful novels. During the next ten years he earned a living as a music and drama critic, and had a reputation for being—in his own words—"an extraordinarily witty, brilliant, and clever man." His major interest at this time was the Fabian Society, a socialist organization, which he helped to found and for which he wrote pamphlets and essays.

Shaw's major literary contribution was the wit, vitality, and intellectual vigor he brought to the English theater. He championed the drama of ideas and had his characters discuss with great exuberance almost every social issue of modern life. In the early 1900's, such discussion both shocked and delighted theater audiences, for Shaw deliberately expressed unpopular opinions and professed not the slightest respect for customary conventions. "My method," he explained, "is to take utmost trouble to find the right thing to say, and then to say it with the utmost levity. And all the time the real joke is that I am in earnest."

Shaw's early plays (1894-1905) are devoted primarily to tearing down false pretensions; his later plays to pointing out that man must, and can, change and mature. The best of these are still among the most popular and successful plays produced by professionals and amateurs in England and abroad. They include such plays as *Arms and the Man, The Devil's Disciple, Candida, Androcles and the Lion, Pygmalion, Man and Superman, Major Barbara, Caesar and Cleopatra, The Doctor's Dilemma,* and *Saint Joan,* which is generally considered his masterpiece.

In 1925, Shaw, then in his sixties, was awarded the Nobel Prize for Literature. When asked later if he would write any more plays, he replied, "Will a duck swim? How can I help it?" In 1933, he visited America as part of a world-wide tour, and in 1938 he allowed *Pygmalion and Major Barbara* to be made into motion pictures. After his death *Pygmalion* was made into the delightful musical comedy, *My Fair Lady.* One of his favorite "causes" was the reform of the non-phonetic English alphabet, and he left the bulk of his considerable estate to a fund dedicated to promoting a phonetic alphabet.

Glossary of Terms

act: one of two or more major divisions of a play, each covering a large block of the action that makes up the *plot*.

action: what takes place – psychological, emotional, and physical – that conveys the story and the meaning of the play.

> **action, rising:** the series of incidents that grow out of the problem to be solved and that build up to the *climax*.

> **action, falling:** the action following the climax; also referred to as *resolution* or *denouement*.

analogy: a comparison of ideas or objects which are essentially different but are alike in one significant way; for example, the analogy between the grasshopper and the man who lives only for the moment.

antagonist: a force that opposes the main character (the *protagonist*). The antagonist may be some weakness, desire, or belief within the protagonist. Or it may be some outside force, such as another character, nature, environment, or fate.

antecedent action: the events which occurred prior to the time covered in the play and about which the audience must be informed through the *dialogue*.

anticlimax: an outcome of a situation or series of events that, by contrast with what was anticipated, is ludicrous or disappointing. The anticlimax often creates a humorous effect.

apron: the part of the stage that is in front of the curtain.

aside: a dramatic *convention* which allows a character to direct a

469

comment either to the audience or to another character presumably without being heard by other characters on the stage.

atmosphere: the general over-all feeling or *mood* of a play, conveyed largely by setting and events.

character: a real or fictional person who is involved in the action of a play and is represented on the stage by an actor.

> **character, consistent:** a character whose actions, decisions, attitudes, etc., are in keeping with what the playwright has led the reader or audience to expect.
>
> **character, dynamic:** a character who changes or develops during the course of the play.
>
> **character, static:** a character who does not change or develop during the course of the play.

characterization: the dramatist's portrayal of a character by what he says and does, and by what other characters say about him and the way they react to him.

cliché: a phrase or an expression used so often that it has lost its freshness and effectiveness.

climax: the moment of highest interest or greatest dramatic intensity. Usually it marks a turning point in the action, after which the reader or audience is no longer in doubt about the outcome.

comedy: a form of drama that is light and amusing and that typically has a happy ending. Many comedies poke fun at—satirize—manners, customs, social or political institutions, or types of people.

high comedy: comedy that appeals to the intellect and arouses "thoughtful" laughter by showing the incongruities of human nature and by displaying the follies of social manners.

low comedy: comedy that appeals to the intellect and arouses "thoughtful" laughter by showing the incongruities of human nature and displaying the follies of social manners.

conflict: the struggle between two opposing forces, ideas, or beliefs that is the basis of the plot. In most plays the conflict is resolved when one force—usually the *protagonist*—succeeds or fails in overcoming the opposing force. Sometimes the protagonist gives up the struggle as too difficult or not worthwhile.

> **conflict, inner:** a struggle between two opposing forces within the heart and mind of the protagonist.
>
> **conflict, external:** a struggle between the protagonist and some outside force.

contrast: the bringing together of ideas, images, or characters to show how they differ.

convention: any device that is not "true to life" but is accepted by the audience as necessary to the presentation of the action of the play. Common theatrical conventions are the scenery, the properties (furniture, etc.), and the opening and closing of the curtain.

denouement: the "unraveling" or *resolution* of the plot, following the *climax*. In this final part of the play—usually brief but sometimes a full act—the playwright brings the conflict to an end and, through the dialogue, reveals how and why everything turned out as it did.

dialogue: the speeches of the characters in a play, usually addressed to one another but sometimes to the audience.

drama: the literary form written to be performed on a stage by actors representing the characters.

dramatic irony: a situation in which the words or actions of a character have a meaning unperceived by the character but understood by the audience. The term also applies to any situation in which the audience knows something that the characters do not. For example, a character—unaware that he has a poisoned drink—might say, "Ah! This will refresh me!"

dramatic purpose: the purpose served by a character, an incident, or a portion of dialogue in (1) furthering the action of the play, (2) creating suspense, (3) changing or intensifying the mood, (4) increasing the emotional effect, (5) contributing to humor, or (6) helping to reveal character.

episode: a group of related incidents—or a major event—that comprises part of the main *plot* or is related to the main plot.

exposition: that part of the play, usually the first act, which reveals "how it all began"; namely, what happened prior to the time covered in a play, what the main characters are like (sometimes before they appear), and what situation has arisen that will lead to a problem that must be solved. See also *antecedent action*.

farce: a *comedy* which begins with an absurd situation and is then developed through ridiculous or hilarious complications involving exaggerated or far-fetched characters.

flashback: an interruption in the main action of a play in order to dramatize an incident or *episode* that occurred prior to the time covered in the play.

foreshadowing: the dropping of hints or suggestions by the playwright that lead the reader or the audience to anticipate events that are to come later in the play.

hero: the central male character, with whom the audience is supposed to sympathize. See *protagonist.*

heroine: the central female character. She may arouse admiration largely because of the hero's regard for her.

humor: the quality that makes something seem funny, amusing, or comic. Humor can arise from action, situation, physical appearance, verbal statement, or from any combination of these.

incident: one of the events (usually minor) that make up the total *action* or *plot* of a play.

initial incident: the event in a play that introduces the *conflict.*

irony: the expression of a meaning that is inappropriate to a situation or that is different from, and even the direct opposite of, the stated, apparent, or literal meaning (verbal irony). The term also applies to a situation or to the outcome of an event or a series of events that is contrary to what would naturally be hoped for or anticipated (irony of situation). See also *dramatic irony* and *tragic irony.*

legitimate theater: drama performed on a stage. The term is used to differentiate stage drama from motion pictures, television plays, etc.

melodrama: a form of drama, usually characterized by sensational or violent action and a happy ending, in which sentiment and passion are intensified or exaggerated for effect.

melodramatic: the quality of a scene, situation, or dialogue that is sensational, violent, or extravagantly emotional.

monologue: a long speech delivered by one character in a play.

mood: the state of mind or feeling created by the *setting*, the speeches of the characters, and the particular situation or sequence of events.

moral: the "lesson" or "teaching" that is brought out through the action of the play or that is explicitly stated or implied by one of the characters.

motivation: the provision by the playwright of a cause or reason that compels a character to behave as he does.

narrator: a storyteller who usually begins and often supplements the dramatic presentation at various points with descriptive information. He is usually either a character in the play or an anonymous voice.

naturalism: the portraying of events, settings, and characters exactly as they appear in real life, even down to the most squalid details, and emphasizing the role of heredity and environment in human life and character development.

paradox: a statement which on the surface seems contradictory, yet if interpreted figuratively, involves an element of truth:
"The child is father of the man."
—William Wordsworth

plot: the series of events or *episodes* that make up the action of the play.

poetic justice: an outcome of events that rewards the virtuous and punishes the vicious; an ending in which each character gets exactly what he deserves.

properties: any of the small, movable articles used as part of the *setting* or used by the actors during the staging of a play.

protagonist: the main character in the play. He faces a problem and in his attempt to solve it becomes involved in a conflict with an opposing force, or *antagonist.*

pun: a play on words, either by using words that sound alike but have different meanings or by using a word with two different meanings, both of which apply.

realism: the portraying of people, scenes, and events as they appear in real life, not as the playwright would like them to be.

resolution: the events following the climax of a work of fiction; sometimes called *falling action.*

romanticism: the portraying of people, scenes, and events not as they are in real life, but as people would like them to be.

satire: the use of *irony,* sarcasm, or ridicule to criticize or poke fun at customs, manners, individuals, or social or political institutions.

scene: (1) the setting of the action of a play. (2) One of two or more clearly defined and separate units that make up an *act.* (3) An incident or situation that develops out of the preceding action and flows into the action that follows.

scenery: the backdrop, walls, furniture, etc., used onstage to represent the place in which the action of a scene occurs.

setting: the time and place in which the action of a play occurs. It may remain the same throughout the entire play, or it may change from act to act or from scene to scene.

slapstick: *low comedy* in which the humor depends upon violent activity, horseplay, and the like. (See *comedy*.)

soliloquy: a dramatic *convention* in which lines are spoken by a character as if to himself rather than to another character; a kind of "thinking out loud" for the purpose of revealing information about the character or his plans which the reader or theater audience needs to know.

stage directions: the words, phrases, sentences, and even paragraphs — generally printed in italics and enclosed in parentheses — through which the playwright indicates what is taking place on the stage and also how the characters should speak, feel, or act. Terms used to refer to specific areas of the stage include *upstage* (at the rear) and *downstage* (at the front), often abbreviated *up* and *down*. *Right* and *left* always refer to the actor's right and left as he is facing the audience.

stereotype: a character who conforms to certain widely accepted ideas of how such a person should look, think, or act.

stock character: a character who has been used in so many plays that the audience immediately recognizes him and knows how he will think and act.

structure: the arrangement of the details and scenes that make up a play.

style: the distinctive manner in which a playwright conveys his meaning to the audience. As generally used, style refers to a writer's language: his choice and arrangement of words.

subplot: a secondary series of events or *episodes* that is subordinate to the main *plot* but, in most cases, contributes to it.

suspense: the reader's or audience's feeling of excitement, curiosity, or expectation about the outcome of a plot.

theme: the idea, view of life, or commentary on human behavior that is dramatized through the words and deeds of the characters and by the outcome of the play.

tone: the feeling conveyed by a playwright through style and choice of words that reveals his attitude toward his subject; for example, a satirical tone.

tragedy: a form of drama in which the *protagonist* undergoes a morally significant struggle and is defeated, sometimes because of a flaw in his own character, more often because he is unable to overcome the force, or forces, that oppose him.

tragic flaw: the flaw of character in a tragic hero which brings about his downfall.

tragic irony: *dramatic irony* involving a tragic hero who is unaware of the disaster that awaits him.

unity: the quality achieved by a play when all its characters, action, language, etc., are interrelated in such a way as to form a harmonious whole.

wit: a term applied to a neatly phrased expression designed to effect comic surprise. In contrast with humor, wit is intentional and verbal, characterized by such devices as irony, pun, paradox, and epigram.